Dedication

To the pilots, students,
and staff at
A Flight Above
helicopter flight school,
St. George, UT

Thanks!

To Nancy Davis and Roslyn Bullas, for their kinder, gentler editing. What a team!

To Connie Jeung-Mills, for another smooth project. I must be getting the hang of this, because you had far fewer comments than I expected.

To Julie Bess, for coming to my rescue at the last minute and producing a fine index for this book. Next time, I'll give you more advance notice!

To Microsoft Corporation, for continuing to revise and improve the world's best word processor.

And to Mike, for the usual reasons.

The Flying M

www.marialanger.com

Table of Contents

VISUAL QuickStart Guide

MICROSOFT OFFICE WORD 2003 FOR WINDOWS

Maria Langer

Peachpit Press

Visual QuickStart Guide
Microsoft Office Word 2003 for Windows
Maria Langer

Peachpit Press
1249 Eighth Street
Berkeley, CA 94710
510-524-2178 • 800-283-9444
510-524-2221 (fax)

Find us on the World Wide Web at: http://www.peachpit.com/

Peachpit Press is a division of Pearson Education

Editors: Roslyn Bullas, Nancy Davis
Indexer: Julie Bess
Cover Design: The Visual Group
Production: Maria Langer, Connie Jeung-Mills

Colophon

This book was produced with Adobe InDesign 2.0 and Adobe Photoshop 7 on a Power Macintosh G4 running Mac OS X 10.2. The fonts used were Utopia, Meta Plus, and PIXymbols Command. Screenshots were created using IMSI Capture and Collage Capture on a Dell Dimension L933r.

Notice of Rights

Notice of Liability

Trademarks

ISBN 0-321-19394-6

9 8 7 6 5 4 3 2 1

Printed and bound in the United States of America.

TABLE OF CONTENTS

Introduction to Word 2003

Introduction

Microsoft Office Word 2003 is the latest version of Microsoft's powerful word processing application for Windows users. Now more powerful than ever, Word enables users to create a wide variety of documents, ranging in complexity from simple, one-page letters to complex, multi-file reports with figures, table of contents, and index.

This Visual QuickStart Guide will help you learn Word 2003 by providing step-by-step instructions, plenty of illustrations, and a generous helping of tips. On these pages, you'll find everything you need to know to get up and running quickly with Word—and more!

This book was designed for page flipping. Use the thumb tabs, index, or table of contents to find the topics for which you need help. If you're brand new to Word or word processing, however, I recommend that you begin by reading at least the first two chapters. **Chapter 1** provides basic information about Word's interface while **Chapter 2** introduces word processing concepts and explains exactly how they work in Word.

If you've used other versions of Word and are interested in information about new Word 2003 features, be sure to browse through this **Introduction**. It'll give you a good idea of the new things Word has in store for you.

New & Improved Features in Word 2003

Word 2003 includes a number of brand new features, as well as improvements to some existing features. Here's a list.

New features

◆ **Reading Layout View.** The new Reading Layout view (**Figure 1**) makes it easier to read documents on screen.

◆ **Research Task Pane.** The Research task pane (**Figure 2**) enables you to search electronic dictionaries, thesauruses, and online research sites from within Word.

◆ **Instant Messaging.** You can now access Windows Instant Messaging (IM) from within Word.

◆ **XML Support.** Word enables you to open and save files in XML (Extensible Markup Language) format. This makes it possible to create Web-based solutions that interact with Word files.

◆ **Microsoft Office Online.** The Microsoft Office Online Web site (**Figure 3**), which offers online help documents, templates, add-ins, and online training, can be accessed from within Word.

◆ **Shared Workspaces.** The shared workspaces feature, which requires Microsoft Windows Server 2003 running Microsoft Windows SharePoint Services, enables you to share documents with other team members.

◆ **Information Rights Management (IRM).** The IRM feature, which requires Microsoft Windows Server 2003 running Microsoft Windows Rights Management Services (RMS), can prevent document recipients from forwarding, copying, or printing documents.

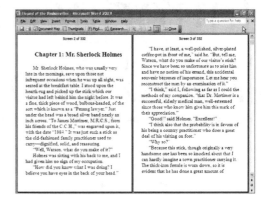

Figure 1 Reading Layout view enables you to read a document as if it were a book.

Figure 2
The Research task pane can display information from online research sites.

Figure 3 Microsoft Office Online offers a wealth of resources for Word users.

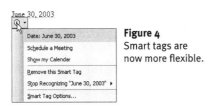

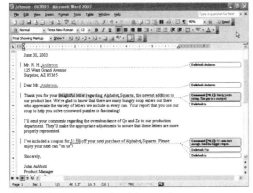

Figure 4
Smart tags are
now more flexible.

Figure 5 Comments and revision marks are now more
visible and easier to track.

Figure 6
Word's built-in Help
feature can retrieve
help documents from
the Microsoft Office
Online Web site.

◆ **Tablet PC Compatibility.** You can annotate Word documents on a Tablet PC, using a pen input device, in your own handwriting.

Improved features

◆ **Smart Tags.** Smart tags (**Figure 4**) can now be associated with specific content so the appropriate tag appears when you point to associated words.

◆ **Comments & Revisions.** Comments and revision marks (**Figure 5**) are now more visible. It's easier to track and merge changes and read comments.

◆ **Word Help.** Word's built-in Help feature (**Figure 6**) can now search the Microsoft Office Online Web site for articles and information to meet your needs.

◆ **Document Protection.** You can now designate certain sections of a document to be modified by specific people, prevent revisions without revision marks enabled, and prevent specific formatting from being applied to protected documents.

NEW & IMPROVED FEATURES IN WORD 2003

The Word Workplace

Meet Microsoft Word

Microsoft Word is a full-featured word processing application that you can use to create all kinds of text-based documents—letters, reports, form letters, mailing labels, envelopes, flyers, and even Web pages.

Word's interface combines common Windows screen elements with buttons, commands, and controls that are specific to Word. To use Word effectively, you must have at least a basic understanding of these elements.

This chapter introduces the Word workplace by illustrating and describing the following elements:

- The Word screen, including window elements

- Menus, shortcut keys, toolbars, palettes, and dialogs

- Views and document navigation techniques

- Word's onscreen Help feature.

✔ Tip

- If you've used previous versions of Word, browse through this chapter to learn about some of the interface elements that are new to this version of Word.

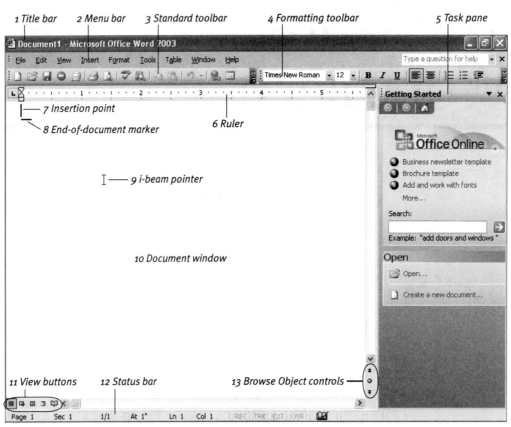

Figure 1 The Word screen displaying a document in Normal view.

Key to the Word screen

1 Title bar

The title bar displays the document's title. You can drag the title bar to move the window.

2 Menu bar

The menu bar appears at the top of the screen and offers access to Word's commands.

3 Standard toolbar

The Standard toolbar offers buttons for basic Word commands.

4 Formatting toolbar

The Formatting toolbar offers buttons and other controls for applying formatting to document contents.

5 Task pane

The task pane offers a quick way to access common Word tasks.

6 Ruler

Word's ruler enables you to set paragraph formatting options such as tabs and indentation.

7 Insertion point

The blinking insertion point indicates where text will appear when typed or inserted with the Paste command.

8 End-of-document marker

The end-of-document marker indicates the end of the document.

9 I-beam pointer

The Click and Type pointer enables you to position the insertion point or select text. This pointer, which is controlled by the mouse, turns into various other pointers depending on its position and the Word view.

10 Document window

The document window is where you create, edit, and view Word documents.

11 View buttons

View buttons enable you to switch between various Word views.

12 Status bar

The status bar displays information about the document, such as the current page number and section and insertion point location.

13 Browse Object controls

These buttons enable you to navigate among various document elements.

✔ Tips

■ **Figure 1** shows the Word screen in Normal view. Other elements that appear in other views are discussed later in this chapter and throughout this book. Word's views are covered later in this chapter.

■ Standard Windows window elements are not discussed in detail in this book. For more information about how to use standard window elements such as the Close button, Minimize button, Maximize button, Restore button, and scroll bars, consult the documentation that came with your computer or Windows online help.

THE WORD SCREEN

The Mouse

As with most Windows programs, you use the mouse to select text, activate buttons, and choose menu commands.

Mouse pointer appearance

The appearance of the mouse pointer varies depending on its location and the item to which it is pointing. Here are some examples:

◆ In the document window, the mouse pointer usually looks like an I-beam pointer (**Figure 1**).

◆ On a menu name, the mouse pointer appears as an arrow pointing up and to the left (**Figure 2**).

◆ In the selection bar between the left edge of the document window and the text, the mouse pointer appears as an arrow pointing up and to the right (**Figure 3**).

◆ On selected text, the mouse pointer appears as an arrow pointing up and to the left (**Figure 4**).

To use the mouse

There are four basic mouse techniques:

◆ **Pointing** means to position the mouse pointer so that its tip is on the item to which you are pointing (**Figure 2**).

◆ **Clicking** means to press the mouse button once and release it. You click to position the insertion point or to activate a button.

◆ **Double-clicking** means to press the mouse button twice in rapid succession. You double-click to open an item or to select a word.

Figure 2
Pointing to a menu name.

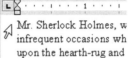

Figure 3
The mouse pointer in the selection bar.

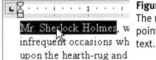

Figure 4
The mouse pointer pointing to selected text.

◆ **Dragging** means to press the mouse button down and hold it while moving the mouse. You drag to resize windows, select text, choose menu commands, or draw shapes.

✔ Tip

■ Throughout this book, when I instruct you to simply *click*, press the left mouse button. When I instruct you to *right-click*, press the right mouse button.

THE MOUSE

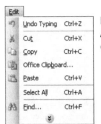

Figure 5
A personalized version
of the Edit menu.

Figure 6
The Edit menu
with all commands
displayed.

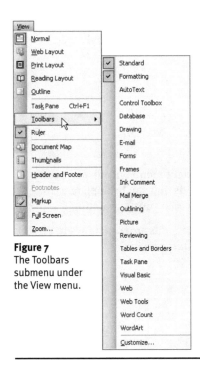

Figure 7
The Toolbars
submenu under
the View menu.

Menus

All of Word's commands are accessible through its menus. Word has three types of menus:

◆ **Personalized menus** appear on the menu bar near the top of the window. These menus automatically track and display only the commands you use most (**Figure 5**).

◆ **Full menus** also appear on the menu bar near the top of the winodw, but only when you either double-click the menu name, pause while displaying the menu, or click the arrows at the bottom of the menu. **Figure 6** shows the menu in **Figure 5** as a full menu with all commands displayed.

◆ **Shortcut menus** appear at the mouse pointer when you right-click on an item (**Figure 8**).

Here are some rules to keep in mind when working with menus:

◆ A menu command that appears in gray cannot be selected.

◆ A menu command followed by an ellipsis (…) displays a dialog.

◆ A menu command followed by a triangle has a submenu. The submenu displays additional commands when the main command is highlighted (**Figure 7**).

◆ A menu command followed by one or more keyboard characters can be chosen with a shortcut key.

◆ A menu command preceded by a check mark has been "turned on" (**Figure 7**). To toggle the command from on to off or off to on, choose it from the menu.

✔ Tip

■ Dialogs and shortcut keys are covered later in this chapter.

To choose a menu command

1. Click the name of the menu from which you want to choose the command. The personalized version of the menu appears (**Figure 5**).

2. If necessary, click the menu name again to display the full menu version of the menu (**Figure 6**).

3. Click the command you want.

   or

   If the command is on a submenu, click on the submenu to display it (**Figure 7**) and then click on the command you want.

✔ Tips

- This book uses the following notation to indicate menu commands: *Menu Name > Submenu Name* (if necessary) *> Command Name*. For example, "choose View > Toolbars > Standard" instructs you to choose the Standard command from the Toolbars submenu under the View menu.

- You can also use mouseless menus. Press (Alt), then use the letter and arrow keys to display and select menus and commands. Press (Enter) to activate a selected command.

To use a shortcut menu

1. Point to the item on which you want to use the shortcut menu.

2. Hold down (Ctrl) and press the mouse button down. The shortcut menu appears (**Figure 8**).

3. Choose the command that you want.

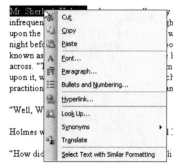

Figure 8 A shortcut menu appears at the mouse pointer when you right-click on an item—in this case, selected text.

✔ Tips

- The shortcut menu only displays the commands that can be applied to the item to which you are pointing.

- Shortcut menus are sometimes referred to as *context-sensitive* or *contextual menus*.

USING MENUS

Shortcut Keys

Shortcut keys are combinations of keyboard keys that, when pressed, choose a menu command without displaying the menu. For example, the shortcut key for the Copy command under the Edit menu (**Figures 5** and **6**) is Ctrl C. Pressing this key combination chooses the command.

✔ Tips

■ All shortcut keys use at least one of the following modifier keys:

Key Name	Keyboard Key
Control	Ctrl
Shift	⇧ Shift
Alt	Alt

■ A menu command's shortcut key is displayed to its right on the menu (**Figures 5** and **6**).

■ Many shortcut keys are standardized from one application to another. The Save and Print commands are good examples; they're usually Ctrl S and Ctrl P.

■ **Appendix A** includes a list of Word's shortcut keys.

To use a shortcut key

1. Hold down the modifier key for the shortcut (normally Ctrl).

2. Press the letter or number key for the shortcut.

For example, to choose the Copy command, hold down Ctrl and press the C key.

Toolbars

Word includes a number of toolbars for various purposes. Each one includes buttons or menus that activate menu commands or set options.

By default, Word automatically displays two toolbars when you launch it:

◆ The **Standard toolbar** (**Figure 9**) offers buttons for a wide range of commonly used commands.

◆ The **Formatting toolbar** (**Figure 10**) offers buttons and menus for formatting selected items.

✔ Tips

■ Other toolbars may appear automatically depending on the task you are performing with Word.

■ Toolbar buttons with faint icon images (for example, Redo in **Figure 9**) cannot be selected.

■ Toolbar buttons with a blue border around them (for example, Align Left in **Figure 10**) are "turned on."

■ You can identify a button by its ScreenTip (**Figure 11**).

■ A toolbar can be **docked** or **floating**. A docked toolbar (**Figures 9** and **10**) is positioned against any edge of the screen. A floating toolbar can be moved anywhere within the screen.

More Buttons button

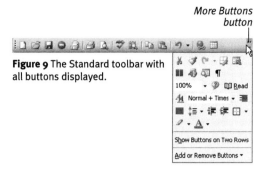

Figure 9 The Standard toolbar with all buttons displayed.

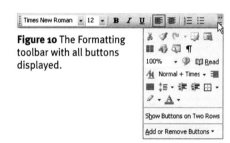

Figure 10 The Formatting toolbar with all buttons displayed.

Figure 11
A ScreenTip appears when you point to a button.

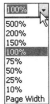

Figure 12
Click the triangle beside the menu to display the menu.

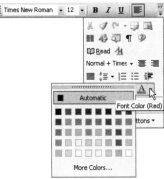

Figure 13 The Font Color menu appears when you click the Font Color button.

Figure 14
The menu appears as a floating menu or palette.

Figure 15 Select the current value,...

Figure 16 ...enter a new value, and press [Enter].

To view more buttons

Click the Toolbar Options button at the far right end of the toolbar. Additional buttons for the toolbar appear in a menu (**Figures 9** and **10**).

To view ScreenTips

Point to a toolbar or palette button. A tiny yellow box containing the name of the button appears (**Figure 11**).

To use a toolbar button

1. Point to the button for the command or option that you want (**Figure 11**).

2. Click once.

To use a toolbar menu

1. Click on the triangle beside the menu to display the menu and its commands (**Figure 12**).

2. Click a command or option to select it.

✔ Tips

■ Button menus that display a gray move handle along the top edge (**Figure 13**) can be "torn off" and used as floating menus or palettes. Simply display the menu and drag it away from the toolbar. When the palette appears, release the mouse button. The menu is displayed as a floating menu with a title bar that displays its name (**Figure 14**).

■ Menus that display text boxes (**Figure 12**) can be changed by typing a new value into the box. Just click the contents of the box to select it (**Figure 15**), then type in the new value and press [Enter] (**Figure 16**).

To display or hide a toolbar

Choose the name of the toolbar that you want to display or hide from the Toolbars submenu under the View menu (**Figure 7**).

If the toolbar name has a check mark beside it, it is displayed and will be hidden.

or

If the toolbar name does not have a check mark beside it, it is hidden and will be displayed.

✔ Tip

■ You can also hide a floating toolbar by clicking its close button.

To float a docked toolbar

Drag the toolbar's move handle (**Figure 17**) away from the toolbar's docked position (**Figure 18**).

✔ Tip

■ Floating a docked toolbar will change the appearance and position of other tool-bars docked in the same row (**Figure 18**).

To dock a floating toolbar

Drag the toolbar's titled bar to the edge of the screen (**Figure 19**).

✔ Tip

■ You can dock a toolbar against the top (**Figure 17**), either side (**Figure 19**), or the bottom of the screen. Buttons may change appearance when the toolbar is docked on the side of the screen.

To move a floating toolbar

Drag the title bar for the toolbar to reposition it on screen.

To resize a floating toolbar

Drag the edge of the toolbar (**Figure 20**).

Move handles

Figure 17 By default, the Standard and Formatting toolbars are docked.

Figure 18 Drag the toolbar into the document window to float it. When you float the Standard toolbar, the Formatting toolbar expands to occupy some of the vacated space.

Figure 19
When you drag a toolbar to the edge of the screen, it becomes docked there. In this example, the Standard toolbar is docked on the left side of the screen.

Figure 20 Drag the edge of a floating toolbar to resize it.

Figure 21
The Getting Started task pane enables you to learn more about using Word, open recently opened documents, and create new documents.

The Task Pane

Microsoft Office XP introduces *task panes*, which appear in all Office applications, including Word. Each task pane includes a number of clickable links and other options to perform common tasks. For example, the Getting Started task pane (**Figure 21**), which appears when you run Word, offers options you might find helpful when you start Word.

Word includes 14 different task panes:

- **Getting Started** (**Figure 21**) enables you to learn more about using Word, open recently opened documents, and create new documents.

- **Help** enables you to search Word's internal and online help. I discuss the Help task pane later in this chapter.

- **Clip Art** enables you to search for clip art items and insert them in your document. I discuss the Clip Art task pane in **Chapter 10**.

- **Research** enables you to search a number of online resources for information about a topic.

- **Clipboard** displays the Microsoft Office Clipboard, which you can use to store multiple items to paste into Office documents. I tell you how to use the Office Clipboard in **Chapter 2**.

- **Search Results** enables you to view the results of a search of Microsoft.com. I discuss the Search Results task pane later in this chapter.

- **New Document** enables you to create a new document from scratch or based on a template. I tell you more about the New Document task pane in **Chapter 2**.

- **Shared Workspace** enables you to set up and manage a document to be shared by multiple users on a network or over the Internet.

- **Document Updates** enables you to manage updates to documents with a copy stored in a shared workspace.

- **Protect Document** enables you to set options for protecting your document from formatting and/or editing. I tell you about protecting documents in **Chapter 15**.

- **Styles and Formatting** enables you to view and set styles for selected text or paragraphs. I cover the Styles and Formatting task pane in **Chapter 4**.

- **Reveal Formatting** enables you to view the formatting options set for selected text. I cover the Reveal Formatting task pane in **Chapter 4**, too.

Continued on next page...

THE TASK PANE

Continued from previous page.

- **Mail Merge** enables you to set up and perform a mail merge. I explain how to use this task pane in **Chapter 14**.

- **XML Structure** enables you to work with XML code in a Word document. Working with XML is beyond the scope of this book.

✔ Tip

- Although the task pane is a handy way to access commonly used commands and features without the use of dialogs that block your work, you may find that it takes up too much space on screen. If you prefer to use all screen real estate for your documents, you can close the task pane, as discussed below.

To perform a task pane task

Click the link or button for the task you want to perform.

To display a different task pane

Choose the name of the task pane you want to display from the pop-up menu in the task pane's title bar (**Figure 22**).

To close the task pane

Click the task pane's close button (**Figure 22**).

To open the task pane

Choose View > Task Pane (**Figure 23**).

Close button

Figure 22
To display a different task pane, choose its name from the pop-up menu in the task pane's title bar.

Figure 23
You can display the task pane by choosing Task Pane from the View menu.

Figure 24
The Word Count dialog just displays information.

Dialogs

Like most other Windows programs, Word uses *dialogs* to communicate with you.

Word can display many different dialogs, each with its own purpose. There are two basic types of dialogs:

◆ Dialogs that simply provide information (**Figure 24**).

◆ Dialogs that offer options to select (**Figure 25**) before Word completes the execution of a command.

✔ Tip

■ Often, when a dialog appears, you must dismiss it by clicking OK, Cancel, or its close button before you can continue working with Word.

Anatomy of a Word dialog

Here are the components of many Word dialogs, along with information about how they work.

◆ **Tabs** (**Figure 25**), which appear at the top of some dialogs, let you move from one group of dialog options to another. To switch to another group of options, click its tab.

◆ **Text boxes** or **entry fields** (**Figures 25** and **26**) let you enter information from the keyboard. You can press Tab to move from one box to the next or click in a box to position the insertion point within it. Then enter a new value.

◆ **List boxes** (**Figure 25**) offer a number of options to choose from. Use the scroll bar to view options that don't fit in the list window. Click an option to select it; it becomes highlighted and appears in the text box.

Tabs   *Text entry box or field*   *List box*

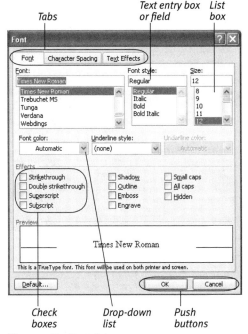

Check boxes   *Drop-down list*   *Push buttons*

Figure 25 The Font dialog.

Continued on next page...

DIALOGS

◆ **Check boxes** (**Figure 25**) let you turn options on or off. Click in a check box to toggle it. When a check mark or X appears in the check box, its option is turned on.

◆ **Option buttons** (**Figure 26**) let you select only one option from a group. Click on an option to select it; the option that was selected before you clicked is deselected.

◆ **Drop-down lists** (**Figure 25**) also let you select one option from a group. Display a list as you would a menu (**Figure 27**), then choose the option that you want.

◆ **Preview areas** (**Figures 25** and **26**), when available, illustrate the effects of your changes before you finalize them by clicking the OK button.

◆ **Push buttons** (**Figures 24, 25,** and **26**) let you access other dialogs, accept the changes and close the dialog (OK), or close the dialog without making changes (Cancel). To choose a button, click it once.

Option buttons

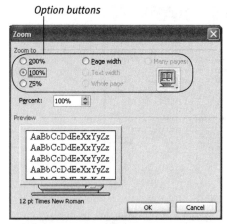

Figure 26 The Zoom dialog.

✔ Tips

■ When the contents of a text box are selected, whatever you type will replace the selection.

■ Word often uses text boxes and list boxes together (**Figure 25**). You can use either one to make a selection.

■ If a pair of tiny triangles appears to the right of an edit box (**Figure 26**), you can click a triangle to increase or decrease the value in the edit box.

■ In some list boxes, double-clicking an option selects it and dismisses the dialog.

■ You can turn on any number of check boxes in a group, but you can select only one option button in a group.

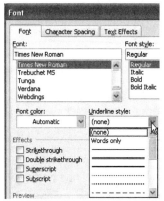

Figure 27
Displaying a drop-down list.

■ Pressing Enter while a push button is active "clicks" that button.

■ You can usually "click" the Cancel button by pressing Esc.

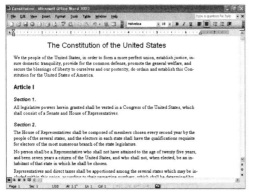

Figure 28 Normal view.

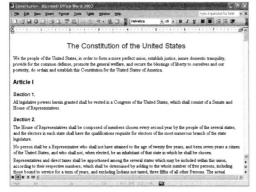

Figure 29 Web Layout View.

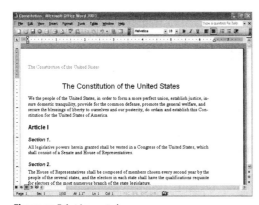

Figure 30 Print Layout view.

Views

Word offers several different ways to view the contents of a document window.

◆ **Normal view (Figure 28)**, which is the default view, shows continuously scrolling text. It is the fastest view for entering and editing text but does not show page layout elements.

◆ **Web Layout view (Figure 29)** displays the contents of a document so they are easier to read on screen. Text appears in a larger font size and wraps to fit the window rather than margins or indentations.

◆ **Print Layout view (Figure 30)** displays the objects on a page positioned as they will be when the document is printed. This is a good view for working with documents that include multiple column text or positioned graphics, such as a newsletter or flyer.

◆ **Outline view (Figure 31)** displays the document's structure—headings and body text—in a way that makes it easy to rearrange the document. Headings can be collapsed to hide detail and simplify the view. Working with Outline view is discussed in **Chapter 8**.

◆ **Reading Layout view (Figure 32)**, which is new in Word 2003, displays the document as an open book with facing pages. Pages "flip" rather than scroll. This view is good for reading long documents but alters font size and text wrap.

✔ Tips

■ Although each view is designed for a specific purpose, you can work with a document in any view.

■ The illustrations throughout this book display windows in Normal view, unless otherwise indicated.

VIEWS

To switch to another view

Choose the desired option from the View menu (**Figure 33**).

or

Click the appropriate view button at the bottom of the window (**Figure 34**).

or

To switch to Reading Layout view, click the Read button 📖 Read on the Standard toolbar.

✔ Tip

- By default, the Outline and Reading Layout commands appear only on the full version of the View menu (**Figure 33**). If you use either of them often enough, however, the one(s) you use should switch to the personalized version of the menu. Full and personalized menus are discussed earlier in this chapter.

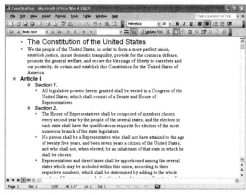

Figure 31 Outline view.

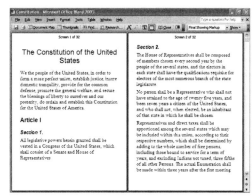

Figure 32 Reading Layout view.

Figure 33
The View menu.

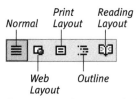

Figure 34 View buttons at the bottom of the document window. The currently selected option is orange with a blue box around it.

SWITCHING VIEWS

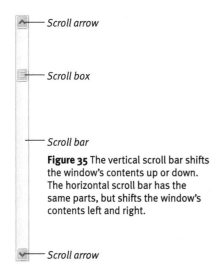

Scroll arrow

Scroll box

Scroll bar

Figure 35 The vertical scroll bar shifts the window's contents up or down. The horizontal scroll bar has the same parts, but shifts the window's contents left and right.

Scroll arrow

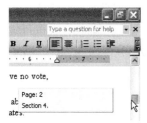

Figure 36 When you drag the scroll box, a yellow box with the page number and heading appears.

✔ Tip

■ Having trouble remembering which scroll arrow to click? Just remember this: click up to see up, click down to see down, click left to see left, and click right to see right.

Document Navigation

Word offers a variety of ways to view different parts of a document.

◆ Use **scroll bars** to shift the contents of the document window.

◆ Use the **Go To command** to view a specific document element, such as a certain page.

◆ Use **Browse Object buttons** to browse a document by its elements.

◆ Use the **Document Map** to move quickly to a specific heading.

◆ Use **Thumbnails**, which are new in Word 2003, to move quickly to a specific page.

✔ Tip

■ Although some keyboard keys change the portion of the document being viewed, they also move the insertion point. I tell you about these keys in **Chapter 2**.

To scroll the contents of the document window

Use one of the following techniques:

◆ Click the scroll arrow (**Figure 35**) for the direction that you want to view. For example, to scroll down to view the end of a document, click the down arrow.

◆ Drag the scroll box (**Figure 35**) in the direction that you want to view. As you drag, a yellow box appears on screen (**Figure 36**). It indicates the page and, if applicable, the heading that you are scrolling to.

◆ Click in the scroll bar above or below the scroll box (**Figure 35**). This shifts the window contents one screenful at a time.

To use the Go To command

1. Choose Edit > Go To (**Figure 6**). The Find and Replace dialog appears with its Go To tab displayed (**Figure 37**).

2. In the Go to what list box, select the type of document element that you want to view.

3. Enter the appropriate reference in the text box.

4. Click the Next button to go to the next reference.

5. Click the dialog's Close button to dismiss it.

For example, to go to page 5 of a document, select Page in step 2 and enter the number 5 in step 3.

To browse a document by its elements

1. Point to the Select Browse Object button (**Figure 38**).

2. Click to display the Select Browse Object pop-up menu.

3. Choose the element by which you want to browse (**Figure 39**).

4. Use the Next and Previous navigation buttons to view the next or previous element.

✔ Tips

■ The name of the object that a button represents appears at the top of the Select Browse Object pop-up menu when you point to the button (**Figure 39**).

■ Some of the buttons on the Select Browse Object pop-up menu (**Figure 39**) display dialogs that you can use for browsing.

Figure 37 The Go To tab of the Find and Replace dialog.

Figure 38 The Browse Object buttons at the bottom of the vertical scroll bar.

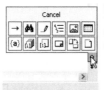

Figure 39
This menu pops up when you click the Select Browse Object button.

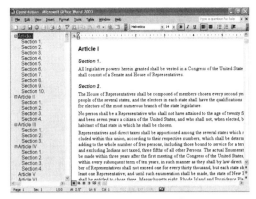

Figure 40 The Document Map in Normal view.

Figure 41 Clicking a heading in the Document Map shifts the document view to display that part of the document.

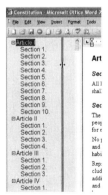

Figure 42 You can resize the Document Map's pane by dragging its right border.

Figure 43 Click a box beside a heading to hide or show its subheadings.

To use the Document Map

1. Choose View > Document Map (**Figure** 33) or click the Document Map button on the Standard toolbar.

   The Document Map appears in a narrow pane on the left side of the window (**Figure 40**).

2. Click the heading that you want to view. The main window pane's view shifts to show the heading that you clicked (**Figure 41**).

✔ Tips

- The Document Map is a good way to navigate documents that use Word's heading styles. I explain how to use headings in **Chapter 12** and styles in **Chapter 4**.

- Navigating with the Document Map also moves the insertion point. Moving the insertion point is discussed in **Chapter 2**.

- You can change the width of the Document Map's pane by dragging the border between it and the main window pane (**Figure 42**). When you release the border, both panes resize.

- You can collapse and expand the headings displayed in the Document Map by clicking the boxes to the left of the heading names (**Figure 43**).

- To hide the Document Map when you are finished using it, choose View > Document Map or double-click the border between the Document Map and the main window pane.

USING THE DOCUMENT MAP

To navigate a document with thumbnails

1. Choose View > Thumbnails (**Figure 33**).

   Thumbnail images for all pages in the document appear in a narrow pane on the left side of the window (**Figure 44**).

2. Click the thumbnail for the page you want to view. The main window pane's view shifts to show the top of the page that you clicked (**Figure 45**).

✔ Tips

■ Thumbnails are especially useful when working with documents that have a variety of page layouts.

■ Navigating with thumbnails also moves the insertion point. Moving the insertion point is discussed in **Chapter 2**.

■ You can change the width of the thumbnails pane by dragging the border between it and the main window pane. When you release the border, both panes resize.

■ To hide the thumbnails when you are finished using them, choose View > Thumbnails or double-click the border between the thumbnails pane and the main window pane.

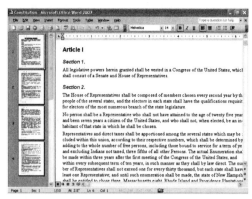

Figure 44 Thumbnails for a document.

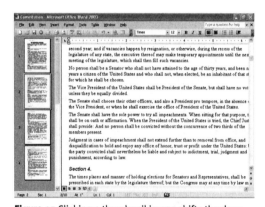

Figure 45 Clicking a thumbnail image shifts the document window's contents to display the top of the page that was clicked.

NAVIGATING WITH THUMBNAILS

Figure 46
The Window menu with three document windows open.

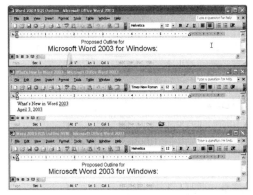

Figure 47 When more than one window is open for a document, the window number appears in the window's title bar.

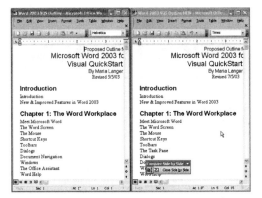

Figure 48 The Arrange All command neatly arranges all windows so you can see inside them.

Figure 49 Word 2003 makes it easy to compare the contents of two windows, side by side.

Windows

Word allows you to open more than one document window at a time. You work with windows using commands on the Window menu (**Figure 46**):

◆ **New Window** opens another window with the same contents as the active window. A number after a colon (:) in the title bar (**Figure 47**) indicates that multiple windows are open for a single document. If you edit the contents of one window, those changes are also displayed in the other(s) for that document.

◆ **Arrange All** resizes and repositions all open windows so you can see into each one (**Figure 48**).

◆ **Compare Side by Side with**, which is new in Word 2003, enables you to compare the contents of two documents, side by side (**Figure 49**). If only two document windows are open, this command will include the name of the inactive window. This command is not available if only one document window is open.

◆ **Split** splits the active document window horizontally (**Figure 50**) so you can scroll the top and bottom halves independently.

◆ *Document Window Name* activates and displays a specific document window.

✔ Tips

■ The active window is the one with the darker title bar. (If the window is maximized, it will be the only one visible.)

■ **Chapter 2** explains how to open and create documents.

WINDOWS

To activate a different window

Choose the name of the window that you want to view from the list on the bottom of the Window menu (**Figure 46**). That window becomes the active window.

To close a window

1. If necessary, activate the window that you want to close.

2. Choose File > Close (**Figure 51**), press Ctrl W, or click the window's close button.

✔ Tips

■ If the document contains unsaved changes, Word warns you and gives you a chance to save it (**Figure 52**). Saving documents is covered in **Chapter 2**.

■ Hold down Shift and display the File menu to change the Close command to the Close All command (**Figure 53**). This command closes all open windows.

To neatly arrange windows

Choose Window > Arrange All (**Figure 46**).

The windows are resized and repositioned so you can see into each one (**Figure 48**).

To split a window

1. Choose Window > Split (**Figure 46**).

2. A black split bar appears across the document window (**Figure 54**) and moves with the mouse pointer. Click to position the split bar (**Figure 50**).

3. Click in the top or bottom half of the window to activate it. You can then use the scroll bars to scroll in that half of the window.

4. When you are finished working with the split window, double-click the split bar to remove it.

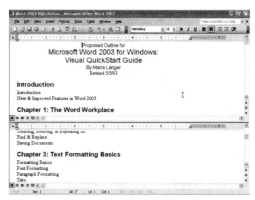

Figure 50 Splitting a window makes it possible to scroll top and bottom halves independently so you can see two parts of a document at once.

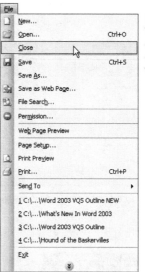

Figure 51 The Close command on the File menu closes the active window.

Figure 52 When you close a window that contains unsaved changes, a dialog like this appears.

Figure 53 Holding down Shift changes the Close command to a Close All command.

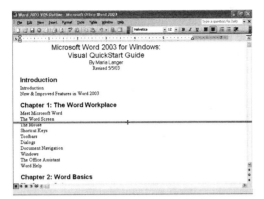

Figure 54 Choosing the Split command displays a split bar in the document window.

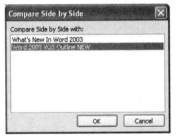

Figure 55 Use the Compare Side by Side dialog to select the document window you want to compare with the active window.

To compare the contents of two windows side by side

1. If only two windows are open, choose Window > Compare Side by Side with *Window Name.*

   or

   If more than two windows are open, choose Window > Compare Side by Side with (**Figure 46**). In the Compare Side by Side dialog that appears (**Figure 55**), select the name of the document you want to compare the active document with and click OK.

   The windows are resized and repositioned so they appear side by side and the Compare Side by Side toolbar appears (**Figure 49**).

2. Use the Synchronize Scrolling button on the Compare Side by Side toolbar to toggle scrolling synchronization. When enabled, scrolling one window automatically scrolls the other.

3. When you are finished comparing documents, click the Close Side by Side button on the Compare Side by Side toolbar.

✔ Tip

- This feature is very useful for comparing two similar documents—for example, the original version of a document and an edited version.

Word Help

Word has an extensive onscreen help feature that draws from help files automatically installed with Word as well as help information available on Microsoft's Web site. This makes it possible to get accurate, up-to-date information for getting assistance and solving problems with Word.

Most of Word's help features can be accessed from its Help menu (**Figure 56**). Here's a quick overview of what each command on that menu does.

◆ **Microsoft Word Help** (F1) displays the Microsoft Word Help task pane (**Figure 57**), which you can use to access a variety of onscreen and online help features.

◆ **Show the Office Assistant** displays the Office Assistant, an animated character (**Figure 58**) that provides an alternative interface for accessing Word Help. The Office Assistant may not be automatically installed with Word; the first time you use this command, a dialog may ask whether you want to install it. Click Yes to install and display it. When the Office Assistant is displayed, this command changes to Hide the Office Assistant.

◆ **Office on Microsoft.com** uses your Web browser to display the Microsoft Office home page on the Microsoft Web site (**Figure 59**).

◆ **Contact Us** uses your Web browser to display the Contact Us page on the Microsoft Web site. This page offers options for contacting Microsoft about Office products.

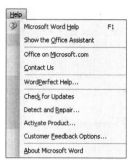

Figure 56
Word's Help menu.

Figure 57
The Microsoft Word Help task pane.

Figure 58
The Office Assistant offers an alternative interface for accessing Word help.

ACCESSING WORD HELP

Figure 59 The Office Online home page on the Microsoft Web site offers a wealth of information about Word and other Office products.

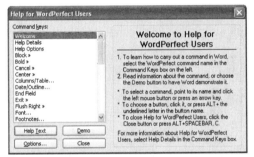

Figure 60 If you just switched from WordPerfect to Word, be sure to install and check out the special help feature written just for you.

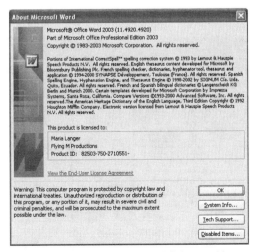

Figure 61 The About Microsoft Word dialog provides version information and more.

◆ **WordPerfect Help** displays help information written specifically for former WordPerfect users (**Figure 60**). This feature may not be automatically installed with Word; the first time you use this command, a dialog may ask if you want to install it. Click Yes to install and display it.

◆ **Check for Updates** uses your Web browser to access the Microsoft Office Downloads page on the Microsoft Web site. This is where you can find updates and add-ins for using Microsoft Office products.

◆ **Detect and Repair** runs an internal Office utility that can detect and repair errors in Microsoft Office files. Use this feature if Word doesn't seem to be running correctly.

◆ **Activate Product** enables you to enter an activation code to activate Word. If you're a registered Word or Office user, you should not need to use this command.

◆ **Customer Feedback Options** displays the Service Options dialog, which you can use to set options for sharing information with Microsoft about how you use Word.

◆ **About Microsoft Word** displays a dialog like the one in **Figure 61** with information about the copy of Word running on your computer. Buttons in this dialog enable you to get information about your system, technical support, and disabled items that can help you or Microsoft support troubleshoot problems.

This part of the chapter explains how to use the Microsoft Word Help task pane to get assistance using Word features. You can explore Word's other Help menu commands on your own.

To use Word Help

1. Click in the Type a question for help box at the right end of the menu bar (**Figure 62**). Enter a word, phrase, or question for which you want help (**Figure 63**) and press Enter.

   or

   Choose Help > Microsoft Word Help, press F1, or click the Microsoft Word Help button 🔍 in the Standard toolbar to display the Microsoft Word Help task pane (**Figure 57**). Enter a word, phrase, or question for which you want help in the Search box and click the green Start Searching button or press Enter.

   Word begins searching and displays the Search Results task pane with topics that may provide the help you need. If you have an active Internet connection, the search results will be from Microsoft's Web site (**Figure 64**). If you don't have an Internet connection, the search results will be from offline help installed with Microsoft Word.

2. Click a blue topic name in the Search Results task pane. The document window resizes and a Microsoft Word Help window appears to its right (**Figure 65**).

3. Read the information in the Help window to learn about the topic.

   or

   Click links in the Help window to display other topics in the window.

4. Repeat steps 2 and 3 to explore the information in all help topics that interest you.

Figure 62 This box, at the right end of the menu bar, offers one way to ask Word for help.

Figure 63 An example of a help request.

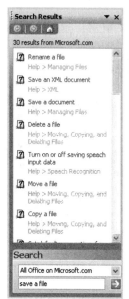

Figure 64
Because my computer is connected to the Internet, the Search Results task pane displays topics from the Microsoft Web site.

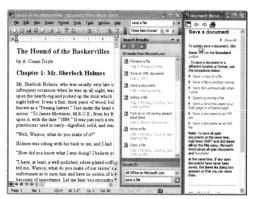

Figure 65 The Microsoft Word Help window appears to the right of the document window when you click a help topic. This is where it really pays to have a big, high-resolution monitor!

USING WORD HELP

Figure 66
You can use the drop-down (or should I say "drop-up"?) list at the bottom of the Search Results task pane to tell Word where to look for help.

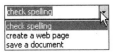

Figure 67 Word remembers all the things you asked during a work session.

5. When you are finished using Help, click the close button in the far right window to close the Microsoft Word Help window and return the document window to its full size. You can also click the close button in the Search Results task pane to dismiss it.

✔ Tips

- In step 1, if you have already used Word's help feature, the last help request you entered may appear in the box at the end of the menu bar. Just click in the box and enter a new word, phase, or question.

- After step 1, to instruct the Help feature to display only results from offline help, choose Offline Help from the drop-down list in the search area (**Figure 66**) and click the green Start Searching button.

- After using the help feature several times, you can quickly go back to search results for a help topic by choosing the topic from the drop-down list at the right end of the menu bar (**Figure 67**).

USING WORD HELP

Word
Basics

Word Processing Basics

Word processing software has revolutionized the way we create text-based documents. Rather than committing each character to paper as you type—as you would do with a typewriter—word processing enables you to enter documents on screen, edit and format them as you work, and save them for future reference or revision. Nothing appears on paper until you use the Print command.

If you're brand new to word processing, here are a few concepts you should understand before you begin working with Microsoft Word or any other word processing software:

◆ Words that you type that do not fit at the end of a line automatically appear on the next line. This feature is called *word wrap*.

◆ Do not press (Enter) at the end of each line as you type. Doing so inserts a Return character, which signals the end of a paragraph, not the end of a line. Press (Enter) only at the end of a paragraph or to skip a line between paragraphs.

◆ Do not use (Spacebar) to indent text or position text in simple tables. Instead, use (Tab) in conjunction with tab settings on the ruler.

◆ Text can be inserted or deleted anywhere in the document.

I tell you more about all of these concepts in this chapter and throughout this book.

Running Word

To use Word, you must run the Word program.

To run Word from the Taskbar

Click Start > Programs > Microsoft Word.

The Word splash screen appears briefly and an empty document window named *Document1* appears, along with the Getting Started task pane (**Figure 1**).

✔ Tip

- You can disable the display of the task pane at startup in the Options dialog. I explain how in **Chapter 19**. Task panes are discussed in **Chapter 1** and elsewhere throughout this book.

To run Word by opening a Word document

1. In Windows Explorer, locate the icon for the document that you want to open (**Figure 2**).

2. Double-click the icon.

   The Word splash screen appears briefly, and then a document window containing the document you opened appears (**Figure 3**).

Figure 1 When you run Word from the Taskbar, it displays a blank document window and the Getting Started task pane.

Figure 2
A Word document icon.

Hound of the Baskervilles

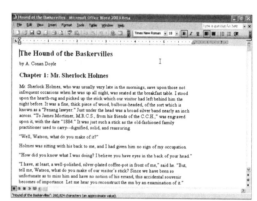

Figure 3 When you run Word by opening a Word document, it displays the document you opened.

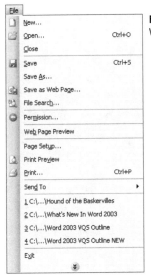

Figure 4
Word's File menu.

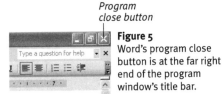

*Program
close button*

Figure 5
Word's program close button is at the far right end of the program window's title bar.

Figure 6 A dialog like this appears if a document with unsaved changes is open when you exit Word.

Exiting Word

When you're finished using Word, you should use the Exit command to close the program. This makes more of the computer's resources available for other programs that you run so your computer can work more efficiently.

✔ Tip

■ Exiting Word also instructs Word to save preference settings and any changes to the Normal template.

To exit Word

Choose File > Exit (**Figure 4**).

or

Click the close button in the upper right corner of the Microsoft Word program window (**Figure 5**).

Here's what happens:

▲ If any documents are open, they close.

▲ If an open document contains unsaved changes, a dialog appears (**Figure 6**) so you can save the changes. Saving documents is discussed later in this chapter.

▲ The Word program closes.

✔ Tip

■ As you've probably guessed, Word automatically exits when you restart or shut down your computer.

Word Documents, Templates, & Wizards

The documents you create and save using Word are Word document files. These files contain all the information necessary to display the contents of the document as formatted using Microsoft Word.

All Word document files are based on *templates*. A template is a collection of styles and other formatting features that determines the appearance of a document. Templates can also include default text, macros, and custom toolbars.

For example, you can create a letterhead template that includes your company's logo and contact information or is designed to be printed on special paper. The template can include styles that utilize specific fonts. It can also include custom toolbars with buttons for commands commonly used when writing letters.

Wizards take templates a step further. They are special Word document files that include Microsoft Visual Basic commands to automate the creation of specific types of documents. Word comes with many wizards, some of which are covered in this book.

Professional Letter

Figure 7
A Word template icon.

Letter Wizard

Figure 8
A Word wizard icon.

✔ Tips

■ A Word document icon (**Figure 2**), template icon (**Figure 7**), and wizard icon (**Figure 8**) are very similar in appearance.

■ Word can open and save files in formats other than Word document format. I tell you more about file formats later in this chapter.

■ When no other template is specified for a document, Word applies the default template, *Normal*.

■ I cover styles in **Chapter 4**, Macros and Visual Basic in **Chapter 18**, and custom toolbars in **Chapter 19**.

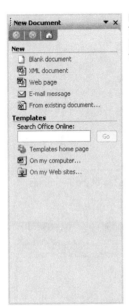

Figure 9
The New
Document
task pane.

Creating Documents

You can create a new document with the New Document task pane.

To create a blank document

1. If the New Document task pane is not displayed, choose File > New (**Figure 4**) to display it (**Figure 9**).

2. In the New area, click Blank Document.

or

Press Ctrl N.

or

Click the New Blank Document button 🗋 on the Standard toolbar.

A blank document based on the Normal template appears (**Figure 10**). If the New Document task pane was showing, it disappears.

✔ Tip

■ The New area of the New Document task pane (**Figure 9**) also enables you to create blank XML documents, Web pages, and e-mail messages. I cover Web pages in **Chapter 17** and e-mail messages in **Chapter 16**. XML documents are beyond the scope of this book.

Figure 10 A blank document window based on the Normal template.

To create a document based on a template other than Normal

1. If the New Document task pane is not displayed, choose File > New (**Figure 4**) to display it (**Figure 9**).

2. In the Template area, click On my computer to display the Templates dialog.

3. Click the tab for the category of template you want to use (**Figure 11**).

4. Select the icon for the template you want to use. A preview of the template may appear in the Preview area.

5. Click OK.

A document based on the template that you selected appears (**Figure 12**). Follow the instructions in the template to replace placeholder text with your text.

✔ Tips

■ The Templates area of the New Document task pane (**Figure 9**) also enables you to access templates on the Microsoft Office Web site and your own Web sites.

■ Once you have created at least one document based on a template, the most recently used templates appear in a list at the bottom of the New Document task pane (**Figure 13**).

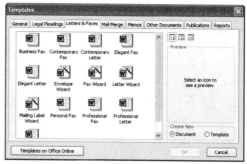

Figure 11 The Letters & Faxes tab of the Templates dialog.

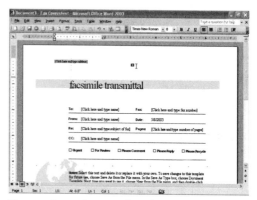

Figure 12 A new document based on a template.

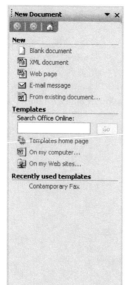

Figure 13
A list of recently used templates appears at the bottom of the New Document task pane after you have used at least one template.

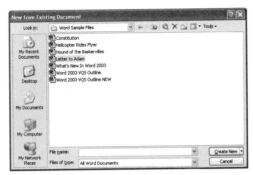

Figure 14 The New from Existing Document dialog enables you to choose an existing document on which to base a new document.

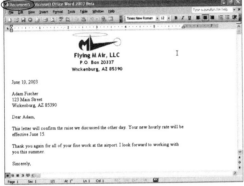

Figure 15 Although this document might look exactly like the original, it is indeed new.

To create a document based on another document

1. If the New Document task pane is not displayed, choose File > New (**Figure 4**) to display it (**Figure 9**).

2. In the New area, click From existing document.

3. Use the New from Existing Document dialog (**Figure 14**) to locate and select the document on which you want to base the new document.

4. Click Create New.

   A new document window appears. Although it appears identical to the one you selected in step 3 (**Figure 15**), the document is untitled; saving it will not overwrite the original document.

✔ Tip

- Creating a document based on an existing document can save time when creating a document that is almost identical to one that already exists.

CREATING DOCUMENTS BASED ON DOCUMENTS

To create a document with a wizard

1. If the New Document task pane is not displayed, choose File > New (**Figure 4**) to display it (**Figure 9**).

2. In the Templates area, click On my computer to display the Templates dialog.

3. Click the tab for the category of wizard you want to use (**Figure 11**).

4. Select the icon for the wizard you want to use. A preview of the wizard may appear in the Preview area.

5. Click OK.

6. A document window appears, along with a series of Wizard dialogs (**Figures 16** through **20**). Enter appropriate information as prompted in each dialog of the Wizard to create the document.

7. When you've finished entering information, click Finish to dismiss the Wizard. The document you created remains open (**Figure 21**) so you can continue to work with it.

✔ Tip

■ When the wizard is finished, you can customize the document it creates (**Figure 21**) to meet your specific needs.

Figure 16 The first dialog of the Letter Wizard.

Figure 17 Step 1 of the Letter Wizard prompts you for the date and formatting information.

Figure 18 Step 2 of the Letter Wizard prompts you for information about who the letter is to.

Figure 19 Step 3 of the Letter Wizard prompts you for additional options to include in the letter.

Figure 20 Step 4 of the Letter Wizard prompts you for information about the sender.

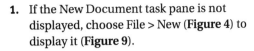

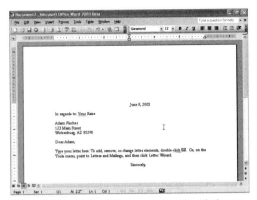

Figure 21 The results of the Letter Wizard, with the settings shown in **Figures 16** though **20**.

Figure 22 The General tab of the Templates dialog.

Figure 23 Use the Create New option buttons to specify whether you want to create a regular document or a template.

To create a template

1. If the New Document task pane is not displayed, choose File > New (**Figure 4**) to display it (**Figure 9**).

2. In the Template area, click On my computer to display the Templates dialog.

3. To create a new blank template, select the Blank Document icon in the General tab (**Figure 22**).

   or

   To create a template based on another template, click the tab for a specific category of template and select the icon for the template you want to use.

4. Select the Template option in the Create New area (**Figure 23**) at the bottom of the Templates dialog.

5. Click OK.

6. A new document window appears. Add text, styles, or other features to the document as discussed throughout this book.

✔ Tip

■ When you save the document, it is automatically saved as a template. Saving documents and templates is covered later in this chapter.

Opening Documents

Once a document has been saved, you can reopen it to read it, modify it, or print it.

To open an existing document

1. Choose File > Open (**Figure 4**) or press [Ctrl] [O].

   or

   Click the Open button 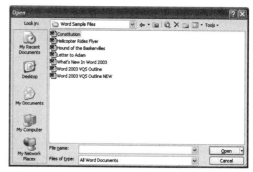 on the Standard toolbar.

Figure 24 The Open dialog.

2. Use the Open dialog that appears (**Figure 24**) to locate the file you want to open:

   ▲ Use the Look in drop-down list near the top of the dialog (**Figure 25**) to go to another location.

   ▲ Double-click a folder to open it.

3. Select the file that you want to open and click the Open button.

   or

   Double-click the file that you want to open.

Figure 25
The Look in drop-down list enables you to look in other locations.

✔ Tips

■ You can also navigate within the Open dialog by using the Places bar along the left side of the Open dialog. Consult the documentation that came with Windows to learn more about using these buttons.

■ To view only specific types of files in the Open dialog, select a format from the Files of type drop-down list at the bottom of the dialog (**Figure 26**).

■ If you select All Files from the Files of type drop-down list (**Figure 26**), you can open just about any kind of file. Be aware, however, that a document in an incompatible format may not appear the way you expect when opened.

Figure 26 The Files of type drop-down list includes file formats that can be read by Word.

■ You can open a recent file by selecting it from the list of recently opened files at the bottom of the File menu (**Figure 4**) or by clicking its name in the Open area of the Getting Started task Pane (**Figure 1**).

Figure 27 Text characters appear at the blinking insertion point as you type.

Figure 28 Word wrap automatically occurs when the text you type won't fit on the current line.

Figure 29 Press [Enter] to start a new paragraph.

Figure 30 Press [Shift][Enter] to start a new line in the same paragraph.

Entering Text

In most cases, you will enter text into a Word document using the keyboard.

✔ Tip

■ A wavy red or green line appearing beneath the text you type indicates that the text has a possible spelling or grammar error. Spelling and grammar checking are covered in **Chapter 7**.

To type text

Type the characters, words, or sentences that you want to enter into the document. Text appears at the blinking insertion point as you type it (**Figure 27**).

✔ Tips

■ I explain how to move the insertion point a little later in this chapter.

■ Do not press [Enter] at the end of a line. A new line automatically begins when a word can't fit on the current line (**Figure 28**).

To start a new paragraph

At the end of a paragraph, press [Enter]. This inserts a paragraph break or return character that ends the current paragraph and begins a new one (**Figure 29**).

To start a new line

To end a line without ending the current paragraph, press [Shift][Enter]. This inserts a line break character in the paragraph (**Figure 30**).

✔ Tip

■ Use a line break instead of a paragraph break to begin a new line without beginning a new paragraph. This makes it easy to apply paragraph formatting to multiple lines that belong together. I cover Paragraph formatting in **Chapters 3** and **4**.

Formatting Marks

Every character you type is entered into a Word document—even characters that normally can't be seen, such as space, tab, return, line break, and optional hyphen characters.

Word enables you to display these *formatting marks* (**Figure 31**), making it easy to see all the characters in a document.

✔ Tips

- Formatting marks are sometimes referred to as *nonprinting* or *invisible characters*.

- By displaying formatting marks, you can get a better understanding of the structure of a document. For example, **Figure 31** clearly shows the difference between the return and line break characters entered in **Figure 30**.

To show or hide formatting marks

Click the Show/Hide ¶ button ¶ on the Standard toolbar. This toggles the display of formatting marks.

To specify which formatting marks should be displayed

1. Choose Tools > Options (**Figure 32**).

2. Click the View tab in the Options dialog that appears (**Figure 33**).

3. Turn on the check boxes in the Formatting marks area of the dialog to specify which characters should appear.

4. Click OK.

✔ Tips

- To display all formatting marks, turn on the All check box in step 3.

- Word's Options dialog is discussed in detail in **Chapter 19**.

Figure 31 Text with formatting marks displayed. This example shows space, paragraph, and line break characters.

Figure 32 Choose Options from the Tools menu.

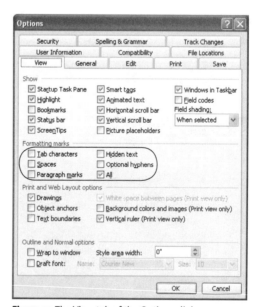

Figure 33 The View tab of the Options dialog.

Table 1

Keystrokes for Moving the Insertion Point	
Press:	**To move the insertion point:**
→	one character to the right
←	one character to the left
↑	one line up
↓	one line down
Ctrl →	one word to the right
Ctrl ←	one word to the left
Ctrl ↑	one paragraph up
Ctrl ↓	one paragraph down
End	to the end of the line
Home	to the beginning of the line
Ctrl End	to the end of the document
Ctrl Home	to the beginning of the document
Page Up	up one screen
Page Down	down one screen
Ctrl Page Up	to the top of the previous page
Ctrl Page Down	to the top of the next page
Ctrl Alt Page Up	to the top of the window
Ctrl Alt Page Down	to the bottom of the window
Shift F5	to the previous edit

Figure 34 Position the mouse's I-beam pointer where you want the insertion point to move.

Figure 35 Click to move the insertion point.

The Insertion Point

The blinking insertion point indicates where the information you type or paste will be inserted. There are two main ways to move the insertion point: with the keyboard and with the mouse.

✔ Tip

- The insertion point also moves when you use the Document Map to navigate within a document. The Document Map is discussed in **Chapter 1**.

To move the insertion point with the keyboard

Press the appropriate keyboard key(s) (**Table 1**).

✔ Tip

- There are additional keystrokes that work within cell tables. I tell you about them in **Chapter 8**, where I discuss tables.

To move the insertion point with the mouse

1. Position the mouse's I-beam pointer where you want to move the insertion point (**Figure 34**).

2. Click once. The insertion point moves (**Figure 35**).

✔ Tips

- Simply moving the I-beam pointer is not enough. You must click to move the insertion point.

- Do not move the mouse while clicking. Doing so will select text.

Inserting & Deleting Text

You can insert or delete characters at the insertion point at any time.

- When you insert characters, any text to the right of the insertion point shifts to the right to make room for new characters (**Figures 36** and **37**).

- When you delete text, any text to the right of the insertion point shifts to the left to close up space left by deleted characters (**Figures 38** and **39**).

- When you insert or delete text, word wrap adjusts if necessary to comfortably fit characters on each line (**Figures 37** and **39**).

To insert text

1. Position the insertion point where you want to insert the text (**Figure 36**).

2. Type the text you want to insert (**Figure 37**).

✔ Tip

- You can also insert text by pasting the contents of the Clipboard at the insertion point. Using the Clipboard to copy and paste text is covered later in this chapter.

To delete text

1. Position the insertion point to the right of the character(s) you want to delete (**Figure 38**).

2. Press Backspace to delete the character to the left of the insertion point (**Figure 39**).

or

1. Position the insertion point to the left of the character(s) you want to delete.

2. Press Delete to delete the character to the right of the insertion point.

Figure 36 Position the insertion point.

Figure 37 Type the text you want to insert.

Figure 38 Position the insertion point to the right of the character(s) you want to delete.

Figure 39 Press Backspace to delete the characters.

✔ Tip

- You can also delete text by selecting it and pressing Backspace or Delete. Selecting text is discussed a little later in this chapter.

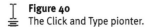

Figure 40
The Click and Type pionter.

Figure 41 Position the Click and Type pointer where you want to enter text.

Figure 42 Double-click to position the insertion point.

Figure 43 Type the text you want to appear.

Click and Type

Click and Type is a feature that makes it easier to position text in a blank area of a page. You simply double-click with the Click and Type pointer (**Figure 40**) and enter the text you want to appear there. Word automatically applies necessary formatting to the text to position it where you want it.

✔ Tip

- Click and Type works only in Print Layout and Web Layout views. Word's views are discussed in **Chapter 1**.

To enter text with Click and Type

1. If necessary, switch to Print Layout or Web Layout view.

2. Position the mouse pointer in an empty area of the document window. The mouse pointer should turn into a Click and Type pointer (**Figure 41**).

3. Double-click. The insertion point appears at the mouse pointer (**Figure 42**).

4. Type the text you want to enter. (**Figure 43**).

✔ Tips

- The appearance of the Click and Type pointer indicates how it will align text at the insertion point. For example, the pointer shown in **Figures 40** and **41** indicates that text will be centered (**Figure 43**). I tell you more about alignment, including how to change it, in **Chapter 3**.

- There are some limitations to where you can use the Click and Type feature. Generally speaking, if the Click and Type pointer does not appear, you cannot use it to position text.

USING CLICK AND TYPE

Selecting Text

You can select one or more characters to delete, replace, copy, cut, or format it. Selected text appears with a colored background or in inverse type.

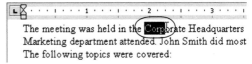

Figure 44 Drag over text to select it.

✔ Tips

■ There are many ways to select text. This section provides just a few of the most useful methods.

■ Word enables you to select multiple blocks of text. To do this, hold down Ctrl while selecting each block, using any of the techniques discussed in this chapter.

To select text by dragging

1. Position the mouse I-beam pointer at the beginning of the text.

2. Press the mouse button down and drag to the end of the text you want to select (**Figure 44**).

3. Release the mouse button.

   All characters between the starting and ending points are selected.

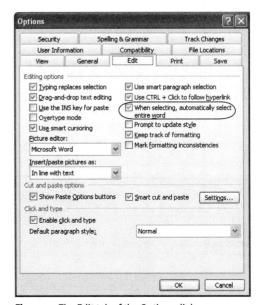

Figure 45 The Edit tab of the Options dialog.

✔ Tips

■ This is the most basic text selection technique. It works for any amount of text.

■ By default, Word automatically selects entire words when you drag through more than one word. To disable this feature, choose Tools > Options (**Figure 32**), click the Edit tab in the Options dialog that appears (**Figure 45**), and turn off the check box for When selecting, automatically select entire word.

Table 2

Techniques for Selecting Text by Clicking	
To select:	Do this:
a word	double-click the word
a sentence	hold down Ctrl and click in the sentence
a line	click in the selection bar to the left of the line (**Figure 46**)
a paragraph	triple-click in the paragraph or double-click in the selection bar to the left of the paragraph
the document	hold down Ctrl and double-click in the selection bar to the left of any line
any text	position the insertion point at the beginning of the text, then hold down Shift and click at the end of the text

Figure 46 Click in the selection bar beside a line to select the line.

Figure 47
The Edit menu.

To select text by clicking

Click as instructed in **Table 2** to select specific amounts of text.

✔ Tips

- You can combine techniques in **Table 2** with dragging to select multiple lines and paragraphs.

- When you select an entire word by double-clicking it, Word also selects any spaces after it.

To select the contents of a document

Choose Edit > Select All (**Figure 47**).

or

Press Ctrl A.

Editing Selected Text

Once you select text, you can delete it or replace it with other text.

To delete selected text

Press Backspace or Delete. The selected text disappears.

To replace selected text

With text selected, type the replacement text. The selected text disappears and the replacement text is inserted in its place.

Copying & Moving Text

Word offers two ways to copy or move text:

◆ Use the Copy, Cut, and Paste commands (or their shortcut keys) to place text on the Clipboard and then copy it from the Clipboard to another location.

◆ Use drag-and-drop editing to copy or move selected text.

You can copy or move text to:

◆ A different location within the same document.

◆ A different document.

◆ A document created with a program other than Word.

✔ Tips

■ Copying and moving text make it possible to reuse text and reorganize a document without a lot of retyping.

■ The Clipboard is a place in your computer's memory (RAM) that is used to temporarily store selected items that are copied or cut. Word supports two Clipboards:

▲ The *Windows Clipboard* is shared among all Windows applications that support the copy and paste commands.

▲ The *Office Clipboard* is shared among all Microsoft Office applications. It offers additional features, which are discussed later in this chapter.

■ Text you copy or cut remains on the Clipboard until you use the Copy or Cut command again or restart your computer. This makes it possible to use Clipboard contents over and over in any document.

■ These techniques also work with objects such as graphics. I tell you more about working with objects in **Chapter 10**.

Figure 48 Select the text that you want to copy.

Figure 49 The Clipboard task pane may appear when you use the Copy command.

Sincerely,

John Aabbott
Product Manager

Figure 50 Position the insertion point where you want the copied text to appear.

Sincerely,

John Aabbott
Product Manager
Alphabet Soup

Figure 51 When you use the Paste command, the contents of the Clipboard appear at the insertion point, along with the Paste Options button.

Thank you for your delightful letter regarding Alphabet Squares, the newest addition to our Alphabet Soup product line. We're glad to know that there are many hungry soup eaters out there who appreciate the variety of letters we include in every can. Your report that you use our soup to help you solve crossword puzzles is fascinating!

I've included a coupon for 75¢ off your next purchase of Alphabet Squares. Please enjoy your next can "on us"!

I'll send your comments regarding the overabundance of Qs and Zs to our production department. They'll make the appropriate adjustments to assure that these letters are more properly represented.

Sincerely,

Figure 52 Select the text that ou want to move.

Thank you for your delightful letter regarding Alphabet Squares, the newest addition to our Alphabet Soup product line. We're glad to know that there are many hungry soup eaters out there who appreciate the variety of letters we include in every can. Your report that you use our soup to help you solve crossword puzzles is fascinating!

I'll send your comments regarding the overabundance of Qs and Zs to our production department. They'll make the appropriate adjustments to assure that these letters are more properly represented.

Sincerely,

Figure 53 The text you cut disappears.

Thank you for your delightful letter regarding Alphabet Squares, the newest addition to our Alphabet Soup product line. We're glad to know that there are many hungry soup eaters out there who appreciate the variety of letters we include in every can. Your report that you use our soup to help you solve crossword puzzles is fascinating!

I'll send your comments regarding the overabundance of Qs and Zs to our production department. They'll make the appropriate adjustments to assure that these letters are more properly represented.

Sincerely,

Figure 54 Position the insertion point where you want the cut text to appear.

Thank you for your delightful letter regarding Alphabet Squares, the newest addition to our Alphabet Soup product line. We're glad to know that there are many hungry soup eaters out there who appreciate the variety of letters we include in every can. Your report that you use our soup to help you solve crossword puzzles is fascinating!

I'll send your comments regarding the overabundance of Qs and Zs to our production department. They'll make the appropriate adjustments to assure that these letters are more properly represented.

I've included a coupon for 75¢ off your next purchase of Alphabet Squares. Please enjoy your next can "on us"!

Sincerely,

Figure 55 The contents of the Clipboard appear at the insertion point, along with the Paste Options button.

To copy text with Copy & Paste

1. Select the text that you want to copy (**Figure 48**).

2. Choose Edit > Copy (**Figure 47**), press Ctrl C, or click the Copy button 📋 on the Standard toolbar.

    The selected text is copied to the Clipboard. The document does not change, however the Clipboard task pane may appear (**Figure 49**).

3. Position the insertion point where you want the text copied (**Figure 50**).

4. Choose Edit > Paste (**Figure 47**), press Ctrl V, or click the Paste button 📋 on the Standard toolbar.

    The text in the Clipboard is copied into the document at the insertion point (**Figure 51**).

To move text with Cut & Paste

1. Select the text that you want to move (**Figure 52**).

2. Choose Edit > Cut (**Figure 47**), press Ctrl X, or click the Cut button ✂ on the Standard toolbar.

    The selected text is copied to the Clipboard and removed from the document (**Figure 53**).

3. Position the insertion point where you want the cut text to appear (**Figure 54**).

4. Choose Edit > Paste (**Figure 47**), press Ctrl V, or click the Paste button 📋 on the Standard toolbar.

    The text in the Clipboard is copied into the document at the insertion point (**Figure 55**).

To copy text with drag-and-drop editing

1. Select the text that you want to copy (**Figure 48**).

2. Position the mouse pointer on the selected text (**Figure 56**).

3. Hold down Ctrl, press the mouse button down, and drag. As you drag, a tiny box and vertical line move with the mouse pointer, which has a plus sign beside it to indicate that it is copying (**Figure 57**).

4. When the vertical line at the mouse pointer is where you want the text copied to, release the mouse button and Ctrl. The selected text is copied (**Figure 51**).

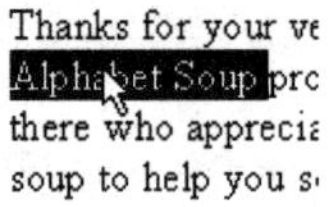

To move text with drag-and-drop editing

1. Select the text that you want to move (**Figure 52**).

2. Position the mouse pointer on the selected text (**Figure 58**).

3. Press the mouse button down and drag. As you drag, a box and vertical line move with the mouse pointer (**Figure 59**).

4. When the vertical line at the mouse pointer is where you want the text moved to, release the mouse button. The selected text is moved (**Figure 55**).

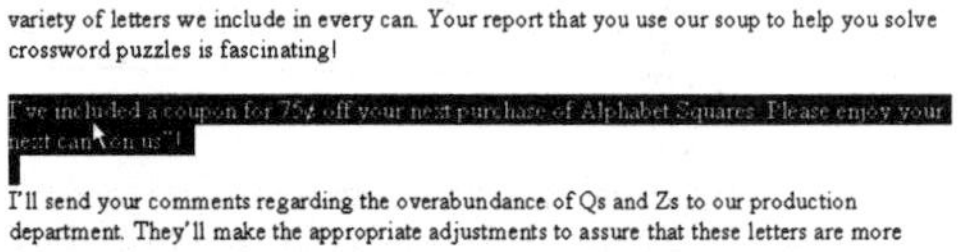

Thanks for your ve
Alphabet Soup prc
there who apprecia
soup to help you s

Figure 56 Point to the selection.

Sincerely,

John Aabbott
Product Manager

Figure 57 Hold down Ctrl and drag to copy the selection.

variety of letters we include in every can. Your report that you use our soup to help you solve crossword puzzles is fascinating!

I've included a coupon for 75¢ off your next purchase of Alphabet Squares. Please enjoy your next can on us!"

I'll send your comments regarding the overabundance of Qs and Zs to our production department. They'll make the appropriate adjustments to assure that these letters are more

Figure 58 Point to the selection.

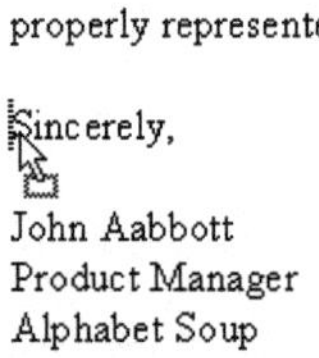

properly represented.

Sincerely,

John Aabbott
Product Manager
Alphabet Soup

Figure 59 Drag to move the selection.

I've included a coupon for 75¢ off your next purchase your next can "on us"!

Sincerely,

John Aabbott
Product Manager
Alphabet Soup

- Keep Source Formatting
- Match Destination Formatting
- Keep Text Only
- Apply Style or Formatting...

Figure 60 Clicking the Paste Options button displays a menu of formatting options for the paste in item.

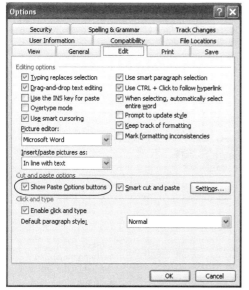

Figure 61 You can disable the Paste Options feature in the Edit tab of the Options dialog.

Paste Options

When you use the Paste command or drag and drop text to copy or move it, the Paste Options button appears (**Figures 51** and **55**). Clicking this icon displays a menu of formatting options (**Figure 60**):

◆ **Keep source formatting** retains the formatting applied to the original item.

◆ **Match destination formatting** changes the formatting to match the new location.

◆ **Keep text only** removes all formatting.

◆ **Apply Style or Formatting** displays the Styles and Formatting task pane so you can apply different formatting to the item.

✔ Tips

■ You do not have to use the Paste Options feature when you copy or move text. Use it only when the formatting of the text you copied or moved needs to be changed.

■ The Paste Options button automatically disappears as you work with Word.

■ Formatting text is discussed in detail in **Chapters 3** and **4**.

To set formatting options with Paste Options

1. Click the Paste Options button to display the Paste Options menu (**Figure 60**).

2. Click to select the option you want.

To disable Paste Options

1. Choose Tools > Options (**Figure 32**).

2. Click the Edit tab in the Options dialog that appears (**Figure 61**).

3. Turn off the check box for Show Paste Options buttons.

4. Click OK.

PASTE OPTIONS

The Office Clipboard

The Office Clipboard enables you to "collect and paste" multiple items. You simply display the Office Clipboard task pane, then copy text or objects as usual. But instead of the Clipboard contents being replaced each time you use the Copy or Cut command, all items are stored on the Office Clipboard (**Figure 62**). You can then paste any of the items on the Office Clipboard into your Word document.

✔ Tip

- The Office Clipboard works with all Microsoft Office applications—not just Word— so you can store items from different types of Office documents.

To display the Office Clipboard

Choose Edit > Office Clipboard (**Figure 47**). The Office Clipboard appears as a task pane beside the document window.

✔ Tip

- The Office Clipboard automatically appears when you copy two items in a row.

To add an item to the Office Clipboard

1. If necessary, display the Office Clipboard (**Figure 62**).

2. Select the text or object you want to copy (**Figure 63**).

3. Choose Edit > Copy (**Figure 47**), press Ctrl C, or click the Copy button on the Standard toolbar. The selection appears on the Office Clipboard (**Figure 64**).

Figure 62 The Office Clipboard appears as a task pane beside the document window.

Figure 63 Select the item you want to add to the Office Clipboard.

Figure 64 The item you copied is added to the Office Clipboard.

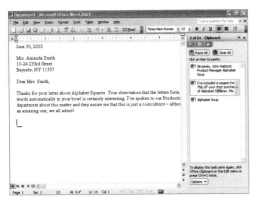

Figure 65 Position the insertion point where you want the item to appear, then click the item in the Office Clipboard.

Figure 66 The item you clicked is pasted in at the insertion point.

Figure 67 Click the button to display a pop-up menu.

Figure 68 The item is removed from the Office Clipboard.

To use Office Clipboard items

1. If necessary, display the Office Clipboard.

2. In the document window, position the insertion point where you want to place the Office Clipboard item (**Figure 65**).

3. In the Office Clipboard task pane, click on the item you want to paste into the document (**Figure 66**).

or

1. If necessary, display the Office Clipboard.

2. Drag the item you want to use from the Office Clipboard window into the document window.

The item you pasted or dragged appears in the document window (**Figure 66**).

✔ Tip

- Clicking the Paste All button at the top of the Office Clipboard (**Figure 66**) pastes all items into the document in the order in which they were added to the Office Clipboard.

To remove Office Clipboard items

1. In the Office Clipboard window, point to the item you want to remove (**Figure 65**). A blue border appears around it and a pop-up menu button appears beside it.

2. Click the pop-up menu button to display a menu of two options (**Figure 67**).

3. Choose Delete. The item is removed from the Office Clipboard (**Figure 68**).

or

Click the Clear All button at the top of the Office Clipboard (**Figure 68**) to remove all items.

Undoing, Redoing, & Repeating Actions

Word offers a trio of commands that enable you to undo, redo, or repeat the last thing you did.

Figures 69, 70, & 71
Some examples of how the Undo, Redo, and Repeat commands can appear on the Edit menu.

♦ **Undo** reverses your last action. Word supports multiple levels of undo, enabling you to reverse more than the last action.

♦ **Redo** reverses the Undo command. This command is only available if the last thing you did was use the Undo command.

♦ **Repeat** performs your last action again. This command is only available when you performed any action other than use the Undo or Redo command.

✔ Tips

■ The exact wording of these commands on the Edit menu varies depending on the last action performed. The Undo command is always the first command under the Edit menu; the Redo or Repeat command (whichever appears on the menu) is always the second command under the full Edit menu. **Figures 69, 70**, and **71** show some examples.

■ By default, the Redo and Repeat commands do not appear on personalized menus. Full and personalized menus are discussed in **Chapter 1**.

■ The Redo and Repeat commands are never both available at the same time.

■ Think of the Undo command as the *Oops!* command—anytime you say "Oops!" you'll probably want to use it.

■ The Repeat command is especially useful for applying formatting to text scattered throughout your document. I tell you more about formatting in **Chapters 3** and **4**.

Figure 72 Use the Undo pop-up menu to select actions to undo.

Figure 73 Use the Redo pop-up menu to select actions to redo.

To undo the last action

Choose Edit > Undo (**Figures 69**, **70**, or **71**), press Ctrl Z, or click the Undo button ⤺ ▾ on the Standard toolbar.

To undo multiple actions

Choose Edit > Undo (**Figures 69**, **70**, or **71**) or press Ctrl Z repeatedly.

or

Click the triangle beside the Undo button ⤺ ▾ on the Standard toolbar to display a pop-up menu of recent actions. Drag down to select all the actions that you want to undo (**Figure 72**). Release the mouse button to undo all selected actions.

To reverse the last undo

Choose Edit > Redo (**Figure 69**), press Ctrl Y, or click the Redo button ↻ ▾ on the Standard toolbar.

To reverse multiple undos

Choose Edit > Redo (**Figure 69**) or press Ctrl Y repeatedly.

or

Click the triangle beside the Redo button ↻ ▾ on the Standard toolbar to display a pop-up menu of recently undone actions. Drag down to select all the actions that you want to redo (**Figure 73**). Release the mouse button to reverse all selected undos.

To repeat the last action

Choose Edit > Repeat (**Figures 70** and **71**) or press Ctrl Y.

UDOING, REDOING, & REPEATING ACTIONS

Find & Replace

Word has a very powerful find and replace feature. With it, you can search a document for specific text strings and, if desired, replace them with other text.

✔ Tip

- By default, the Find and Replace commands search the entire document, beginning at the insertion point.

To find text

1. Choose Edit > Find (**Figure 47**) or press Ctrl F.

2. In the Find tab of the Find and Replace dialog that appears (**Figure 74**), enter the text that you want to find.

3. Click the Find Next button. One of two things happens:

   ▲ If Word finds the search text, it selects the first occurrence that it finds (**Figure 75**). Repeat step 3 to find all occurrences, one at a time. When the last occurrence has been found, Word tells you with a dialog (**Figure 76**).

   ▲ If Word does not find the search text, it tells you with a dialog (**Figure 77**). Repeat steps 2 and 3 to search for different text.

4. When you're finished, dismiss the Find and Replace dialog by clicking its close button.

✔ Tips

- To select all occurrences of the search criteria at once (**Figure 78**), turn on the Highlight all items found in check box and click Find All.

- If desired, you can fine-tune search criteria. I tell you how a little later in this chapter.

FINDING TEXT

Figure 74 The Find tab of the Find and Replace dialog.

Figure 75 Word selects each occurrence of the text that it finds.

Figure 76 When Word has finished showing all occurrences of the search text, it tells you.

Figure 77 Word also tells you when it can't find the search text at all.

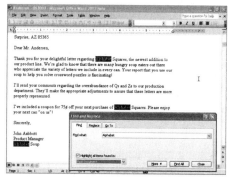

Figure 78 Word can select all occurrences of the search text at once.

Figure 79 The Replace tab of the Find and Replace dialog.

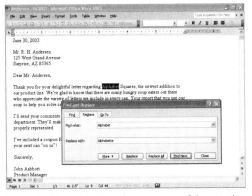

Figure 80 Word selects each occurrence of the search text it finds.

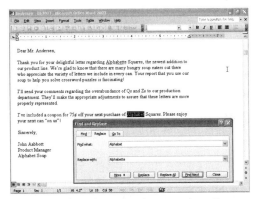

Figure 81 Clicking the Replace button replaces the selected occurrence and finds the next one.

Figure 82 Clicking the Replace All button replaces all occurrences. Word tells you how many replacements it made when it's finished.

To replace text

1. Choose Edit > Replace (**Figure 47**) or press Ctrl H. The Replace tab of the Find and Replace dialog appears (**Figure 79**).

2. Enter the text that you want to find in the Find what text box.

3. Enter the text that you want to replace the found text with in the Replace with text box.

4. Click the Find Next button to start the search. One of two things happens:
   - ▲ If Word finds the search text, it selects the first occurrence that it finds (**Figure 80**). Continue with step 5.
   - ▲ If Word does not find the search text, it tells you with a dialog (**Figure 77**). You can repeat steps 2 and 4 to search for different text.

5. Do one of the following:
   - ▲ To replace the selected occurrence and automatically find the next occurrence, click the Replace button (**Figure 81**). You can repeat this step until Word has found all occurrences (**Figure 76**).
   - ▲ To replace all occurrences, click the Replace All button. Word tells you how many changes it made (**Figure 82**).
   - ▲ To skip the current occurrence and move on to the next one, click the Find Next button. You can repeat this step until Word has found all occurrences (**Figure 76**).

6. When you're finished, dismiss the Find and Replace dialog by clicking its close button.

✔ Tip

- ■ If desired, you can fine-tune search criteria. I tell you how on the next page.

To fine-tune search criteria

1. In the Find (**Figure 74**) or Replace (**Figure 79**) tab of the Find and Replace dialog, click the More button. The dialog expands to show additional search criteria options (**Figure 83**).

2. Click in the Find what or Replace with text box to indicate which criterion you want to fine-tune.

3. Set search criteria options as desired:

   ▲ The **Search** pop-up menu (**Figure 84**) lets you specify whether you want to search the current document or all documents and which direction you want to search.

   ▲ The **Match case** check box exactly matches capitalization.

   ▲ The **Find whole words only** check box finds the search text only when it is a separate word or phrase.

   ▲ The **Use wildcards** check box lets you include wildcard characters (such as *?* for a single character and *** for multiple characters).

   ▲ The **Sounds like** check box finds homonyms—words that sound alike but are spelled differently.

   ▲ The **Find all word forms** check box searches for all verb, noun, or adjective forms of the search text.

4. Set search or replace criteria options as desired:

   ▲ The **Format** pop-up menu (**Figure 85**) lets you specify formatting options. Choosing one of these options displays the corresponding dialog. I explain how to use these dialogs in **Chapters 3** and 4.

   ▲ The **Special** pop-up menu (**Figure 86**) lets you find and replace special characters.

Figure 83 The Replace tab of the Find and Replace dialog expanded to show additional search and replace criteria options.

Figure 84
The Search pop-up menu in the Find and Replace dialog.

Figure 85
The Format pop-up menu in the Find and Replace dialog.

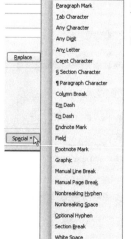

Figure 86
The Special pop-up menu in the Find and Replace dialog.

FINE-TUNING SEARCH CRITERIA

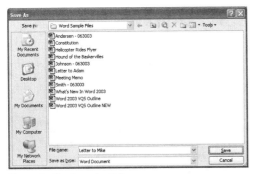

Figure 87 The Save As dialog.

Figure 88
The Save in pop-up menu at the top of the Save As dialog.

Figure 89 The New Folder dialog.

Figure 90 The name you give a document appears in its title bar after you save it.

Saving Documents

When you save a document, you put a copy of it on disk.

✔ Tips

- Until you save a document, its information is stored only in your computer's RAM. Your work on the document could be lost in the event of a power outage or system crash.

- It's a good idea to save documents frequently as you work. This ensures that the most recent versions are always saved to disk.

To save a document for the first time

1. Choose File > Save or File > Save As (**Figure 4**), press [Ctrl][S], or click the Save button on the Standard toolbar.

2. Use the Save As dialog that appears (**Figure 87**) to navigate to the folder in which you want to save the file:

   ▲ Use the Save in menu near the top of the dialog (**Figure 88**) to go to another location.

   ▲ Double-click a folder to open it.

   ▲ Click the Create New Folder button on the command bar to create a new folder within the current folder. Enter the name for the folder in the New Folder dialog (**Figure 89**) and click OK.

3. Enter a name for the file in the File name box.

4. Click Save.

   The file is saved to disk. Its name appears on the window's title bar (**Figure 90**).

To save changes to a document

Choose File > Save (**Figure 4**), press (Ctrl)(S), or click the Save button  on the Standard toolbar.

The document is saved with the same name in the same location on disk.

To save a document with a different name or in a different disk location

1. Choose File > Save As (**Figure 4**).

2. Follow steps 2 and/or 3 on the previous page to select a new disk location and/or enter a different name for the file.

3. Click the Save button.

✔ Tips

- You can use the Save as type pop-up menu at the bottom of the Save As dialog (**Figure 91**) to specify a different format for the file. This enables you to save the document in a format that can be opened and read by other versions of Word or other applications.

- If you save a file with the same name and same disk location as another file, a dialog offering three options (**Figure 92**):

  ▲ **Replace existing file** replaces the file already on disk with the file you are saving.

  ▲ **Save changes with a different name** redisplays the Save As dialog box so you can change the name or location of the file you are saving.

  ▲ **Merge changes into existing file** uses Word's collaboration features to add the current file's contents to the one already on disk. Collaboration features are discussed in **Chapter 15**.

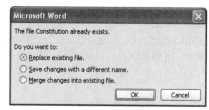

Figure 91 You can use the Save as type pop-up menu to specify a file format.

Figure 92 This dialog appears when you attempt to save a file with the same name and same disk location as another file.

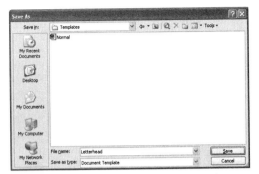

Figure 93 The Save As dialog when you save a document as a template.

Figure 94 When a file has been saved as a template, it appears in the Templates dialog.

To save a document as a template

1. Choose File > Save As (**Figure 4**).

2. Enter a name for the file in the Name box.

3. Choose Document Template from the Save as type pop-up menu (**Figure 91**). The file list portion of the dialog automatically displays the contents of the Templates folder (**Figure 93**).

4. Click the Save button.

   The file is saved as a template. Its name appears in the document title bar.

✔ Tips

- To begin using a template right after you created it, close it, then follow the instructions near the beginning of this chapter to open a new file based on a template. The template appears in the General tab of the Templates dialog (**Figure 94**).

- I tell you more about templates in the beginning of this chapter.

Text Formatting Basics

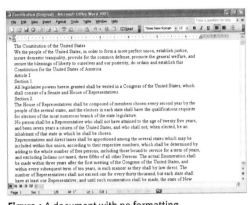

Figure 1 A document with no formatting.

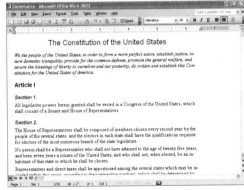

Figure 2 The same document with font and paragraph formatting applied.

Text Formatting Basics

Microsoft Word offers a wide range of text formatting options that you can use to make your documents more interesting and readable. Most text formatting can be broken down into two types:

◆ **Font** or **character formatting** applies to individual characters of text. Examples include bold, italic, underline, and font color. The actual font or typeface used to display characters is also a part of font formatting.

◆ **Paragraph formatting** applies to entire paragraphs of text. Examples are indentation, justification, line spacing, bullets, and numbering.

This chapter introduces text formatting using basic formatting techniques. **Chapter 4** continues the discussion of text formatting by covering advanced formatting techniques.

✔ Tips

■ When properly applied, formatting can make the document easier to read, as illustrated in **Figures 1** and **2**.

■ Don't get carried away with formatting—especially font formatting. Too much formatting distracts the reader, making the document difficult to read.

■ *Page formatting*, which enables you to format document pages or sections, is covered in **Chapter 5**.

Font Formatting

Font formatting, which is sometimes referred to as *character formatting*, can be applied to individual characters of text. Word offers a wide variety of options.

◆ **Font (Figure 3)** is the typeface used to display characters.

◆ **Font style (Figure 4)** is the appearance of font characters: regular, italic, bold, or bold italic.

◆ **Size (Figure 5)** is the size of characters, expressed in points.

◆ **Font Color** is the color applied to text characters.

◆ **Underline style (Figure 6)** options allow you to apply a variety of underlines beneath characters.

◆ **Underline color** is the color of the applied underline.

◆ **Effects (Figure 7)** are special effects that change the appearance of characters. Options include strikethrough, double strikethrough, superscript, subscript, shadow, outline, emboss, engrave, small caps, all caps, or hidden.

◆ **Scale (Figure 8)** determines the horizontal size of font characters. Scale is specified as a percentage of normal character width.

◆ **Spacing (Figure 9)** determines the amount of space between each character of text. Spacing can be normal or can be expanded or condensed by the number of points you specify.

◆ **Position (Figure 10)** determines whether text appears above or below the baseline. Position can be normal or can be raised or lowered by the number of points you specify.

Arial
Bookman Old Style
Century Gothic
Courier New
Forte
Garamond
Impact
Συμβολ
Verdana
Times New Roman
✳◉▢✢✦✳■✖✦◉▼▲

Figure 3
Some font examples using some of the fonts installed on my system. Your system's fonts may differ.

Regular
Bold
Italic
Bold Italic

Figure 4
The font styles offered by Word.

10 points
12 points
14 points
18 points
24 points
36 points

Figure 5
Examples of font sizes. This illustration is not at actual size.

No underline
Words Only
Underline Example
Underline Example
Underline Example
Underline Example
Underline Example
Underline Example
Underline Example
Underline Example
Underline Example
Underline Example
Underline Example
Underline Example
Underline Example
Underline Example
Underline Example
Underline Example

Figure 6
Examples of underlines offered by Word.

~~Strikethrough~~
~~Double Strikethrough~~
^{Super}script
_{Sub}script
Shadow
Outline
Emboss
Engrave
SMALL CAPS
ALL CAPS

Figure 7
Examples of effects.

Characters at 200% Scale
Characters at 150% Scale
Characters at 100% Scale
Characters at 75% Scale
Characters at 50% Scale

Figure 8 Examples of various scale settings.

Spacing Expanded by 2 points
Spacing Expanded by 1 point
Spacing Set to Normal
Spacing Condensed by 1 point
Spacing Condensed by 2 points

Figure 9 Examples of various spacing settings.

An example of text ^{raised by 3 points}
An example of text neither raised nor lowered
An example of text _{lowered by 3 points}

Figure 10 Examples of various position settings.

We Talk

We Talk

Figure 11 Example of text with kerning turned off (top) and turned on (bottom). Note the way the lowercase e and a tuck under the uppercase W and T.

◆ **Kerning** (**Figure 11**) determines how certain combinations of letters "fit" together.

◆ **Animations** are special animated effects that alter the appearance of font characters when viewed onscreen.

✔ Tips

■ Although some fonts come with Microsoft Office, Word enables you to apply *any* font that is properly installed in your system.

■ A *point* is 1/72 inch. The larger the point size, the larger the characters.

■ Hidden characters do not show onscreen unless formatting marks are displayed. Formatting marks are discussed in **Chapter 2**.

■ Don't confuse character position with superscript and subscript. Although all three of these font formatting options change the position of text in relation to the baseline, superscript and subscript also change the size of characters.

■ The effect of kerning varies depending on the size and font applied to characters for which kerning is enabled. Kerning is more apparent at larger point sizes and requires that the font contain *kerning pairs*—predefined pairs of letters to kern. In many instances, you may not see a difference in spacing at all.

Applying Font Formatting

Font formatting is applied to selected characters or, if no characters are selected, to the characters you type at the insertion point after setting formatting options. Here are two examples:

◆ To apply a bold font style to text that you have already typed, select the text (**Figure 12**), then apply the formatting. The appearance of the text changes immediately (**Figure 13**).

◆ To apply a bold font style to text that you have not yet typed, position the insertion point where the text will be typed (**Figure 14**), apply (or "turn on") the bold formatting, and type the text. The text appears in bold (**Figure 15**). You must remember, however, to "turn off" bold formatting before you continue to type (**Figure 16**).

Word offers several methods of applying font formatting:

◆ The Formatting toolbar enables you to apply font, size, some font styles, and font color formatting.

◆ Shortcut keys enable you to apply some font formatting.

◆ The Font dialog enables you to apply all kinds of font formatting.

✔ Tips

■ In my opinion, it's easier to type text and apply formatting later than to format as you type.

■ I explain how to select text in **Chapter 2**.

We the people of the United States, in domestic tranquility, provide for the co blessings of liberty to ourselves and or

Figure 12 Select the text that you want to format,...

We the people of the **United States**, in domestic tranquility, provide for the comm blessings of liberty to ourselves and our r

Figure 13 ...then apply the formatting.

We the people of the|

Figure 14 Position the insertion point where you want the formatted text to appear,...

We the people of the **United States**|

Figure 15 ...then "turn on" the formatting and type the text.

We the people of the **United States**, in order to|

Figure 16 Be sure to "turn off" the formatting before continuing to type.

Figure 17
The Font menu on the Formatting toolbar.

Figure 18
The Font Size menu on the Formatting toolbar.

Figure 19 Select the contents of the Font box.

Figure 20 Enter the name of the font that you want to apply.

Figure 21 The Font Color menu on the Formatting toolbar.

Figure 22 The Highlight Color menu on the Formatting toolbar.

Figure 23 Word tells you when you've entered a font that isn't installed.

To apply font formatting with the Formatting toolbar

Choose the font or size that you want to apply from the Font [Times New Roman ▾] or Font Size [12 ▾] menu (**Figures 17** and **18**).

or

1. Click the Font (**Figure 19**) or Font Size text box to select its contents.

2. Enter the name of the font (**Figure 20**) or the size that you want to apply.

3. Press (Enter).

or

Click the button for the font style you want to apply: Bold [B], Italic [I], or Underline [U].

or

Click the Font Color button [A▾] to apply the currently selected color or choose another color from the Font Color toolbar menu (**Figure 21**).

Click the Highlight button [▾] to apply the currently selected color or choose another color from the Highlight Color toolbar menu (**Figure 22**).

✔ Tips

■ Font names appear on the Font menu in their typefaces (**Figure 17**).

■ Recently applied fonts appear at the top of the Font menu (**Figure 17**).

■ If you enter the name of a font that is not installed on your system, Word warns you (**Figure 23**). If you use the font anyway, the text appears in the document in the default paragraph font. The text will appear in the specified font after the font is installed on your system or when the document is opened on a system on which the font is installed.

USING THE FORMATTING TOOLBAR

65

To apply font formatting with shortcut keys

Press the shortcut key combination (**Table 1**) for the formatting that you want to apply.

✔ Tip

- The shortcut key to change the font requires that you press the first key combination, enter the name of the font desired, then press Enter. This command activates the Font box on the Formatting toolbar (**Figure 19**).

Table 1

Shortcut Keys for Font Formatting	
Formatting	Keystroke
Font	Ctrl Shift F *Font Name* Enter
Symbol font	Ctrl Shift Q
Grow font	Ctrl Shift .
Grow font 1 point	Ctrl]
Shrink font	Ctrl Shift ,
Shrink font 1 point	Ctrl [
Bold	Ctrl B or Ctrl Shift B
Italic	Ctrl I or Ctrl Shift I
Underline	Ctrl U or Ctrl Shift U
Word underline	Ctrl Shift W
Double underline	Ctrl Shift D
Superscript	Ctrl Shift =
Subscript	Ctrl =
All caps	Ctrl Shift A
Small caps	Ctrl Shift K
Hidden	Ctrl Shift H

Figure 24
The Format menu.

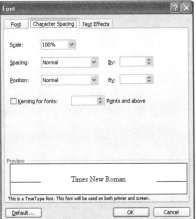

Figures 25, 26, & 27 The three tabs of the Font dialog: Font (top), Character Spacing (middle), and Text Effects (bottom).

To apply font formatting with the Font dialog

1. Choose Format > Font (**Figure 24**) or press [Ctrl] [D].

2. Click the tab for the type of font formatting you want to set:

   ▲ **Font** (**Figure 25**) enables you to set basic font formatting options, including font, size, style, color, underline, and effects.

   ▲ **Character Spacing** (**Figure 26**) enables you to set font scale, spacing, position, and kerning options.

   ▲ **Text Effects** (**Figure 27**) enables you to set animation options.

3. Set formatting options as desired.

4. Repeat steps 2 and 3 for each type of formatting you want to set.

5. Click OK.

✔ Tip

■ The Preview area of the Font dialog illustrates what text will look like with the selected formatting applied.

USING THE FONT DIALOG

Paragraph Formatting

Paragraph formatting is applied to entire paragraphs of text. Word offers a variety of paragraph formatting options:

♦ **Alignment** (**Figure 28**) is the way lines of text line up between the indents.

♦ **Indentation** (**Figure 29**) is the spacing between text and margins. Word allows you to set left and right margins, as well as special indentations for first line and hanging indents.

♦ **Bullets** (**Figure 30**) combines hanging indentation and bullet characters for each paragraph.

♦ **Numbering** (**Figure 31**) combines hanging indentation and automatic numbering for each paragraph.

♦ **Line spacing** (**Figure 32**) is the amount of space between lines. Spacing can be set as single, 1.5 lines, double, at least a certain amount, exactly a certain amount, or multiple lines.

♦ **Paragraph spacing** (**Figure 33**) is the amount of space before and after the paragraph.

♦ **Pagination** options, including widow/orphan control, keep lines together, keep with next, and page break before, determine how automatic page breaks occur in the document.

♦ **Line numbering** and **hyphenation** options determine whether the paragraph should be excluded from line number and hyphenation.

✔ Tip

■ Tabs are also a paragraph formatting option. Because of their relative complexity, however, I discuss them separately later in this chapter.

Left aligned text lines up with the left indent which, in this example, is the same as the left margin.

Centered text is centered between the left and right indents, which, in this example, is the same as the margins.

Right aligned text lines up with the right indent which, in this example, is the same as the right margin.

Justified text lines up with both the left and right indents, which, in this example, is the same as the margins. Spacing between words is adjust, if necessary, to force the justification. You can't really see that text is fully justified unless there are at least three lines in the paragraph. That's why I have to type so much in this example.

Figure 28 Examples of alignment options.

In this example, the left and right indents are set at the margins. There is no special indentation.

In this example, both the left and right indents are moved in 1/2 inch from the margins. This indentation is commonly used for long quotations in the body of documents.

In this example, the first line is indented by shifting the first line left indent to the right while leaving the left indent at the margin. This is common, first line indentation.

In this example, there's a hanging indent created by shifting the left indent to the right while leaving the first line left indent at the margin.

• Here's another example of a hanging indent. Most bullet lists are created with hanging indents. Word has its own built-in bullet formatting.

Figure 29 Examples of indentation options. The ruler in this illustration shows the indent markers set for the first sample paragraph.

• Speaking of bullets, here's an example of Word's built-in bullet formatting at work.
• You can use standard bullets like these nice fat ones or any other character.
• You can even use pictures as bullets!

Figure 30 Example of bullet formatting.

1. And if you're interested in numbering paragraphs, Word has you covered.
2. Not only will it insert a number before each paragraph formatted with its built-in number formatting, but it will keep track of the numbers for you.
3. You can even insert or delete paragraphs and Word will renumber them for you!

Figure 31 Example of numbering format.

This paragraph has single line spacing. Line spacing is not apparent unless there are at least two lines in the paragraph.

This paragraph has 1.5 line spacing. Line spacing is not apparent unless there are at least two lines in the paragraph.

This paragraph has double line spacing. Line spacing is not apparent unless there are at least two lines in the paragraph.

This paragraph has at least 12 point line spacing. If a line needs more than 12 points because of the size of characters in the line, the spacing adjusts. Otherwise, line spacing is 12 points.

This paragraph has exactly 12 point line spacing. If a line needs more than 12 points because of the size of characters in the line, that's just too darn bad. The spacing is always 12 points.

This paragraph has 2.7 line spacing. This option is set with the Multiple option in the Paragraph dialog box. As you can see, you can set spacing exactly the way you want it.

Figure 32 Example of line spacing options.

This paragraph has no spacing between it and other paragraphs.

This paragraph has 8 points of space between it and other paragraphs.

This paragraph has 18 points of space between it and other paragraphs.

Figure 33 Example of paragraph spacing options.

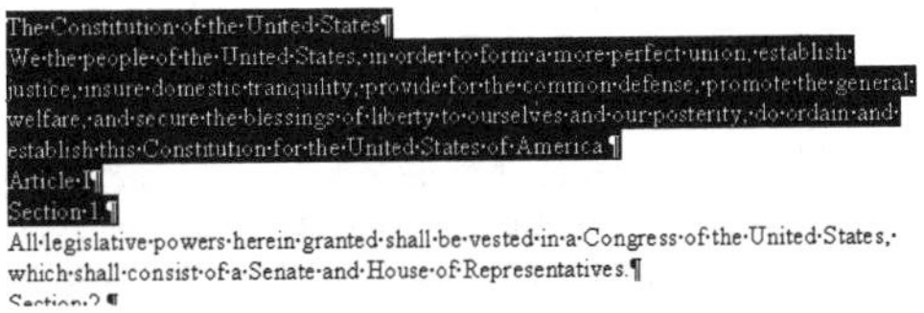
The·Constitution·of·the·United·States¶
We·the·people·of·the·United·States,·in·order·to·form·a·more·perfect·union,·establish·justice,·insure·domestic·tranquility,·provide·for·the·common·defense,·promote·the·general·welfare,·and·secure·the·blessings·of·liberty·to·ourselves·and·our·posterity,·do·ordain·and·establish·this·Constitution·for·the·United·States·of·America.¶
Article·I¶
Section·1.¶
All·legislative·powers·herein·granted·shall·be·vested·in·a·Congress·of·the·United·States,·which·shall·consist·of·a·Senate·and·House·of·Representatives.¶

Figure 34 In this example, the first four paragraphs are completely selected and will be affected by any paragraph formatting applied.

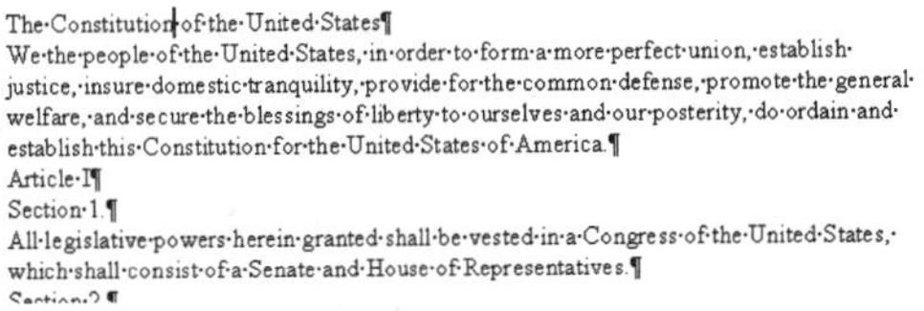
The·Constitution·of·the·United·States¶
We·the·people·of·the·United·States,·in·order·to·form·a·more·perfect·union,·establish·justice,·insure·domestic·tranquility,·provide·for·the·common·defense,·promote·the·general·welfare,·and·secure·the·blessings·of·liberty·to·ourselves·and·our·posterity,·do·ordain·and·establish·this·Constitution·for·the·United·States·of·America.¶
Article·I¶
Section·1.¶
All·legislative·powers·herein·granted·shall·be·vested·in·a·Congress·of·the·United·States,·which·shall·consist·of·a·Senate·and·House·of·Representatives.¶

Figure 35 In this example, the insertion point is in the first paragraph. That entire paragraph will be affected by any paragraph formatting applied.

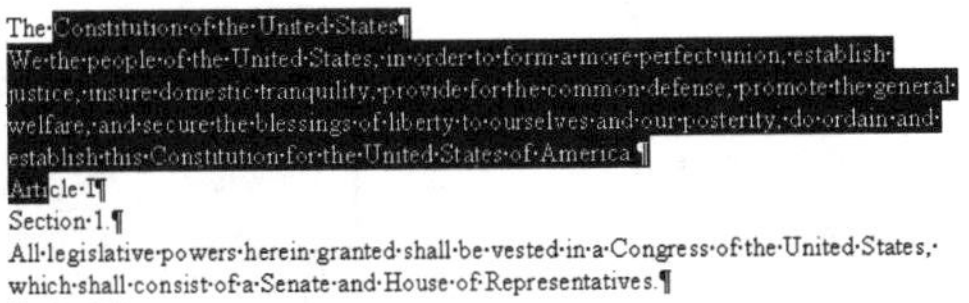
The·Constitution·of·the·United·States¶
We·the·people·of·the·United·States,·in·order·to·form·a·more·perfect·union,·establish·justice,·insure·domestic·tranquility,·provide·for·the·common·defense,·promote·the·general·welfare,·and·secure·the·blessings·of·liberty·to·ourselves·and·our·posterity,·do·ordain·and·establish·this·Constitution·for·the·United·States·of·America.¶
Article·I¶
Section·1.¶
All·legislative·powers·herein·granted·shall·be·vested·in·a·Congress·of·the·United·States,·which·shall·consist·of·a·Senate·and·House·of·Representatives.¶

Figure 36 In this example, only part of the first paragraph and part of the third paragraph are selected, along with all of the second paragraph. All three paragraphs will be affected by any paragraph formatting applied.

Applying Paragraph Formatting

Paragraph formatting is applied to selected paragraphs (**Figure 34**) or, if no paragraphs are selected, to the paragraph in which the insertion point is blinking (**Figure 35**).

Word offers several methods of applying paragraph formatting:

- The Formatting toolbar enables you to apply some paragraph formatting.
- Shortcut keys enable you to apply some paragraph formatting.
- The ruler enables you to apply indentation and tab formatting.
- The Paragraph dialog enables you to apply most kinds of paragraph formatting.
- The Bullets and Numbering dialog enables you to apply bullet and numbering formats.

✔ Tips

- Paragraph formatting applies to the entire paragraph, even if only part of the paragraph is selected (**Figure 36**).
- A *paragraph* is the text that appears between paragraph marks. You can see paragraph marks when you display formatting marks (**Figures 34** through **36**). Formatting marks are discussed in **Chapter 2**.
- When you press Enter, the paragraph formatting of the current paragraph is carried forward to the new paragraph.
- Selecting paragraphs is explained in **Chapter 2**.

To apply paragraph formatting with Formatting toolbar buttons

To set alignment, click Align Left ▤, Center ▤, Align Right ▤, or Justify ▤.

or

To set left indentation, click Decrease Indent ▦ or Increase Indent ▦.

or

To enable automatic bullets or numbering, click Bullets ▤ or Numbering ▤.

or

To set line spacing, click the arrow beside the Line Spacing button ▤▾ and choose an option from the menu that appears (**Figure 37**).

✔ Tip

■ Choosing More from the Line Spacing button's menu (**Figure 37**) displays the Paragraph dialog, which is discussed on the next page.

To apply paragraph formatting with shortcut keys

Press the shortcut key combination (**Table 2**) for the formatting that you want to apply.

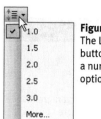

Figure 37
The Line Spacing button's menu offers a number of spacing options.

Table 2

Shortcut Keys for Paragraph Formatting	
Formatting	Keystroke
Align left	Ctrl L
Center	Ctrl E
Align right	Ctrl R
Justify	Ctrl J
Indent	Ctrl M
Unindent	Ctrl Shift M
Hanging indent	Ctrl T
Unhang indent	Ctrl Shift T
Single line space	Ctrl 1
1.5 line space	Ctrl 5
Double line space	Ctrl 2
Open/Close Up Paragraph	Ctrl 0 (zero)

USING TOOLBAR BUTTONS & SHORTCUT KEYS

Figure 38 Indent markers on the ruler.

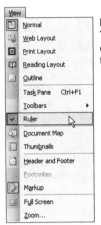

Figure 39
To display the ruler, choose Ruler from the View menu.

To set indentation with the ruler

Drag the indent markers (**Figure 38**) to set indentation as desired:

◆ **First Line Indent** sets the left boundary for the first line of a paragraph.

◆ **Hanging Indent** sets the left boundary for all lines of a paragraph other than the first line.

◆ **Left Indent** sets the left boundary for all lines of a paragraph. (Dragging this marker moves the First Line Indent and Hanging Indent markers.)

◆ **Right Indent** sets the right boundary for all lines of a paragraph.

✔ Tips

■ If the ruler is not showing, choose View > Ruler (**Figure 39**) to display it.

■ Dragging the First Line Indent marker to the right creates a standard indent.

■ Dragging the Hanging Indent marker to the right creates a hanging indent.

SETTING INDENTATION WITH THE RULER

To apply paragraph formatting with the Paragraph dialog

1. Choose Format > Paragraph (**Figure 24**) to display the Paragraph dialog.

2. Click the Indents and Spacing tab to display its options (**Figure 40**). Then set options as desired:

   ▲ **Alignment** (**Figure 41**) sets paragraph alignment.

   ▲ **Outline level** (**Figure 42**) applies a style corresponding to one of Word's outline levels. (Styles are covered in **Chapter 4**; outlines are covered in detail in **Chapter 12**.)

   ▲ **Left** sets the left indentation. Enter a measurement or use the arrow buttons beside the box to set the value.

   ▲ **Right** sets the right indentation. Enter a measurement or use the arrow buttons beside the box to set the value.

   ▲ **Special** (**Figure 43**) applies First Line or Hanging indentation. If you choose an option other than (none), you can enter a value in the box beside the menu to set the indentation spacing.

   ▲ **Before** sets the amount of space before the paragraph. Enter a measurement or use the arrow buttons beside the box to set the value.

   ▲ **After** sets the amount of space after the paragraph. Enter a measurement or use the arrow buttons beside the box to set the value.

   ▲ **Line spacing** (**Figure 44**) sets the spacing between lines in the paragraph. If you choose At least, Exactly, or Multiple, enter a value in the box beside the menu.

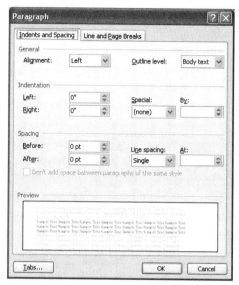

Figure 40 The Indents and Spacing tab of the Paragraph dialog.

Figure 41
Use the Alignment menu in the Paragraph dialog to set paragraph alignment.

Figure 42
Use the Outline level menu in the Paragraph dialog to specify an outline level style.

Figure 43
Use the Special menu in the Paragraph dialog to apply first line or hanging indentation.

Figure 44
Use the Line spacing menu in the Paragraph dialog to set line spacing for the paragraph.

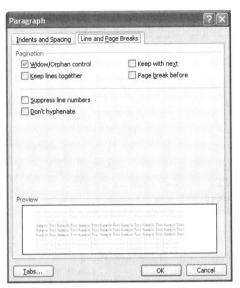

Figure 45 The Line and Page Breaks tab of the Paragraph dialog.

▲ **Don't add space between paragraphs of the same style** tells Word not to use the paragraph spacing options specified above if the paragraphs have the same style applied to them. I tell you about Word's style feature in **Chapter 4**.

3. Click the Line and Page Breaks tab to display its options (**Figure 45**). Then set options as desired:

   ▲ **Widow/Orphan Control** prevents a page break from occurring right after the first line in a paragraph or right before the last line in a paragraph.

   ▲ **Keep lines together** prevents a page break from occurring within the selected paragraph, thus keeping all lines of the paragraph together on the same page.

   ▲ **Keep with next** prevents a page break from occurring between the selected paragraph and the next paragraph.

   ▲ **Page break before** puts a page break before the selected paragraph.

   ▲ **Suppress line numbers** excludes the paragraph from line numbering when line numbering is enabled.

   ▲ **Don't hyphenate** excludes the paragraph from hyphenation when the document is manually or automatically hyphenated.

4. Click OK to save your settings and dismiss the Paragraph dialog.

✔ Tips

■ The Preview area of the Paragraph dialog illustrates what text will look like with formatting applied.

■ I tell you more about page formatting, including how to insert manual page breaks, in **Chapter 5**.

To apply bulleted list formatting with the Bullets and Numbering dialog

1. Choose Format > Bullets and Numbering (**Figure 24**).

2. In the Bullets and Numbering dialog that appears, click the Bulleted tab to display its options (**Figure 46**).

3. Click the box that displays the type of bullet character that you want.

4. Click OK.

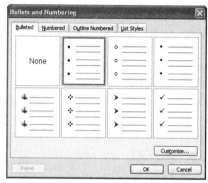

Figure 46 The Bulleted tab of the Bullets and Numbering dialog.

✔ Tips

- Clicking the Bullets button 🔳 on the Formatting toolbar applies the last style of bullet set in the Bullets and Numbering dialog (**Figure 24**) or Customize Bulleted List dialog (**Figure 47**).

- To further customize a bullet list, after step 3 above, click the Customize button in the Bullets and Numbering dialog (**Figure 46**). Set options in the Customize Bulleted List dialog that appears (**Figure 47**), and click OK.

- You can also use pictures for bullets. Click the Picture button in the Customize Bulleted List dialog (**Figure 47**). Then select one of the pictures in the Picture Bullet dialog that appears (**Figure 48**) and click OK. Word automatically uses the same picture for all bullets in the list.

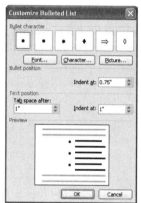

Figure 47
The Customize Bulleted List dialog.

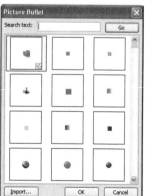

Figure 48
Use the Picture Bullet dialog to select a picture to use for all bullets in a bulleted list.

Figure 49 The Numbered tab of the Bullets and Numbering dialog.

Figure 50
The Customize Numbered List dialog.

To apply numbered list formatting with the Bullets and Numbering dialog

1. Choose Format > Bullets and Numbering (**Figure 24**).

2. In the Bullets and Numbering dialog that appears, click the Numbered tab to display its options (**Figure 49**).

3. Click the box that displays the numbering format that you want.

4. Click OK.

✔ Tips

- Clicking the Numbering button 📄 on the Formatting toolbar applies the last style of numbering set in the Bullets and Numbering dialog (**Figure 49**) or Customize Numbered List dialog (**Figure 50**).

- To further customize a numbered list, after step 3 above, click the Customize button in the Bullets and Numbering dialog (**Figure 49**). Set options in the Customize Numbered List dialog that appears (**Figure 50**), and click OK.

- If your document already includes a numbered list, you can use the option buttons at the bottom of the Numbered tab of the Bullets and Numbering dialog to determine whether Word should restart numbering or continue the previous list's numbering. These options are only available if the document contains multiple numbered lists.

- I tell you about the Outline Numbered tab of the Bullets and Numbering dialog in my discussion of Word's outlining feature in **Chapter 12**.

To remove bulleted or numbered list formatting

1. Choose Format > Bullets and Numbering (**Figure 24**).

2. In the Bullets and Numbering dialog (**Figure 46** or **49**), click the None box.

3. Click OK.

or

To remove bulleted list formatting from a selected paragraph, click the Bullets button ⊞ on the Formatting toolbar.

or

To remove numbered list formatting from a selected paragraph, click the Numbering button ⊞ on the Formatting toolbar.

Tab marker icon

Figure 51 Default tab stops appear as tiny gray lines on the ruler.

Figure 52 Word's five tab stops in action. In order, they are: left, bar, right, center, decimal. Examine the ruler to see how they're set.

Figure 53 Word's tab leader options: none, dotted, dashed, and underscore.

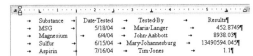

Figure 54 Displaying formatting marks enables you to see the tab characters.

✔ Tips

- Tabs are a type of paragraph formatting; when set, they apply to an entire paragraph.

- Tabs are often used to create simple tables.

- When trying to align text in a simple table, use tabs, not spaces. Tabs always align to tab stops while text positioned with space characters may not align properly due to the size and spacing of characters in a font.

Tabs

Tab stops determine the horizontal position of the insertion point when you press Tab.

By default, a blank document includes tab stops every half inch. They appear as gray marks on the bottom of the ruler (**Figure 51**). You can use the ruler or Tabs dialog to set tabs that override the defaults.

Word supports five kinds of tabs (**Figure 52**):

- **Left tab** aligns tabbed text to the left against the tab stop.

- **Center tab** centers tabbed text beneath the tab stop.

- **Right tab** aligns tabbed text to the right against the tab stop.

- **Decimal tab** aligns the decimal point (or period) of tabbed numbers beneath the tab stop. When used with text, a decimal tab works just like a right tab.

- **Bar tab** is a vertical line that appears beneath the tab stop.

Word also supports four types of *tab leaders* (**Figure 53**)—characters that appear in the space otherwise left by a tab: none, periods, dashes, and underscores.

- It's a good idea to display formatting marks when working with tabs (**Figure 54**) so you can distinguish tabs from spaces. Formatting marks are discussed in **Chapter 2**.

TABS

To set tab stops with the ruler

1. Click the tab marker icon at the far-left end of the ruler (**Figure 51**) until it displays the icon for the type of tab stop that you want to set (**Figure 55**).

2. Click on the ruler where you want to position the tab stop to set it there.

3. Repeat steps 1 and 2 until all desired tab stops have been set (**Figure 52**).

✔ Tips

■ When you set a tab stop, all default tab stops to its left disappear (**Figures 52 and 54**).

■ Repeatedly clicking the tab marker icon will cycle through all the tab markers, as well as two indentation markers. I discuss using the indentation markers on the ruler to set indentation earlier in this chapter.

To move a tab stop with the ruler

1. Position the mouse pointer on the tab stop that you want to move.

2. Press the mouse button and drag the tab stop to its new position.

✔ Tip

■ Don't click on the ruler anywhere except on the tab stop that you want to move. Doing so will set another tab stop.

To remove a tab stop from the ruler

1. Position the mouse pointer on the tab stop that you want to remove.

2. Press the mouse button and drag the tab stop down into the document. When you release the mouse button, the tab stop disappears.

Figure 55 The tab marker icons for left, center, right, decimal, and bar tabs.

Figure 56
The Tabs dialog.

Figure 57
When you add a tab, it appears in the list in the Tabs dialog.

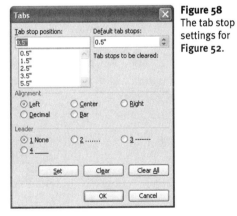

Figure 58
The tab stop settings for Figure 52.

Figure 59
When you click Clear to remove a tab stop, it is removed from the tab list.

To open the Tabs dialog

Use one of the following techniques:

- Choose Format > Tabs (**Figure 24**).

- Click the Tabs button in the Paragraph dialog (**Figures 40** and **45**).

- Double-click a tab stop on the ruler.

To set tab stops with the Tabs dialog

1. Open the Tabs dialog (**Figure 56**).

2. In the Alignment area, select the option button for the type of tab that you want.

3. In the Leader area, select the type of leader that you want the tab stop to have.

4. Enter a ruler measurement in the Tab stop position box.

5. Click Set. The tab stop is added to the tab list (**Figure 57**).

6. Repeat steps 2 through 5 for each tab stop that you want to set (**Figure 58**).

7. Click OK.

To remove tab stops with the Tabs dialog

1. In the Tabs dialog, select the tab stop that you want to remove.

2. Click Clear. The tab stop is removed from the list and added to the list of Tab stops to be cleared in the dialog (**Figure 59**).

3. Repeat steps 1 and 2 for each tab stop that you want to remove.

4. Click OK.

✔ Tip

- To remove all tab stops, click the Clear All button in the Tabs dialog (**Figure 58**) and then click OK.

To change the default tab stops

1. In the Tabs dialog (**Figure 56**), enter a new value in the Default tab stops box.

2. Click OK.

✔ Tip

■ Remember, tab stops that you set manually on the ruler or with the Tabs dialog override default tab stops to their left.

To create a simple table with tab stops

1. Position the insertion point in the paragraph in which you set tabs (**Figure 60**).

2. To type at a tab stop, press Tab, then type (**Figure 61**).

3. Repeat step 2 to type at each tab stop.

4. Press Enter or Shift Enter to end the paragraph or line and begin a new one. The tab stops in the paragraph are carried forward (**Figure 62**).

5. Repeat steps 2 through 4 to finish typing your table (**Figure 54**).

✔ Tips

■ You can move tabs at any time—even after you have begun using them. Be sure to select all of the paragraphs that utilize the tab stops before you move them. Otherwise, you may only adjust tabs for part of the table.

■ Another way to create tables is with Word's table feature, which is far more flexible than using tab stops. I tell you about it in **Chapter 8**.

Figure 60 Position the insertion point in the paragraph for which you have set tab stops.

Figure 61 Press Tab to type at the first tab stop, then type. In this example, text is typed at a right-aligned tab stop.

Figure 62 When you are finished typing a line, press Enter to start a new paragraph with the same tab stops.

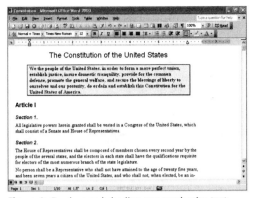

Figure 63 Borders and shading can emphasize text.

Borders & Shading

Borders and shading are two separate features that can work together to emphasize text:

◆ **Borders** enables you to place lines above, below, to the left, or to the right of selected characters or paragraphs (**Figure 63**).

◆ **Shading** enables you to add color or shades of gray to selected characters or paragraphs (**Figure 63**).

✔ Tips

■ How borders or shading are applied depends on how text is selected:

▲ To apply borders or shading to characters, select the characters.

▲ To apply borders or shading to a paragraph, click in the paragraph or select the entire paragraph.

▲ To apply borders or shading to multiple paragraphs, select the paragraphs.

■ When applying borders to selected text characters (as opposed to selected paragraphs), you must place a border around each side, creating a box around the text.

■ I tell you about page borders, which can be applied to entire pages, in **Chapter 5**.

To apply text borders with the Formatting toolbar

1. Select the text to which you want to apply borders.

2. Click the arrow beside the Border button  to display a menu of border options (**Figure 64**).

3. Click the button for the border you want to apply.

Figure 64 The Border menu on the Formatting toolbar.

✔ Tips

■ You can apply more than one border to selected paragraphs. For example, if you want a top and bottom border, choose the top border option and then choose the bottom border option. Both are applied.

■ Some border options apply more than one border. For example, the outside border option (top left button) applies the outside border as well as the top, bottom, left, and right borders.

To apply text borders with the Borders and Shading dialog

1. Select the text to which you want to apply borders.

2. Choose Format > Borders and Shading (**Figure 24**).

3. Click the Borders tab in the Borders and Shading dialog that appears to display its options (**Figure 65**).

4. Click a Setting icon to select the type of border. All options except None and Custom place borders around each side of the selected text.

5. Click a style in the Style list box to select a line style.

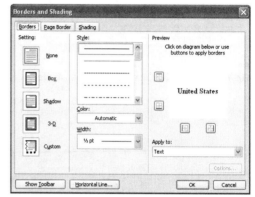

Figure 65 The Borders tab of the Borders and Shading dialog.

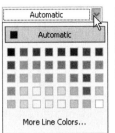

Figure 66
Use the Color menu in the Borders and Shading dialog to set the color of a border.

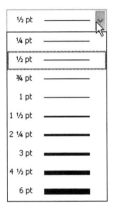

Figure 67
Use the Width menu in the Borders and Shading dialog to set the thickness of a border line.

Figure 68 If necessary, use the Apply to menu in the Borders and Shading dialog to specify what the border or shading settings should apply to.

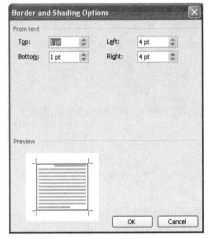

Figure 69 The Border and Shading Options dialog.

6. Choose a line color from the Color pop-up menu (**Figure 66**). If you choose Automatic, Word applies the color that is specified in the paragraph style that was applied to the text.

7. Choose a line thickness from the Width drop-down list (**Figure 67**).

8. If necessary, choose an option from the Apply to drop-down list (**Figure 68**). The Preview area changes accordingly.

9. To apply custom borders, click the buttons in the Preview area to add or remove lines using the settings in the dialog.

10. When the Preview area illustrates the kind of border that you want to apply, click OK.

✔ Tips

■ You can repeat steps 5 through 7 and 9 to customize each border of a custom paragraph border.

■ You can further customize a paragraph border by clicking the Options button to display the Border and Shading Options dialog (**Figure 69**). Set options as desired and click OK to return to the Borders and Shading dialog.

APPLYING TEXT BORDERS

To remove text borders

1. Select the text from which you want to remove borders.

2. Click the arrow beside the Border button ▣▾ to display a pop-up menu of border options (**Figure 64**).

3. Click the No Borders button (the second button on the bottom row).

or

1. Select the text from which you want to remove borders.

2. Choose Format > Borders and Shading (**Figure 24**) and click the Borders tab in the Borders and Shading dialog that appears (**Figure 65**).

3. Click the None icon.

4. Click OK.

REMOVING TEXT BORDERS

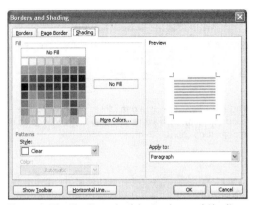

Figure 70 The Shading tab of the Borders and Shading dialog.

Figure 71
Use the Style menu in the Borders and Shading dialog to set a shading pattern.

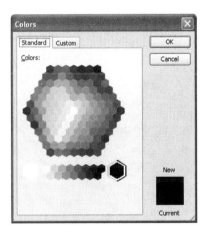

Figure 72 The Colors dialog offers two tabs of additional color options.

To apply shading

1. Select the text to which you want to apply shading.

2. Choose Format > Borders and Shading (**Figure 24**).

3. Click the Shading tab in the Borders and Shading dialog to display its options (**Figure 70**).

4. Click a Fill color or shade to select it.

5. To create a pattern, choose an option from the Style drop-down list (**Figure 71**) and then choose a color from the Color pop-up menu (**Figure 66**).

6. If necessary, choose an option from the Apply to drop-down list (**Figure 68**). The Preview area changes accordingly.

7. When the Preview area shows the kind of shading that you want to apply, click OK.

✔ Tips

- Use text shading with care. If the pattern is too dark or "busy," the shaded area may be impossible to read!

- Clicking the More Colors button in the Borders and Shading dialog displays the Colors dialog (**Figure 72**), which you can use to select different colors.

To remove shading

1. Select the text from which you want to remove shading.

2. Choose Format > Borders and Shading (**Figure 24**) and click the Shading tab in the Borders and Shading dialog (**Figure 70**).

3. Click the No Fill button in the Fill area.

4. Choose Clear from the Style drop-down list (**Figure 71**).

5. Click OK.

APPLYING & REMOVING SHADING

Drop Caps

A drop cap is an enlarged and/or repositioned character at the beginning of a paragraph. Word supports two types of drop caps (**Figure 73**):

◆ **Dropped** enlarges the character and wraps the rest of the text in the paragraph around it.

◆ **In Margin** enlarges the character and moves it into the margin.

✔ Tips

■ Word creates drop caps using frames, a feature that enables you to precisely position text on a page or in relation to a paragraph. Frames is an advanced feature of Word that is beyond the scope of this book.

■ To see drop caps, you must be in Print Layout view or Print Preview. A drop cap appears as an enlarged character in its own paragraph in Normal view (**Figure 74**).

■ A drop cap can consist of more than just the first letter of a paragraph (**Figure 75**).

We the people of the United States, in order to form a more perfect union, establish justice, insure domestic tranquility, provide for the common defense, promote the general welfare, and secure the blessings of liberty to ourselves and our posterity, do ordain and establish this Constitution for the United States of America.

We the people of the United States, in order to form a more perfect union, establish justice, insure domestic tranquility, provide for the common defense, promote the general welfare, and secure the blessings of liberty to ourselves and our posterity, do ordain and establish this Constitution for the United States of America.

We the people of the United States, in order to form a more perfect union, establish justice, insure domestic tranquility, provide for the common defense, promote the general welfare, and secure the blessings of liberty to ourselves and our posterity, do ordain and establish this Constitution for the United States of America.

Figure 73 The same paragraph three ways: without a drop cap (top), with a drop cap (middle), and with an in margin drop cap (bottom).

W

e the people of the United States, in order to form a more perfect union, establish justice, insure domestic tranquility, provide for the common defense, promote the general welfare, and secure the blessings of liberty to ourselves and our posterity, do ordain and establish this Constitution for the United States of America.

Figure 74 A paragraph with a drop cap when viewed in Normal view.

We the people of the United States, in order to form a more perfect union, establish justice, insure domestic tranquility, provide for the common defense, promote the general welfare, and secure the blessings of liberty to ourselves and our posterity, do ordain and establish this Constitution for the United States of America.

Figure 75 A drop cap can consist of more than just one character.

Figure 76 Use the Drop Cap dialog to enter settings for a drop cap.

To create a drop cap

1. Position the insertion point anywhere in the paragraph for which you want to create a drop cap.

2. Choose Format > Drop Cap (**Figure 24**).

3. In the Drop Cap dialog that appears (**Figure 76**), click the icon for the type of drop cap that you want to create.

4. Choose a font for the drop cap from the Font drop-down list.

5. Enter the number of lines for the size of the drop cap character in the Lines to drop box.

6. Enter a value for the amount of space between the drop cap character and the rest of the text in the paragraph in the Distance from text box.

7. Click OK.

✔ Tip

■ To create a drop cap with more than one character (**Figure 75**), select the characters that you want to appear as drop caps, then follow steps 2 through 7 above. You cannot select more than one word to include in drop caps.

To remove a drop cap

Follow the steps above, but select the icon for None in step 3.

CREATING & REMOVING DROP CAPS

Advanced Text Formatting

Advanced Text Formatting Techniques

Microsoft Word offers a number of formatting techniques that go beyond the basics discussed in **Chapter 3**:

- ◆ **Reveal Formatting** enables you to get information about the formatting applied to selected text.

- ◆ **Format Painter** enables you to copy font and paragraph formats from one selection to another.

- ◆ **Styles** enables you to define and apply named sets of formatting options for individual characters or paragraphs.

- ◆ **Themes** and the **Style Gallery** enable you to apply predefined sets of styles to a document.

- ◆ **AutoFormat** instructs Word to automatically format text you type.

This chapter covers these advanced formatting techniques and shows you how they can help you format your documents more quickly, effectively, or consistently.

✔ Tip

- ■ It's a good idea to have a solid understanding of the concepts covered in **Chapter 3** before you read this chapter.

Revealing Formatting

Word offers an easy way to see what kind of formatting is applied to text: the Reveal Formatting command (**Figure 1**). This command displays a task pane that tells you exactly what kind of formatting is applied to the text you select (**Figures 2** and **3**).

✔ Tip

- The Reveal Formatting feature shows formatting details in three categories: Font, Paragraph, and Section (**Figure 4**). I cover section formatting in **Chapter 5**.

To reveal formatting

1. Choose Format > Reveal Format (**Figure 1**) or press ⇧Shift F1 . The Reveal Formatting task pane appears to the right of the document window. Its Formatting of selected text scrolling window lists all of the formatting applied to selected text (**Figures 2** and **3**).

2. To learn about the formatting applied to text, click on or select the text.

3. Repeat step 2 for any text for which you want to reveal formatting.

4. When you are finished revealing formatting, click the close button in the Reveal Formatting task pane to dismiss it.

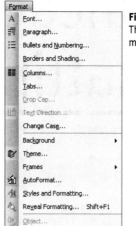

Figure 1
The Format menu.

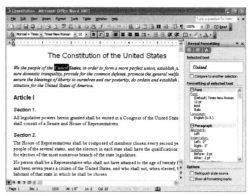

Figure 2 One example of revealing formatting.

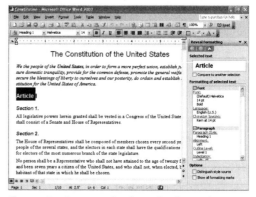

Figure 3 Another example of revealing formatting.

Figure 4
Scrolling through the Formatting of selected text box displays formatting information in three categories.

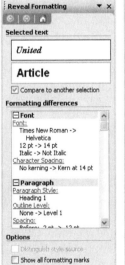

Figure 5 You can use the Reveal Formatting task pane to compare the formatting of two text selections.

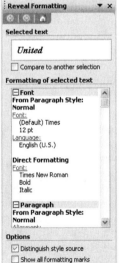

Figure 6 The Reveal Formatting task pane can also provide information about styles and directly applied formatting.

✔ Tips

■ In step 2, you can click the box to the left of a formatting category name to expand or collapse the formatting information display.

■ You can use check boxes in the Reveal Formatting task pane to get more formatting information:

▲ **Compare to another selection** enables you to make another text selection and see the difference between it and the first selection (**Figure 5**).

▲ **Distinguish style source** includes the style information for the selected text as well as directly applied formatting that makes the text different from the style's definition (**Figure 6**). I cover styles later in this chapter.

▲ **Show all formatting marks** displays formatting marks in the document window. This is the same as clicking the Show/Hide ¶ button 📖 on the standard toolbar. I tell you about formatting marks in **Chapter 2**.

REVEALING FORMATTING

91

To format text with the Reveal Formatting task pane

1. If necessary, chose Format > Reveal Formatting (**Figure 1**) or press Shift F1 to display the Reveal Formatting task pane (**Figures 2** and **3**).

2. Select the text for which you want to change formatting.

3. Click the arrow on the right side of the Selected text box to display a menu of formatting options (**Figure 7**) and choose one of the commands::

   ▲ **Select All text With Similar Formatting** selects all text in the document with the same formatting as the selected text. You can then apply different formatting to all of the selected text at once.

   ▲ **Apply Formatting of Surrounding Text** applies the formatting of the text around the selected text to the selected text.

   ▲ **Clear Formatting** clears the formatting of the selected text, returning its formatting to that of the style applied to the text.

   or

   Click an underlined link in the Formatting of selected text box to display a dialog for changing the formatting of the selection. (For example, clicking Font displays the Font tabof the Font dialog, which is covered in **Chapter 3**.) Use options in the dialog to change the formatting and click OK.

4. Repeat steps 2 though 3 for any text you want to reformat.

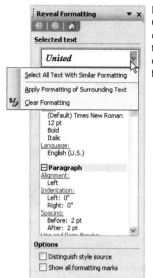

Figure 7
Clicking the arrow on the right side of the Selected text box displays a menu of formatting options.

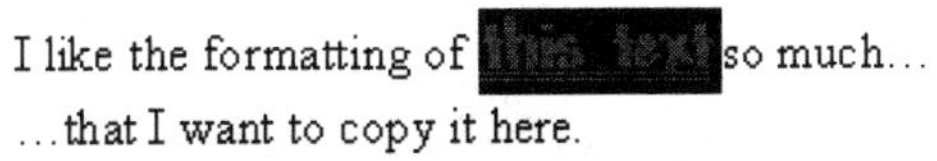

I like the formatting of this text so much…

…that I want to copy it here.

Figure 8 Select the text with the formatting you want to copy.

Figure 9 When you click the Format Painter button, the mouse pointer turns into a Format Painter pointer.

I like the formatting of this text so much…

…that I want to copy it here.

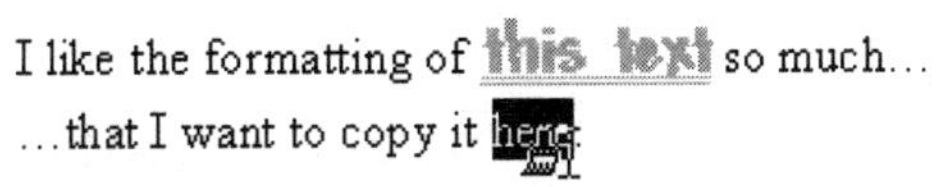

Figure 10 Use the Format Painter pointer to select the text you want to apply the formatting to.

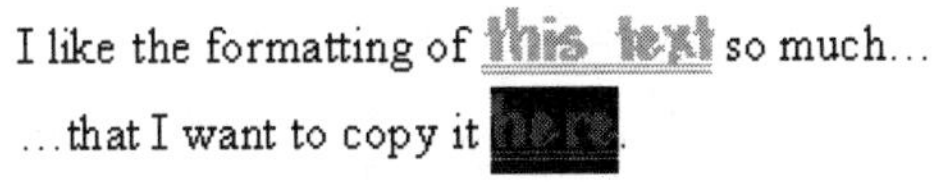

I like the formatting of this text so much…

…that I want to copy it here.

Figure 11 When you release the mouse button, the formatting is applied.

The Format Painter

The Format Painter enables you to copy the font or paragraph formatting of selected text and apply it to other text. This can save time and effort when applying the same formatting in multiple places throughout a document.

✔ Tip

■ Another way to apply the same formatting in various places throughout a document is with styles. I begin my discussion of Word's styles feature on the next page.

To use the Format Painter

1. Select the text whose formatting you want to copy (**Figure 8**).

2. Click the Format Painter button on the Standard toolbar. The Format Painter button becomes selected and the mouse pointer turns into an I-beam pointer with a plus sign beside it (**Figure 9**).

3. Use the mouse pointer to select the text to which you want to copy the formatting (**Figure 10**). When you release the mouse button, the formatting is applied (**Figure 11**) and the mouse pointer returns to normal.

✔ Tips

■ To copy paragraph formatting, be sure to select the entire paragraph in step 1, including the paragraph formatting mark (¶) at the end of the paragraph. I tell you about formatting marks in **Chapter 2**.

■ To copy the same formatting to more than one selection, double-click the Format Painter button. The mouse pointer remains a Format Painter pointer (**Figure 9**) until you press Esc or click the Format Painter button again.

THE FORMAT PAINTER

Styles

Word's styles feature enables you to define and apply sets of paragraph and/or font formatting to text throughout a document. This offers two main benefits over applying formatting using the basic techniques covered so far:

◆ **Consistency.** All text with a particular style applied will have the same formatting (**Figure 12**)—unless additional formatting has also been applied.

◆ **Flexibility.** Changing a style's definition is relatively easy. Once changed, the change automatically applies to all text formatted with that style (**Figure 13**).

Word supports four kinds of styles:

◆ **Character styles** affect the formatting of characters.

◆ **Paragraph styles** affect the formatting of entire paragraphs. The default paragraph style is called *Normal*.

◆ **Table styles** affect the formatting of tables.

◆ **List styles** affect the formatting of bulleted and numbered lists.

✔ Tips

■ Like font or paragraph formatting, you can apply styles as you type or to text that has already been typed. Check **Chapter 3** for details.

■ Styles are sometimes known as *style sheets*.

■ Word includes a number of predefined styles that you can apply to text.

■ Word's outline feature automatically applies predefined Heading styles as you create an outline. You can learn more about outlines in **Chapter 12**.

■ Tables are covered in **Chapter 9**.

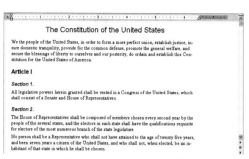

Figure 12 In this example, styles are applied to all text for consistent formatting.

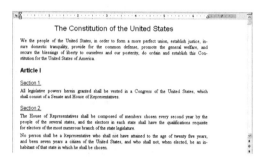

Figure 13 When two of the styles are modified, the formatting of text with those styles applied changes automatically. In this example, Normal style's paragraph formatting was changed from align left to justified and Heading 2 style's font formatting was changed from bold italic to regular with underline.

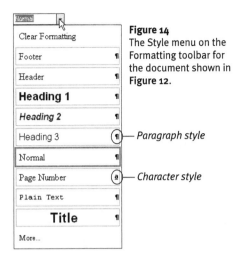

Figure 14
The Style menu on the Formatting toolbar for the document shown in **Figure 12**.

— *Paragraph style*

— *Character style*

Figure 15 Click the style name to select it.

Figure 16 Type in the name of the style that you want to apply.

To apply a style with the Formatting toolbar

Choose a style from the Style menu on the Formatting toolbar (**Figure 14**).

or

1. Click the name of the style in the Style box [Normal] to select it (**Figure 15**).

2. Type in the exact name of the style that you want to apply (**Figure 16**).

3. Press [Enter].

✔ Tips

- The Style menu displays only the styles that have been applied in the document, the first three Heading styles, Normal, and the Clear Formatting option (**Figure 14**).

- Choosing More from the Style menu (**Figure 14**) displays the Styles and Formatting task pane (**Figure 17**), which I discuss on the next page.

- To include all built-in template styles on the Style menu, hold down [Shift] while clicking to display the menu.

- The Style menu displays each style name using the formatting of that style (**Figure 14**).

- You can distinguish between character styles and paragraph styles in the Style pop-up menu by the symbol to the right of the style name (**Figure 14**).

- If you enter the name of a style that does not yet exist in the document in step 2 above, Word creates a new style for you, based on the selected paragraph. The formatting of the paragraph does not change, but the new style name appears on the Style pop-up menu.

To apply a style with the Styles and Formatting task pane

1. Choose Format > Styles and Formatting (**Figure 1**) or click the Styles and For-matting button 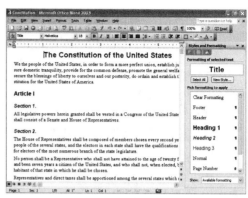 on the Formatting toolbar. The Styles and Formatting task pane appears (**Figure 17**).

2. If desired, use the Show drop-down list (**Figure 18**) to display a group of styles:

   ▲ **Available formatting** are the formats and styles that have been used in the document.

   ▲ **Formatting in use** are the styles applied within the document.

   ▲ **Available styles** are the styles that have been used in the document.

   ▲ **All styles** are all of the styles included within the template on which the document is based.

   ▲ **Custom** displays the Format Settings dialog (**Figure 19**), which you can use to specify which styles appear in the list.

3. Click the name of the style you want to apply.

✔ Tips

■ You can distinguish between character styles and paragraph styles in the Style dialog by the symbol to the right of the style name (**Figure 17**).

■ The name of the currently applied style appears in the box at the top of the Styles and Formatting task pane (**Figure 17**). In addition, a border appears around the name of the currently applied style.

■ When you point to the name of a style in the Styles and Formatting task pane, a box with a description of the style appears (**Figure 20**).

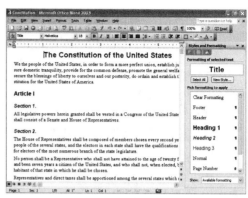

Figure 17 The Styles and Formatting task pane appears beside the document window.

Figure 18 The Show drop-down list in the Styles and Formatting task pane.

Figure 19 The Format Settings dialog enables you to customize the display of the Styles and For-matting task pane.

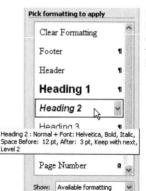

Figure 20 Pointing to a style displays a list of the formatting it includes.

Figure 21
Clicking the arrow beside a style's name displays a menu of options for that style.

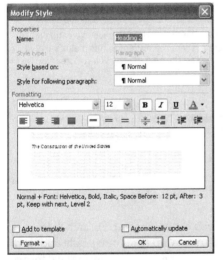

Figure 22 The Modify Style dialog.

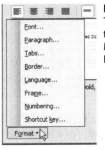

Figure 23
The Format menu at the bottom of the Modify Style and New Style dialogs.

To modify a style

1. If necessary, choose Format > Styles and Formatting (**Figure 1**) or click the Styles and Formatting button 🔲 on the Formatting toolbar to display the Styles and Formatting task pane (**Figure 17**).

2. If necessary, use the Show drop-down list (**Figure 18**) to display a group of styles.

3. Point to the name of the style you want to modify, and then choose Modify from its menu (**Figure 21**). The Modify Style dialog appears (**Figure 22**).

4. To change the style's name, enter a new name in the Name box.

5. To change basic style formatting options, use the drop-down lists and buttons in the Formatting area.

6. To change other formatting options, choose a type of formatting from the dialog's Format menu (**Figure 23**). Each option displays the appropriate formatting dialog. Make changes as desired in the dialog that appears and click OK.

7. Repeat step 6 as necessary to make all desired formatting changes.

8. To add the revised style to the template on which the document is based, turn on the Add to template check box.

9. To instruct Word to automatically update the style's definition whenever you apply manual formatting to text with the style applied, turn on the Automatically update check box.

10. Click OK.

✔ Tip

- The Options that appear in the Modify style dialog vary depending on the type of style you are modifying.

To create a new style

1. If necessary, choose Format > Styles and Formatting (**Figure 1**) or click the Styles and Formatting button 🖊 on the Formatting toolbar to display the Styles and Formatting task pane (**Figure 17**).

2. Click the New Style button to display the New Style dialog (**Figure 24**).

3. Enter a name for the style in the Name box.

4. Choose the type of style that you want to create from the Style type drop-down list (**Figure 25**).

5. To base the style on an existing style, choose the style from the Style based on drop-down list. This drop-down list includes all styles of the type you selected in step 4 that are included in the template on which the document is based.

6. If you chose Paragraph in step 4, choose a style from the Style for following paragraph drop-down list. This tells Word what style to apply to the next paragraph when you press ⌐Return⌐.

7. To set basic style formatting options, use the drop-down lists and buttons in the Formatting area.

8. To set other formatting options, choose a type of formatting from the dialog's Format menu (**Figure 23**). Each option displays the appropriate formatting dialog. Set options as desired in the dialog that appears and click OK.

9. Repeat step 8 as necessary to set all desired formatting options.

10. To add the new style to the template on which the document is based, turn on the Add to template check box.

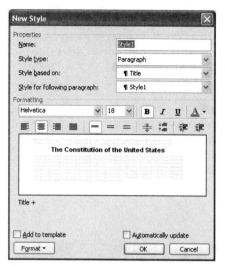

Figure 24 The New Style dialog when creating a paragraph style. The options in this dialog vary depending on the type of style you are creating.

Figure 25 The Style type drop-down list.

11. If you chose Paragraph in step 4, to instruct Word to automatically update the style whenever you apply manual formatting to text with the style applied, turn on the Automatically update check box.

12. Click OK.

✔ Tips

- The Options that appear in the New style dialog vary depending on the type of style you are creating.

- I tell you more about list formatting in **Chapter 2** and about tables in **Chapter 8**.

Figure 26 Word confirms that you want to delete a style.

To delete a style

1. If necessary, choose Format > Styles and Formatting (**Figure 1**) or click the Styles and Formatting button ![A] on the Formatting toolbar to display the Styles and Formatting task pane (**Figure 17**).

2. Point to the name of the style you want to delete, and then choose Delete from its menu (**Figure 21**).

3. In the confirmation dialog that appears (**Figure 26**), click Yes.

✔ Tips

- When you delete a paragraph style, the default style (Normal) is applied to any text to which the deleted style was applied.

- Not all styles can be deleted. For example, you cannot delete the Normal style or the Heading styles that are predefined by Word. That's why the Delete command appears gray in **Figure 21**.

Templates & Styles

As discussed in **Chapter 2**, each Word document is based on a template. The most commonly used template is Normal—the one that's used when you create a Blank new document—but Word comes with a variety of other templates and you can create your own.

Templates can include styles, as well as other Word features. The styles that are part of a template make it possible to create consistently formatted documents. Simply create the document based on the template and apply its styles as you build the document.

But what if you didn't create your document based on the template with the styles you want to use? That's where the Style Gallery, Templates and Add-Ins, and Organizer dialogs can help.

Word's Style Gallery enables you to copy styles from another template to the currently open document. You can then apply those styles to the document. If the document has already been formatted using the original template's styles, it will be automatically reformatted using the style definitions of any copied styles that have the same style name as originally applied styles.

The Templates and Add-Ins dialog goes a step further by enabling you to attach a different template to an existing file. This replaces all of the original templates elements—which can also include custom AutoText entries, toolbars, and macros—with the newly applied template's elements.

Finally, the Organizer dialog enables you to copy specific template elements, such as styles, from one document to another. This is particularly handy if the styles you'd like to use have already been created and saved in another Word document.

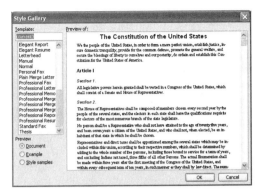

Figure 27 The Style Gallery window starts by displaying the document with its current styles.

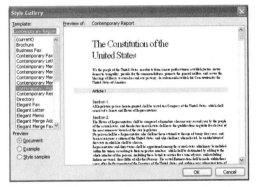

Figure 28 Clicking a template name displays the document with that template's styles applied.

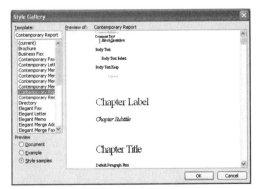

Figure 29 The Style Gallery also enables you to view samples of a template's styles.

To use the Style Gallery

1. Choose Format > Theme (**Figure 1**).

2. In the Theme dialog that appears, click the Style Gallery button to display the Style Gallery dialog (**Figure 27**).

3. Click the name of a template in the Template list to select it. An example of the document with the template's styles applied appears in the Preview area of the dialog (**Figure 28**).

4. To copy and apply the the styles of a selected template to the current document, click OK.

   or

   To close the Style Gallery dialog without copying styles, click Cancel.

✔ Tips

- I tell you about Word's Themes feature in **Chapter 17**.

- If the template you select in step 3 has not yet been installed, a message will appear at the top of the Preview area. Click OK to install the template and apply it to your document. You cannot preview a template or its styles unless it has been installed.

- You can use the Preview option buttons at the bottom of the Style Gallery dialog to change the display within the dialog:

  ▲ **Document** (**Figure 28**) shows the current document with the template's styles applied.

  ▲ **Example** shows an example document with the template's styles applied.

  ▲ **Style samples** (**Figure 29**) shows each of the documents' styles with the style's formatting applied.

To attach a template to a document with the Templates & Add-Ins dialog

1. Choose Tools > Templates and Add-Ins (**Figure 30**) to display the Templates and Add-ins dialog.

2. If necessary, click the Templates tab to display its options (**Figure 31**).

3. To update the current document's styles with styles from the template you are attaching, turn on the Automatically update document styles check box.

4. Click the Attach button.

5. Use the Attach Template dialog that appears (**Figure 32**) to locate, select, and open the template you want to attach to the document.

6. Back in the Templates and Add-ins dialog, click OK.

✔ Tips

- You can attach any Word template to a Word document—not just one of the templates that came with Microsoft Word.

- When you attach a template to a document, you make all the styles stored in the template available for use in the document.

- Attaching a template to a document is a good way to get an existing document to use standard formatting stored in a template file, even if the template was not available when the document was originally created.

Figure 30
Word's Tools menu.

Figure 31 The Templates tab of the Templates and Add-Ins dialog.

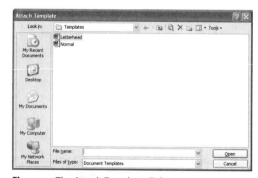

Figure 32 The Attach Template dialog.

Figure 33 The Styles tab of the Organizer dialog starts off by listing the styles in the active document and the template on which it is based.

Figure 34 When you click a Close file button, the contents of its scrolling list disappear and the button turns into an Open File button.

Figure 35 Use the Open dialog to locate and open a template or Word document containing the styles you want to copy.

Figure 36 Select the style you want to copy...

Figure 37 ...and click Copy to copy it to the other document.

To copy styles from one document to another with the Organizer

1. Choose Tools > Templates and Add-Ins (**Figure 30**) to display the Templates and Add-ins dialog (**Figure 31**).

2. Click the Organizer button to display the Organizer dialog.

3. If necessary, click the Styles tab to display its options. As shown in **Figure 33**, the dialog shows the styles in the active document on the left and the styles in the attached template on the right.

4. To select a different document or template on either side of the dialog, use one or both of the following techniques:

   ▲ Choose a different document or template from the Styles available in drop-down list.

   ▲ Click the Close File button to remove the document or template from the dialog, then click the Open File button that appears in its place (**Figure 34**) and use the Choose a File dialog that appears (**Figure 35**) to locate, select, and open the document or file you want.

   When you're finished, two different file names should appear at the top of the scrolling lists in the dialog. **Figure 36** shows an example.

5. Select the style you want to copy from one file to the other (**Figure 36**) and click the Copy button. The style is copied (**Figure 37**).

6. Repeat steps 4 and 5 for each style you want to copy.

7. Click Close to dismiss the Organizer dialog.

COPYING STYLES WITH THE ORGANIZER

Reformatting with Find and Replace

The Find and Replace dialog, which I discuss in **Chapter 2**, offers yet another way to change the formatting of a document. Although this dialog is used primarily to find and replace document text, it can also be used to find and replace document formatting, whether the formatting is directly applied or applied with styles.

To change formatting with the Find and Replace dialog

1. Choose Edit > Find (**Figure 38**) or press ⌃F to display the Find and Replace dialog.

2. If necessary, click the Replace tab to display its options.

3. If necessary, click the More button to expand the dialog so it looks like **Figure 39**.

4. To change the formatting of specific text, enter the text in both the Find what and Replace with boxes.

   or

   To change the formatting of any text, make sure the Find what and Replace with boxes are empty.

5. Position the insertion point in the Find what box.

6. Use the Format pop-up menu (**Figure 40**) to select the type of formatting you want to find. The appropriate dialog appears. **Figure 41** shows an example of what the Find Font dialog might look like. Change settings as desired and click OK.

7. Repeat step 6 for each type of formatting that you expect to find. Remember, Word will find text with all the formatting settings you specify.

Figure 38
The Edit menu.

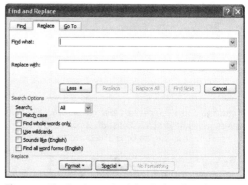

Figure 39 The Replace tab of the Find and Replace dialog, expanded to show all options.

Figure 40
Use the Format pop-up menu to choose the type of formatting you want to find or apply.

REFORMATTING WITH FIND AND REPLACE

Figure 41 The Find Font dialog. When you first display this dialog, nothing is selected, indicating that Word will find any font formatting.

Figure 42 In this example, Word will find any text that's underlined and has the Normal paragraph style applied and replace it with the same text formatted with bold, italic, Verdana font.

8. Position the insertion point in the Replace with box.

9. Use the Format pop-up menu (**Figure 40**) to select the type of formatting you want to apply to found text. The appropriate dialog appears. Change settings as desired and click OK.

10. Repeat step 9 for each type of formatting that you want to apply to found text. Remember, Word will apply all of the formatting you specify. **Figure 42** shows an example of how the Find and Replace dialog might look when you're finished.

11. Use the Replace or Replace All buttons as discussed in **Chapter 2** to replace formatting occurrences, thus reformatting the found text.

✔ Tips

■ As shown in **Figure 41**, formatting dialog boxes that are accessed from the Find and Replace dialog do not indicate any formatting settings—nothing is selected and check boxes are green, indicating that an option is neither selected nor deselected. Your settings in these dialogs should indicate the type of formatting you expect to find. For example, to find any text that was underlined, no matter what font, size, or other formatting option is applied, you'd select just the Underline style option you expect to find. Making changes for other options includes those options in your settings.

■ If you're not familiar with the Find and Replace dialog, be sure to read about it in **Chapter 2** before following the instructions here.

REFORMATTING WITH FIND AND REPLACE

AutoFormat

Word's AutoFormat feature can automatically format a document either as you type or when the document is finished. Word formats documents by applying appropriate styles to text based on how it is used in the document—for example, as titles, lists, headings, or body text. Word can also format Internet addresses as hyperlinks and replace typed symbols (such as --) with actual symbols (such as —).

Figure 43 The AutoFormat dialog.

✔ Tips

- AutoFormat As You Type is automatically turned on when you first use Word.

- I tell you more about Internet addresses and hyperlinks in **Chapter 17** and about symbols in **Chapter 9**.

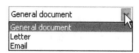

Figure 44 Use this drop-down list to tell Word what kind of document it must format.

To use AutoFormat on a completed document

1. Choose Format > AutoFormat (**Figure 1**) to display the AutoFormat dialog (**Figure 43**).

2. To use AutoFormat without reviewing changes, select the AutoFormat now option.

   or

   To review changes as you use Auto-Format, select the AutoFormat and review each change option.

3. Select the appropriate type of document from the drop-down list (**Figure 44**).

4. Click OK to begin the AutoFormat process.

   ▲ If you selected the AutoFormat now option in Step 2, Word formats the document and displays the changes. The AutoFormat process is complete; the rest of the steps do not apply.

   ▲ If you selected the AutoFormat and review each change option in step 2, Word formats the document. Continue with step 5.

Figure 45 This AutoFormat dialog appears when Word has finished the AutoFormat process and is waiting for you to review its changes.

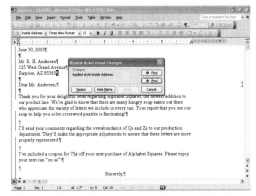

Figure 46 The Review AutoFormat Changes dialog lets you accept or reject each change as it is selected in the document window.

Figure 47 Word tells you when you reach the end of a document.

5. A different AutoFormat dialog appears (**Figure 45**). Click one of its four buttons to proceed:

 ▲ **Accept All** accepts all changes to the document. The AutoFormat process is complete; the rest of the steps do not apply.

 ▲ **Reject All** rejects all changes to the document. The AutoFormat process is reversed; the rest of the steps do not apply.

 ▲ **Review Changes** enables you to review the changes one by one. The Review AutoFormat Changes dialog appears (**Figure 46**). Continue with step 6.

 ▲ **Style Gallery** displays the Style Gallery dialog (**Figure 27**) so you can select a different template's styles. I tell you how to use the Style Gallery earlier in this chapter. When you are finished using the Style Gallery, you will return to this dialog; click one of the other buttons to continue.

6. In the Review AutoFormat Changes dialog (**Figure 46**), review the information in the Changes area and click the appropriate button:

 ▲ To accept a change, click a Find button to display the next change.

 ▲ To reject a change and move to the next change, click the Reject button.

7. Repeat step 6 until you have reviewed every change.

8. Word displays a dialog like the one in **Figure 47** when you reach the end of the document. Click Cancel to dismiss it.

9. Click Cancel again to return to the AutoFormat Dialog (**Figure 45**).

10. Click Accept All to accept all changes that you did not reject.

To set AutoFormat options

1. Choose Format > AutoFormat (**Figure 1**) to display the AutoFormat dialog (**Figure 43**).

2. Click Options. The AutoFormat tab of the AutoCorrect dialog appears (**Figure 48**).

3. Set options as desired:

   ▲ **Built-in Heading styles** applies Word's Heading styles to heading text.

   ▲ **List styles** applies list and bullet styles to numbered, bulleted, and other lists.

   ▲ **Automatic bulleted lists** applies bulleted list formatting to paragraphs beginning with *, o, or - followed by a space or tab.

   ▲ **Other paragraph styles** applies other styles such as Body Text, Inside Address, and Salutation.

   ▲ **"Straight quotes" with "smart quotes"** replaces plain quote characters with curly quote characters.

   ▲ **Ordinals (1st) with superscript** formats ordinals with superscript. For example, 1st becomes 1st.

   ▲ **Fractions (1/2) with fraction character** ($\frac{1}{2}$) replaces fractions typed with numbers and slashes with fraction characters.

   ▲ **Hyphens (- -) with dash (—)** replaces a single hyphen with an en dash (–) and a double hyphen with an em dash (—).

   ▲ ***Bold* and _italic_ with real formatting** formats text enclosed within asterisk characters (*) as bold and text enclosed within underscore characters as italic. For example, *hello* becomes **hello** and _goodbye_ becomes *goodbye*.

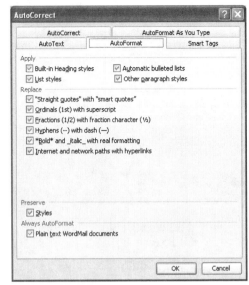

Figure 48 The AutoFormat tab of the AutoCorrect dialog.

   ▲ **Internet and network paths with hyperlinks** formats e-mail addresses and URLs as clickable hyperlink fields.

   ▲ **Styles** prevents styles already applied in the document from being changed.

   ▲ **Plain text WordMail documents** enables you to format e-mail messages when you use Word as your e-mail editor.

4. Click OK to save your settings.

✔ Tips

■ To convert other characters to corresponding symbols, such as (tm) to ™ or (c) to ©, use the AutoCorrect feature, which I explain in **Chapter 7**.

■ I tell you about hyperlinks and other Internet-related features in **Chapter 17**.

Figure 49 The AutoFormat As You Type tab of the AutoCorrect dialog.

To set automatic formatting options

1. Choose Format > AutoFormat (**Figure 1**) to display the AutoFormat dialog (**Figure 43**).

2. Click the Options button. The Auto-Format tab of the AutoCorrect dialog appears (**Figure 48**).

3. Click the AutoFormat As You Type tab to display its options (**Figure 49**).

4. Set options as desired. Most of the options are the same as those in the AutoFormat tab, which is discussed on the previous page. Here are the others:

   ▲ **Automatic numbered lists** applies numbered list formatting to paragraphs beginning with a number or letter followed by a space or tab.

   ▲ **Border lines** automatically applies paragraph border styles when you type three or more hyphens, underscores, or equal signs.

   ▲ **Tables** creates a table when you type a series of hyphens with plus signs to indicate column edges, such as +----------+-----+.

   ▲ **Format beginning of list item like the one before it** repeats character formatting that you apply to the beginning of a list item. For example, if the first word of the previous list item was formatted as bold, the first word of the next list item is automatically formatted as bold.

   ▲ **Set left- and first-indent with tabs and backspaces** sets left indentation on the ruler based on tabs and backspaces you type.

   ▲ **Define styles based on your formatting** automatically creates or modifies styles based on manual formatting that you apply in the document.

5. Click OK to save your settings.

✔ Tips

■ I tell you about borders and list formatting in **Chapter 3**, about styles earlier in this chapter, and about tables in **Chapter 8**.

■ Most AutoFormatting As You Type options are turned on by default. The only way to disable this feature is to turn off all options in the AutoFormat As You Type tab of the AutoCorrect dialog (**Figure 49**).

SETTING AUTOMATIC FORMATTING OPTIONS

Page & Section Formatting

Page & Section Formatting

Chapters 3 and **4** provide a wealth of information about formatting text—the types of formatting you can apply and the various methods you can use to apply them. But if your document is destined for the printer, you should also be interested in page formatting.

Page formatting is is formatting that is applied to an entire document or section of a document. For example, *margins*, which determine the spacing between the edge of the paper and the text indents, are applied to entire pages—you can't have different margins for different words or paragraphs. *Page borders*, which are another example of page formatting, surround the contents of a page, not just parts of it.

Many types of page formatting can be applied to document *sections* or parts. For example, a *header* is text or other information that appears at the top of each page. Rather than have the same thing appear at the top of every page in a document, you can create different document sections, each with its own custom header. *Multiple-column text* is another example of formatting that can be applied to document sections.

In this chapter, I tell you about the different types of page formatting and explain how you can apply them to entire documents and document sections.

Page, Section, & Column Breaks

As you work with a document, Word automatically sets page breaks based on paper size, margins, and contents. A *page break* marks the end of a page; anything after the page break will appear on the next page when the document is printed. This is easy to see in Print Layout view (**Figure 1**). In Normal view, automatic page breaks appear as dotted lines across the document (**Figure 2**).

Although you cannot change an automatic page break directly, you can change it indirectly by inserting a manual page break before it (**Figure 3**). This forces the page to end where you specify and, in most cases, forces subsequent automatic page breaks in the document to change.

In addition to page breaks, Word also enables you to insert section and column breaks. A *section break* marks the end of a document section. Sections are commonly used to divide a document into logical parts, each of which can have its own settings in the Page Setup dialog. A *column break* marks the end of a column of text. Column breaks are usually used in conjunction with multi-column text.

✔ Tips

- Automatic page breaks do not appear in Web Layout or Outline view. The page breaks that appear in Reading Layout view do not correspond to those that appear when the document is printed.

- As discussed later in this chapter, section breaks may be automatically inserted by Word in a document when you change page formatting settings.

- Columns and multi-column text are discussed a little later in this chapter.

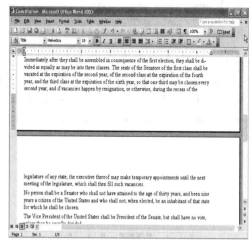

Figure 1 A page break in Print Layout view.

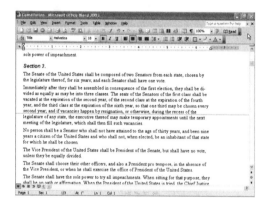

Figure 2 The same page break in Normal view.

Figure 3 A manual page break adjusts all of the subsequent automatic page breaks.

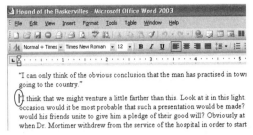

Figure 4 Position the insertion point where you want the break to occur.

Figure 5
Choose Break from the Insert menu.

Figure 6
Use the Break dialog to select the type of break to insert.

Figure 7 Click in the selection bar to the left of the break to select it.

To insert a break

1. Position the insertion point where you want the break to occur (**Figure 4**).

2. Choose Insert > Break (**Figure 5**) to display the Break dialog (**Figure 6**).

3. Choose the option for the type of break you want to insert:

   ▲ **Page break** inserts a page break. **Figure 3** shows an inserted page break.

   ▲ **Column break** inserts a column break. This forces any text after the break into the next column.

   ▲ **Text wrapping break** ends the current line and forces the text to continue after a picture or table.

   ▲ **Next page** inserts a section break that also acts as a page break.

   ▲ **Continuous** inserts a section break in the middle of a page.

   ▲ **Odd page** inserts a section break that also acts as a page break. The following page will always be odd-numbered.

   ▲ **Even page** inserts a section break that also acts as a page break. The following page will always be even-numbered.

   or

   Use one of the following shortcut keys:

   ▲ To insert a page break, press [Shift][Enter].

   ▲ To insert a column break, press [Ctrl][Shift][Enter].

To remove a break

1. In Normal view, select the break by clicking in the selection bar beside it (**Figure 7**).

2. Press [Backspace].

The Page Setup Dialog

The Page Setup dialog (**Figures 8** through **10**) enables you to set a number of page and section formatting options. The dialog offers three tabs of options:

◆ **Margins** (**Figure 8**) enables you to set margins, gutter, orientation, and multiple page options for a document.

◆ **Paper** (**Figure 9**) enables you to set the paper size and source for a print job.

◆ **Layout** (**Figure 10**) enables you to set section options, header and footer locations, and vertical alignment for a document or section.

One very important aspect of the Page Setup dialog is the Apply to drop-down list (**Figures 11** and **12**) in the Preview area of each tab. This menu determines how page formatting options in the dialog are applied to the document. The options on this menu vary depending on what is selected in the document window:

◆ **Whole document** applies the formatting to all of the pages in the document. This option always appears.

◆ **Selected text** applies the formatting to only the text that is selected in the document. Choosing this option automatically inserts a section break before and after the selected text. This option only appears if text is selected when you open the Page Setup dialog.

◆ **This point forward** applies the formatting to the document's pages from the insertion point to the end of the document. Choosing this option automatically inserts a section break at the insertion point. This option only appears if no text is selected when you open the Page Setup dialog.

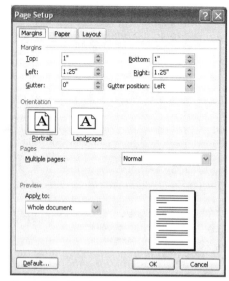

Figure 8 The Margins tab of the Page Setup dialog.

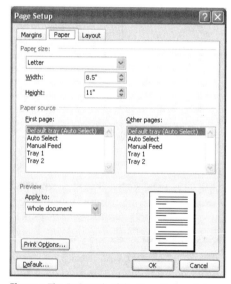

Figure 9 The Paper tab of the Page Setup dialog.

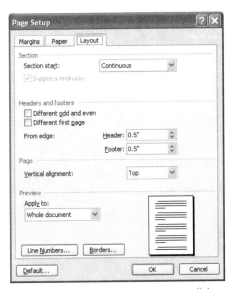

Figure 10 The Layout tab of the Page Setup dialog.

Figures 11 & 12
The Apply to drop-down list with nothing selected in a single-section document (top) and with one section selected in a multi-section document (bottom).

◆ **This section** applies the formatting to the current section—the section in which the insertion point is blinking. This option only appears if the document already contains at least one section break and no text is selected.

◆ **Selected sections** applies the formatting to the currently selected document sections. This option only appears if at least one section is selected in its entirety.

This part of the chapter explains how to set page and section formatting options in the Page Setup dialog.

✔ Tip

■ Some Page Setup options—such as margins, paper size, and orientation—affect the dimensions of a page's printable area. If you plan to use non-standard Page Setup options, consider setting them *before* you create and format your document.

To open the Page Setup dialog

Choose File > Page Setup (**Figure 13**).

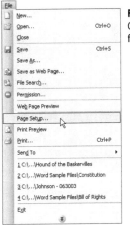

Figure 13
Choose Page Setup from the File menu.

To set margins & orientation

1. In the Page Setup dialog, click the Margins tab to display its options (**Figure 8**).

2. Enter values in the Top, Bottom, Left, and Right boxes.

3. To set a gutter width, enter a value in the Gutter box. If necessary, use the Gutter Position drop-down list to specify whether the gutter should be on the Left or Top of each page.

4. Select the button for the orientation option you want. The images on the buttons illustrate each option.

5. To apply your settings to the entire document, make sure Whole document is selected from the Apply to drop-down list (**Figures 11** and **12**). Otherwise, choose the desired option from the Apply to drop-down list.

6. Click OK.

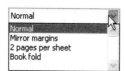

Figure 14
The Multiple pages drop-down list in the Margins tab of the Page Setup dialog.

✔ Tips

- You can select an option from the Multiple Pages drop-down list (**Figure 14**) to set up the document for special multiple-page printing.

  - ▲ **Normal** prints all pages with the same settings.

  - ▲ **Mirror margins** turns the Left and Right margin options to Inside and Outside options. Use this for double-sided printing and facing pages.

  - ▲ **Two pages per sheet** prints two document pages per sheet of paper.

  - ▲ **Book fold** prints two pages per sheet of paper and shuffles the print order of the pages so they can be folded into a booklet after printing.

- The Preview area of the Page Setup dialog illustrates all page formatting settings.

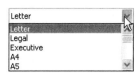

Figure 15
The Paper size
drop-down list.

To set paper size & source

1. In the Page Setup dialog, click the Paper tab to display its options (**Figure 9**).

2. Choose a size from the Paper size drop-down list (**Figure 15**).

   or

   Enter custom values in the Width and Height boxes.

3. If necessary, set Paper source options to determine how your printer will feed paper. (These options are not available for all printers.)

4. To apply your settings to the entire document, make sure Whole document is selected from the Apply to drop-down list (**Figures 11** and **12**). Otherwise, choose the desired option from the Apply to drop-down list.

5. Click OK.

✔ Tips

■ The Paper source options that appear in the Paper tab of the Page Setup dialog are printer-specific. Unless you have the same printer I have (or one with the same features), the options that appear on your screen will differ from what appears in **Figure 9**.

■ Clicking the Print Options button at the bottom of the Paper tab (**Figure 9**) displays the Print tab of the Options dialog. I discuss Print options in **Chapter 19**.

To set section start options

1. In the Page Setup dialog, click the Layout tab to display its options (**Figure 10**).

2. Choose an option from the Section start drop-down list (**Figure 16**). These options correspond to the options in the Break dialog (**Figure 6**), which is discussed earlier in this chapter.

3. Choose the appropriate option from the Apply to drop-down list (**Figures 11** and **12**) to determine which section break(s) the settings should apply to.

4. Click OK.

To set header & footer options

1. In the Page Setup dialog, click the Layout tab to display its options (**Figure 10**).

2. Set options as desired in the Headers and Footers area:

   ▲ **Different odd and even** enables you to specify different headers and footers for odd and even pages of the document or section.

   ▲ **Different first page** enables you to specify a different header and footer for the first page of the document or section.

   ▲ **From edge** enables you to enter the amount of space between the edge of the paper and the header and footer.

3. To apply your settings to the entire document, make sure Whole document is selected from the Apply to drop-down list (**Figures 11** and **12**). Otherwise, choose the desired option from the Apply to drop-down list.

4. Click OK.

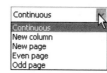

Figure 16
The Section start drop-down list.

✔ Tip

■ I explain how to insert headers and footers later in this chapter.

Figure 17
The Vertical alignment drop-down list.

Figure 18 Examples of vertical alignment: top (top left), center (top right), justified (bottom left), and bottom (bottom right).

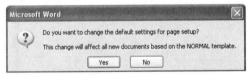

Figure 19 This dialog appears when you click the Default button in the Page Setup dialog. Click Yes only if you want to change the default Page Setup settings for the template on which the document is based—in this example, Normal.

To set vertical alignment for pages

1. In the Page Setup dialog, click the Layout tab to display its options (**Figure 10**).

2. Choose an option from the Vertical alignment drop-down list (**Figure 17**). **Figure 18** shows page previews of what each option looks like when applied to the same document page.

3. To apply your settings to the entire document, make sure Whole document is selected from the Apply to drop-down list (**Figures 11** and **12**). Otherwise, choose the desired option from the Apply to drop-down list.

4. Click OK.

✔ Tips

■ Vertical alignment is only apparent on pages that are less than a full page in length.

■ On screen, you can only view vertical alignment in Print Layout view and Print Preview.

To set default page formatting

1. In the Page Setup dialog, set options as desired in the Margins, Paper, and Layout tabs (**Figures 8** through **10**).

2. Click the Default button.

3. Word displays a dialog like the one in **Figure 19**, asking if you want to change the default settings for the template on which the document is based. Click Yes only if you want the settings to apply to all new documents that you create with that template.

Headers & Footers

A header is a part of the document that appears at the top of every page. A footer is a part of the document that appears at the bottom of every page. Headers and footers are commonly used to place page numbers, revision dates, or other document information on document pages.

To display a header or footer

Choose View > Header and Footer (**Figure 20**).

If necessary, Word switches to Print Layout view and displays the Header area of the current document section, as well as the Header and Footer toolbar (**Figure 21**).

◆ To view the footer for the current section, click the Switch Between Header and Footer button 📄 on the Header and Footer toolbar. The Footer area appears (**Figure 22**).

◆ To view the header or footer for the previous or next section of a multi-section document, click the Show Previous 📄 or Show Next 📄 button on the Header and Footer toolbar.

✔ Tip

■ In Print Layout view, you can view a header or footer by double-clicking in the Header or Footer area of a page.

To hide a header or footer

Click the Close button [Close] on the Header and Footer toolbar.

or

Double-click anywhere in the document window other than in the Header or Footer.

The document returns to the view you were in before you viewed the header or footer. The Header and Footer toolbar disappears.

Figure 20
Choose Header and Footer from the View menu.

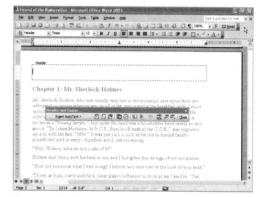

Figure 21 The Header area of a document window.

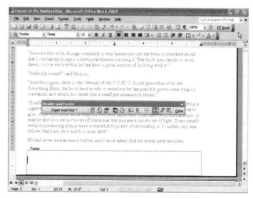

Figure 22 The Footer area of a document window.

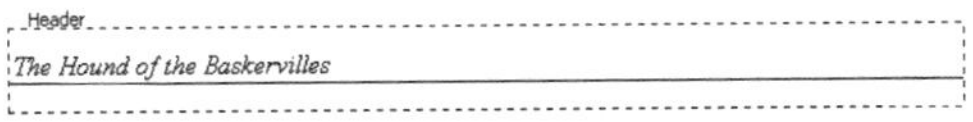

Header
The Hound of the Baskervilles

Figure 23 An example of a header with text formatting applied.

Footer
Revised 15-October-1897

Figure 24 A simple footer.

To create a header or footer

1. Display the header or footer area (**Figure 21 or 22**) for the header or footer that you want to create.

2. Enter the header (**Figure 23**) or footer (**Figure 24**) information.

3. When you're finished, hide the header or footer area to continue working on the document.

✔ Tip

- You can format the contents of a header or footer the same way that you format any other part of the document. In **Figure 23**, for example, the header text has italic font formatting and a bottom paragraph border applied. You can find detailed text formatting instructions in **Chapters 3 and 4**.

To edit a header or footer

1. Display the header (**Figure 23**) or footer (**Figure 24**) area for the header or footer that you want to change.

2. Edit the header or footer information.

3. When you're finished, hide the header or footer area to continue working on the document.

To remove a header or footer

1. Display the Header or Footer area for the header or footer that you want to remove.

2. Select its contents and press Backspace. The header or footer is removed.

3. Hide the header or footer area to continue working on the document.

WORKING WITH HEADERS & FOOTERS

To insert AutoText entries or Word fields in a header or footer

1. Position the insertion point in the Header or Footer area where you want the AutoText entry or field to appear.

2. To insert an AutoText entry, click the Insert AutoText button on the Header and Footer toolbar to display a menu of entries (**Figure 25**). Choose the one that you want to insert.

3. To insert a Word field, click the appropriate button on the Header and Footer toolbar (**Figure 26**) to insert the field:

   ▲ **Insert Page Number** 🔲 inserts the page number.

   ▲ **Insert Number of Pages** 🔲 inserts the total number of pages in the document.

   ▲ **Insert Date** 🔲 inserts the current date.

   ▲ **Insert Time** 🔲 inserts the current time.

✔ Tips

■ I tell you about AutoText entries and Word fields in **Chapter 9**.

■ To number pages, use the Insert Page Number button 🔲 on the Header and Footer toolbar or one of the first three options or the last option on the Insert AutoText button's menu (**Figure 25**) to insert a page number in the header or footer. **Figure 27** shows an example using the "Author, Page #, Date" AutoText Entry. In my opinion, using these options is the best way to number pages in a document. Using the Page Numbers command on the Insert menu inserts page numbers in frames that can be difficult to work with. The Page Numbers command is not covered in this book.

Figure 25
The AutoText pop-up menu on the Header and Footer toolbar.

Figure 26 The Header and Footer toolbar.

Figure 27 This footer example uses the "Author, Page #, Date" AutoText entry to insert Word fields.

Figure 28 Examples of headers for the first three sections of a document with multiple sections and different first page headers and footers. (The first section has only one page.) As you can see, the header and its link status is clearly identified.

To create a different first page or odd and even header and footer

1. Choose File > Page Setup (**Figure 13**) to display the Page Setup dialog. If necessary, click the Layout tab (**Figure 10**).

2. To create a different header and footer on odd- and even-numbered pages of the document, turn on the Different odd and even check box.

3. To create a different header and footer on the first page of the document or document section, turn on the Different first page check box.

4. Click OK.

5. Follow the instructions on the previous pages to create headers and footers as desired. Use the Show Previous [icon] and Show Next [icon] buttons on the Header and Footer toolbar to display and edit each header and footer.

✔ Tips

■ As illustrated in **Figure 28**, the Header or Footer area clearly identifies the current Header or Footer.

■ By default, if your document is set up to have multiple headers or footers, each header and footer is linked to the previous one (**Figure 28**), thus ensuring that they are the same. Use the Link to Previous button [icon] on the Header and Footer toolbar to toggle this feature. You must disable this feature to change a header or footer without changing the previous one(s).

Columns

Word enables you to format text with multiple columns, like those in a newspaper.

✔ Tips

- Although you can edit multi-column text in any view, you must be in Print Layout view (**Figure 29**) to see the columns side by side. In Normal view, the text appears in the same narrow column (**Figure 30**).

- Column formatting applies to sections of text. You can insert section breaks as discussed earlier in this chapter to set up various multi-column sections.

To set the number of columns

1. Select the text for which you want to set the number of columns (**Figure 31**).

2. Click the Columns button 🏢 on the Standard toolbar to display a menu of columns and choose the number of columns (**Figure 32**).

If you are not in Print Layout view, Word switches to that view. The text is reformatted with the number of columns you specified (**Figure 29**).

✔ Tips

- To set the number of columns for an entire single-section document, in step 1 above, position the insertion point anywhere in the document.

- To set the number of columns for one section of a multi-section document, in step 1 above, position the insertion point anywhere in the section.

- If necessary, Word inserts section breaks to mark the beginning and end of multi-column text (**Figure 30**).

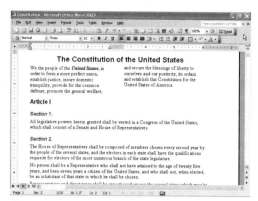

Figure 29 A section of multi-column text in Print Layout view.

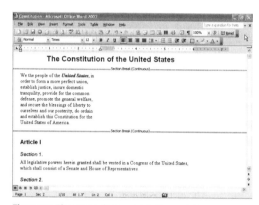

Figure 30 The same document in Normal view.

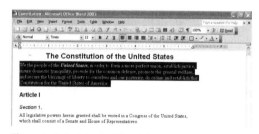

Figure 31 Select the text for which you want to set columns.

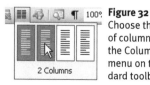

Figure 32 Choose the number of columns from the Columns button menu on the Standard toolbar.

Figure 33
The Format menu.

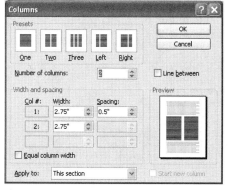

Figure 34 The Columns dialog.

To set column options

1. Position the insertion point in the section for which you want to change column options.

   or

   Select the sections for which you want to change column options.

2. Choose Format > Columns (**Figure 33**) to display the Columns dialog (**Figure 34**).

3. To set the number of columns, click one of the icons in the Presets section or enter a value in the Number of columns box.

4. To set different column widths for each column, make sure the Equal column width check box is turned off, then enter values in the Width boxes for each column. You can also enter values in the Spacing boxes to specify the amount of space between columns.

5. To put a vertical line between columns, turn on the Line between check box.

6. To specify the part of the document that you want the changes to apply to, choose an option from the Apply to drop-down list (**Figures 11** and **12**).

   or

   To insert a column break at the insertion point, choose This point forward from the Apply to drop-down list (**Figure 11**), then turn on the Start new column check box.

7. Click OK.

✔ Tip

■ You can see the effect of your changes in the Preview area as you change settings in the Columns dialog.

SETTING COLUMN OPTIONS

Page Borders

Page borders are borders that apply to entire pages of a document. They enable you to, in effect, frame document pages.

✔ Tips

- Page borders make it easy to create official-looking certificates and other "suitable for framing" documents.

- Page borders can be applied to all pages in a document or only the pages in a specific document section.

To apply page borders

1. If necessary, position the insertion point in the section of the document to which you want to apply page borders.

2. Choose Format > Borders and Shading (**Figure 33**) to display the Borders and Shading dialog.

3. If necessary, click the Page Border tab to display its options (**Figure 35**).

4. Click a Setting icon to select the type of border. All options except None and Custom place borders around each side of the page.

5. Click a style in the Style scrolling list to select a line style. Then choose a line color from the Color drop-down list (**Figure 36**) and a line thickness from the Width drop-down list (**Figure 37**).

   or

   Select a graphic from the Art drop-down list (**Figure 38**).

6. If necessary, choose an option from the Apply to drop-down list (**Figures 11** and **12**).

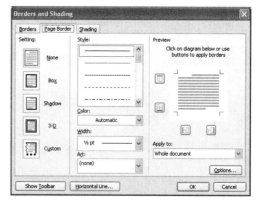

Figure 35 The Page Borders tab of the Borders and Shading dialog.

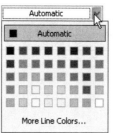

Figure 36 The Color drop-down list.

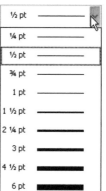

Figure 37 The Width drop-down list.

Figure 38 The Art drop-down list.

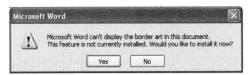

Figure 39 This dialog appears if the border art feature is not installed.

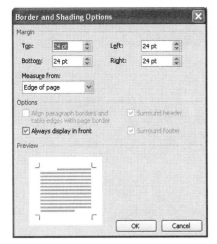

Figure 40 The Border and Shading Options dialog for page borders.

7. To apply custom borders, click the buttons in the Preview area to add or remove a line using the settings in the dialog.

8. When the Preview area illustrates the kind of border that you want to apply, click OK.

✔ Tips

■ If a dialog like the one in **Figure 39** appears when you attempt to select a graphic in step 5, the border art feature is not installed. To install it, click Yes and follow the prompts that appear on screen. You will then be able to choose an option from the Art drop-down list.

■ You can repeat steps 5 and 7 to customize each border of a custom border.

■ You can further customize a border by clicking the Options button in the Borders and Shading dialog to display the Border and Shading Options dialog (**Figure 40**). Set options as desired and click OK to return to the Borders and Shading dialog.

■ I tell you about the other tabs of the Borders and Shading dialog in **Chapter** 3.

To remove page borders

1. Position the insertion point in the section from which you want to remove borders.

2. Choose Format > Borders and Shading (**Figure 33**) and click the Page Border tab in the Borders and Shading dialog that appears (**Figure 35**).

3. Click the None icon.

4. Click OK.

REMOVING PAGE BORDERS

Printing
Documents

Printing Documents

In most cases, when you've finished writing, formatting, and proofreading a document, you'll want to print it. This chapter tells you about the Microsoft Word features you'll use to complete the printing process:

- ◆ **Print Preview** enables you to view the document on screen before you print it. You can also use this view to set page breaks and margins to fine-tune printed appearance.

- ◆ The printer's **Properties** dialog enables you to set options specific to your printer.

- ◆ The **Print** dialog enables you to specify the page range, number of copies, and other options for printing. It then sends the document to your printer.

✔ Tips

- ■ The Page Setup dialog , which is covered in **Chapter 5**, offers many options that affect the way a document prints. If you're not familiar with page formatting options such as paper size, orientation, and margins, consult **Chapter 5**.

- ■ This chapter assumes that your computer is already set up for printing. If it is not, consult the documentation that came with your printer for setup information.

- ■ Information about printing mailing labels, form letters, and envelopes is provided in **Chapters 13** and **14**.

Print Preview

Word's Print Preview (**Figure 1**) displays one or more pages of a document exactly as they will appear when printed. It also enables you to make last-minute changes to margins and document contents before printing.

✔ Tip

■ Print Preview can save time and paper—it's a lot quicker to look at a document on screen than to wait for it to print, and it doesn't use a single sheet of paper.

To switch to Print Preview

Choose File > Print Preview (**Figure 2**), or click the Print Preview button  on the Standard toolbar.

✔ Tip

■ The Print Preview toolbar (**Figure 3**) appears automatically at the top of the screen when you switch to Print Preview.

To zoom in or out

1. Select the Magnifier button on the Print Preview toolbar (**Figure 3**).

2. Click on the page. With each click, the view toggles between 100% and the current Zoom percentage `100%` on the Print Preview toolbar.

or

Choose an option from the Zoom drop-down list on the Print Preview toolbar (**Figure 4**).

or

1. Click in the Zoom box `100%` on the Print Preview toolbar.

2. Enter a value.

3. Press Enter.

Figure 1 A single page of a document in Print Preview.

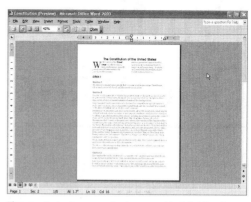

Figure 2 Commands for printing a document can be found on the File menu.

Figure 3 The Print Preview toolbar.

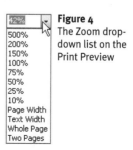

Figure 4 The Zoom drop-down list on the Print Preview

Figure 5
Use the Multiple Pages button's menu to choose a layout for displaying multiple document pages in Print Preview.

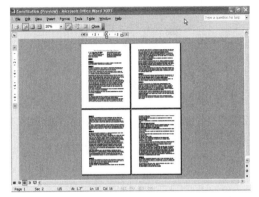

Figure 6 Four pages of a document displayed in Print Preview.

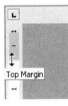

Figure 7
The mouse pointer changes when you position it on a margin on the ruler.

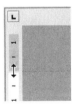

Figure 8
Drag to change the margin.

To view multiple pages

Click the Multiple Pages button ▣ on the Print Preview toolbar to display a menu of page layouts and choose the one that you want (**Figure 5**).

The view and magnification change to display the pages as you specified (**Figure 6**).

✔ Tip

■ To return to a single-page view, click the One Page button ▣ on the Print Preview toolbar.

To change margins

1. If necessary, click the View Ruler button ▣ on the Print Preview toolbar to display the ruler in the Print Preview window (**Figure 1**).

2. Position the mouse pointer on the ruler in the position corresponding to the margin you want to change. The mouse pointer turns into a box with arrows on either end and a yellow box appears, identifying the margin (**Figure 7**).

3. Press the mouse button down and drag to change the margin. As you drag, a dotted line indicates the position of the margin (**Figure 8**). When you release the mouse button, the margin changes.

✔ Tips

■ A better way to change margins is with the Margins tab of the Page Setup dialog, which is covered in **Chapter 5**.

■ You can also use the ruler to change indentation for selected paragraphs. **Chapter 3** explains how.

WORKING WITH PRINT PREVIEW

To move from page to page

In Print Preview, click the Previous Page or Next Page button at the bottom of the vertical scroll bar (**Figure 9**).

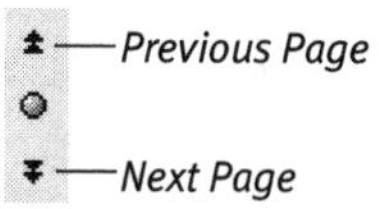

To edit the document

1. If necessary, zoom in to get a better look at the text you want to edit.

2. Deselect the Magnifier button 📷 on the Print Preview toolbar.

3. Click in the document window to position the insertion point.

4. Edit the document as desired.

✔ Tip

■ You may find that your computer responds more quickly when you edit in Page Layout or Normal view than in Print Preview.

To reduce the number of pages

Click the Shrink to Fit button 📄 on the Print Preview toolbar.

Word squeezes the document onto one less page by making minor adjustments to font size and paragraph spacing. It then displays the revised document.

✔ Tip

■ This feature is useful for squeezing a two-page letter onto one page when the second page only has a line or two.

— Previous Page

— Next Page

Figure 9 Use the Previous Page and Next Page buttons at the bottom of the vertical scroll bar to move from one page to another.

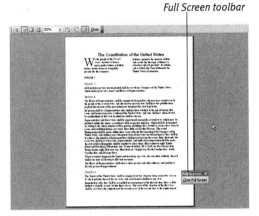

Full Screen toolbar

Figure 10 Full Screen view in Print Preview.

To switch to a full-screen view

Click the Full Screen button ⬜ on the Print Preview toolbar.

The screen redraws to remove the status bar (**Figure 10**). This enables you to get a slightly larger view of the document page(s).

✔ Tip

- To return to a regular Print Preview view, click the Close Full Screen button on the Full Screen toolbar.

To leave Print Preview

Click the Close button on the Print Preview toolbar (**Figure 3**).

The document returns to whatever view you were in before you switched to Print Preview.

Printer Properties

Your printer's Properties dialog, which is specific to your brand and model of printer, may offer additional printing options. In some cases, you may want to set options in this dialog for a specific printing job.

Although it is impossible for this book to cover all options that may appear in the Properties dialog, these two pages provide a quick look at what's in the Properties dialog for my printer (**Figures 11, 12, 13**, and **16**), an HP LaserJet 2100TN, which is connected to my network. The options for your printer may be similar. Explore the Properties dialog for your printer on your own.

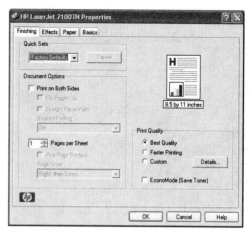

Figure 11 The Finishing tab of the Properties dialog for a LaserJet 2100TN printer.

✔ Tips

- If an option appears in both the Properties dialog and the Print or Page Setup dialog, modify it in the Print or Page Setup dialog. This saves your changes for the document rather than for the printer.

- You can use the Quick Sets feature in the Properties dialog to save groups of settings for reuse. Consult the Windows documentation for more inforamtion.

- For more information about your printer and the options it offers, consult its owner's manual.

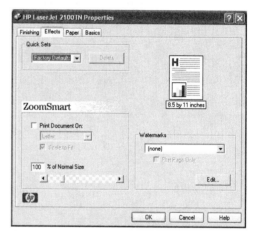

Figure 12 The Effects tab of the Properties dialog for a LaserJet 2100TN printer.

To open the printer's Properties dialog

1. Choose File > Print (**Figure 2**) to display the Print dialog.

2. If necessary, choose the name of the printer you want to use from the Name drop-down list.

3. Click the Properties button. The Properties dialog for the printer you chose appears (**Figures 11, 12, 13**, and **16**).

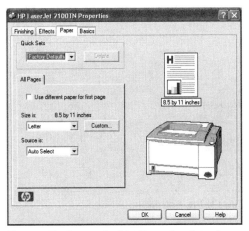

Figure 13 The Paper tab of the Properties dialog for a LaserJet 2100TN printer.

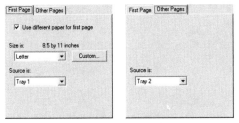

Figures 14 & 15 Turning on the check box labeled Use different paper for first page enables me to set different paper sources for the first page of a document (left) and its subsequent pages (right).

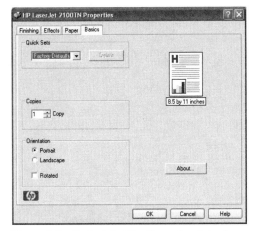

Figure 16 The Basics tab of the Properties dialog for a LaserJet 2100TN printer.

A look at a LaserJet 2100TN printer's Properties dialog

The LaserJet 2100TN network printer offers options in four tabs. Here's a quick discussion of each.

◆ **Finishing (Figure 11)** offers options for multi-sided printing, printing multiple pages on one sheet, and print quality.

◆ **Effects (Figure 12)** includes something called ZoomSmart for printing at different magnifications and watermarks, which is background text that can appear on every page.

◆ **Paper (Figure 13)** is probably the most useful tab. It enables me to take advantage of the multiple paper feed tray features of my printer to print the first page from one paper source (**Figure 14**)—perhaps one containing letterhead—and the remaining pages from another source (**Figure 15**). These options are also available in the Page Setup dialog, which is covered in **Chapter 5**.

◆ **Basics (Figure 16)** include the number of copies and orientation. This is better set in the Print and Page Setup dialogs respectively.

PRINTER PROPERTIES

Printing

You use the Print dialog (**Figure 17**) to set options for a print job and send it to the printer.

To set print options & print

1. Choose File > Print (**Figure 2**), press `Ctrl P`, or click the Print button in the Page Setup dialog to display the Print dialog (**Figure 17**).

2. If more than one printer is available to you, choose a printer from the Name drop-down list.

3. Select a Page range option:

    ▲ **All** prints all pages.

    ▲ **Current** page prints the currently selected page or the page in which the insertion point is blinking.

    ▲ **Selection** prints only selected document contents. This option is only available if something is selected in the document window when you open the Print dialog.

    ▲ **Pages** enables you to enter one or more page ranges. Separate first and last page numbers with a hyphen; separate multiple page ranges with a comma.

4. Choose an option from the Print what drop-down list (**Figure 18**):

    ▲ **Document** prints the Word document.

    ▲ **Document properties** prints information about the document.

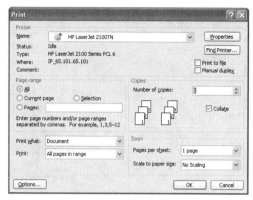

Figure 17 The Print dialog.

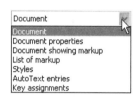

Figure 18
The Print what drop-down list enables you to specify what you want to print.

Figure 19 Use the Print drop-down list to specify which pages in the range to print.

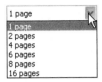

Figure 20
To print more than one page per sheet of paper, choose an option from the Pages per sheet drop-down list.

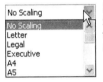

Figure 21
Set scaling options with the Scale to paper size drop-down list.

▲ **Document showing markup** prints the document with any revision marks.

▲ **List of markup** prints a list of document markups.

▲ **Styles** prints style information.

▲ **AutoText entries** prints a list of AutoText entries.

▲ **Key assignments** prints a list of shortcut keys available throughout Word.

5. If desired, choose an option from the Print drop-down list (**Figure 19**):

   ▲ **All pages in range** prints all pages in the range specified in step 3.

   ▲ **Odd pages** prints only the odd pages in the range specified in step 3.

   ▲ **Even pages** prints only the even pages in the range specified in step 3.

6. Enter the number of copies to print in the Copies box.

7. To print more than one page on each sheet of paper, choose an option from the Pages per sheet drop-down list (**Figure 20**).

8. To scale the printout so it fits on a specific paper size, choose an option from the Scale to paper size drop-down list (**Figure 21**).

9. Click OK to send the document to the printer.

USING THE PRINT DIALOG

Continued on next page...

Continued from previous page.

✔ Tips

- Clicking the Print button 🖨 on the Standard or Print Preview toolbar sends the document directly to the printer without displaying the Print dialog.

- The options on the Name menu in step 2 vary depending on the printers set up for your computer.

- Word's revision feature is covered in **Chapter 15**, styles are covered in **Chapter 4**, AutoText is covered in **Chapter 9**, and shortcut keys are covered in **Chapter 1**.

- If you enter a value greater than 1 in the Copies box in step 6, you can use the Collate check box to determine whether copies should be collated as they are printed.

- Clicking the Options button displays the Print tab of the Options dialog (**Figure 22**), which I discuss in **Chapter 19**.

- To print the document as a file on disk, turn on the Print to file check box in the Print dialog (**Figure 17**). When you click OK, you can use the Print to file dialog that appears (**Figure 23**) to save the document as a .PRN file.

Figure 22 The Print tab of the Options dialog.

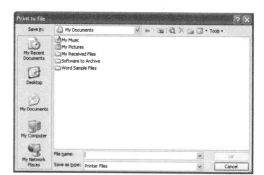

Figure 23 Use the Print to file dialog to name and save a document as a .PRN file.

Writing Tools

Word's Writing Tools

Microsoft Word includes a number of features that can help you be a better writer. Some of these features can help you find and fix errors in your documents, while other features can help you fine tune your documents for publication.

This chapter covers the following writing tools of interest to most Word users:

◆ The **spelling checker** compares words in your document to words in dictionary files to identify unknown words.

◆ The **grammar checker** checks sentences against a collection of grammar rules to identify questionable sentence construction.

◆ **AutoCorrect** automatically corrects common errors as you type.

◆ The **thesaurus** enables you to find synonyms or antonyms for words in your document.

◆ **Hyphenation** automatically hyphenates words based on hyphenation rules.

◆ **Word count** counts the words in a selection or the entire document.

◆ The **Change Case** command changes the capitalization of words you select.

This chapter also introduces a number of new writing tools, including AutoSummarize, research, and translation.

✔ Tip

■ No proofing tool is a complete substitute for carefully rereading a document to manually check it for errors. Use Word's writing tools to help you find and fix errors, but don't depend on them to find all errors in your documents.

The Spelling & Grammar Checkers

Word's spelling and grammar checkers help you to identify potential spelling and grammar problems in your documents. They can be set to check text automatically as you type or when you have finished typing.

The spelling checker compares the words in a document to the words in its main spelling dictionary, which includes many words and names. If it cannot find a match for a word, it then checks the active custom dictionaries—the dictionary files that you create. If Word still cannot find a match, it flags the word as unknown so you can act on it.

The grammar checker works in much the same way. It compares the structure of sentences in the document with predetermined rules for a specific writing style. When it finds a sentence or sentence fragment with a potential problem, it identifies it for you so you can act on it.

Both the spelling and grammar checkers are highly customizable so they work the way that you want them to.

✔ Tips

■ The spelling checker cannot identify a misspelled word if it correctly spells another word. For example, if you type *from* when you meant to type *form*, the spelling checker would not find the error. The grammar checker, on the other hand, might find this particular error, depending on its usage.

■ Do not add a word to a custom dictionary unless you *know* it is correctly spelled. Otherwise, the word will never be flagged as an error.

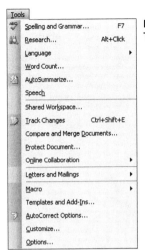

Figure 1
The Tools menu.

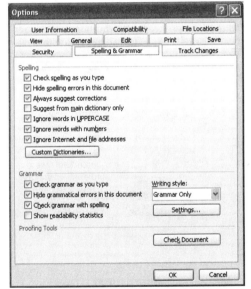

Figure 2 The default settings in the Spelling & Grammar tab of the Options dialog.

To enable or disable automatic spelling and/or grammar checking

1. Choose Tools > Options (**Figure 1**).

2. In the Options dialog that appears, click the Spelling & Grammar tab to display its options (**Figure 2**).

3. To enable automatic spelling checking, turn on the Check spelling as you type check box.

   or

   To disable automatic spelling checking, turn off the Check spelling as you type check box.

4. To enable automatic grammar checking, turn on the Check grammar as you type check box.

   or

   To disable automatic grammar checking, turn off the Check grammar as you type check box.

5. Click OK.

✔ Tips

- By default, Word is set up to automatically check spelling and grammar as you type.

- I explain how to set other spelling and grammar options in **Chapter 19**.

To check spelling as you type

1. Make sure that the automatic spelling checking feature has been enabled.
2. As you enter text into the document, a red wavy underline appears beneath each unknown word (**Figure 3**).
3. Right-click on a flagged word. The spelling shortcut menu appears (**Figure 4**).
4. Choose the appropriate option:
   - ▲ Suggested spellings appear at the top of the shortcut menu. Choosing one of these spellings changes the word and removes the wavy underline.
   - ▲ **Ignore All** tells Word to ignore the word throughout the document. Choosing this option removes the wavy underline from all occurrences of the word.
   - ▲ **Add to Dictionary** adds the word to the current custom dictionary. The wavy underline disappears and the word is never flagged again as unknown.
   - ▲ **AutoCorrect** enables you to create an AutoCorrect entry for the word using one of the suggested spellings (**Figure 5**). The word is replaced in the document and will be automatically replaced with the word you chose each time you type in the unknown word.
   - ▲ **Language** enables you to set language options for the word. Choose Set Language from the Language submenu (**Figure 6**), select a language in the Language dialog that appears (**Figure 7**), and click OK.

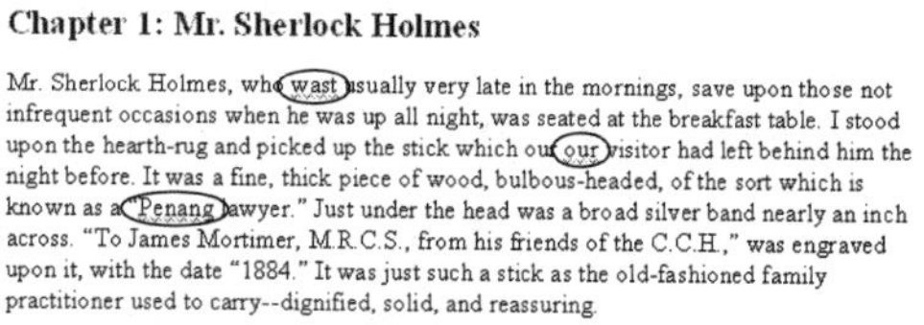

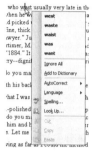

Chapter 1: Mr. Sherlock Holmes
Mr. Sherlock Holmes, who wast usually very late in the mornings, save upon those not infrequent occasions when he was up all night, was seated at the breakfast table. I stood upon the hearth-rug and picked up the stick which our our visitor had left behind him the night before. It was a fine, thick piece of wood, bulbous-headed, of the sort which is known as a Penang lawyer." Just under the head was a broad silver band nearly an inch across. "To James Mortimer, M.R.C.S., from his friends of the C.C.H.," was engraved upon it, with the date "1884." It was just such a stick as the old-fashioned family practitioner used to carry--dignified, solid, and reassuring.

Figure 3 Three possible errors identified by the spelling checker.

west
waste
waist
was
want
Ignore All
Add to Dictionary
AutoCorrect
Language
Spelling...
Look Up...
Cut
Copy
Paste

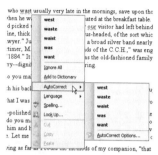

Figure 4 A shortcut menu displays options to fix a spelling problem.

AutoCorrect
west
waste
waist
was
want
AutoCorrect Options...

Figure 5 The AutoCorrect option displays a submenu with the suggested words. Choose one to create an AutoCorrect entry.

favor
favors
flavor
Ignore All
Add to Dictionary
AutoCorrect
Language
Spelling...
Look Up...
English (U.S.)
Set Language...

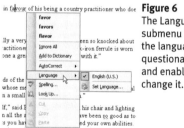

Figure 6 The Language submenu indicates the language of the questionable word and enables you to change it.

Language
Mark selected text as:
English (Trinidad and Tobago)
English (U.K.)
English (U.S.)
English (Zimbabwe)
Estonian
Faeroese
The speller and other proofing tools automatically use dictionaries of the selected language, if available.
Do not check spelling or grammar
Detect language automatically
Default...
OK
Cancel

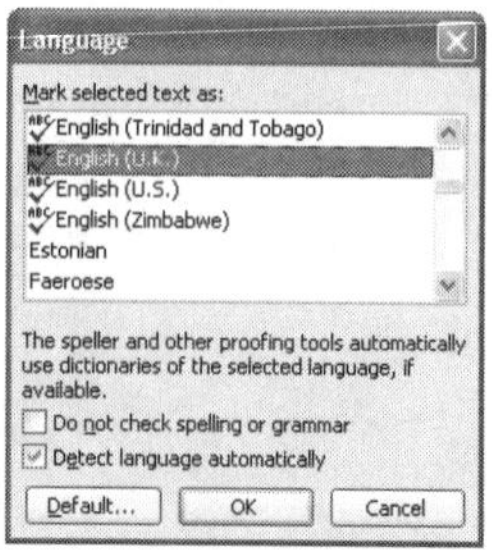

Figure 7 Use the Language dialog to select the language for a questionable word. Languages preceded by the ABC icon are those for which a dictionary is available for spelling check.

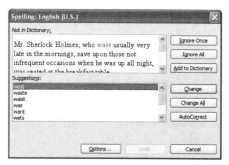

Figure 8 The Spelling dialog offers additional options for dealing with possible spelling errors. This dialog is very similar to the Spelling and Grammar dialog shown in **Figures 15** and **16**.

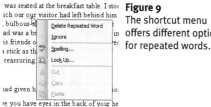

Figure 9
The shortcut menu offers different options for repeated words.

▲ **Spelling** opens the Spelling dialog (**Figure 8**) for the word.

▲ **Look Up** displays the Research task pane and, if you have a connection to the Internet, information about the word from a variety of online resources.

✔ Tips

■ As shown in **Figure 9**, Word's spelling checker also identifies repeated words and offers appropriate options.

■ Setting a different language for a word instructs Word to use that language's dictionary (if available) to check its spelling. This is an extremely useful feature for working with multilanguage documents. In fact, you can include language as part of a character or paragraph style to automatically use a correct dictionary for text formatted with that style. I tell you about styles in **Chapter 4**.

■ AutoCorrect, the Spelling dialog, and the Research task pane are discussed later in this chapter.

To check grammar as you type

1. Make sure that the automatic grammar checking feature has been enabled.

2. As you enter text into the document, a green wavy underline appears beneath each questionable word, phrase, or sentence (**Figure 10**).

3. Right-click on a flagged problem. The grammar shortcut menu appears (**Figures 11** and **12**).

4. Choose the appropriate option:

   ▲ Suggested corrections appear near the top of the shortcut menu (**Figures 11** and **12**). Choosing one of these corrections changes the text and removes the wavy underline.

   ▲ **Ignore Once** tells Word to ignore the problem. Choosing this option removes the wavy underline.

   ▲ **Grammar** opens the Grammar dialog (**Figure 13**).

   ▲ **About this Sentence** provides information about the grammar rule that caused the sentence to be flagged (**Figure 14**). (The Office Assistant must be displayed for this option to be accessible.)

   ▲ **Look Up** displays the Research task pane and, if you have a connection to the Internet, information about the word from a variety of online resources.

✔ Tips

■ I tell you more about the Grammar dialog later in this chapter.

■ Word's grammar checker doesn't always have a suggestion to fix a problem.

■ Don't choose a suggestion without examining it carefully. The suggestion Word offers may not be correct.

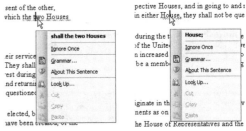

Figure 10 Three possible errors identified by the grammar checker.

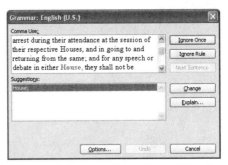

Figures 11 & 12 Using the grammar shortcut menu to correct possible grammar problems.

Figure 13 The Grammar dialog offers additional options for working with possible grammar problems. This dialog is very similar to the Spelling and Grammar dialog shown in **Figures 15** and **16**.

Figure 14 The Office Assistant can explain grammar rules.

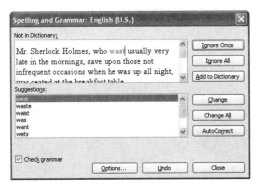

Figure 15 The Spelling and Grammar dialog displaying options for a spelling problem.

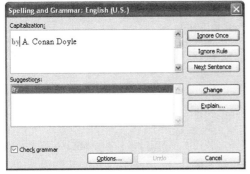

Figure 16 The Spelling and Grammar dialog displaying options for a grammar problem.

To check spelling and grammar all at once

1. Choose Tools > Spelling and Grammar (**Figure 1**) or press F7.

   or

   Click the Spelling and Grammar button 🔲 on the Standard toolbar.

   Word begins checking spelling and grammar. When it finds a possible error, it displays the Spelling and Grammar dialog (**Figures 15** and **16**).

2. For a spelling or grammar problem:

   ▲ To ignore the problem, click Ignore Once.

   ▲ To ignore all occurrences of the problem in the document, click Ignore All.

   ▲ To use one of Word's suggested corrections, click to select the suggestion and then click Change.

   ▲ To change the problem without using a suggestion, edit it in the top part of the Spelling and Grammar dialog. Then click Change.

   For a spelling problem only:

   ▲ To add the word to the current custom dictionary, click Add to Dictionary.

   ▲ To change the word throughout the document to one of the suggested corrections, click to select it and then click Change All.

   ▲ To create an AutoCorrect entry for the word, select one of the suggestions and click AutoCorrect.

Continued on next page...

CHECKING SPELLING & GRAMMAR AT ONCE

Continued from previous page.

For a grammar problem only:

▲ To skip the current sentence without ignoring it, click Next Sentence.

▲ To get an explanation of a grammar rule (**Figure 14**), click Explain.

3. Word continues checking. It displays the Spelling and Grammar dialog for each possible error. Repeat step 2 until the entire document has been checked.

✔ Tips

■ The Spelling and Grammar dialog contains elements found in both the Spelling dialog (**Figure 6**) and the Grammar dialog (**Figure 13**).

■ To disable grammar checking during a manual spelling check, turn off the Check grammar check box in the Spelling and Grammar dialog (**Figures 15** and **16**).

■ Clicking the Options button in the Spelling and Grammar dialog (**Figures 15** and **16**) displays Spelling & Grammar options (**Figure 2**). I explain how to use these options to customize a spelling and grammar check in **Chapter 19**.

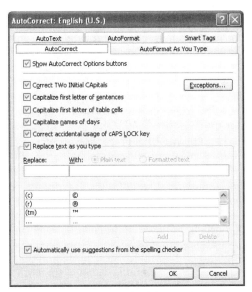

Figure 17 The AutoCorrect tab of the AutoCorrect dialog.

Figure 18 When Word makes an automatic correction, it displays a button you can click to display a menu of options.

AutoCorrect

Word's AutoCorrect feature can correct common typographical errors as you make them. You set up AutoCorrect entries by entering the incorrect and correct text in the AutoCorrect dialog (**Figure 17**). Then, each time you make an error for which an Auto-Correct entry exists, Word automatically corrects the error.

✔ Tips

- Word comes preconfigured with hundreds of AutoCorrect entries based on abbreviations, special symbols, and common errors.

- AutoCorrect is enabled by default.

To set AutoCorrect options

1. Choose Tools > AutoCorrect Options (**Figure 1**).

2. The AutoCorrect dialog appears. If necessary, click the AutoCorrect tab to display its options (**Figure 17**).

3. Set options as desired:

   ▲ **Show AutoCorrect Options buttons** displays a tiny blue button beneath text that was automatically corrected when you point to the text. Clicking this button displays a menu that you can use to reverse the correction or set AutoCorrect options (**Figure 18**).

   ▲ **Correct TWo INitial CApitals** changes the second letter in a pair of capital letters to lowercase.

   ▲ **Capitalize first letter of sentences** capitalizes the first letter following the end of a sentence.

Continued on next page...

SETTING UP AUTOCORRECT

Continued from previous page.

▲ **Capitalize first letter of table cells** capitalizes the first letter of a word in a table cell.

▲ **Capitalize names of days** capitalizes the names of the days of the week.

▲ **Correct accidental usage of cAPS LOCK key** corrects capitalization errors that occur when you type with Caps Lock down. (It also turns off Caps Lock.)

▲ **Replace text as you type** enables the AutoCorrect feature for the Auto-Correct entries in the bottom of the dialog.

▲ **Automatically use suggestions from the spelling checker** tells Word to replace spelling errors with words from the dictionary as you type.

4. Click OK to save your settings.

✔ Tip

■ To disable AutoCorrect, turn off all check boxes in the AutoCorrect tab of the AutoCorrect dialog.

To add an AutoCorrect entry

1. Choose Tools > AutoCorrect Options (**Figure 1**).

2. The AutoCorrect dialog appears. If necessary, click the AutoCorrect tab to display its options (**Figure 17**).

3. Type the text that you want to automatically replace in the Replace box.

4. Type the text that you want to replace it with in the With box (**Figure 19**).

5. Click the Add button.

6. Click OK.

Figure 19 Each AutoCorrect entry has two parts.

✔ Tips

■ To add a formatted text entry, enter and format the replacement text in your document. Then select that text and follow the steps above. Make sure the Formatted text option button is selected before clicking the Add button in step 5.

■ As the example in **Figures 19** through **21** illustrates, you can use AutoCorrect to do more than just correct typos and frequent spelling errors. You can also use it to enter lengthy bits of text when you type abbreviations.

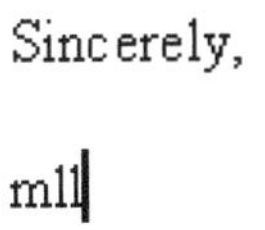

Sincerely,

mll

Figure 20
To use an AutoCorrect entry, type the text from the Replace part of the entry...

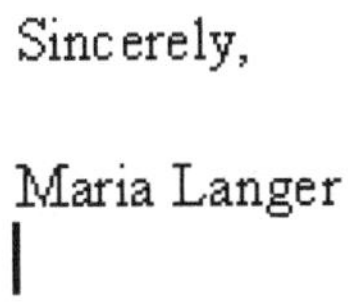

Sincerely,

Maria Langer

Figure 21
...and the With part of the entry appears automatically as you continue typing.

To use AutoCorrect

In a document, type the text that appears on the Replace side of the AutoCorrect entries list (**Figure 20**). When you press (Spacebar), (Enter), (Shift)(Enter), or some punctuation, the text you typed changes to the corresponding text on the With side of the AutoCorrect entries list (**Figure 21**).

To delete an AutoCorrect entry

1. Choose Tools > AutoCorrect Options (**Figure 1**).

2. The AutoCorrect dialog appears. If necessary, click the AutoCorrect tab to display its options (**Figure 17**).

3. Scroll through the list of AutoCorrect entries in the bottom half of the dialog to find the entry that you want to delete and click it once to select it.

4. Click the Delete button.

5. Click OK.

USING AUTOCORRECT

The Thesaurus

Word's thesaurus enables you to find synonyms or antonyms for words in your document—without leaving Word. This feature makes it easy to find just the right word to get your message across.

To find a synonym quickly

1. Right-click on the word for which you want to find a synonym.

2. A shortcut menu appears. If the Synonyms option is available, select it to display a submenu of synonyms for the word (**Figure 22**).

3. To replace the word with one of the synonyms, choose it from the submenu.

To find synonyms or antonyms with the Research task pane

1. Select the word for which you want to find a synonym or antonym.

2. Choose Tools > Language > Thesaurus (**Figure 23**) or press ⬚Shift⬚⬚F7⬚ to display the Research task pane. As shown in **Figure 24**, it indicates Thesaurus as the reference source and displays a list of meanings with synonyms and antonyms.

3. To replace the selected word, point to the word you want to replace it with and click the button that appears to display a menu (**Figure 25**). Choose Insert.

   or

   To look up a synonym or antonym, double-click it. It appears in the box near the top of the Research task pane and the meanings, synonyms, and antonyms change accordingly.

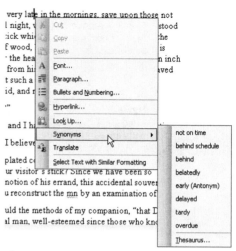

Figure 22 The shortcut menu for a word may include synonyms.

Figure 23 The Language submenu under the Tools menu.

Word being looked up   Reference source

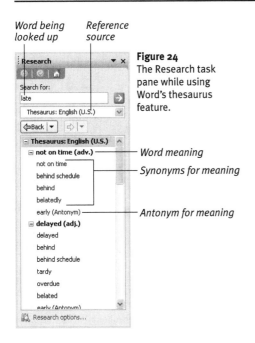

Figure 24
The Research task pane while using Word's thesaurus feature.

Word meaning

Synonyms for meaning

Antonym for meaning

Figure 25
Use a word's menu to insert it in place of a selected word, copy it for use elsewhere, or look it up.

✔ Tips

- You can click the button beside a word meaning in the Research task pane (**Figure 24**) to expand or collapse the list of synonyms and antonyms.

- Word keeps track of all the words you looked up while using the Research task pane. Click the Back button near the top of the task pane (**Figure 24**) to go back to previously looked-up words.

- To close the Research task pane when you are finished with it, click its close button (**Figure 24**).

- I tell you more about Word's Research feature and the Research task pane later in this chapter.

Hyphenation

Word's hyphenation feature can hyphenate words so they fit better on a line. Word can hyphenate the words in your documents automatically as you type or manually when you have finished typing.

✔ Tips

- Hyphenation helps prevent ragged right margins in left aligned text and large gaps between words in full justified text. I tell you about alignment in **Chapter 3**.

- To prevent text from being hyphenated, select it and then turn on the Don't hyphenate option in the Line and Page Breaks tab of the Paragraph dialog (**Figure 26**). I explain options in the Paragraph dialog in **Chapter 3**.

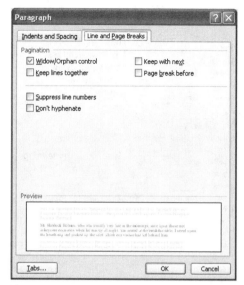

Figure 26 Use the Line and Page Breaks tab of the Paragraph dialog to prevent hyphenation in selected paragraphs.

To set hyphenation options

1. Choose Tools > Language > Hyphenation (**Figure 23**) to display the Hyphenation dialog (**Figure 27**).

2. Set options as desired:

   ▲ **Automatically hyphenate document** enables automatic hyphenation as you type. (By default, this option is turned off.)

   ▲ **Hyphenate words in CAPS** hyphenates words entered in all uppercase letters, such as acronyms.

   ▲ **Hyphenation zone** is the distance from the right indent within which you want to hyphenate the document. The lower the value you enter, the more words are hyphenated.

   ▲ **Limit consecutive hyphens to** is the maximum number of hyphens that can appear in a row.

3. Click OK.

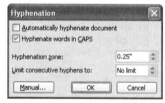

Figure 27 The default settings in the Hyphenation dialog.

✔ Tip

- To remove hyphenation inserted with the automatic hyphenation feature, turn off the Automatically hyphenate document check box in the Hyphenation dialog (**Figure 27**).

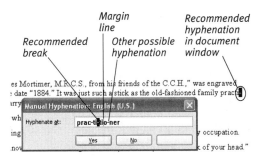

Recommended break *Margin line* *Other possible hyphenation* *Recommended hyphenation in document window*

Figure 28 The Manual Hyphenation dialog.

To manually hyphenate text

1. Follow steps 1 and 2 on the previous page to open the Hyphenation dialog (**Figure 27**) and set options. Be sure to leave the Automatically hyphenate document check box turned off.

2. Click the Manual button. Word begins searching for hyphenation candidates. When it finds one, it displays the Manual Hyphenation dialog (**Figure 28**).

3. Do one of the following:

   ▲ To hyphenate the word at the recommended break, click Yes.

   ▲ To hyphenate the word at a different break, click the hyphen at the desired break and then click Yes. (The hyphen that you click must be to the left of the margin line.)

   ▲ To continue without hyphenating the word, click No.

4. Word continues looking for hyphenation candidates. It displays the Manual Hyphenation dialog for each one. Repeat step 3 until the entire document has been hyphenated.

✔ Tips

■ To hyphenate only part of a document, select the part that you want to hyphenate before following the above steps.

■ You can also manually insert two types of special hyphens within words:

   ▲ Press Ctrl - to insert an optional hyphen, which only breaks the word when necessary. Use this to manually hyphenate a word without using the Manual Hyphenation dialog.

   ▲ Press Shift Ctrl - to insert a non-breaking hyphen, which displays a hyphen but never breaks the word.

Word Count

The word count feature counts the pages, words, characters, paragraphs, and lines in a selection or the entire document.

✔ Tip

- The word count feature is especially useful for writers who often have word count limitations or get paid by the word.

To count pages, words, characters, paragraphs, & lines

1. If necessary, select the text that you want to count.

2. Choose Tools > Word Count (**Figure 1**) to display the Word Count dialog (**Figure 29**).

   After a moment, complete count figures appear.

3. To include footnotes and endnotes in the count, turn on the Include footnotes and endnotes check box.

4. When you are finished working with the count figures, click Close to dismiss the dialog.

✔ Tip

- To display word count on screen as you work, click the Show Toolbar button in the Word Count dialog. This displays the Word Count toolbar (**Figure 30**), which offers quick and easy access to count figures. Use the drop-down list on the toolbar to display counts (**Figure 31**). When you're finished using the Word Count toolbar, you can click its close button to dismiss it.

Figure 29 The Word Count dialog.

Figure 30 The Word Count toolbar.

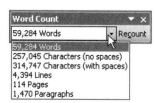

Figure 31 The Word Count toolbar puts count figures on screen where you can reference them as you work.

COUNTING WORDS & MORE

Figure 32 The Change Case dialog.

You can use the Change Case dialog box to change the case of typed characters.
You can use the Change Case dialog box to change the case of typed characters.
you can use the change case dialog box to change the case of typed characters.
YOU CAN USE THE CHANGE CASE DIALOG BOX TO CHANGE THE CASE OF TYPED CHARACTERS.
You Can Use The Change Case Dialog Box To Change The Case Of Typed Characters.
yOU CAN USE THE cHANGE cASE DIALOG BOX TO CHANGE THE CASE OF TYPED CHARACTERS.

Figure 33 Change Case in action—from top to bottom: original text, Sentence case, lowercase, UPPERCASE, Title Case, and tOGGLE cASE.

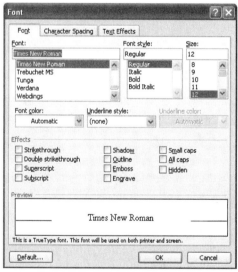

Figure 34 The Font tab of the Font dialog.

Change Case

You can use the Change Case dialog (**Figure 32**) to change the case of selected characters. There are five options (**Figure 33**):

◆ **Sentence case** capitalizes the first letter of a sentence.

◆ **lowercase** changes all characters to lowercase.

◆ **UPPERCASE** changes all characters to uppercase.

◆ **Title Case** capitalizes the first letter of every word.

◆ **tOGGLE cASE** changes uppercase characters to lowercase and lowercase characters to uppercase.

✔ Tips

■ You might be wondering: if the Change Case command is under the Format menu, why is it being discussed with features under the Tools menu? Technically speaking, changing the case of characters with the Change Case dialog (**Figure 32**) does *not* format the characters. Instead, it changes the actual characters that were originally entered into the document. To emphasize this point, I decided to discuss it in this chapter, as a writing tool.

■ To change the case of characters without changing the characters themselves, use the All caps or Small caps option in the Font tab of the Font dialog (**Figure 34**). I tell you how in **Chapter 3**.

CHANGING CHARACTER CASE

To change the case of characters

1. Select the characters whose case you want to change.

2. Choose Format > Change Case (**Figure 35**).

3. In the Change Case dialog that appears (**Figure 32**), select the option you want.

4. Click OK.

✔ Tip

■ If you use the Change Case dialog to change the case of characters and get unexpected results, use the Undo command to reverse the action, then try the Change Case dialog again. I cover the Undo command in **Chapter 2**.

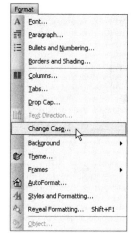

Figure 35
Choosing Change Case from the Format menu.

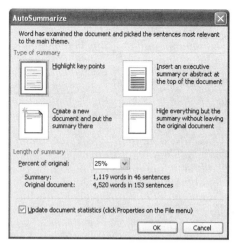

Figure 36 The AutoSummarize dialog.

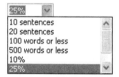

Figure 37 Use this drop-down list to specify how long you want the summary to be.

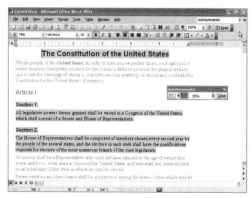

Figure 38 Here's what the U.S. Constitution might look like after Word has highlighted its key points. Note the AutoSummarize toolbar that appears when you automatically summarize with the Highlight key points option in the AutoSummarize dialog.

AutoSummarize

Word's AutoSummarize feature can automatically summarize a document to identify its key points. It does this by analyzing words and sentences and assigning them a score. More frequently used words get a higher score, identifying them as key points.

✔ Tips

- AutoSummarize works best with documents that are highly structured, such as reports and articles.

- Review a summary before relying on it. It may not be as complete as it needs to be.

To automatically summarize a document

1. Open the document you want to summarize.

2. Choose Tools > AutoSummarize (**Figure 1**) to display the AutoSummarize dialog (**Figure 36**).

3. Select the icon for the type of summary you want. The description beside each icon clearly explains what it does.

4. If desired, use the Percent of original drop-down list (**Figure 37**) to tell Word how long (or short!) the summary should be.

5. To include the summary in the Summary tab of the Properties dialog, make sure the Update document statistics check box is turned on.

6. Click OK. Word prepares the summary to your specifications. **Figure 38** shows an example.

✔ Tip

- I tell you about the Properties dialog in **Chapter 15**.

Research

Word's new research feature enables you to get more information about words or phrases in a document right from within Word. This feature works with reference material that is installed with Word 2003 (or Office 2003) as well as with online resources, if you have an Internet connection.

✔ Tip

■ Word's thesaurus feature, which is discussed earlier in this chapter, uses Word's new Research task pane.

To research a topic

1. If the text you want to research is in the document, select it.

2. Choose Tools > Research (**Figure 1**) or hold down Alt while clicking the selected text. The Research task pane appears.

3. If necessary, enter the text you want to research in the Search for box.

4. Choose a reference source from the drop-down list beneath the Search for box (**Figure 39**).

5. Click the Green arrow button.

6. Word searches the source(s) you specified in step 4 and displays a list of results in the Research task pane's scrolling list (**Figure 40**).

7. Click links in the list of results to explore them further.

✔ Tip

■ In step 7, it may be necessary to click the tiny plus sign icon beside an item (**Figure 40**) to view its contents (**Figure 41**) and click related links.

Figure 39
Choose the reference source you want to search.

Figure 40
The Research task pane at the conclusion of a successful search of research sites.

Figure 41
Clicking the tiny plus sign icon beside an item expands the item to show its details. This example includes a link to an article preview. The dollar sign beside the link indicates that there's a fee to obtain the entire article (not just the preview).

RESEARCHING TOPICS

Figure 42
The Research task pane at the start of a translation.

Figure 43 The From and To drop-down lists include all supported languages.

Translation

Word's translation feature, which requires an Internet connection, makes it possible to create rough translations of documents. For example, suppose you've written a report in English and need to send it to someone in your company's Mexico City office who might not speak English fluently. You can use the translation feature to translate the document and send the translation to him.

✔ Tip

- Keep in mind that the translation feature makes a *rough* translation. It may not be accurate or grammatically correct, so don't rely on it if you need to share vital information or want to make an impression on someone.

To translate a document

1. Open the document you want to translate.

2. Choose Tools > Language > Translate (**Figure 23**). The Research task pane appears with Translation chosen from its research source drop-down list (**Figure 42**).

3. Select the languages you want to translate between from the From and To (**Figure 43**) drop-down lists.

4. Click the Green arrow button beneath Translate whole document.

5. Word launches your Web browser, connects to the Internet, and displays a page containing the translation on the World Lingo Web site (**Figure 44**).

6. If desired, use the Copy and Paste techniques discussed in **Chapter 2** to copy the translation and paste it into a new Word document.

Figure 44 The translated document appears in a Web browser window.

✔ Tips

- To translate just a word, select the word or sentence after step 1. The translation appears in the Research pane after step 3.

- The first time you use the translation feature, a dialog telling you that the feature is not installed may appear. Click Yes to install it.

TRANSLATING DOCUMENTS

Tables

Item Name	Description	Item Number	Price
Envelopes, #10	#10 envelopes, 20 lb. white, all-purpose. 500 per box.	ENV10	$15.99/box
Envelopes, #9	#9 envelopes, 20 lb. white, all-purpose. 500 per box.	ENV09	$12.99/box
Permanent Marker, Blue	Mark of Zorro brand permanent marker. 0.5 mm felt tip. Airtight cap. Blue.	MRK01	$2.99 each
Permanent Marker, Red	Mark of Zorro brand permanent marker. 0.5 mm felt tip. Airtight cap. Red.	MRK03	$2.99 each
Laser Paper, White	White, 20 lb. paper, designed for use in laser printers. 8-1/2 x 11 inches. 500 sheets per ream.	PAP05	$5.99/ream
InkJet Paper, White	White, 20 lb. paper, designed for use in inkjet printers. 8-1/2 x 11 inches. 500 sheets per ream.	PAP11	$7.99/ream
Copier Paper, White	White, 20 lb. paper, designed for use in copy machines. 8-1/2 x 11 inches. 500 sheets per ream.	PAP01	$4.99/ream
Shipping Boxes, 9 x 12	9 x 12 inches, corrugated cardboard shipping boxes. White.	BOX05	$10.99/pkg

Figure 1 A four-column, nine-row table with borders. Each box is an individual cell.

Tables

Microsoft Word's table feature enables you to create tables of information.

A table consists of table cells arranged in columns and rows (**Figure 1**). You enter information into each cell, which is like a tiny document of its own. You can put multiple paragraphs of text into a cell and format characters or paragraphs as discussed in **Chapters 3** and **4**.

Table structure and format are extremely flexible and can be modified to meet your needs. A cell can expand vertically to accommodate long blocks of text or graphics; you can also resize it manually as desired. You can format cells, merge cells, and split cells. You can even put a table within a table cell. These capabilities make the table feature a good choice for organizing a wide variety of data.

✔ Tip

- You can also use tab stops and tab characters to create simple tables without cells. **Chapter 3** explains how to do this. This method, however, is not nearly as flexible as using cell tables.

Creating a Table

Word offers four ways to create a table:

◆ Use the **Insert Table** command and dialog to create a table at the insertion point.

◆ Use the **Insert Table** toolbar button to create a table at the insertion point.

◆ Use the **Draw Table** command and toolbar button to draw a table anywhere on a page.

◆ Use the **Convert Text to Table** command to convert existing text to a table.

To insert a table with the Insert Table dialog

1. Position the insertion point where you want the table to appear.

2. Choose Table > Insert > Table (**Figure 2**) to display the Insert Table dialog (**Figure 3**).

3. Enter the number of columns and rows for the table in the Number of columns and Number of rows boxes.

4. Choose an AutoFit behavior option:

▲ **Fixed column width** sets the width of each column regardless of its contents or the window width. If you select this option, enter Auto in the text box to set the table as wide as the print area and divide the table into columns of equal width or enter a value in the text box to specify the width of each column.

▲ **AutoFit to contents** sets each column to fit the contents of the widest cell in the column and makes the table as wide as all of the columns combined.

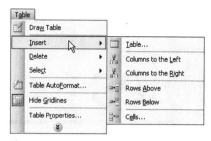

Figure 2 Use commands at the top of the Table menu to create a table.

Figure 3 The Insert Table dialog.

INSERTING TABLES

Figure 4 An empty three-column, four-row table inserted after some text.

▲ **AutoFit to window** sets the table's width based on the width of the window and divides the table into columns of equal width.

5. Click OK. The table appears, with the insertion point in the top left cell (**Figure 4**).

✔ Tips

- You can click the AutoFormat button in the Insert Table dialog (**Figure 3**) to format the table as you create it. Automatically formatting tables is covered later in this chapter.

- To set the options in the Insert Table dialog (**Figure 3**) as the default options for all new tables you create, turn on the Remember dimensions for new tables check box.

- You can use this technique to insert a table into a table cell. Just make sure the insertion point is within a table cell before you choose Table > Insert > Table (**Figure 2**).

To insert a table with the Insert Table button

1. Position the insertion point where you want the table to appear.

2. Click the Insert Table button on the Standard toolbar to display a menu of columns and rows.

3. Select the number of columns and rows you want in the table (**Figure 5**).

   The table appears, with the insertion point in the top left cell (**Figure 4**).

✔ Tips

■ This is probably the fastest way to insert an empty table into a document.

■ You can use this technique to insert a table into a table cell. Just make sure the insertion point is within a table cell before you use the Insert Table button's menu.

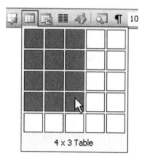

Figure 5
The Insert Table button's menu of columns and rows.

4 x 3 Table

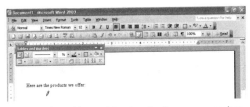

Figure 6 The Tables and Borders toolbar appears when you draw a table.

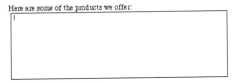

Figure 7 Drag diagonally to draw a box the size and shape of the table you want.

Figure 8 The outside border for a single-cell table appears.

Figure 9 Draw vertical lines for column boundaries...

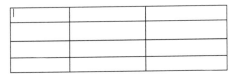

Figure 10 ...and horizontal lines for row boundaries.

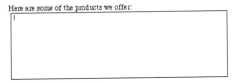

Figure 11 A drawn table.

To draw a table

1. Choose Table > Draw Table (**Figure 2**) or click the Tables and Borders button 🔲 on the Standard toolbar.

2. If you are not in Print Layout view, Word switches to that view. The Tables and Borders toolbar appears (**Figure 6**). If necessary, click the Draw Table button 🔲 to select it.

3. Position the Draw Table tool, which looks like a pencil (**Figure 6**) where you want the upper-left corner of the table.

4. Press the mouse button down and drag diagonally to draw a box the size and shape of the table you want (**Figure 7**). When you release the mouse button, the outside border of the table appears (**Figure 8**).

5. Drag the Draw Table tool from the top border of the table to the bottom to draw each column boundary (**Figure 9**).

6. Drag the Draw Table tool from the left border of the table to the right to draw each row boundary (**Figure 10**).

   When you're finished, the table might look something like the one in **Figure 11**.

✔ Tip

■ Don't worry if you can't draw column and row boundaries exactly where you want them. Changing column widths and row heights is discussed later in this chapter.

DRAWING TABLES

To convert text to a table

1. Select the text that you want to convert to a table (**Figure 12**).

2. Choose Table > Convert > Text to Table (**Figure 13**).

3. In the Convert Text to Table dialog that appears (**Figure 14**), confirm that the correct separator has been selected and the correct values appear in the text boxes. Make any required changes.

4. Click OK.

The text turns into a table (**Figure 15**).

✔ Tips

■ This method works best with tab- or comma-separated text.

■ The AutoFit behavior options in the Convert Text to Table dialog (**Figure 14**) are the same as in the Insert Table dialog. I explain them earlier in this chapter.

■ In most instances, Word will correctly "guess" the settings for the Convert Text to Table dialog (**Figure 14**) and no changes will be required in step 3 above.

Figure 12 Tab-separated text selected for conversion.

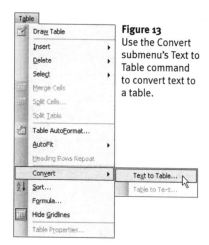

Figure 13 Use the Convert submenu's Text to Table command to convert text to a table.

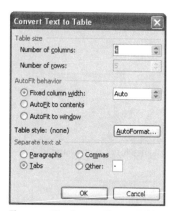

Figure 14 The Convert Text to Table dialog.

Substance	Date Tested	Tested By	Results
MSG	5/18/02	Maria Langer	452.3516
Magnesium	6/4/02	John Aabbott	51.84
Sulfur	6/15/02	Mary Johannesburg	145236.145872
Aspirin	10/17/02	Tim Jones	1.1

Figure 15 The text in **Figure 12** converted to a table.

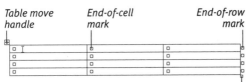

Table move handle   End-of-cell mark   End-of-row mark

Table resize handle

Figure 16 Table elements include column, row, and cell boundaries, end-of-cell and end-of-row marks, and, in this example borders.

Figure 17 When a table has no borders, gridlines can identify the boundaries.

Anatomy of a Table

A table includes a variety of elements (**Figure 16**):

◆ **Column boundaries** appear on either side of a column.

◆ **Row boundaries** appear on the top and bottom of a row.

◆ **Cell boundaries** are the portions of column and row boundaries that appear around an individual cell.

◆ **End-of-cell marks** appear within each table cell. They indicate the end of the cell's contents—just like the end-of-document marker marks the end of a Word document.

◆ **End-of-row marks** appear to the right of the last cell in a row. They indicate the end of the row.

◆ **Table move handle** enables you to select the entire table and drag it to a new position in the document.

◆ **Table resize handle** enables you to resize the table by dragging.

◆ **Borders** are lines that can appear on any column, row, or cell boundary. These lines print when the table is printed.

◆ **Gridlines** (**Figure 17**) are lines that appear on any column, row, or cell boundary. Unlike borders, however, gridlines don't print.

Continued on next page...

ANATOMY OF A TABLE

Continued from previous page.

✔ Tips

■ To see end-of-cell and end-of-row marks, display nonprinting characters by enabling the Show/Hide ¶ button ¶ on the Standard toolbar. I tell you more about formatting marks and the Show/Hide ¶ button in **Chapter 1**.

■ The table move handle and table resize handle only appear in Page Layout view when the mouse pointer is on the table (**Figure 16**).

■ By default, Word creates tables with borders on all column and row boundaries. You can change or remove them using techniques discussed in **Chapter 4**.

■ You can only see gridlines on boundaries that do not have borders (**Figure 17**). In addition, the Gridlines option on the Table menu (**Figure 18**) must be enabled for gridlines to appear.

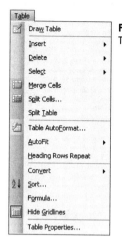

Figure 18
The Table menu.

Figure 19 Position the mouse pointer in the cell's selection bar.

Figure 20 Click to select the cell.

Permanent Marker, Red	Mark of Zorro brand permanent marker. 0.5 mm felt tip. Airtight cap. Red.	MRK03
Laser Paper, White	White, 20 lb. paper, designed for use in laser printers. 8-1/2 x 11 inches. 500 sheets per ream.	PAP05
Inkjet Paper, White	White, 20 lb. paper, designed for use in inkjet printers. 8-1/2 x 11 inches. 500 sheets per ream.	PAP11

Figure 21 Position the I-beam pointer at the beginning of the cell's contents.

Permanent Marker, Red	Mark of Zorro brand permanent marker. 0.5 mm felt tip. Airtight cap. Red.	MRK03
Laser Paper, White	White, 20 lb. paper, designed for use in laser printers. 8-1/2 x 11 inches. 500 sheets per ream.	PAP05
Inkjet Paper, White	White, 20 lb. paper, designed for use in inkjet printers. 8-1/2 x 11 inches. 500 sheets per ream.	PAP11

Figure 22 Drag through the cell's contents to select it.

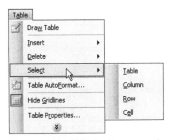

Figure 23 The Select submenu under the Table menu offers commands for selecting all or part of a table.

Selecting Table Cells

In many cases, to format the contents of table cells or restructure a table, you must begin by selecting the cells you want to change. Selecting table cells is very similar to selecting other document text, but Word offers some tricks to make it easier.

To select a cell

1. Position the mouse pointer in the far left side of the cell so it points to the right (**Figure 19**). This is the cell's selection bar.

2. Click once. The cell becomes selected (**Figure 20**).

or

1. Position the mouse pointer at the beginning of a cell's contents. The mouse pointer must look like an I-beam pointer (**Figure 21**).

2. Press the mouse button down and drag through the contents of the cell. When you release the mouse button, the cell is selected (**Figure 22**).

or

1. Position the insertion point anywhere within the cell you want to select.

2. Choose Table > Select > Cell (**Figure 23**).

SELECTING CELLS

169

To select a row

1. Position the mouse pointer in the selection bar of any cell in the row (**Figure 19**) in the selection bar at the far left side of the window.

2. Double-click. The entire row becomes selected (**Figure 24**).

or

1. Click to position the blinking insertion point in any cell in the row (**Figure 25**) or select any cell in the row (**Figure 22**).

2. Choose Table > Select > Row (**Figure 23**). The entire row is selected (**Figure 26**).

To select a column

1. Position the mouse pointer over the top boundary of the column that you want to select. It turns into an arrow pointing down (**Figure 27**).

2. Click once. The column is selected (**Figure 28**).

or

Hold down Alt while clicking anywhere in the column that you want to select.

or

1. Click to position the blinking insertion point in any cell in the column (**Figure 25**) or select any cell in the column (**Figure 22**).

2. Choose Table > Select > Column (**Figure 23**). The entire column is selected (**Figure 29**).

Figure 24 Double-click in a cell's selection bar to select the entire row.

Permanent Marker, Red	Mark of Zorro brand permanent marker. 0.5 mm felt tip. Airtight cap. Red.	MRK03
Laser Paper, White	White, 20 lb. paper, designed for use in laser printers. 8-1/2 x 11 inches. 500 sheets per ream.	PAP05
Inkjet Paper, White	White, 20 lb. paper, designed for use in inkjet printers. 8-1/2 x 11 inches. 500 sheets per ream.	PAP11

Figure 25 Position the insertion point in any cell in the row.

Permanent Marker, Red	Mark of Zorro brand permanent marker. 0.5 mm felt tip. Airtight cap. Red.	MRK03
Laser Paper, White	White, 20 lb. paper, designed for use in laser printers. 8-1/2 x 11 inches. 500 sheets per ream.	PAP05
Inkjet Paper, White	White, 20 lb. paper, designed for use in inkjet printers. 8-1/2 x 11 inches. 500 sheets per ream.	PAP11

Figure 26 When you choose Table > Select > Row, the entire row is selected.

Figure 27 Position the mouse pointer over the top boundary of the column.

Figure 28 Click once to select the column.

Permanent Marker, Red	Mark of Zorro brand permanent marker. 0.5 mm felt tip. Airtight cap. Red.	MRK03
Laser Paper, White	White, 20 lb. paper, designed for use in laser printers. 8-1/2 x 11 inches. 500 sheets per ream.	PAP05
Inkjet Paper, White	White, 20 lb. paper, designed for use in inkjet printers. 8-1/2 x 11 inches. 500 sheets per ream.	PAP11

Figure 29 When you choose Table > Select > Column, the entire column is selected.

Figure 30 A selected table.

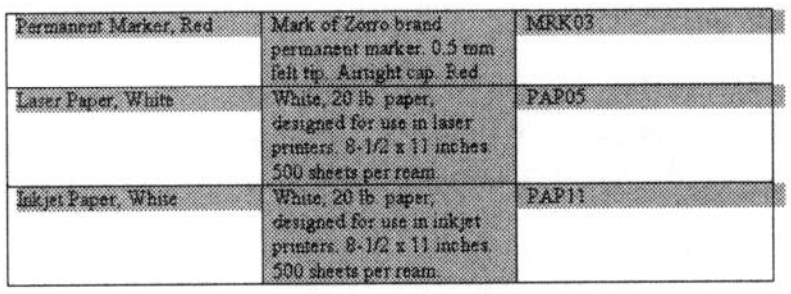

Permanent Marker, Red	Mark of Zorro brand permanent marker. 0.5 mm felt tip. Airtight cap. Red	MRK03
Laser Paper, White	White, 20 lb. paper, designed for use in laser printers. 8-1/2 x 11 inches. 500 sheets per ream.	PAP05
Inkjet Paper, White	White, 20 lb. paper, designed for use in inkjet printers. 8-1/2 x 11 inches. 500 sheets per ream.	PAP11

Figure 31 Another selected table.

To select an entire table

Hold down Alt while double-clicking anywhere in the table. The table is selected (**Figure 30**).

or

In Page Layout view, click the table move handle (**Figure 16**). The entire table is selected (**Figure 30**).

or

1. Click to position the blinking insertion point in any cell in the table (**Figure 25**) or select any cell in the table (**Figure 22**).

2. Choose Table > Select > Table (**Figure 23**). The entire table is selected (**Figure 31**).

✔ Tip

■ Although the table move handle's true purpose is to enable you to move a table by dragging it, clicking the move handle automatically selects the entire table.

Entering & Formatting Table Information

You enter text and other information into a table the same way you enter it into any document: type, paste, or drag it in. Then format it as desired using techniques in **Chapters** 3 and 4.

✔ Tips

- Think of each cell as a tiny document window. The cell boundaries are like document margins. You can enter as much information as you like and apply any kind of formatting.

- As you enter information into a cell, the cell expands vertically as necessary to accommodate the text.

- I tell you about copying and moving text with the Cut, Copy, and Paste commands and drag-and-drop text editing in **Chapter 2**.

To enter text into a cell

1. Position the insertion point in the cell (**Figure 32**).

2. Type the text that you want to appear in the cell (**Figure 33**).

   or

   Use the Edit menu's Paste command to paste the Clipboard contents (a previously copied or cut selection) into the cell.

or

1. Select text in another part of the document (**Figure 34**) or another document.

2. Drag the selected text into the cell in which you want it to appear (**Figure 35**). When you release the mouse button, the text appears in the cell (**Figure 36**).

Figure 32 Position the insertion point in the cell in which you want to enter text.

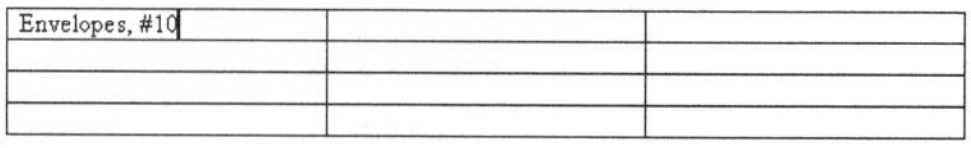

Figure 33 Type to enter the text.

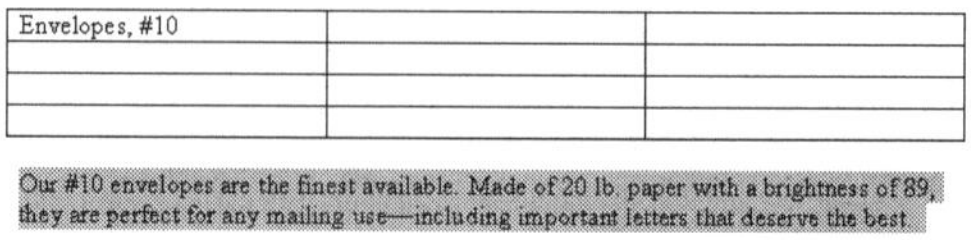

Figure 34 Select the text that you want to move into a cell.

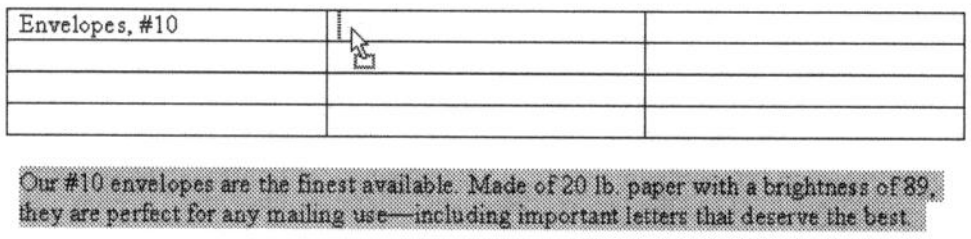

Figure 35 Drag the selection into the cell.

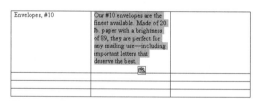

Figure 36 When you release the mouse button, the selection moves into the cell.

✔ Tip

- To enter a tab character in a cell, press Control Tab.

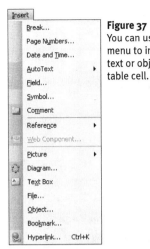

Figure 37
You can use the Insert menu to insert special text or objects into a table cell.

Envelopes, #10 | Our #10 envelopes are the finest available. Made of 20 lb. paper with a brightness of 89, they are perfect for any mailing use—including important letters that deserve the best.

Figure 38 Select the object that you want to move into a cell.

Envelopes, #10 | Our #10 envelopes are the finest available. Made of 20 lb. paper with a brightness of 89, they are perfect for any mailing use—including important letters that deserve the best.

Figure 39 Drag the object into the cell.

Envelopes, #10 | Our #10 envelopes are the finest available. Made of 20 lb. paper with a brightness of 89, they are perfect for any mailing use—including important letters that deserve the best.

Figure 40 When you release the mouse button, the object moves.

To enter special text or objects into a cell

1. Position the insertion point in the cell.

2. Choose the appropriate command from the Insert menu (**Figure 37**) to insert special text or objects.

   or

   Use the Edit menu's Paste command to paste the Clipboard contents (a previously copied or cut selection) into the cell.

or

1. Select special text or objects in another part of the document (**Figure 38**) or another document.

2. Drag the selection into the cell in which you want it to appear. When you release the mouse button (**Figure 39**), it appears in the cell (**Figure 40**).

✔ Tip

■ I tell you about options under the Insert menu in **Chapter 9**.

To move the insertion point from one cell to another

To advance to the next cell in the table, press Tab.

or

To advance to the previous cell in the table, press Shift Tab.

✔ Tip

■ If you use either of these techniques to advance to a cell that is not empty, the cell's contents become selected. Otherwise, the insertion point appears in the cell.

ENTERING OTHER INFO INTO TABLE CELLS

173

To format characters or paragraphs in a cell

1. Select the characters that you want to format.

2. Apply font formatting (such as font, font size, and font style) and/or paragraph formatting (such as alignment, indentation, and line spacing) as discussed in **Chapters 3** and **4**.

✔ Tips

■ Almost every kind of font or paragraph formatting can be applied to the contents of individual cells.

■ I tell you more about formatting tables when I discuss the Table AutoFormat feature later in this chapter.

To align a table

1. Select the entire table (**Figure 41**).

2. Click one of the alignment buttons on the Formatting toolbar:

   ▲ **Align Left** ![] shifts the table against the left margin. This is the default setting.

   ▲ **Center** ![] shifts the table to center it between the left and right margins (**Figure 42**).

   ▲ **Align Right** ![] shifts the table against the right margin.

✔ Tips

■ The Justify button ![] does not move the table. Instead it applies full justification to all paragraphs within the table.

■ You will only notice a change in a table's alignment if the table is narrower than the printable area between the document's left and right margins.

Figure 41 Select the table that you want to align.

Figure 42 When you click the Center button on the Formatting toolbar, the table centers between the left and right document margins.

Substance	Date Tested	Tested By	Results
MSG	5/18/02	Maria Langer	452.3516
Magnesium	6/4/02	John Aabbott	51.84
Sulfur	6/15/02	Mary Johannesburg	145236.145872
Aspirin	10/17/02	Tim Jones	1.1

Figure 43 Select the column adjacent to where you want to insert a column.

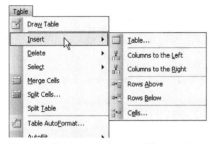

Figure 44 The Insert submenu offers options for inserting tables, columns, rows, or cells.

Substance		Date Tested	Tested By	Results
MSG		5/18/02	Maria Langer	452.3516
Magnesium		6/4/02	John Aabbott	51.84
Sulfur		6/15/02	Mary Johannesburg	145236.145872
Aspirin		10/17/02	Tim Jones	1.1

Figure 45 When you choose Columns to the Left from the Insert submenu, a column is inserted to the left of the selected column.

Substance	Date Tested	Tested By	Results
MSG	5/18/02	Maria Langer	452.3516
Magnesium	6/4/02	John Aabbott	51.84
Sulfur	6/15/02	Mary Johannesburg	145236.145872
Aspirin	10/17/02	Tim Jones	1.1

Figure 46 Select a row adjacent to where you want to insert the row.

Substance	Date Tested	Tested By	Results
MSG	5/18/02	Maria Langer	452.3516
Magnesium	6/4/02	John Aabbott	51.84
Sulfur	6/15/02	Mary Johannesburg	145236.145872
Aspirin	10/17/02	Tim Jones	1.1

Figure 47 When you choose Rows Above from the Insert submenu, a row is inserted above the selected row.

Inserting & Deleting Cells

You can insert or remove columns, rows, or individual cells at any time to change the structure of a table.

To insert a column

1. Select a column adjacent to where you want to insert a column (**Figure 43**).

2. To insert a column to the left of the selected column, choose Table > Insert > Columns to the Left (**Figure 44**) or click the Insert Columns button ▦ on the Standard toolbar.

   or

   To insert a column to the right of the selected column, choose Table > Insert > Columns to the Right (**Figure 44**).

   An empty column is inserted (**Figure 45**).

✔ Tip

- To insert multiple columns, select the same number of columns that you want to insert (if possible) in step 1 or repeat step 2 until the number of columns that you want to insert have been inserted.

To insert a row

1. Select a row adjacent to where you want to insert a row (**Figure 46**).

2. To insert a row above the selected row, choose Table > Insert > Rows Above (**Figure 44**) or click the Insert Rows button ▦ on the Standard toolbar.

   or

   To insert a row below the selected row, choose Table > Insert > Rows Below (**Figure 44**).

   An empty row is inserted (**Figure 47**).

Continued on next page...

INSERTING COLUMNS & ROWS

Continued from previous page.

✔ Tips

- Another way to insert a row at the bottom of the table is to position the insertion point in the last cell of the table and press Tab. An empty row is inserted (**Figure 48**).

- To insert multiple rows, select the same number of rows that you want to insert (if possible) in step 1 or repeat step 2 until the number of rows that you want to insert have been inserted.

To insert a cell

1. Select the cell at the location where you want to insert a cell (**Figure 49**).

2. Choose Table > Insert > Cells (**Figure 44**) or click the Insert Cells button 🔳 on the Standard toolbar.

3. In the Insert Cells dialog that appears (**Figure 50**), select an option:

   ▲ **Shift cells right** inserts a cell in the same row and moves the cells to its right to the right (**Figure 51a**).

   ▲ **Shift cells down** inserts a cell in the same column and moves the cells below it down (**Figure 51b**).

   ▲ **Insert entire row** inserts a row above the selected cell.

   ▲ **Insert entire column** inserts a column to the left of the selected cell.

4. Click OK.

✔ Tip

- To insert multiple cells, select the same number of cells that you want to insert (if possible) in step 1 or repeat steps 2 and 3 until the number of cells that you want to insert have been inserted.

Substance	Date Tested	Tested By	Results
MSG	5/18/02	Maria Langer	452.3516
Magnesium	6/4/02	John Aabbott	51.84
Sulfur	6/15/02	Mary Johannesburg	145236.145872
Aspirin	10/17/02	Tim Jones	1.1

Figure 48 Pressing Tab while the insertion point is in the last cell of the table adds a row at the bottom of the table.

Substance	Date Tested	Tested By	Results
MSG	5/18/02	Maria Langer	452.3516
Magnesium	6/4/02	John Aabbott	51.84
Sulfur	6/15/02	Mary Johannesburg	145236.145872
Aspirin	10/17/02	Tim Jones	1.1

Figure 49 Select the cell where you want to insert a cell.

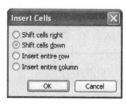

Figure 50
The Insert Cells dialog.

Substance	Date Tested	Tested By	Results	
MSG	5/18/02	Maria Langer		452.3516
Magnesium	6/4/02	John Aabbott	51.84	
Sulfur	6/15/02	Mary Johannesburg	145236.145872	
Aspirin	10/17/02	Tim Jones	1.1	

Substance	Date Tested	Tested By	Results
MSG	5/18/02	Maria Langer	
Magnesium	6/4/02	John Aabbott	452.3516
Sulfur	6/15/02	Mary Johannesburg	51.84
Aspirin	10/17/02	Tim Jones	145236.145872
			1.1

Figures 51a & 51b You can shift cells to the right (top) or down (bottom) when you insert a cell.

INSERTING CELLS

Substance	Date Tested	Tested By	Results
MSG	5/18/02	Maria Langer	452.3516
Magnesium	6/4/02	John Aabbott	51.84
Sulfur	6/15/02	Mary Johannesburg	145236.145872
Aspirin	10/17/02	Tim Jones	1.1

Figure 52 Select the column that you want to delete.

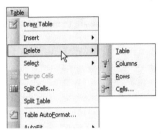

Figure 53 Use commands on the Delete submenu to delete a selected table, column, row, or cell.

Substance	Date Tested	Results
MSG	5/18/02	452.3516
Magnesium	6/4/02	51.84
Sulfur	6/15/02	145236.145872
Aspirin	10/17/02	1.1

Figure 54 The column is deleted.

Substance	Date Tested	Tested By	Results
MSG	5/18/02	Maria Langer	452.3516
Magnesium	6/4/02	John Aabbott	51.84
Sulfur	6/15/02	Mary Johannesburg	145236.145872
Aspirin	10/17/02	Tim Jones	1.1

Figure 55 Select the row that you want to delete.

Substance	Date Tested	Tested By	Results
MSG	5/18/02	Maria Langer	452.3516
Sulfur	6/15/02	Mary Johannesburg	145236.145872
Aspirin	10/17/02	Tim Jones	1.1

Figure 56 The row is deleted.

Substance	Date Tested	Tested By	Results
MSG	5/18/02	Maria Langer	452.3516
Magnesium	6/4/02	John Aabbott	51.84
Sulfur	6/15/02	Mary Johannesburg	145236.145872
Aspirin	10/17/02	Tim Jones	1.1

Figure 57 Select the cell that you want to delete.

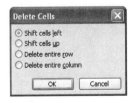

Figure 58 The Delete Cells dialog.

Substance	Date Tested	Tested By	Results
MSG	5/18/02	Maria Langer	
Magnesium	6/4/02	John Aabbott	51.84
Sulfur	6/15/02	Mary Johannesburg	145236.145872
Aspirin	10/17/02	Tim Jones	1.1

Substance	Date Tested	Tested By	Results
MSG	5/18/02	Maria Langer	51.84
Magnesium	6/4/02	John Aabbott	145236.145872
Sulfur	6/15/02	Mary Johannesburg	1.1
Aspirin	10/17/02	Tim Jones	

Figures 59a & 59b You can shift cells to the left (top) or up (bottom) when you delete a cell.

To delete a column, row, or cell

1. Select the column (**Figure 52**), row (**Figure 55**), or cell (**Figure 57**) that you want to remove.

2. Choose the appropriate command from the Table menu's Delete submenu (**Figure 53**) to delete the selected column, row, or cell.

   or

   Press [Backspace].

3. If you delete a column, it disappears and the columns to its right shift to the left (**Figure 54**).

   or

   If you delete a row, it disappears and the rows below it shift up (**Figure 56**).

   or

   If you delete a cell, choose an option in the Delete Cells dialog that appears (**Figure 58**):

   ▲ **Shift cells left** deletes the cell and moves the cells to its right to the left (**Figure 59a**).

   ▲ **Shift cells up** deletes the cell and moves the cells below it up (**Figure 59b**).

   ▲ **Delete entire row** deletes the row.

   ▲ **Delete entire column** deletes the column.

   Then click OK.

✔ Tips

■ The contents of a column, row, or cell are deleted with it.

■ You can select multiple contiguous columns, rows, or cells in step 1 above to delete them all at once.

177

Merging & Splitting Cells & Tables

You can modify the structure of a table by merging and splitting cells or splitting the table:

◆ Merging cells turns multiple cells into one cell that spans multiple columns or rows.

◆ Splitting a cell turns a single cell into multiple cells in the same column or row.

◆ Splitting a table turns a single table into two separate tables.

To merge cells

1. Select the cells that you want to merge (**Figure 60**).

2. Choose Table > Merge Cells (**Figure 18**). The cells become a single cell (**Figure 61**).

✔ Tip

■ When you merge cells containing text, each cell's contents appear in a separate paragraph of the merged cell (**Figure 61**).

To split cells

1. Select the cell(s) that you want to split (**Figure 62**).

2. Choose Table > Split Cells (**Figure 18**) to display the Split Cells dialog (**Figure 63**).

3. Enter the number of columns and rows for the cell split in the Number of columns and Number of rows text boxes.

4. Click OK. The cell splits as specified (**Figure 64**).

Item Name	Description	Number	Price
Permanent Marker, Red	Mark of Zorro brand permanent marker. 0.5 mm felt tip. Airtight cap. Red.	MRK03	$2.99 each
Laser Paper, White	White, 20 lb. paper, designed for use in laser printers. 8-1/2 x 11 inches. 500 sheets per ream.	PAP05	$12.99/ream

Figure 60 Select the cells that you want to merge.

Item Name	Description	Number	Price
Permanent Marker, Red Mark of Zorro brand permanent marker. 0.5 mm felt tip. Airtight cap. Red.		MRK03	$2.99 each
Laser Paper, White	White, 20 lb. paper, designed for use in laser printers. 8-1/2 x 11 inches. 500 sheets per ream.	PAP05	$12.99/ream

Figure 61 The cells are merged into one cell.

Item Name	Description	Number	Price
Permanent Marker, Red	Mark of Zorro brand permanent marker. 0.5 mm felt tip. Airtight cap. Red.	MRK03	$2.99 each
Laser Paper, White	White, 20 lb. paper, designed for use in laser printers. 8-1/2 x 11 inches. 500 sheets per ream.	PAP05	$12.99/ream

Figure 62 Select the cell that you want to split.

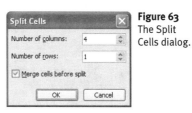

Figure 63 The Split Cells dialog.

Item Name	Description	Number	Price
Permanent Marker, Red	Mark of Zorro brand permanent marker. 0.5 mm felt tip. Airtight cap. Red.	MRK03	$2.99 each
Laser Paper, White	White, 20 lb. paper, designed for use in laser printers. 8-1/2 x 11 inches. 500 sheets per ream.	PAP05	$12.99/ream

Figure 64 A cell split into one column and two rows.

Item Name	Description	Number	Price
Permanent Marker, Red Mark of Zorro brand permanent marker. 0.5 mm felt tip. Airtight cap. Red.		MRK03	$2.99 each
Laser Paper, White	White, 20 lb. paper, designed for use in laser printers. 8-1/2 x 11 inches. 500 sheets per ream.	PAP05	$12.99/ream

Figure 65 The cells selected in **Figure 60** after merging and splitting them into one column and three rows.

Item Name	Description	Number	Price
Permanent Marker, Red	Mark of Zorro brand permanent marker. 0.5 mm felt tip. Airtight cap. Red.	MRK03	$2.99 each
Laser Paper, White	White, 20 lb. paper, designed for use in laser printers. 8-1/2 x 11 inches. 500 sheets per ream.	PAP05	$12.99/ream
Inkjet Paper, White	White, 20 lb. paper, designed for use in inkjet printers. 8-1/2 x 11 inches. 500 sheets per ream.	PAP11	$12.99/ream
Paper Clips, Small	Standard small paperclips. Silver in color. 100 per box.	FAS04	$2.95/box

Figure 66 Position the insertion point in the row below where you want the split to occur.

Item Name	Description	Number	Price
Permanent Marker, Red	Mark of Zorro brand permanent marker. 0.5 mm felt tip. Airtight cap. Red.	MRK03	$2.99 each
Laser Paper, White	White, 20 lb. paper, designed for use in laser printers. 8-1/2 x 11 inches. 500 sheets per ream.	PAP05	$12.99/ream
Inkjet Paper, White	White, 20 lb. paper, designed for use in inkjet printers. 8-1/2 x 11 inches. 500 sheets per ream.	PAP11	$12.99/ream
Paper Clips, Small	Standard small paperclips. Silver in color. 100 per box.	FAS04	$2.95/box

Figure 67 The table splits above the insertion point.

✔ Tips

■ To split a cell in the middle of its contents, in step 1 above position the insertion point where you want the split to occur.

■ To merge and split multiple cells at the same time, in step 1, select all the cells (**Figure 60**). Then, in step 3, make sure the Merge cells before split check box is turned on (**Figure 63**). When you click OK, the cells are merged and split (**Figure 65**).

To split a table

1. Position the insertion point anywhere in the row below where you want the split to occur (**Figure 66**).

2. Choose Table > Split Table (**Figure 18**).

   The table splits above the row you indicated (**Figure 67**).

SPLITTING TABLES

179

Resizing Columns & Rows

Word offers two ways to manually change the width of columns or height of rows:

◆ Drag to change column widths and row heights.

◆ Use the Table Properties dialog to change column widths and row heights.

To change a column's width by dragging

1. Position the mouse pointer on the boundary between the column that you want to change and the one to its right. The mouse pointer turns into a double line with arrows (**Figure 68**).

2. Press the mouse button down and drag:

   ▲ Drag to the right to make the column wider.

   ▲ Drag to the left to make the column narrower.

   As you drag, a dotted line indicating the new boundary moves with the mouse pointer (**Figure 69**).

3. Release the mouse button. The column boundary moves to the new position, resizing both columns (**Figure 70**).

✔ Tips

■ To resize a column without changing the width of other columns, in step 1, position the mouse pointer on the Move Table Column area for the column's right boundary (**Figure 71**). Because this method changes only one column's width, it also changes the width of the table.

■ If a cell is selected when you drag to resize a column, only the selected cell's width changes.

Item Name	Description	Number	Price
Permanent Marker, Red	Mark of Zorro brand permanent marker. 0.5 mm felt tip. Airtight cap. Red.	MRK03	$2.99 each
Laser Paper, White	White, 20 lb. paper, designed for use in laser printers. 8-1/2 x 11 inches. 500 sheets per ream.	PAP05	$12.99/ream

Figure 68 Position the mouse pointer on the column's right boundary.

Item Name	Description	Number	Price
Permanent Marker, Red	Mark of Zorro brand permanent marker. 0.5 mm felt tip. Airtight cap. Red.	MRK03	$2.99 each
Laser Paper, White	White, 20 lb. paper, designed for use in laser printers. 8-1/2 x 11 inches. 500 sheets per ream.	PAP05	$12.99/ream

Figure 69 Drag the column boundary.

Item Name	Description	Number	Price
Permanent Marker, Red	Mark of Zorro brand permanent marker. 0.5 mm felt tip. Airtight cap. Red.	MRK03	$2.99 each
Laser Paper, White	White, 20 lb. paper, designed for use in laser printers. 8-1/2 x 11 inches. 500 sheets per ream.	PAP05	$12.99/ream

Figure 70 When you release the mouse button, the column and the column to its right resize.

Item Name	Description	Number	Price
Permanent Marker, Red	Mark of Zorro brand permanent marker. 0.5 mm felt tip. Airtight cap. Red.	MRK03	$2.99 each
Laser Paper, White	White, 20 lb. paper, designed for use in laser printers. 8-1/2 x 11 inches. 500 sheets per ream.	PAP05	$12.99/ream

Figure 71 You can also resize a column by dragging the Move Table Column area for the column's right boundary.

Item Name ⊕	Description	Number	Price
Permanent Marker, Red	Mark of Zorro brand permanent marker. 0.5 mm felt tip. Airtight cap. Red.	MRK03	$2.99 each
Laser Paper, White	White, 20 lb. paper, designed for use in laser printers. 8-1/2 x 11 inches. 500 sheets per ream.	PAP05	$12.99/ream

Figure 72 Position the mouse pointer on the bottom boundary.

Item Name	Description	Number	Price
Permanent Marker, Red ‡	Mark of Zorro brand permanent marker. 0.5 mm felt tip. Airtight cap. Red.	MRK03	$2.99 each
Laser Paper, White	White, 20 lb. paper, designed for use in laser printers. 8-1/2 x 11 inches. 500 sheets per ream.	PAP05	$12.99/ream

Figure 73 Drag the row boundary.

Item Name	Description	Number	Price
Permanent Marker, Red	Mark of Zorro brand permanent marker. 0.5 mm felt tip. Airtight cap. Red.	MRK03	$2.99 each
Laser Paper, White	White, 20 lb. paper, designed for use in laser printers. 8-1/2 x 11 inches. 500 sheets per ream.	PAP05	$12.99/ream

Figure 74 When you release the mouse button, the boundary moves, changing the row's height.

Figure 75 You can also resize a row by dragging the Adjust Table Row area for the row's bottom boundary.

To change a row's height by dragging

1. If necessary, switch to Print Layout view.

2. Position the mouse pointer on the boundary between the row that you want to change and the one below it. The mouse pointer turns into a double line with arrows (**Figure 72**).

3. Press the mouse button down and drag:

   ▲ Drag up to make the row shorter.

   ▲ Drag down to make the row taller.

   As you drag, a dotted line indicating the new boundary moves with the mouse pointer (**Figure 73**).

4. Release the mouse button. The row boundary moves to the new position. The rows beneath it shift accordingly (**Figure 74**).

✔ Tips

- Another way to resize a row by dragging is to position the mouse pointer on the Adjust Table Row area of the row's bottom boundary (**Figure 75**). Then follow steps 3 and 4 above.

- Changing a row's height changes the total height of the table.

- You can't make a row's height shorter than the height of the text within the row.

To change a table's size by dragging

1. If necessary, switch to Print Layout view.

2. Position the mouse pointer on the table resize handle. The mouse pointer turns into a two-headed arrow (**Figure 76**).

3. Press the mouse button down and drag in any direction:

   ▲ Drag to the left to to make the table narrower.

   ▲ Drag to the right to make the table wider.

   ▲ Drag up to make the table shorter.

   ▲ Drag down to make the table longer.

   As you drag, a dotted line indicating the new table boundary moves with the mouse pointer (**Figure 77**).

4. Release the mouse button. The table resizes (**Figure 78**).

✔ Tips

■ Dragging the table resize handle to resize a table resizes each column and row proportionally.

■ You cannot make a table any shorter than it needs to be to display table contents.

■ Although you can make a table wider than the page boundaries, the table may be cropped when printed. It's best to keep table width within the page margins. You can change page orientation to landscape (in the Page Setup dialog, as discussed in **Chapter 5**) to print a wide table.

Substance	Date Tested	Tested By	Results
MSG	5/18/02	Maria Langer	452.3516
Magnesium	6/4/02	John Aabbott	51.84
Sulfur	6/15/02	Mary Johannesburg	145236.145872
Aspirin	10/17/02	Tim Jones	1.1

Figure 76 When you position the mouse pointer on the table resize handle, it turns into a two-headed arrow.

Substance	Date Tested	Tested By	Results
MSG	5/18/02	Maria Langer	452.35;6
Magnesium	6/4/02	John Aabbott	51.84
Sulfur	6/15/02	Mary Johannesburg	145236;145872
Aspirin	10/17/02	Tim Jones	1.1

Figure 77 Drag the table resize handle.

Substance	Date Tested	Tested By	Results
MSG	5/18/02	Maria Langer	452.3516
Magnesium	6/4/02	John Aabbott	51.84
Sulfur	6/15/02	Mary Johannesburg	145236.145872
Aspirin	10/17/02	Tim Jones	1.1

Figure 78 When you release the mouse button, the table is resized.

Figure 79 The Row tab of the Table Properties dialog.

Figure 80 Use this drop-down list to specify how the row height measurement you enter should be used.

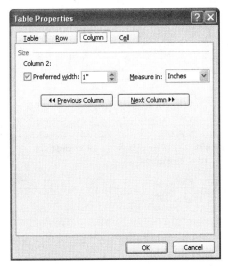

Figure 81 The Column tab of the Table Properties dialog.

Figure 82 Use this drop-down list to specify how the column width measurement you enter should be used.

To set row height or column width

1. Select a cell in the row or column for which you want to set height or width.

2. Choose Table > Table Properties (**Figure 18**) to display the Table Properties dialog.

3. To set row height, click the Row tab to display its options (**Figure 79**). Turn on the Specify Height check box, enter a value in the box beside it, and choose an option from the Row Height Is drop-down list (**Figure 80**).

   or

   To set column width, click the Column tab to display its options (**Figure 81**). Turn on the Preferred Width check box, enter a value in the box beside it, and choose an option from the Measure In drop-down list (**Figure 82**).

4. Click OK.

✔ Tips

- To set column width and row height at the same time, in step 1, select a cell that is in both the column and row that you want to change. Then follow the remaining steps, including both parts of step 3.

- You can click the Previous Row and Next Row buttons in the Row tab (**Figure 79**) and the Previous Column and Next Column buttons in the Column tab (**Figure 81**) of the Table Properties dialog to cycle through and set values for all the rows and columns in the table.

- The Table Properties dialog also offers a number of advanced features for formatting tables, rows, columns, and cells. Explore them on your own.

SETTING ROW HEIGHT & COLUMN WIDTH

Using AutoFit

Table AutoFit options (**Figure 84**) instruct Word to automatically set the column width or row height depending on the table or window width or cell contents. The options are:

◆ **AutoFit to Contents** automatically sizes a column's width based on its contents.

◆ **AutoFit to Window** automatically sizes a table's width to fill the space between the margins.

◆ **Fixed Column Width** locks a column's width so it does not automatically change.

◆ **Distribute Rows Evenly** equalizes the height of rows.

◆ **Distribute Columns Evenly** equalizes the width of columns.

To adjust columns to best fit contents

1. To adjust all table columns, click anywhere in the table (**Figure 83**).

   or

   To adjust just one or more columns, select the column(s).

2. Choose Table > AutoFit > AutoFit to Contents (**Figure 84**).

   The column(s) adjust to minimize word wrap (**Figure 85**).

Item Name	Description	Number	Price
Permanent Marker, Red	Mark of Zorro brand permanent marker. 0.5 mm felt tip. Airtight cap. Red.	MRK03	$2.99 each
Laser Paper, White	White, 20 lb. paper, designed for use in laser printers. 8-1/2 x 11 inches. 500 sheets per ream.	PAP05	$12.99/ream
Inkjet Paper, White	White, 20 lb. paper, designed for use in inkjet printers. 8-1/2 x 11 inches. 500 sheets per ream.	PAP11	$12.99/ream
Paper Clips, Small	Standard small paperclips. Silver in color. 100 per box.	FAS04	$2.95/box

Figure 83 Position the insertion point anywhere in the table.

Figure 84 Use commands under the AutoFit submenu to automatically resize columns or rows.

Item Name	Description	Number	Price
Permanent Marker, Red	Mark of Zorro brand permanent marker. 0.5 mm felt tip. Airtight cap. Red.	MRK03	$2.99 each
Laser Paper, White	White, 20 lb. paper, designed for use in laser printers. 8-1/2 x 11 inches. 500 sheets per ream.	PAP05	$12.99/ream
Inkjet Paper, White	White, 20 lb. paper, designed for use in inkjet printers. 8-1/2 x 11 inches. 500 sheets per ream.	PAP11	$12.99/ream
Paper Clips, Small	Standard small paperclips. Silver in color. 100 per box.	FAS04	$2.95/box

Figure 85 The AutoFit to Contents command minimizes word wrap within cells.

Item Name	Description	Number	Price
Permanent Marker, Red	Mark of Zorro brand permanent marker. 0.5 mm felt tip. Airtight cap. Red.	MRK03	$2.99 each
Laser Paper, White	White, 20 lb. paper, designed for use in laser printers. 8-1/2 x 11 inches. 500 sheets per ream.	PAP05	$12.99/ream
Inkjet Paper, White	White, 20 lb. paper, designed for use in inkjet printers. 8-1/2 x 11 inches. 500 sheets per ream.	PAP11	$12.99/ream
Paper Clips, Small	Standard small paperclips. Silver in color. 100 per box.	FAS04	$2.95/box

Figure 86 The AutoFit to Window command resizes columns proportionally so the table fits in the space between the margins.

Item Name	Description	Number	Price
Permanent Marker, Red	Mark of Zorro brand permanent marker. 0.5 mm felt tip. Airtight cap. Red.	MRK03	$2.99 each
Laser Paper, White	White, 20 lb. paper, designed for use in laser printers. 8-1/2 x 11 inches. 500 sheets per ream.	PAP05	$12.99/ream
Inkjet Paper, White	White, 20 lb. paper, designed for use in inkjet printers. 8-1/2 x 11 inches. 500 sheets per ream.	PAP11	$12.99/ream
Paper Clips, Small	Standard small paperclips. Silver in color. 100 per box.	FAS04	$2.95/box

Figure 87 Select the columns for which you want to equalize width.

Item Name	Description	Number	Price
Permanent Marker, Red	Mark of Zorro brand permanent marker. 0.5 mm felt tip. Airtight cap. Red.	MRK03	$2.99 each
Laser Paper, White	White, 20 lb. paper, designed for use in laser printers. 8-1/2 x 11 inches. 500 sheets per ream.	PAP05	$12.99/ream
Inkjet Paper, White	White, 20 lb. paper, designed for use in inkjet printers. 8-1/2 x 11 inches. 500 sheets per ream.	PAP11	$12.99/ream
Paper Clips, Small	Standard small paperclips. Silver in color. 100 per box.	FAS04	$2.95/box

Figure 88 The space used by the columns is distributed evenly between them.

Item Name	Description	Number	Price
Permanent Marker, Red	Mark of Zorro brand permanent marker. 0.5 mm felt tip. Airtight cap. Red.	MRK03	$2.99 each
Laser Paper, White	White, 20 lb. paper, designed for use in laser printers. 8-1/2 x 11 inches. 500 sheets per ream.	PAP05	$12.99/ream
Inkjet Paper, White	White, 20 lb. paper, designed for use in inkjet printers. 8-1/2 x 11 inches. 500 sheets per ream.	PAP11	$12.99/ream
Paper Clips, Small	Standard small paperclips. Silver in color. 100 per box.	FAS04	$2.95/box

Figure 89 Select the rows for which you want to equalize height.

Item Name	Description	Number	Price
Permanent Marker, Red	Mark of Zorro brand permanent marker. 0.5 mm felt tip. Airtight cap. Red.	MRK03	$2.99 each
Laser Paper, White	White, 20 lb. paper, designed for use in laser printers. 8-1/2 x 11 inches. 500 sheets per ream.	PAP05	$12.99/ream
Inkjet Paper, White	White, 20 lb. paper, designed for use in inkjet printers. 8-1/2 x 11 inches. 500 sheets per ream.	PAP11	$12.99/ream
Paper Clips, Small	Standard small paperclips. Silver in color. 100 per box.	FAS04	$2.95/box

Figure 90 The row heights change as necessary so each selected row is the same height.

To adjust a table's width to fill the window

1. Click anywhere in the table (**Figure 83**).

2. Choose Table > AutoFit > AutoFit to Window (**Figure 84**).

   The table's width adjusts to fill the space between the margins (**Figure 86**). Columns are resized proportionally.

To equalize the width of columns

1. Select the columns for which you want to equalize width (**Figure 87**).

2. Choose Table > AutoFit > Distribute Columns Evenly (**Figure 84**). The column widths change to evenly distribute space within the same area (**Figure 88**).

To equalize the height of rows

1. Select the rows for which you want to equalize height (**Figure 89**).

2. Choose Table > AutoFit > Distribute Rows Evenly (**Figure 84**). The row heights change so that all selected rows are the same height (**Figure 90**).

✔ Tip

- Using the Distribute Rows Evenly command usually increases the height of the table, since all selected rows become the same height as the tallest row.

USING AUTOFIT

Table Headings

A table heading consists of one or more rows that appear at the top of the table. If page breaks occur within a table, the table heading appears at the top of each page of the table (**Figure 91**).

✔ Tip

- Setting a row as a table heading does not change its appearance. You must manually apply formatting or use the Table AutoFormat command to make headings look different from other data in the table. I tell you about formatting text in **Chapters** 3 and 4 and about the Table AutoFormat command on the next page.

To set a table heading

1. Select the row(s) that you want to use as a table heading (**Figure 92**).

2. Choose Table > Heading Rows Repeat (**Figure 93**).

   The selected rows are set as headings.

To remove a table heading

1. Select the row(s) that comprise the heading (**Figure 92**).

2. Choose Table > Heading Rows Repeat (**Figure 93**).

   The headings setting is removed from the selected rows.

✔ Tip

- Removing the heading feature from selected row(s) does not delete the row(s) from the table.

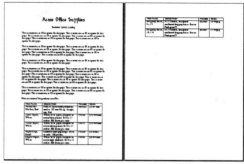

Figure 91 If a page break splits a table into multiple pages, the headings appear at the top of each page of the table.

ITEM NAME	DESCRIPTION	NUMBER	PRICE
Permanent Marker, Red	Mark of Zorro brand permanent marker. 0.5 mm felt tip. Airtight cap. Red.	MRK03	$2.99 each
Laser Paper, White	White, 20 lb. paper, designed for use in laser printers. 8-1/2 x 11 inches. 500 sheets per ream.	PAP05	$12.99/ream
Inkjet Paper, White	White, 20 lb. paper, designed for use in inkjet printers. 8-1/2 x 11 inches. 500 sheets per ream.	PAP11	$12.99/ream
Paper Clips, Small	Standard small paperclips. Silver in color. 100 per box.	FAS04	$2.95/box
Copier Paper, White	White, 20 lb. paper, designed for use in copy machines. 8-1/2 x 11 inches. 500 sheets per ream.	PAP01	$8.99/ream
Shipping Boxes, 9 x 12	9 x 12 inches, corrugated cardboard shipping boxes. Brown. Package of 5.	BOX05	10.99/pkg
Shipping Boxes, 10 x 14	9 x 14 inches, corrugated cardboard shipping boxes. Brown. Package of 5.	BOX07	11.99/pkg

Figure 92 Select the row(s) that you want to use as a heading.

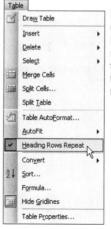

Figure 93 Choose Heading Rows Repeat from the Table menu a second time to remove the heading feature from selected row(s).

Item Name	Description	Number	Price
Permanent Marker, Red	Mark of Zorro brand permanent marker. 0.5 mm felt tip. Airtight cap. Red.	MRK03	$2.99 each
Laser Paper, White	White, 20 lb. paper, designed for use in laser printers. 8-1/2 x 11 inches. 500 sheets per ream.	PAP05	$12.99/ream
Inkjet Paper, White	White, 20 lb. paper, designed for use in inkjet printers. 8-1/2 x 11 inches. 500 sheets per ream.	PAP11	$12.99/ream
Paper Clips, Small	Standard small paperclips. Silver in color. 100 per box.	FAS04	$2.95/box
Copier Paper, White	White, 20 lb. paper, designed for use in copy machines. 8-1/2 x 11 inches. 500 sheets per ream.	PAP01	$8.99/ream
Shipping Boxes, 9 x 12	9 x 12 inches, corrugated cardboard shipping boxes. Brown. Package of 5.	BOX05	10.99/pkg
Shipping Boxes, 10 x 14	9 x 14 inches, corrugated cardboard shipping boxes. Brown. Package of 5.	BOX07	11.99/pkg

Figure 94 Select the table that you want to

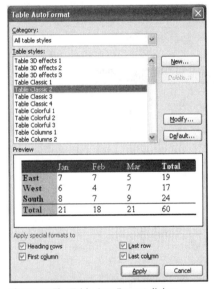

Figure 95 The Table AutoFormat dialog.

Item Name	Description	Number	Price
Permanent Marker, Red	Mark of Zorro brand permanent marker. 0.5 mm felt tip. Airtight cap. Red.	MRK03	$2.99 each
Laser Paper, White	White, 20 lb. paper, designed for use in laser printers. 8-1/2 x 11 inches. 500 sheets per ream.	PAP05	$12.99/ream
Inkjet Paper, White	White, 20 lb. paper, designed for use in inkjet printers. 8-1/2 x 11 inches. 500 sheets per ream.	PAP11	$12.99/ream
Paper Clips, Small	Standard small paperclips. Silver in color. 100 per box.	FAS04	$2.95/box
Copier Paper, White	White, 20 lb. paper, designed for use in copy machines. 8-1/2 x 11 inches. 500 sheets per ream.	PAP01	$8.99/ream
Shipping Boxes, 9 x 12	9 x 12 inches, corrugated cardboard shipping boxes. Brown. Package of 5.	BOX05	10.99/pkg
Shipping Boxes, 10 x 14	9 x 14 inches, corrugated cardboard shipping boxes. Brown. Package of 5.	BOX07	11.99/pkg

Figure 96 The table from **Figure 91** with the Table Classic 2 format applied.

Table AutoFormat

Word's Table AutoFormat feature offers a quick and easy way to combine many formatting options for an entire table.

To use Table AutoFormat

1. Select the table that you want to format (**Figure 94**).

2. Choose Table > Table AutoFormat (**Figure 18**) to display the Table Auto-Format dialog (**Figure 95**).

3. Click to select one of the formats in the scrolling list.

4. Toggle check boxes in the Apply special formats to area to specify which part(s) of the table should get the special formatting.

5. When you're finished setting options, click OK. The formatting for the Auto-Format is applied to the table (**Figure 96**).

✔ Tips

- Each time you make a change in the Table AutoFormat dialog (**Figure 95**), the Preview area changes to show the effect of your changes.

- The Table AutoFormat dialog (**Figure 95**) applies table styles to the selected cells. You can also use this dialog to create new table styles or modify existing ones. Styles are discussed in **Chapter 4**.

- If you don't like the formatting applied by the Table AutoFormat feature, use the Undo command to reverse them. Then try again or format the table manually.

To remove AutoFormatting

Follow steps 1 and 2 above, but select Table Grid in the scrolling list (**Figure 95**) in step 3, and then click OK.

Removing a Table

You can remove a table two ways:

◆ Delete the table, thus removing it and its contents from the document.

◆ Convert the table to text, thus removing the structure of the table from the document but not the table's contents.

To delete a table

1. Select the table that you want to delete.

2. Choose Table > Delete > Table (**Figure 53**).

   or

   Press (Backspace).

   The table, and all of its data, is removed from the document.

To convert a table to text

1. Select the table that you want to convert to text.

2. Choose Table > Convert > Table to Text (**Figure 97**).

3. In the Convert Table to Text dialog that appears (**Figure 98**), select the radio button for the type of delimiter that you want to use to separate the contents of table cells when the cell boundaries are removed.

4. Click OK.

   The table is converted to text.

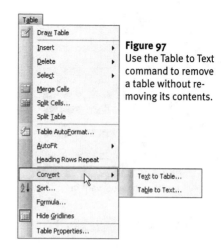

Figure 97
Use the Table to Text command to remove a table without removing its contents.

Figure 98
The Convert Table to Text dialog.

Inserting Special Text

Figure 1
The Insert menu.

✔ Tip

■ I discuss other Insert menu commands throughout this book:

▲ Break, in **Chapter 4**

▲ Comment, in **Chapter 15**

▲ Reference submenu commands and Bookmark, in **Chapter 11**

▲ Picture submenu commands, Diagram, and Text Box, in **Chapter 10**

▲ Object, in **Chapter 16**

▲ Hyperlink, in **Chapter 17**

Special Text

Microsoft Word's Insert menu (**Figure 1**) includes a number of commands that you can use to insert special text into your documents:

◆ **AutoText** submenu commands enable you to create and insert AutoText entries, which are commonly used text snippets, such as your name or the closing of a letter.

◆ **Field** enables you to insert Word fields, which are pieces of information that change as necessary, such as the date, file size, or page number.

◆ **Date and Time** inserts a date or time field than can automatically update to reflect the current date or time.

◆ **Page Numbers** inserts a page number field on each page of the document. When viewed onscreen or printed, the field indicates the number of the page on which it appears.

◆ **Symbol** enables you to insert symbols and special characters such as bullets, smiley faces, and the registered trademark symbol (®).

◆ **File** enables you to insert another file.

AutoText & AutoComplete

Word's AutoText feature makes it quick and easy to insert text snippets that you use often in your documents. First, create the AutoText entry that you want to use. Then use one of two methods to insert it:

◆ Use options on the AutoText submenu under the Insert menu (**Figure 3**) to insert the entry.

◆ Begin to type the entry or entry name. When an AutoComplete suggestion box appears (**Figure 7**), press Enter to enter the rest of the entry. This feature is known as AutoComplete.

✔ Tip

■ Word comes preconfigured with dozens of AutoText entries.

To create an AutoText entry

1. Select the text that you want to use as an AutoText entry (**Figure 2**).

2. Choose Insert > AutoText > New (**Figure 3**).

3. The Create AutoText dialog appears (**Figure 4**). It displays a default name for the entry. If desired, change the name.

4. Click OK.

or

1. Choose Insert > AutoText > AutoText (**Figure 3**) to display the AutoText tab of the AutoCorrect dialog (**Figure 5**).

2. Enter the text that you want to use as an AutoText entry in the Enter AutoText entries here box.

3. Click Add. The entry appears in the list.

4. Repeat steps 2 and 3, if desired, to add additional entries.

5. When you are finished, click OK.

Figure 2 Select the text that you want to use as an AutoText entry.

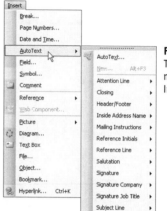

Figure 3 The AutoText menu under the Insert menu.

Figure 4 The Create AutoText dialog.

Figure 5 The AutoText tab of the AutoCorrect dialog.

Figure 6 Selecting an AutoText entry.

To delete an AutoText entry

1. Choose Insert > AutoText > AutoText
   (**Figure 3**) to display the AutoText tab of
   the AutoCorrect dialog (**Figure 5**).

2. In the scrolling list of AutoText entries,
   click to select the entry that you want to
   delete (**Figure 6**). You can confirm that
   you have selected the correct entry by
   checking its contents in the Preview area.

3. Click Delete. The entry is removed from
   the scrolling list.

4. Repeat steps 2 and 3, if desired, to delete
   other entries.

5. When you are finished, click OK.

To enable or disable the AutoComplete feature

1. Choose Insert > AutoText > AutoText
   (**Figure 3**) to display the AutoText tab of
   the AutoCorrect dialog (**Figure 5**).

2. To enable the AutoComplete feature, turn
   on the Show AutoComplete suggestions
   check box.

   or

   To disable the AutoComplete feature,
   turn off the Show AutoComplete suggestions check box.

3. Click OK.

✔ Tip

- The AutoComplete feature is turned on
  by default.

AutoText Entries & AutoComplete

191

To insert an AutoText entry with the AutoText submenu

1. Position the insertion point where you want the AutoText entry to appear.

2. Use your mouse to display the AutoText submenu under the Insert menu (**Figure 3**).

3. Select the submenu option that contains the entry that you want (**Figure 7**) and select the entry. It is inserted into the document.

✔ Tip

■ The AutoText entries you create appear on the Normal submenu under the AutoText submenu.

To insert an AutoText entry with AutoComplete

1. Type text into your document.

2. When you type the first few characters of an AutoText entry, an AutoComplete suggestion box appears (**Figure 8**).

3. To enter the text displayed in the Auto-Complete suggestion, press (Enter). The text you were typing is completed with the text from the AutoText entry (**Figure 9**).

   or

   To ignore the AutoComplete suggestion, keep typing.

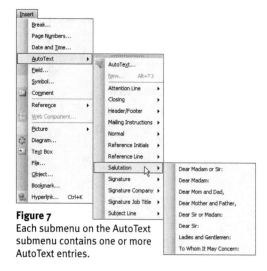

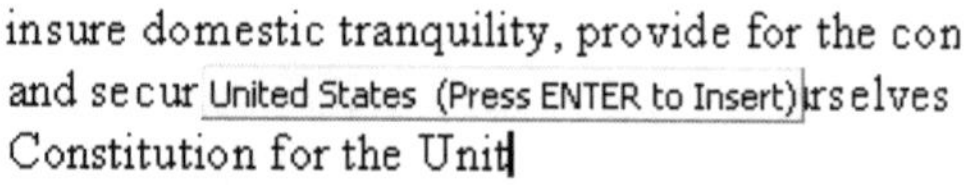

Figure 7
Each submenu on the AutoText submenu contains one or more AutoText entries.

insure domestic tranquility, provide for the con and secur United States (Press ENTER to Insert) rselves Constitution for the Unit

Figure 8 When you begin to type text for which there is an AutoText entry, an AutoComplete suggestion box appears.

insure domestic tranquility, provide for the cor and secure the blessings of liberty to ourselves Constitution for the United States

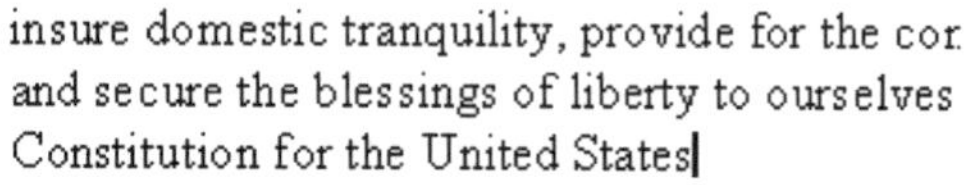

Figure 9 Press (Enter) to complete the text you are typing with the AutoText entry.

INSERTING AUTOTEXT ENTRIES

Word Fields

Word *fields* are special codes that, when inserted in a document, display specific information. But unlike typed text, fields can change when necessary so the information they display is always up-to-date.

For example, the LastSavedBy field displays the name of the last person who saved the document. If someone else saves the document, the contents of the LastSavedBy field will change to that person's name. Similarly, the PrintDate field displays the date the document was last printed. If the document is printed again at a later date, the contents of the PrintDate field will change to reflect the new date.

The Insert menu includes three commands for inserting Word fields:

◆ **Field** enables you to insert any Word field.

◆ **Date and Time** enables you to insert a date or time field.

◆ **Page Number** inserts a page number field in a frame in the document's header or footer. This makes it possible to position a page number anywhere on a page.

This part of the chapter explains how to use these three commands to insert Word fields into your documents. It also explains how to select, update, and delete Word fields.

✔ Tip

■ Word fields is a complex and extremely powerful feature of Microsoft Word—one that an entire book could be written about. Although a thorough discussion of Word fields is beyond the scope of this book, the following pages provide the basic information you need to get started using Word fields in your documents.

To insert any Word field

1. Position the insertion point where you want the field information to appear (**Figure 10**).

2. Choose Insert > Field (**Figure 1**) to display the Field dialog (**Figure 11**).

3. Choose a code category from the Categories drop-down list (**Figure 12**).

4. In the Field names list, click to select the name of the field you want to insert.

5. In the Formats list, click to select the format for the field. The options vary for each field and are generally self-explanatory.

6. Click OK. The field is inserted in the document (**Figure 13**).

✔ Tip

- If field codes appear instead of field contents (**Figure 14**), choose Tools > Options, click the View tab in the Options dialog that appears, and turn off the Field codes check box (**Figure 15**).

Aviation Department
Monthly Report

Prepared by: |

Figure 10
Position the insertion point where you want the field to appear.

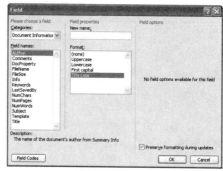

Figure 11 The Field dialog.

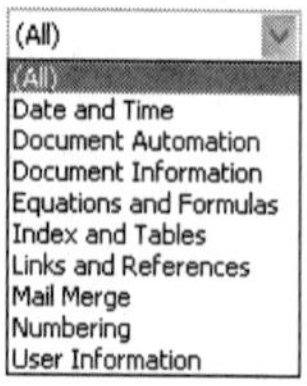

Figure 12
The Categories drop-down list.

Prepared by: Maria Langer|

Figure 13 In this example, the Author field was inserted.

Prepared by: { AUTHOR * Caps * MERGEFORMAT }|

Figure 14 Here's the same field with the field codes rather than the field contents displayed.

Figure 15 Make sure Field codes is turned off in the View tab of the Options dialog.

Aviation Department
Monthly Report

Prepared by: Maria Langer
Revision Date: |

Figure 16 Position the insertion point
where you want the date or time to appear.

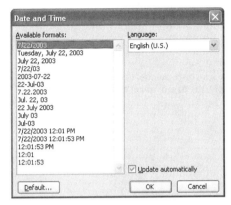

Figure 17 The Date and Time dialog.

Revision Date: 7/22/2003|

Figure 18 This example shows the
Date field inserted in a document.

To insert a date or time field

1. Position the insertion point where you
   want the field information to appear
   (**Figure 16**).

2. Choose Insert > Date and Time (**Figure 1**)
   to display the Date and Time dialog
   (**Figure 17**).

3. Select one of the options in the Available
   formats list.

4. To insert the date or time in a specific
   language format, choose an option from
   the Language drop-down list.

5. To insert the date or time as a field that
   automatically updates when you save or
   print the document, turn on the Update
   automatically check box.

6. Click OK. The current date or time is
   inserted in the document (**Figure 18**).

✔ Tips

- As shown in Figure 17, some of the
  options in the Available formats list
  include both the date and the time.

- If you do not turn on the Update automatically check box in step 5, the current
  date or time is inserted as plain text
  rather than as a Word field.

- If field codes appear instead of field
  contents (**Figure 14**), choose Tools >
  Options, click the View tab in the Options
  dialog that appears, and turn off the Field
  codes check box (**Figure 15**).

To insert a page number

1. Choose Insert > Page Numbers (Figure 1) to display the Page Numbers dialog (**Figure 19**).

2. Choose an option from the Position drop-down list. The options are Top of page (Header) or Bottom of page (Footer).

3. Choose an option from the Alignment drop-down list:

   ▲ **Left** aligns the page number at the left margin of all pages.

   ▲ **Center** centers the page number between margins on all pages.

   ▲ **Right** aligns the page number at the right margin of all pages.

   ▲ **Inside** aligns the page number at the left margin of odd numbered pages and at the right margin of even numbered pages.

   ▲ **Outside** aligns the page number at the right margin of odd numbered pages and at the left margin of even numbered pages.

4. To include the page number on the first page, make sure the Show page number on first page check box is turned on.

5. Click OK. A page number field is inserted in a frame at the location you specified (**Figure 20**).

Figure 19 The Page Numbers dialog.

Figure 20 A page number inserted in a footer. In this example, the page number's frame is selected so it's easier to see.

Figure 21 The Page Number Format dialog.

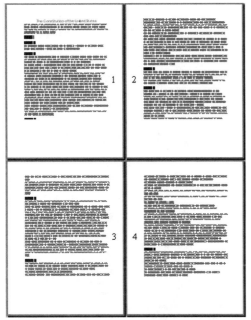

Figure 22 Four pages of a lengthy document in Print Preview. In this example, I used the Page Numbers command to insert a page number in the footer, then formatted the page number and used the Frame dialog to position it in the outside margin.

✔ Tips

- You can click the Format button in the Page Numbers dialog and use the Page Number Format dialog that appears (**Figure 21**) to set number formatting options for the page number.

- To see an inserted page number, choose View > Header and Footer. Then, if necessary, click the Switch Between Header and Footer button 📧 on the Header and Footer toolbar to switch to the footer (**Figure 20**). I tell you more about headers and footers in **Chapter 5**.

- The Page Numbers command inserts a page number in a frame. This makes it possible to position the page number *anywhere* on the page (**Figure 22**). Simply drag the frame into position while in Print Layout View or use the Frame dialog to specify precise position settings. I tell you more about working with frames in **Chapter 10**.

- In my opinion, the Page Numbers command is *not* the best way to insert page numbers into a document. A better way is to use the Header and Footer toolbar's Insert Page Number button 🔳 to insert a page number field in the header or footer, as I explain in **Chapter 5**. This inserts the page number without the frame, which keeps things simple.

To select a field

1. In the document window, click the field once. It turns light gray and the insertion point appears within it (**Figure** 23).

2. Drag over the field. The field turns dark gray (or black) and is selected (**Figure** 24).

✔ Tip

- Once you have selected a field, you can format it using formatting techniques discussed in **Chapter** 3 or delete it by pressing (Backspace).

To update a field

1. Right-click on the field to display its shortcut menu (**Figure** 25).

2. Choose Update Field. If necessary, the contents of the field changes.

✔ Tips

- To ensure that all fields are automatically updated before the document is printed, choose Tools > Options, click the Print tab in the Options dialog that appears, and turn on the Update fields check box (**Figure** 26).

- Choosing Edit Field from the field's shortcut menu (**Figure** 25) displays the Field dialog (**Figure** 11), which you can use to select a different field or different format for the field.

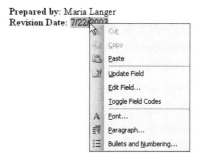

Prepared by: Maria Langer

Prepared by: Maria Langer

Figures 23 & 24 When you click a field, it turns light gray and the insertion point appears within it (top). When you drag over the field, it turns dark gray or black and is selected (bottom).

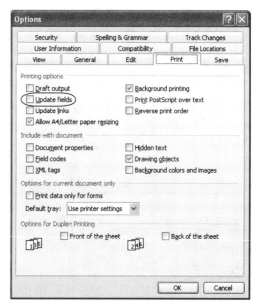

Prepared by: Maria Langer
Revision Date: 7/22/2003

Figure 25 A field's shortcut menu includes the Update Field command.

Figure 26 To ensure that all fields are updated before a document is printed, turn on the Update fields check box in the Print tab of the Options dialog.

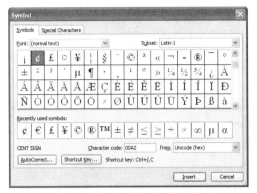

Figure 27 The Symbols tab of the Symbol window.

Figure 28 The Special Characters tab of the Symbol window.

Symbols & Special Characters

Symbols are special characters that don't appear on the keyboard. They include special characters within a font, such as ®, ©, ™, or é, and characters that appear only in special "dingbats" fonts, such as ■, ▲, →, and ♣.

Word offers the Symbol window (**Figures 27** and **28**), which makes it easy to insert all kinds of symbols and special characters in your documents.

✔ Tips

- You don't need to use the Symbol window to insert symbols or special characters in your documents. You just need to know the keystrokes and, if necessary, the font to apply. The Symbol window takes all the guesswork out of inserting these characters.

- A *dingbats font* is a typeface that displays graphic characters rather than text characters. Monotype Sorts, Webdings, Wingdings, and Zapf Dingbats are four examples.

- In the Special Characters tab of the Symbol window (**Figure 28**), special characters appear in the current font.

To insert a symbol or special character

1. Position the insertion point where you want the character to appear (**Figure 29**).

2. Choose Insert > Symbol (**Figure 1**).

3. If necessary, click the Symbols tab in the Symbol window that appears to display its options (**Figure 27**).

4. Choose the font that you want to use to display the character from the Font drop-down list (**Figure 30**). The Characters displayed in the Symbol window change accordingly.

5. Click the character that you want to insert to select it (**Figure 31**).

6. Click Insert. The character that you clicked appears at the insertion point (**Figure 32**).

7. Repeat steps 4 though 6, if desired, to insert additional characters.

8. When you are finished inserting characters, click the close box to dismiss the Symbol window.

✔ Tips

■ The (normal text) option on the Font drop-down list (**Figure 30**) uses the default font for the paragraph or character style applied to the text at the insertion point. Styles are discussed in **Chapter 4**.

■ When inserting a symbol or special character in the normal font, you may prefer to use the Special Characters tab of the Symbol window (**Figure 28**). The list of special characters includes the shortcut key you can use to type the character without using the Symbol window.

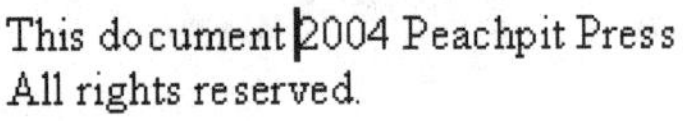

This document 2004 Peachpit Press
All rights reserved.

Figure 29 Position the insertion point where you want the symbol or special character to appear.

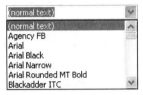

Figure 30 The Font drop-down list in the Symbol window.

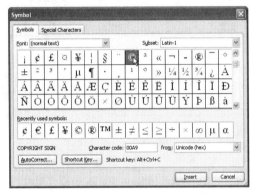

Figure 31 An example of the Symbols tab of the Symbol window being used to insert a special character in the default font.

This document ©2004 Peachpit Press
All rights reserved.

Figure 32 The character you selected appears at the insertion point.

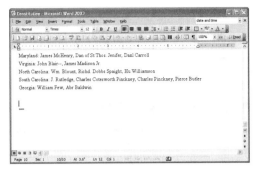

Figure 33 Position the insertion point where you want to insert the file.

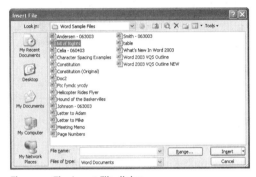

Figure 34 The Insert File dialog.

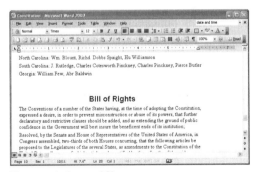

Figure 35 An inserted file.

Figure 36
The Files of type drop-down list.

Files

You can use the File command under the Insert menu to insert one file (the *source* file) within another file (the *destination* file). The source file then becomes part of the destination file.

✔ Tips

- The source file can be in any format that Word recognizes.

- Copy and paste and drag and drop are two other methods for inserting the contents of one file into another. These techniques are explained in **Chapter 2**.

- A file can be inserted with or without a link. If the source file is linked, when you update the link, the destination file is updated with fresh information from the source. This means that changes in the source file are reflected in the destination file.

To insert a file

1. Position the insertion point where you want the source file to be inserted (**Figure 33**).

2. Choose Insert > File (**Figure 1**).

3. Use the Insert File dialog that appears (**Figure 34**) to locate and select the file that you want to insert.

4. Click the Insert button. The file is inserted (**Figure 35**).

✔ Tip

- You can use the Files of type drop-down list (**Figure 36**) to view only specific types of files in the Insert File dialog (**Figure 34**).

To insert a file as a link

Follow all of the steps on the previous page to insert a file. In step 4, choose Insert As File from the Insert button's menu (**Figure 37**).

Figure 37
The Insert button's menu.

✔ Tips

■ When you click the contents of a linked file, it turns gray (**Figure 38**).

■ Any changes you make in the destination file to the contents of a linked file are lost when the link is updated.

■ A linked file is inserted as a field. I tell you about fields earlier in this chapter.

To update a link

1. Right-click on the linked file to display its shortcut menu (**Figure 39**).

2. Choose Update Field.

   The link's contents are updated to reflect the current contents of the source file.

✔ Tip

■ If Word cannot find the source file when you attempt to update a link, it replaces the contents of the source file with an error message (**Figure 40**). There are three ways to fix this problem:

   ▲ Undo the update.

   ▲ Remove the linked file and reinsert it.

   ▲ Choose Edit > Links to fix the link with the Links dialog.

To remove an inserted file

1. Select the contents of the inserted file.

2. Press [Backspace].

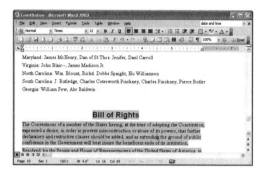

Figure 38 When you click the contents of a linked file, it turns gray.

Figure 39 The shortcut menu for a linked file.

Figure 40 Word displays an error message in the document window when you attempt to update a link and it can't find the source file.

Working with Graphics

Figure 1
The Insert menu.

Working with Graphics

Microsoft Word includes support for inserting and formatting graphic objects, including pictures, line drawings, diagrams, and charts. Graphic elements like these can make your documents more interesting or more informative to readers.

This chapter explores options under the Insert menu (**Figure 1**) and its Picture submenu (**Figure 2**) for inserting graphic elements in your Word documents:

- ◆ **Picture** submenu options enable you to insert a variety of picture types, including clip art, image files, drawings, AutoShapes, and WordArt.

- ◆ **Diagram** enables you to create and insert a custom diagram.

- ◆ **Text Box** inserts a box in which you can enter and format text.

This chapter also provides some basic information for formatting and working with the graphic elements in your Word documents.

✔ Tip

- ■ I discuss other Insert menu commands throughout this book:
  - ▲ Break, in **Chapter 4**
  - ▲ Page Numbers, Date and Time, Auto-Text submenu commands, and File, in **Chapter 9**
  - ▲ Comment, in **Chapter 15**
  - ▲ Reference submenu commands and Bookmark, in **Chapter 11**
  - ▲ Object, in **Chapter 16**
  - ▲ Hyperlink, in **Chapter 17**

Pictures

Pictures are graphic objects. Word's Picture submenu (**Figure 2**) enables you to insert a variety of picture types:

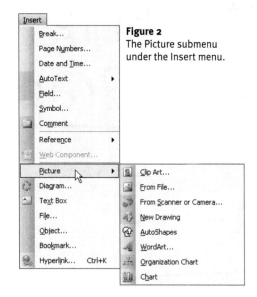

Figure 2
The Picture submenu under the Insert menu.

- ◆ **Clip Art** inserts clip art, pictures, sounds, and videos from the Clip Gallery.

- ◆ **From File** inserts an existing picture file.

- ◆ **From Scanner or Camera** enables you to import images directly from a scanner or digital camera into a Word document.

- ◆ **New Drawing** inserts a blank drawing.

- ◆ **AutoShapes** displays the AutoShapes and Drawing toolbars, which you can use to draw shapes and lines.

- ◆ **WordArt** inserts stylized text.

- ◆ **Organization Chart** inserts an organization chart.

- ◆ **Chart** inserts a Microsoft Graph chart.

This section introduces all of these options.

✔ Tip

- ■ When a graphic object is inserted into a Word document, it is usually inserted in the *document layer* as an *inline image*— an image that appears on text baselines like any other text. Some graphics, however, can be drawn on or moved to the *drawing layer*. This layer is separate from the text in your Word documents and text can wrap around it.

Figure 3 The Insert Clip Art task pane appears beside the document window.

Figures 4 & 5 The Search in (left) and Results should be (above) drop-down lists.

Figure 6 Clip art that matches the criteria you specified appears in the task pane.

Figure 7 Click a thumbnail to insert its image.

To insert clip art

1. Position the insertion point where you want the clip art to appear.

2. Choose Insert > Picture > Clip Art (**Figure 2**) to display the Insert Clip Art task pane beside the document window (**Figure 3**).

3. Enter a search word in the Search text box.

4. To search only some collections, display the Search in drop-down list (**Figure 4**) and click check boxes to toggle search location options on or off.

5. To specify the type of media you want to find, display the Results should be drop-down list (**Figure 5**) and click check boxes to toggle media type options on or off.

6. Click Search.

7. Wait while Word searches for clip art that matches the criteria you specified. When it's done, it displays matches in the Insert Clip Art task pane (**Figure 6**).

8. Click the thumbnail view of a Clip Art item to insert it as an inline image in the document (**Figure 7**).

✔ Tips

- You can click the plus or minus button beside an item in the Search in or Results should be drop-down list to collapse or expand its display.

- A globe icon in the bottom-left corner of an image thumbnail indicates that the image resides on the Web. If you insert one of these images into your document, Word automatically downloads a copy of the image and saves it on your hard disk.

To insert a picture from a file

1. Position the insertion point where you want the picture to appear.

2. Choose Insert > Picture > From File (**Figure 2**) to display the Insert Picture dialog (**Figure 8**).

3. Locate and select the file that you want to insert.

4. Click the Insert button. The file is inserted as an inline image at the insertion point (**Figure 9**).

✔ Tip

■ Be aware that not all images may display as thumbnails in the Insert Picture dialog. Instead, some may display as generic image icons.

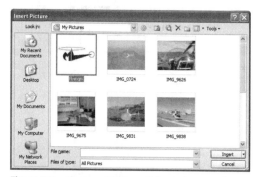

Figure 8 Use the Insert Picture dialog to insert a picture from a file on disk.

Figure 9 When you insert a picture from a file on disk, it appears at the insertion point.

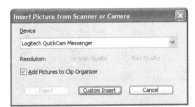

Figure 10 Use this dialog to select the scanner or camera you want to access.

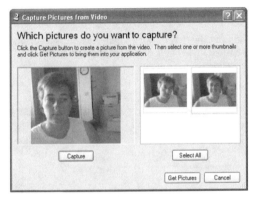

Figure 11 Word displays a dialog you can use to scan, select, or capture the image. In this example, the Capture Pictures from Video dialog lets me capture a still image from a QuickCam Messenger digital camera.

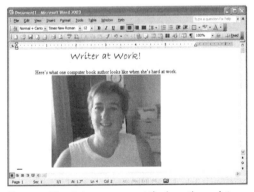

Figure 12 The picture appears at the insertion point.

To insert a picture from a scanner or a digital camera

1. Make sure the scanner software is properly installed and that the scanner is connected to your computer and turned on. Then place the image you wish to scan on the scanning surface.

   or

   Make sure the digital camera software is properly installed and that the camera is connected to your computer and turned on.

2. In the Word document, position the insertion point where you want the picture to appear.

3. Choose Insert > Picture > From Scanner or Camera (**Figure 2**).

4. The Insert Picture from Scanner or Camera dialog appears (**Figure 10**). Use the drop-down list to choose a device.

5. Click Custom Insert. A dialog with options for your device appears (**Figure 11**).

6. Follow the instructions that appear on screen to scan, select, or capture the image. When you are finished, the image appears in the Word document as an inline image (**Figure 12**).

✔ Tips

- If the Insert Picture from Scanner or Camera dialog (**Figure 10**) does not appear after step 3, your scanner or camera is probably not installed correctly. Consult the documentation that came with the device to set it up before trying again.

- The procedure in step 6 varies depending on the device you are using. Word may launch your scanner or digital camera software to complete the scan or download an image. If so, consult the device's documentation for instructions.

To insert a drawing

1. Position the insertion point where you want the drawing to appear.

2. Choose Insert > Picture > New Drawing (**Figure** 2). An empty drawing canvas appears, along with the floating Drawing Canvas toolbar. The Drawing toolbar also appears anchored to the bottom of the window. You can see all this in **Figure** 13.

3. Use buttons and tools on the Drawing toolbar to create a drawing:

   ▲ To draw a line or shape, click a button or choose a menu option to select a tool and then drag in the drawing canvas.

   ▲ To move a line or shape, drag it to a new position within the drawing canvas.

   ▲ To remove a line or shape, select it and press (Backspace).

4. When you are finished drawing, click anywhere outside the drawing canvas. The completed drawing appears as an inline image in the document and the Drawing Canvas toolbar disappears (**Figure** 14).

✔ Tip

■ In general, Word's drawing tools work very much like the drawing tools in other Windows programs. A complete discussion of Word's drawing feature is beyond the scope of this book. Experiment with Word's tools to see how you can use them to create drawings in your documents.

Figure 13 The New Drawing command inserts an empty drawing canvas in the document and displays two toolbars.

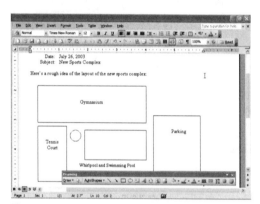

Figure 14 A completed drawing in a Word document. (Now you know why I'm a writer and not an artist.)

INSERTING DRAWINGS

Figure 15 The AutoShapes and Drawing toolbars appear when you choose the AutoShapes command.

Figure 16
Click a button to display a menu of related shapes or lines.

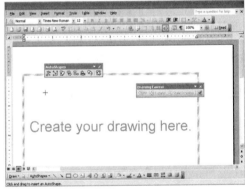

Figure 17 Selecting a drawing tool displays a drawing canvas and the Drawing Canvas toolbar.

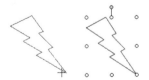

Figures 18 & 19 Drag the mouse to begin drawing the shape (left). When you release the mouse button, the shape appears with selection handles around it (right).

To insert a shape or line

1. Choose Insert > Picture > AutoShapes (**Figure 2**). The AutoShapes and Drawing toolbars appear (**Figure 15**).

2. To draw an AutoShape, click a button on the AutoShapes toolbar to display a pop-up menu of shapes (**Figure 16**) or lines and choose the shape or line that you want to draw.

   or

   To draw a basic shape, click a button on the Drawing toolbar to select a drawing tool.

3. A drawing canvas and the Drawing Canvas toolbar appears (**Figure 17**). You have two options:

   ▲ To draw inside the drawing canvas drag to draw the shape within the drawing canvas box. When you do so, the drawing canvas remains in place so you can draw additional shapes and lines within it.

   ▲ To draw outside the drawing canvas, drag to draw the shape outside the drawing canvas box (**Figure 18**). When you do so, the drawing canvas disappears and the shape or line becomes an independent object on the document's drawing layer (**Figure 19**).

✔ Tip

■ The shape or line pop-up menu that appears when you click an AutoShapes toolbar button (**Figure 16**) can be dragged off the toolbar to create its own toolbar.

INSERTING SHAPES & LINES

209

To insert WordArt

1. Display the Word document in which you want the WordArt image to appear.

2. Choose Insert > Picture > WordArt (**Figure 2**).

3. In the WordArt Gallery dialog that appears (**Figure 20**), click to select a WordArt style.

4. Click OK.

5. In the Edit WordArt Text dialog that appears next (**Figure 21**), change the sample text to the text that you want to display. You can also select a different font and font size and turn on bold and/ or italic formatting.

6. Click OK. The WordArt image is inserted as an inline image in your document (**Figure 22**).

✔ Tip

■ Once you have created a WordArt image, you can use buttons on the WordArt toolbar, which appears when the WordArt image is selected (**Figure 23**). You can click the image to select it.

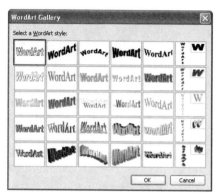

Figure 20 The WordArt Gallery dialog.

Figure 21 The default text in the Edit WordArt Text dialog.

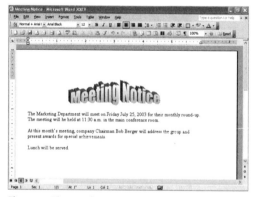

Figure 22 The WordArt image is inserted at the insertion point.

Figure 23 The WordArt toolbar appears when a WordArt image is selected.

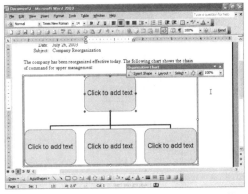

Figure 24 Word inserts a basic organization chart, all ready for customization, and displays the Organization Chart toolbar.

Figure 25 Type the text you want to appear within the box.

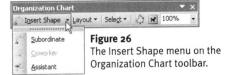

Figure 26 The Insert Shape menu on the Organization Chart toolbar.

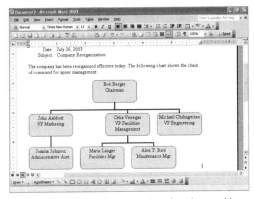

Figure 27 A completed organization chart inserted in a Word document.

To insert an organization chart

1. Position the insertion point where you want the organization chart to appear.

2. Choose Insert > Picture > Organization Chart (**Figure 2**). A box containing a basic organization chart structure appears, along with the Organization Chart toolbar (**Figure 24**).

3. Modify the basic chart to build your own custom chart:

   ▲ To enter information into a box, click inside the box, then type the text you want to appear (**Figure 25**).

   ▲ To add a box, select the box you want to attach it to and choose an option from the Insert Shape menu on the Organization Chart toolbar (**Figure 26**).

   ▲ To remove a box, select the box you want to remove and press (Backspace).

4. When you are finished modifying the chart, click anywhere outside it. The completed chart appears as an inline image in the document and the Organization Chart toolbar disappears (**Figure 27**).

✔ Tips

■ You can format the contents of the organization chart boxes as you can any other text. Consult **Chapter 3** for details.

■ In step 2, the Drawing toolbar also appears (anchored to the bottom of the window in **Figures 24** and **27**) but it is not used to create an organization chart. The Drawing toolbar is discussed briefly on the next page.

To insert a chart

1. Activate the Word document in which you want the chart to appear.

2. Choose Insert > Picture > Chart (**Figure** 2). Word inserts a chart in the document and displays the corresponding Datasheet window (**Figure 28**).

3. Edit the contents of the Datasheet window to reflect the data that you want to chart; the Chart window is updated automatically.

4. When you are finished, click the Datasheet window's close button. The chart is inserted as an inline image in the document (**Figure 29**).

✔ Tips

- You can edit a chart by right-clicking the chart and choosing Datasheet from the shortcut menu that appears.

- You can format a chart by double-clicking its components to display various formatting dialogs.

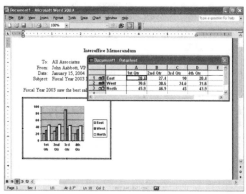

Figure 28 Word inserts a default chart and displays the corresponding Datasheet window.

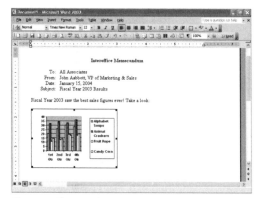

Figure 29 The completed chart appears as an inline image in the document.

Figure 30
Use the Diagram Gallery dialog to select the type of diagram you want to create.

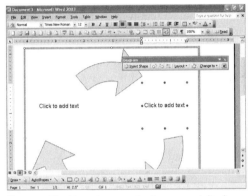

Figure 31 Word inserts a sample diagram and displays the Diagram toolbar.

Figure 32
Enter the text you want to appear for a shape.

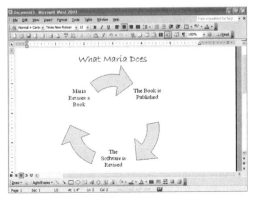

Figure 33 A completed diagram.

Diagrams

The Insert menu's Diagram command (Figure 1), enables you to insert a variety of diagrams as inline images in your Word documents.

To insert a diagram

1. Position the insertion point where you want the diagram to appear.

2. Choose Insert > Diagram (**Figure 1**) to display the Diagram Gallery dialog (**Figure 30**).

3. Select the icon for the type of diagram you want to create. The name and a brief description of the diagram appears near the bottom of the dialog (**Figure 30**).

4. Click OK. A sample chart is inserted in the document and the Diagram toolbar appears (**Figure 31**).

5. Modify the basic diagram to build your own custom diagram:

   ▲ To enter text, click where indicated and type the text you want to appear (**Figure 32**).

   ▲ To add a shape and accompanying text, click the Insert Shape button on the Diagram toolbar.

   ▲ To remove a shape and its text, select the text box for the shape you want to remove and press (Backspace).

6. When you are finished modifying the chart, click anywhere outside it. The completed chart appears as an inline image in the document and the Diagram toolbar disappears (**Figure 33**).

Continued on next page...

INSERTING DIAGRAMS

Continued from previous page.

✔ Tips

- Choosing the first diagram type in step 3 creates an organization chart, which is discussed earlier in this chapter. Follow the instructions earlier there to complete the chart.

- In step 4, the Drawing toolbar also appears (anchored to the bottom of the window in **Figures 24** and **27**) but it is not used to create an organization chart. The Drawing toolbar is discussed briefly on the next page.

- You can format the contents of the diagram's text boxes the same way you format any other text. Consult **Chapter 3** for details.

INSERTING DIAGRAMS

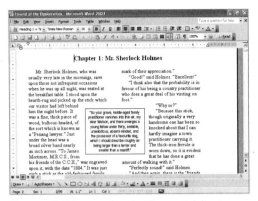

Figure 34 In this example, a text box containing a quote from the document is used as a design element. Text boxes only appear exactly as positioned in Print Layout view (shown here) and Print Preview.

Text Boxes & Frames

Text boxes and *frames* are containers for text and graphics. Word enables you to position them just about anywhere on a page, format them and their contents, and flow text around them (**Figure 34**).

Frames have been a Word feature for as long as I can remember—and I've been using Word since 1990. Text boxes were introduced a few versions ago as part of Word's drawing features. But as Word evolved, Microsoft added more and more functionality to text boxes. In Word 2002 and 2003, you can use a command on the Insert menu (**Figure 1**) to insert a text box in your document; previous versions enabled you to insert a frame instead.

Clearly, Microsoft is encouraging Word users to use text boxes instead of frames. But what's more important is that there are specific instances when you must use one instead of the other.

You must use a text box to do any of the following:

◆ Make text flow from one container to another. This is done by linking text boxes; frames cannot be linked.

◆ Change the orientation of text in a container using the Format menu's Text Direction command.

◆ Format a text container using options on the Drawing toolbar. This includes changing the shape of the text box to one of Word's AutoShapes.

◆ Group text containers and change the alignment or distribution of them as a group.

Continued on next page...

TEXT BOXES & FRAMES

Continued from previous page.

♦ Create a watermark that appears on document pages when printed. This feature differs from any watermark capabilities that your printer may support.

On the other hand, you must use frames if your text container includes any of the following:

♦ Inserted comments, which are indicated by comment marks.

♦ Footnotes or endnotes, which are indicated by note reference marks.

♦ Certain Word fields, including AUTONUM, AUTONUMLGL, and AUTONUMOUT, which are used for numbering lists and paragraphs in legal documents and outlines, or TC, TOC, RD, XE, TA, and TOA, which are used for various indexes and tables.

This part of the chapter will concentrate on text boxes that are inserted with the Insert menu's Text Box command (**Figure 1**).

✔ Tips

■ When you open a document that contains frames created with a previous version of Word, Word keeps the frames.

■ You can convert a text box into a frame. I explain how later in this part of the chapter.

■ I tell you about footnotes and endnotes in **Chapter 11**. I tell you about Word fields and explain how to insert a page number in a frame in **Chapter 9**.

Mr. Sherlock Holmes, who was usually very late in the mornings, save upon those not infrequent occasions when he was up all night, was seated at the hearth-rug and picked up the stick which our visitor had left behind him the night before. It was a fine, thick piece of wood, bulbous-headed, of the sort which is known as a "Penang lawyer." Just under the head was a broad silver band nearly an inch across. "To James Mortimer, M.R.C.S., from his friends of the C.C.H.," was engraved upon it, with the date "1884." It was just such a stick as the old-fashioned family practitioner used to carry--dignified, solid, and reassuring.

"Well, Watson, what do you make of it?"

head."

"I have, at least, a well-polished, silver-plated coffee-pot in front of me," said he. "But, tell me, Watson, what do you make of our visitor's stick? Since we have been so unfortunate as to miss him and have no notion of his errand, this accidental souvenir becomes of importance. Let me hear you reconstruct the mn by an examination of it."

"I think," said I, following as far as I could the methods of my companion, "that Dr. Mortimer is a successful, elderly medical man, well-esteemed since those who know him give him this mark of their appreciation."

"Good!" said Holmes. "Excellent!"

"I think also that the probability is in favour of his being a country practitioner

Figure 35 Use a crosshairs pointer to draw a text box.

Figure 36 When you release the mouse button, the text box and the Text Box toolbar appear.

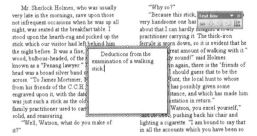

Figure 37 You can enter text into a text box by typing or pasting it in.

To insert a text box

1. In an open Word document, choose Insert > Text Box. A number of things happen:

   ▲ If the document was in any view other than Page Layout view, it switches to Page Layout view.

   ▲ The Drawing toolbar appears with the Text Box tool selected.

   ▲ The mouse pointer appears as a crosshairs pointer.

2. Use the crosshairs pointer to draw a box the approximate size and shape of the text box you want in the location you want it (**Figure 35**).

3. Release the mouse button. The text box appears with selection handles around it and a blinking insertion point within it (**Figure 36**).

4. Enter the text you want to appear in the text box (**Figure 37**).

✔ Tips

- In step 1, if a drawing canvas labeled *Create your drawing here* appears, ignore it. You can draw a text box anywhere in the document—not just on a drawing canvas. The drawing canvas disappears automatically if not used.

- If the Drawing toolbar is already showing, skip step 1 and click the Text Box tool instead. Then follow the remaining steps.

- Once text has been entered into a text box, it can be formatted like any other text. Consult **Chapter 3** for more information about formatting text.

- You can use the Text Box toolbar to change the orientation of text in a text box or link text in one text box to another. Explore the toolbar buttons on your own.

To select a text box

Click anywhere inside the text box. A thick hashmark border and round white selection handles appear around the text box (**Figure 38**).

✔ Tip

- To select multiple text boxes at the same time, hold down (Shift) while clicking the border of each one.

To delete a text box

1. Select the text box you want to delete (**Figure 38**).

2. Press (Backspace). The text box disappears.

✔ Tip

- To delete a text box without deleting its contents, first select and copy its contents to another part of the document or to another document.

To convert a text box to a frame

1. Select the text box you want to convert.

2. Choose Format > Text Box. The Format Text Box dialog appears.

3. Click the Text Box tab to display its options (**Figure 39**).

4. Click the Convert to Frame button.

5. A warning dialog like the one in **Figure 40** appears. Click OK. The text box is converted into a frame (**Figure 41**).

✔ Tip

- You cannot directly convert a frame to a text box. Instead, create a text box, copy the contents of the frame, paste them into the text box, and delete the frame.

Figure 38
A selected text box.

Figure 39 The Text Box tab of the Format Text Box dialog enables you to set text box options or convert a text box to a frame.

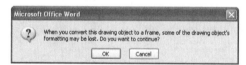

Figure 40 Word warns you before it converts a text box.

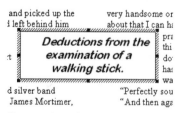

Figure 41 A text box converted to a frame. Note that the selection handles are black and text automatically wraps around a frame. I explain how to wrap text around a text box or other graphic object later in this chapter.

Figure 42 When you click a graphic object in the document layer, a black selection box and handles appear around it and the Picture toolbar appears.

Figure 43 Drag the selection handle toward the center of the picture to make the picture smaller.

Figure 44 When you release the mouse button, the picture resizes.

Working with Graphic Objects

Word includes many powerful image-editing tools that you can use to work with the graphic objects in your Word documents. Although a complete discussion of all of these tools is far beyond the scope of this book, here are some instructions for performing some common layout-related tasks on graphic objects and text boxes in your Word documents.

To move a graphic object

Drag it with the mouse pointer.

◆ A graphic object in the document layer can be moved like a text character.

◆ A graphic object in the drawing layer can be moved anywhere on a page.

To resize a graphic object

1. Click the object to select it. White or black selection handles appear around it (**Figure 42**).

2. Position the mouse pointer on a handle, press the mouse button, and drag as follows:

   ▲ Drag away from the object to make it larger.

   ▲ Drag toward the center of the object to make it smaller (**Figure 43**).

   When you release the mouse button, the object resizes (**Figure 44**).

✔ Tip

■ To resize the object proportionally, hold down (Shift) while dragging a corner handle.

To wrap text around a graphic object

1. Click the object you want to wrap text around to select it.

2. Choose the last command under the Format menu. As shown in **Figures 45a**, **45b**, and **45c**, this command's name changes depending on what is selected.

3. In the Format dialog that appears, click the Layout tab to display its options (**Figure 46**).

4. Select one of the Wrapping style options:

   ▲ **In line with text** places the object in the document layer as an inline image. This is the default setting for inline images.

   ▲ **Square** wraps text around all sides of the object with some space to spare.

   ▲ **Tight** wraps text tightly around all sides of the object.

   ▲ **Behind text** places the object behind the document layer. There is no word wrap.

   ▲ **In front of text** places the object in front of the document layer. There is no word wrap. This is the default setting for text boxes.

5. Choose one of the Horizontal alignment options to determine how the object will be aligned in the document window.

6. Click OK.

7. If you selected a Wrapping style option other than In line with text in step 4, the image is moved from the document layer to the drawing layer. Drag it into position in the document and text wraps around it (**Figure 47**).

Figures 45a, 45b, and 45c The last command on the Format menu changes depending on what kind of object is selected in the document window. (These figures show the short, personalized Format menu.)

Figure 46 The Layout tab of the Format dialog enables you to set Word wrap options for a selected graphic object or, in this case, a text box.

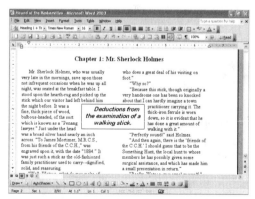

Figure 47 Once an object is set for text wrapping, text flows around it.

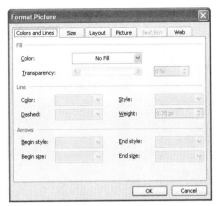

Figure 48 The Colors and Lines tab of the Format Picture dialog.

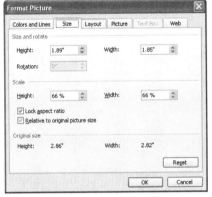

Figure 49 The Size tab of the Format Picture dialog.

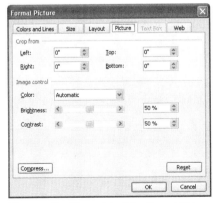

Figure 50 The Picture tab of the Format Picture dialog.

To set advanced formatting options

1. Click the object you want to format to select it.

2. Choose the last command under the Format menu. As shown in **Figures 45a**, **45b**, and **45c**, this command's name changes depending on what is selected.

3. In the Format dialog that appears, click the tab for the type of formatting option you want to set:

   ▲ **Colors and Lines (Figure 48)** enables you to set options for the object's fill and border color and transparency.

   ▲ **Size (Figure 49)** enables you to set size, rotation, and scaling options for the object.

   ▲ **Layout (Figure 46)** enables you to set wrapping style and alignment options for the object.

   ▲ **Picture (Figure 50)** enables you to set cropping and image control options for the object.

   ▲ **Text Box (Figure 39)** enables you to set internal margin and word wrap options for a text box.

   ▲ **Web** enables you to set alternative text to appear in place of the object while it is loading into a Web browser. This option is for use with documents that are saved as Web pages. I tell you about creating Web pages with Word in **Chapter 17**.

4. Set options in the tab as desired.

5. Repeat steps 3 and 4.

6. When you are finished setting formatting options, click OK to save your settings. The object changes accordingly.

Continued on next page...

USING ADVANCED FORMATTING OPTIONS

Continued from previous page.

✔ Tips

- The options that are available in each tab of the Format dialog vary, depending on the object you are formatting.

- A complete discussion of all formatting options is far beyond the scope of this book. Experiment with these options on your own. Remember, the Undo command is always available to get you out of trouble if formatting goes wrong.

To remove a graphic object

1. Click the object once to select it.

2. Press (Backspace). The object disappears.

Reference Features

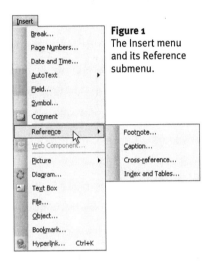

Figure 1
The Insert menu and its Reference submenu.

Reference Features

Microsoft Word includes several features you can use to insert references within a document. These commands can be found on the Insert menu and its Reference submenu (**Figure 1**):

◆ **Bookmark** enables you to mark a document location for use with the Go To command or other reference features.

◆ **Footnote** inserts a footnote or endnote marker and enables you to enter corresponding reference text.

◆ **Caption** inserts a labeled caption above or below a table, graphic object, or equation.

◆ **Cross-reference** inserts a cross-reference to another part of the document.

◆ **Index and Tables** enables you to create an index or table of contents.

Word's Reference features all have one thing in common: they work with Word fields, which I discuss in **Chapter 9**, to create dynamic document content. But instead of requiring you to insert the correct field, the command you use inserts it for you, making the process easier and keeping Word fields out of sight.

This chapter explains how to use each of these reference features in your Word documents.

Bookmarks

A bookmark is an item or location in a document that you identify with a name. You can then reference it by name to jump to the location quickly, create cross-references, and perform other tasks.

For example, suppose you're writing a book about Word and there's a chapter with a section covering captions. You can select all of the text in that section and mark it with a bookmark named "Captions." You can then use the Go To dialog to quickly display the Captions section. You can also use the bookmark when you create an index, as discussed later in this chapter, to reference all of the pages covering the captions topic.

This part of the chapter explains how to create, modify, and delete bookmarks in Word documents.

To create a bookmark

1. Select the text or item you want to name with a bookmark.

   or

   Position the insertion point where you want to insert the bookmark (**Figure 2**).

2. Choose Insert > Bookmark (**Figure 1**) to display the Bookmark dialog (**Figure 3**).

3. Enter a name for the Bookmark in the Bookmark name box.

4. Click Add. The bookmark is created and the dialog disappears.

✔ Tips

- Bookmark names cannot begin with a number or contain nonalphanumeric characters (including spaces) except an underscore character (_). A bookmark name that begins with an underscore character is hidden.

"How can you say that, sir?"

"You have presented an inch or two of it to my examination talking. It would be a poor expert who could not give the date of so. You may possibly have read my little monograph upon the

"The exact date is 1742." Dr. Mortimer drew it from his bre was committed to my care by Sir Charles Baskerville, whose su months ago created so much excitement in Devonshire. I may s as well as his medical attendant. He was a strong-minded man,

Figure 2 Position the insertion point where you want to insert the bookmark. In this example, the bookmark will be inserted at the beginning of a paragraph.

Figure 3 The Bookmark dialog with a bookmark name entered but not yet saved.

- Normally, bookmarks are not visible in a document. I explain how to display them later in this section.

Figure 4 The Bookmark dialog with several bookmarks created.

Figure 5 The Go To tab of the Find and Replace dialog.

Figure 6 All bookmark names appear on the Enter bookmark name drop-down list in the Go To tab of the Find and Replace dialog.

To go to a bookmark

1. Choose Insert > Bookmark (**Figure** 1).

2. In the Bookmark dialog that appears (**Figure** 4), select the name of the bookmark you want to go to.

3. Click Go To. One of two things happens:

   ▲ If the bookmark was for a selection, that text or item is selected.

   ▲ If the bookmark was for a location, the insertion point moves to that location.

or

1. Choose Edit > Go To or press ⌃⌘G to display the Go To tab of the Find and Replace dialog (**Figure** 5).

2. Select Bookmark in the scrolling list.

3. Choose the bookmark you want to go to from the Enter bookmark name drop-down list (**Figure** 6).

4. Click Go To.

✔ Tips

■ If your document contains many bookmarks, select a Sort by option in the Bookmark dialog (**Figure** 4) to sort them by name or location.

■ No matter which method you use to go to a bookmark, the dialog remains on screen when you're finished so you can go to another bookmark if desired.

GOING TO BOOKMARKS

To delete a bookmark

1. Choose Insert > Bookmark (**Figure 1**).

2. In the Bookmark dialog that appears (**Figure 4**), select the name of the bookmark you want to delete.

3. Click Delete. The bookmark is removed from the list.

✔ Tip

■ Deleting a bookmark does not delete the text or item that the bookmark refers to.

To display bookmarks

1. Choose Tools > Options to display the Options dialog.

2. Click the View tab to display its options (**Figure 7**).

3. Turn on the Bookmarks check box.

4. Click OK.

   Bookmarks appear in the document as either brackets around a selection (**Figure 8**) or as an I-beam in a location (**Figure 9**).

✔ Tip

■ Although bookmarks may appear on screen, they don't print.

Figure 7 The View tab of the Options dialog.

Figure 8 Brackets appear around a bookmark for a selection.

Figure 9 An I-beam appears as a bookmark for a location.

DELETING & DISPLAYING BOOKMARKS

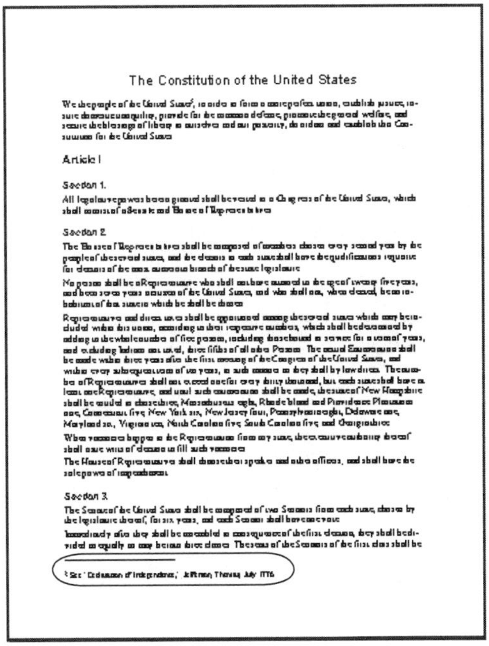
The Constitution of the United States

Article I

Section 1.

Section 2.

Section 3.

Figure 10 A page with a footnote. Word automatically inserts the footnote separator line, too.

Footnotes & Endnotes

Footnotes and endnotes are annotations for specific document text. You insert a marker—usually a number or symbol—right after the text, tell Word where you want the note to go, and enter the note. When you view the document in Print Layout view or Print Preview, or print the document, the note appears where you specified.

The difference between a footnote and an endnote is its position in the document:

- **Footnotes** appear either after the last line of text on the page on which the annotated text appears or at the bottom of the page on which the annotated text appears (**Figure 10**).
- **Endnotes** appear either at the end of the section in which the annotated text appears or at the end of the document.

✔ Tips

- Footnotes and endnotes are commonly used to show the source of a piece of information or provide additional information that may not be of interest to every reader.
- Multiple-section documents are covered in **Chapter 5**.
- Word automatically renumbers footnotes or endnotes when necessary when you insert or delete a note.
- If you're old enough to remember preparing high school or college term papers on a typewriter, you'll recognize this feature as another example of how easy kids have it today. (Sheesh! I sound like my mother!)

To insert a footnote or endnote

1. Position the insertion point immediately after the text that you want to annotate (**Figure 11**).

2. Choose Insert > Reference > Footnote (**Figure 1**) to display the Footnote and Endnote dialog (**Figure 12**).

3. In the Location part of the dialog, select the Location option for the type of note you want to insert.

4. Use the drop-down list beside the option you selected (**Figures 13a** and **13b**) to specify where the note should appear.

5. Choose an option from the Number format drop-down list (**Figure 14**).

   or

   Enter a character for the mark in the Custom mark box.

6. Choose an option from the Numbering drop-down list (**Figure 15**).

7. Click OK. Word inserts a marker at the insertion point, then one of two things happens:

   ▲ If you are in Normal or Online Layout view, the window splits to display a footnote or endnote pane with the insertion point blinking beside the marker (**Figure 16**).

   ▲ If you are in Print Layout view, the view shifts to the location of the footnote or endnote where a separator line is inserted. The insertion point blinks beside the marker (**Figure 17**).

8. Enter the footnote or endnote text (**Figure 18**).

The Constitution

We the people of the United States, in order insure domestic tranquility, provide for the c and secure the blessings of liberty to ourselv Constitution for the United States.

Figure 11 Position the insertion point immediately after the text that you want to annotate.

Figure 12 The Footnote and Endnote dialog.

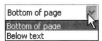 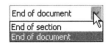

Figures 13a & 13b The Location drop-down lists for footnotes (left) and endnotes (right).

Figure 14 The Number format drop-down list.

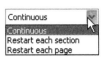

Figure 15 The Numbering drop-down list in the Footnote and Endnote dialog.

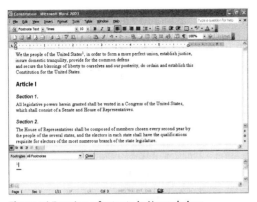

Figure 16 Entering a footnote in Normal view.

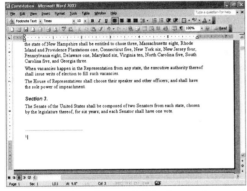

Figure 17 Entering a footnote in Print Layout view.

[1] See "Declaration of Independence," Jefferson, Thomas, July 1776|

Figure 18 Enter footnote text right after the marker.

Figure 19 You can use the Symbol window to select a symbol (instead of a number) to use as a marker.

✔ Tips

■ In step 5, you can click the Symbol button to display the Symbol window (**Figure 19**), click a symbol to select it, and click OK to insert it in the Custom mark box. I explain how to use the Symbol dialog in **Chapter 9**.

■ In Normal view, to close the footnote pane, click the Close button at the top of the pane.

■ You can also use the Footnote and Endnote dialog (**Figure 12**) to change the options for existing footnotes and endnotes in the document. Follow the instructions on the previous page to open the dialog and set options. Click the Apply button to apply your settings and click the close button to close the dialog without inserting a note.

To convert notes

1. Choose Insert > Reference > Footnote (**Figure** 1) to display the Footnote and Endnote dialog (**Figure 12**).

2. Click the Convert button to display the Convert Notes dialog (**Figure 20**).

3. Select the option for the type of conversion that you want to do.

4. Click OK.

5. Click the close button to dismiss the Footnote and Endnote dialog.

✔ Tip

■ The options available in the Convert Notes dialog (**Figure 20**) vary depending on the type(s) of notes in the document.

To delete a note

1. In the document window (not the note area or pane), select the note marker (**Figure 21**).

2. Press (Backspace). The note marker and corresponding note are removed from the document. If the note was numbered using the AutoNumber option, all notes after it are properly renumbered.

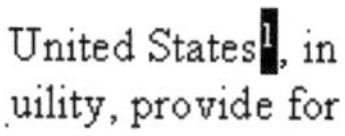

✔ Tip

■ If you have trouble selecting the tiny note marker in the document, use the Zoom drop-down list on the Standard toolbar (**Figure 22**) to increase the window's magnification so you can see it better. Zooming a window's view is covered in **Chapter 1**.

Figure 20
The Convert Notes dialog for a document that contains both footnotes and endnotes.

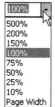

United States, in
uility, provide for

Figure 21 To delete a footnote or endnote, begin by selecting the note marker.

Figure 22
You can use the Zoom drop-down list on the Standard toolbar to increase the window's magnification so you can see the tiny note markers.

CONVERTING & DELETING NOTES

Date	Time	Event Name
3/1/03	9:00 AM	Museum Tour
3/8/03	10:30 AM	Horseback Ride
3/15/03	2:00 PM	Pot Luck Barbeque
3/22/03	10:00 AM	Hummer Tour
3/29/03	8:00 AM	Poker Run

Table 1: Schedule of Events for March 2003

Label   Text
    Number

Figure 23 A Word table with a caption attached.

Captions

A caption is a numbered label that you can attach to a table, graphic, equation, or other item. It consists of three parts (**Figure 23**):

◆ **Caption label** is text that identifies the type of item. Word comes preconfigured with three caption labels—Equation, Figure, and Table—but you can add others.

◆ **Caption number** is the number assigned to the caption. This number is dynamic and can change when other labels are inserted or deleted before it.

◆ **Caption text** is text that you type for the caption. This is optional—a caption can consist of just the label and number.

There are two ways to add captions:

◆ Manually add captions to items in your document using the Caption command under the Insert menu.

◆ Set up Word to automatically insert captions when you insert a table, graphic, or equation in your document.

This part of the chapter explains how to manually insert, modify, and delete captions, as well as how to set up Word to automatically insert them for you.

✔ Tips

■ Although this book wasn't written in Word, each of its figure captions follows the standard format used by Word. (Unfortunately, I had to number—and renumber—them manually.)

■ Note that Word maintains separate numbering for each caption label. For example, if your document contains captions using the Figure and Table labels, Word numbers each type of caption starting with 1 (or A or i).

■ Captions are formatted using the Caption style. You can change the formatting of all captions in a document by modifying the Caption style.

To insert a caption

1. Select the item for which you want to insert a caption (**Figure 24**).

   or

   Position the insertion point where you want the caption to appear.

2. Choose Insert > Reference > Caption (**Figure 1**) to display the Caption dialog (**Figure 25**).

3. Set basic options for the caption:

   ▲ **Label** is the caption label. The pre-defined choices are Equation, Figure, or Table.

   ▲ **Position** is the position of the caption in relation to the selected item: above it or below it.

4. To change numbering options for the caption, click the Numbering button. The Caption Numbering dialog (**Figure 26**) appears. Set options and click OK:

   ▲ **Format** is the number format. You can choose among Arabic, alphabetical, and Roman numeral styles (**Figure 27**).

   ▲ **Include chapter number** automatically inserts the chapter number as part of the caption number. If you enable this option, you must choose a heading level from the "Chapter starts with style" drop-down list and a separator from the Use separator drop-down list (**Figure 28**).

5. If desired, enter caption text after the caption label and number that appears in the Caption box.

6. Click OK. The caption is inserted to your specifications (**Figure 23**).

Date	Time	Event Name
3/1/03	9:00 AM	Museum Tour
3/8/03	10:30 AM	Horseback Ride
3/15/03	2:00 PM	Pot Luck Barbeque
3/22/03	10:00 AM	Hummer Tour
3/29/03	8:00 AM	Poker Run

Figure 24 Select the item you want to insert the caption for.

Figure 25 Use the Caption dialog to set options for the captions you insert.

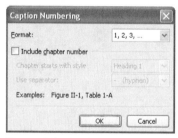

Figure 26 The Caption Numbering dialog.

Figure 27
The Format drop-down list lets you choose from among number formats.

Figure 28
The Use separator drop-down list.

Figure 29 The New label dialog.

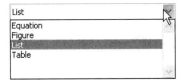

Figure 30 The new label is added to the Label drop-down list.

Figure 31 When a custom label is selected from the Label pop-up menu, the Delete Label button can be clicked.

✔ Tips

- In step 3, to create a new label, click the New Label button (**Figure 25**), enter the desired label in the New Label dialog that appears (**Figure 29**), and click OK. The new label appears in the Label pop-up menu (**Figure 30**).

- You can delete a custom label. In the Caption dialog, select the label you want to delete from the Label pop-up menu (**Figure 31**). Click Delete Label. The label is removed from the list. If the deleted label is used in a document caption, it is not deleted where it appears in the document.

- In step 3, if you choose Above selected item from the Position pop-up menu, Word automatically formats the caption so that it stays with the next paragraph. This ensures that the caption and the item to which it applies are always on the same page.

- In step 4 (**Figure 26**), you can only include the chapter number in the caption number if the chapter name and number is formatted with a heading style and you have set up that heading style with automatic numbering.

- If you want a colon or other punctuation to appear between the caption number and the caption text as shown in **Figure 23**, you must type that punctuation as part of the caption text in step 5.

To modify a caption

1. Select the caption you want to modify (**Figure 32**).

2. Choose Insert > Reference > Caption (**Figure 1**). The Caption dialog appears with the caption settings displayed (**Figure 33**).

3. Change settings as discussed in the section titled "To insert a caption."

4. Click OK. The caption changes accordingly.

✔ Tip

■ You must use this method to change the caption label or number format. You can change the caption text, however, using standard editing techniques right in the document window.

To delete a caption

1. Select the caption you want to delete (**Figure 32**).

2. Press [Backspace]. The caption disappears.

✔ Tip

■ When you delete a caption, subsequent caption numbers may not automatically update. I explain how to update captions and cross-references near the end of this chapter.

Date	Time	Event Name
3/1/03	9:00 AM	Museum Tour
3/8/03	10:30 AM	Horseback Ride
3/15/03	2:00 PM	Pot Luck Barbeque
3/22/03	10:00 AM	Hummer Tour
3/29/03	8:00 AM	Poker Run
Table 1: Schedule of Events for March 2003		

Figure 32 When you select an entire caption, it turns black.

Figure 33 The Caption dialog for the caption selected in **Figure 32**.

Figure 34 The AutoCaption dialog. In this illustration, the automatic caption feature is enabled for several types of items.

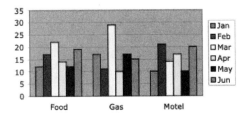

Figure 1

Figure 35 An automatically inserted caption beneath an Excel chart inserted in a Word document.

To automatically insert captions

1. Choose Insert > Reference > Caption (**Figure 1**) to display the Caption dialog (**Figure 25**).

2. Click the AutoCaption button to display the AutoCaption dialog (**Figure 34**).

3. Turn on the check box beside a type of item you want to automatically insert captions for.

4. With the item you enabled in step 3 selected, set options in the bottom half of the window:

   ▲ **Use label** enables you to choose a caption label for that type of item.

   ▲ **Position** enables you to specify whether the caption should appear above or below the item.

   ▲ **New Label** displays the New Label dialog (**Figure 29**), which you can use to create a new label. I explain how to use this dialog earlier in this section.

   ▲ **Numbering** displays the Caption Numbering dialog (**Figure 26**), which you can use to set numbering options. I explain how to use this dialog earlier in this section.

5. Repeat steps 3 and 4 for each type of item you want to automatically insert captions for.

6. Click OK. From that point forward, each time you use Insert menu commands to insert a type of item for which you enabled automatic captions, a caption appears for that item (**Figure 35**).

AUTOMATICALLY INSERTING CAPTIONS

Continued on next page...

235

Continued from previous page.

✔ Tips

■ To add caption text to an automatically inserted caption, position the insertion point at the end of the caption in the document window and type the text you want to appear (**Figure 36**).

■ To disable the automatic caption feature for a type of item, follow steps 1 and 2 to display the AutoCaption dialog (**Figure 34**), turn off the check box beside the item, and click OK. The automatic caption feature for that item is disabled.

■ Changes you make in the AutoCaption dialog are saved in the document template, not the document itself. I tell you more about templates in **Chapter 2**.

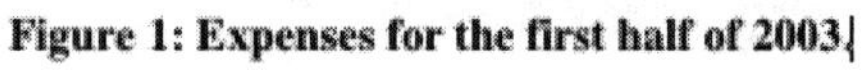

Figure 1: Expenses for the first half of 2003.

Figure 36 You can add caption text to an automatically inserted caption by simply typing it in.

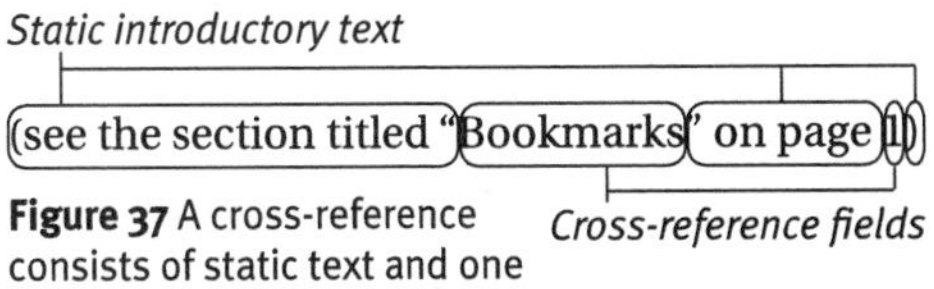

Static introductory text

(see the section titled "Bookmarks" on page 1)

Figure 37 A cross-reference consists of static text and one or more cross-reference fields.

Cross-reference fields

Cross-References

A cross-reference is a reference to an item that appears in another location in a document. "See Table 2 in Chapter 3" and "See the section titled 'Bookmarks' on page 5" are two examples of cross-references. Cross-references are commonly used in technical documents, like computer how-to books. (In fact, if Adobe InDesign had a cross-reference feature like Word's, this book would have a lot more cross-references, complete with page numbers.)

Word's cross-reference feature is extremely powerful. It enables you to create cross-references to headings, footnotes, bookmarks, captions, numbered paragraphs, and other items in your Word documents. If an item moves or is modified, the cross-reference can be easily updated for the change. And if you're creating a document that will be read on screen, you can take advantage of the hyperlink feature to make cross-references clickable links to the referenced item.

Cross-references are made up of two components (**Figure 37**):

◆ **Static introductory text** is text you type as part of the cross-reference. This text does not change.

◆ **Cross-reference field** is text inserted by the cross-reference feature as a Word field. This text can change if the information it refers to changes.

This part of the chapter explains how to insert and delete cross-references in your Word documents.

To insert a cross-reference

1. Position the insertion point where you want the cross-reference to appear (**Figure 38**).

2. Enter the first part of the static text of the cross-reference (**Figure 39**).

3. Choose Insert > Reference > Cross-reference (**Figure 1**) to display the Cross-reference dialog (**Figure 40**).

4. Choose a type of reference from the Reference type drop-down list (**Figure 41**).

5. Choose an option from the Insert reference to drop-down list. The options that appear vary based on what you chose in step 4. **Figure 42** shows the options for a Heading reference.

6. To insert the reference as a clickable hyperlink, turn on the Insert as hyperlink check box.

7. To instruct Word to include the word "above" or "below" as part of the reference, turn on the Include above/below check box. (This option is only available for some reference types.)

8. Select the item you want to refer to in the scrolling list. For example, to duplicate the reference that appears in **Figure 37**, I'd select "Bookmarks."

9. Click Insert. The reference is inserted, but the Cross-reference dialog remains active (**Figure 43**).

10. If necessary, click in the document window and position the insertion point where additional static text should appear. Enter the additional text (**Figure 44**).

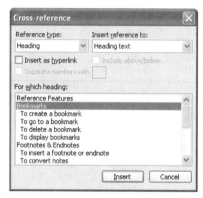

Reference Features

Microsoft Word includes several features you can use to insert references within a document. These commands can be found on the Insert menu and its Reference submenu (Figure 1):

• Bookmark enables you to mark a document location for use with the Go To command or other reference features.

Figure 38 Position the insertion point where you want the cross-reference to begin.

• Bookmark (see the section titled) enables you to mark a document location for use with the Go To command or other reference features.

Figure 39 Enter the first part of the static text.

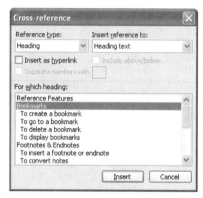

Figure 40 The Cross-reference dialog.

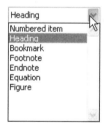

Figure 41 The Reference type drop-down list.

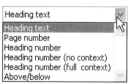

Figure 42 The Insert reference to drop-down list with Heading chosen from the Reference type drop-down list.

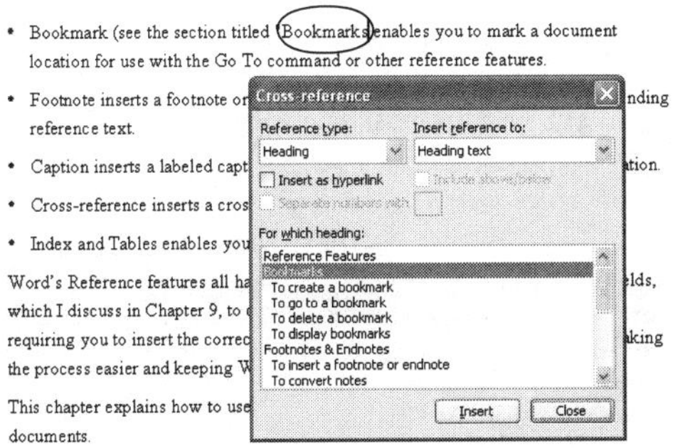
• Bookmark (see the section titled Bookmarks) enables you to mark a document location for use with the Go To command or other reference features.
• Footnote inserts a footnote or ... nding reference text.
• Caption inserts a labeled capt... tion.
• Cross-reference inserts a cros...
• Index and Tables enables you...
Word's Reference features all ha... lds, which I discuss in Chapter 9, to ... requiring you to insert the correc... king the process easier and keeping W...
This chapter explains how to use... documents.
Cross-reference
Reference type:
Heading
Insert reference to:
Heading text
Insert as hyperlink
Include above/below
Separate numbers with
For which heading:
Reference Features
Bookmarks
To create a bookmark
To go to a bookmark
To delete a bookmark
To display bookmarks
Footnotes & Endnotes
To insert a footnote or endnote
To convert notes
Insert
Close

Figure 43 A cross-reference inserted into a document.

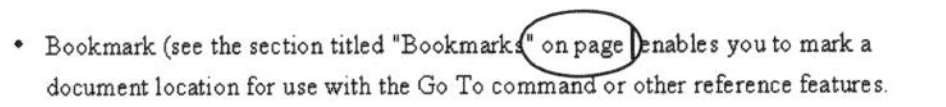
• Bookmark (see the section titled "Bookmarks" on page) enables you to mark a document location for use with the Go To command or other reference features.

Figure 44 Additional static text inserted after the first cross-reference.

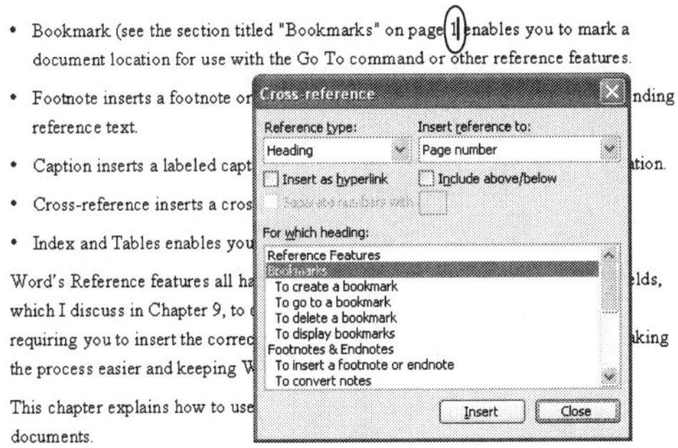
• Bookmark (see the section titled "Bookmarks" on page 1) enables you to mark a document location for use with the Go To command or other reference features.
• Footnote inserts a footnote or ... nding reference text.
• Caption inserts a labeled capt... tion.
• Cross-reference inserts a cros...
• Index and Tables enables you...
Word's Reference features all ha... lds, which I discuss in Chapter 9, to ... requiring you to insert the correc... king the process easier and keeping W...
This chapter explains how to use... documents.
Cross-reference
Reference type:
Heading
Insert reference to:
Page number
Insert as hyperlink
Include above/below
Separate numbers with
For which heading:
Reference Features
Bookmarks
To create a bookmark
To go to a bookmark
To delete a bookmark
To display bookmarks
Footnotes & Endnotes
To insert a footnote or endnote
To convert notes
Insert
Close

Figure 45 Another cross-reference inserted into a document. In this case, the reference is the page number for a specific heading.

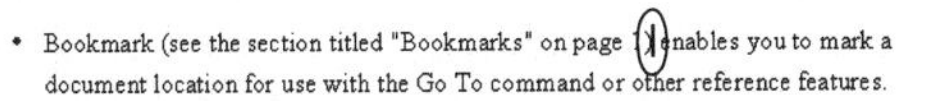
• Bookmark (see the section titled "Bookmarks" on page 1) enables you to mark a document location for use with the Go To command or other reference features.

Figure 46 The final bit of static text—a close parenthesis character—inserted into the document. The cross-reference shown in **Figure 37** is now complete.

11. To insert another cross-reference, click the Cross-reference dialog to make it active, then follow steps 4 through 9 to insert it (**Figure 45**).
12. If necessary, repeat steps 10 and 11 for additional static text (**Figure 46**) and/or cross-references.
13. When you're finished with the Cross-reference dialog, click its close button to dismiss it.

✔ Tips

- It is impossible to cover all options available in the Cross-reference dialog, since they vary based on the reference type and the contents of a document. The instructions here provide enough information to get you started exploring the options on your own. Remember, if you insert the wrong cross-reference, you can always delete it and try again.
- Cross-references can be formatted like any other document text.

To delete a cross-reference

1. In the document window, select the cross-reference you want to delete. It becomes highlighted in black (**Figure 47**).

2. Press (Backspace). The cross-reference disappears, like any other text.

To change what a cross-reference refers to

1. Select the cross-reference you want to modify. (Do not select any introductory text.) The cross-reference is highlighted in black (**Figure 47**).

2. Choose Insert > Reference> Cross-reference (**Figure 1**) to display the Cross-reference dialog (**Figure 48**).

3. Choose options from the Reference type (**Figure 41**) and Insert reference to (**Figure 41**) drop-down lists to set revised cross-reference options (**Figure 35**).

4. Click Insert. The new cross-reference replaces the one that was selected (**Figure 49**).

• Bookmark (see the section titled "Bookmarks" on page 1) enables you to mark a document location for use with the Go To command or other reference features.

Figure 47 Select the cross-reference you want to delete or modify.

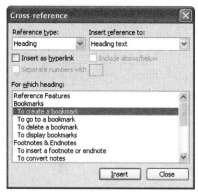

Figure 48 The Cross-reference dialog also enables you to change a selected cross-reference.

• Bookmark (see the section titled "To create a bookmark" on page 1) enables you to mark a document location for use with the Go To command or other reference features.

Figure 49 The cross-reference you selected is replaced with the new one.

Indexes

An index is an alphabetical list of topics with page references for the topic's location within a document. Word indexes can include two levels of index entries: main entries and subentries. Indexes may also include *See* cross-references to other topics and special formatting of page numbers.

Creating an index in Word is a two-step process:

1. **Mark index entries.** This tells Word what text should be included in the index.

2. **Generate the index.** This gathers together all index entries, alphabetizes them, and displays them with page numbers in index format.

This part of the chapter explains, in detail, how to create an index in a Word document.

✔ Tips

- The indexing feature can use bookmarks, which I discuss earlier in this chapter, to include ranges of pages in an index entry. If you plan on indexing topic discussions that span multiple pages, it's a good idea to bookmark those topics *before* marking index entries.

- Indexes, like other reference features, are created with Word fields. If pagination or document content changes after an index has been generated, you'll need to update the index before finalizing the document. I explain how to update indexes at the end of this chapter.

To manually mark an index entry

1. In the document window, select the text you want to index (**Figure 50**).

2. Choose Insert > Reference > Index and Tables (**Figure 1**) to display the Index and Tables dialog.

3. If necessary, click the Index tab to display its options (**Figure 51**).

4. Click the Mark Entry button to display the Mark Index Entry dialog (**Figure 52**).

5. In the Main entry box, enter the text you want to appear in the index. By default, the selected text appears there, but you can enter something else if desired.

6. If the entry should be a subentry under the main entry, in the Subentry box enter the text you want to appear as a subentry. **Figure 53** shows an example for the text selected in **Figure 50**.

7. Select one of the Options options:

   ▲ **Cross-reference** enables you to create a textual cross-reference to another index entry. Since a cross-reference normally appears after the word *See*, that word is entered in italics by default. Enter the cross-reference text in the box after *See*.

   ▲ **Current page** sets the index entry's page reference to the page on which the selected text appears. This is the most commonly used option.

   ▲ **Page range** enables you to choose a bookmark to correspond to the range of pages you want to index. Use the pop-up menu to select the bookmark.

8. To set special formatting for the index entry's page number, turn on one or both of the Page number format check boxes.

My friends Janet and Steve were in Colorado for six weeks, doing art shows in the western part of the state. I tracked them down on their cell phone and found out where they were. Then I started to plan for a trip that would take me from Wickenburg, AZ to Gypsum, CO, high on the west side of the Rockies.

Figure 50 Select the text you want to create an index entry for.

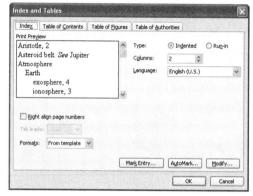

Figure 51 The Index tab of the Index and Tables dialog.

Figure 52 The Mark Index Entry dialog.

Figure 53 An example of an index entry with a main entry and subentry. The subentry text will appear indented beneath the main entry text in the index.

MANUALLY MARKING INDEX ENTRIES

My·friends·Janet·and·Steve·were·in·Colorado·for·six·weeks,·doing·art·shows·in·the· western·part·of·the·state.·I·tracked·them·down·on·their·cell·phone·and·found·out·where· they·were.·Then·I·started·to·plan·for·a·trip·that·would·take·me·from·Wickenburg{·XE· "Arizona:Wickenburg"·}·,·AZ·to·Gypsum,·CO,·high·on·the·west·side·of·the·Rockies.¶

Figure 54 If formatting marks are displayed, the field codes for each index entry appear after the text it was inserted for.

Figure 55 The View options of the Options dialog. When Formatting marks are set as shown here, all formatting marks except hidden text will appear. The field codes for index entries do not appear.

9. Click Mark. The index entry is marked with an XE field. If formatting marks are displayed, you can see the field codes for the entry (**Figure 54**), which are formatted as hidden text. The Mark Index Entry dialog remains on screen.

10. To index another entry, follow step 1, then click the Mark Index Entry dialog to activate it and follow steps 5 through 9.

11. Repeat step 10 for every index entry you want to mark.

12. When you are finished marking index entries, click the Mark Index Entry dialog's Close button.

✔ Tips

- A quicker way to open the Mark Index Entry dialog (**Figure 3**) is to press [Alt][Shift][X]. By doing this, you can skip steps 2 through 4.

- In step 9, if you click Mark All, Word automatically searches through the document and marks all occurrences of the selected word as an index entry using the options you set in the Mark Index Entry dialog. Although this is a quick way to consistently mark text for indexing, it may create far more index entries for selected text than you need. Use this option with care!

- If you find the index entry fields distracting (I do!), you can hide them by clicking the Show/Hide ¶ button ¶ on the Standard toolbar. Or, to show all formatting marks except hidden characters, set options in the Formatting marks area of the Option dialog's View options (**Figure 55**).

- I cover bookmarks in detail earlier in this chapter.

MANUALLY MARKING INDEX ENTRIES

To automatically mark index entries

1. Choose File > New Blank Document, press ⌃N, or click the New Blank Document button 🗋 on the Standard toolbar to create a blank Word document.

2. Choose Table > Insert > Table (**Figure 56**) to display the Insert Table dialog (**Figure 57**).

3. Enter 2 in the Number of columns box and 1 in the Number of rows box.

4. Click OK. A two-by-one table appears in the document window (**Figure 58**).

5. In the left cell, enter a word that appears in your document that you want to be automatically marked as an index entry.

6. Press Tab.

7. In the right cell, enter the text you want to appear in the index:

   ▲ If you want just a main entry to appear, enter just the main entry text.

   ▲ If you want a main entry and subentry to appear, enter the main entry followed by a colon (:) and then the subentry.

Figure 59 shows what a completed entry might look like.

8. To add another entry, press Tab to add another row to the table. Then follow steps 5 through 7 to add entry information.

9. Repeat step 8 for each entry you want to add. When you're finished, you should have a table of indexable words with corresponding index entry text (**Figure 60**).

10. Choose File > Save, press ⌃S, or click the Save button 🖫 on the Standard toolbar. Then use the Save dialog that appears to save the document.

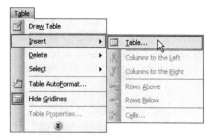

Figure 56 Choose Table from the Table menu's Insert submenu.

Figure 57 Use the Insert Table dialog to insert a cell table in the document window.

Figure 58 A table in a Word document.

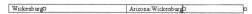

Figure 59 A completed concordance file entry.

Wickenburg□	Arizona:Wickenburg□
Page□	Arizona:Page□
Moab□	Utah:Moab□
Grand-Canyon□	Arizona:Grand-Canyon□
Monument-Valley□	Monument-Valley□

Figure 60 Each entry in a concordance file appears in its own row.

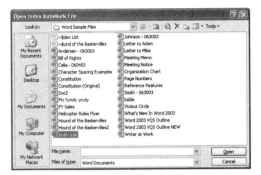

Figure 61 The Open Index AutoMark File dialog.

My·friends·Janet·and·Steve·were·in·Colorado·for·six·weeks,·doing·art·shows·in·the· western·part·of·the·state.·I·tracked·them·down·on·their·cell·phone·and·found·out·where· they·were.·Then·I·started·to·plan·for·a·trip·that·would·take·me·from·Wickenburg[··· ·Arizona.·Wickenburg··],·AZ·to·Gypsum,·CO,·high·on·the·west·side·of·the·Rockies.¶

Figure 62 To select an index entry, select the { and } characters and all text between them.

11. Open or switch to the document you want to index.

12. Choose Insert > Reference > Index and Tables (**Figure 1**) to display the Index and Tables dialog.

13. If necessary, click the Index tab to display its options (**Figure 51**).

14. Click the AutoMark button to display the Open Index AutoMark File dialog (**Figure 61**).

15. Locate and select the file you created in step 10. Then click Open.

Word searches the document for the words you entered in the left column and inserts index entries from the right column.

✔ Tips

- The document you create with steps 1 through 10 is referred to in Word documentation as a *concordance file* or an *Index AutoMark* file.

- Use this feature with care! If you include a word in the left column that has multiple meanings—for example, *Page* in **Figure 60**—all occurences will be indexed the same way. Is this really what you want?

To delete an index entry

1. Select the entire index entry, including the { and } characters (**Figure 62**).

2. Press Backspace. The entry disappears and will not be included in the index.

To generate an index

1. Position the insertion point where you want the index to appear. Normally, this will be at the end of the document, but it can be anywhere you like.

2. Choose Insert > Reference> Index and Tables (**Figure 1**) to display the Index and Tables dialog.

3. If necessary, click the Index tab to display its options (**Figure 51**).

4. Select one of the Type options:

   ▲ **Indented** indents each subentry beneath the main entry. This is the type of index used in this book.

   ▲ **Run-in** displays all subentries with the main entry, in the same paragraph.

5. Enter the number of columns the index should occupy on each page in the Columns box.

6. If necessary, choose a different language from the Language drop-down list. This modifies the entry sort order according to the rules of that language.

7. Set other formatting options as desired:

   ▲ **Right align page numbers** shifts page numbers to the right side of the column. This option is only available if you chose Indented in step 4.

   ▲ **Tab leader** enables you to choose the characters that appear between the index text and page number reference. This option is only available if you turned on the Right align page numbers check box.

   ▲ **Formats** enables you to choose one of several predefined index formats.

8. Click OK. Word generates the index and displays it at the insertion point (**Figure 63**).

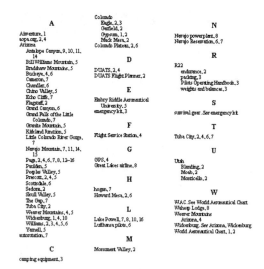

Figure 63 A completed index in Print Preview. This index uses the Indented type, Classic format, and 3 columns.

GENERATING INDEXES

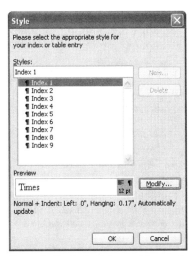

Figure 64 The Style dialog enables you to modify style definitions for Index styles.

`{ INDEX \h "A" \c "2" \z "1033" }`

Figure 65 The index field codes for the Index in **Figure 63**.

✔ Tips

- You can see the effect of changes you make in steps 4 through 7 in the Print Preview area of the Index and Tables dialog (**Figure 51**).

- You can further define the appearance of an index by clicking the Modify button in the Index tab of the Index and Tables dialog (**Figure 51**) when From Template is chosen from the Formats drop-down list. This displays the Style dialog (**Figure 64**), which you can use to modify style definitions for Index styles. I tell you more about styles in **Chapter 4**.

- If you don't like the way an index looks, you can delete it and start over. Just select the entire index and press Backspace, then follow the steps on the previous page to generate a new index.

- If your index looks more like **Figure 65** than **Figure 63**, View preferences are set to display field codes. To display the index instead, turn off the Field codes option in the Option dialog's View options (**Figure 55**).

- As illustrated in **Figure 65**, an index is created with an index (INDEX) field.

GENERATING INDEXES

Table of Contents

A table of contents lists, in order of appearance, the major headings within a document. The table of contents for this book, for example, lists the chapters and first level headings with their corresponding page numbers. Although not as detailed as an index, a table of contents can help readers find specific content within a lengthy document.

Creating a table of contents for a Word document is a two-step process:

1. **Format document headings for a table of contents.** This tells Word what text should be included in the table of contents. The easiest way to do this is using Word's built-in heading styles, but you can use any style you want.

2. **Generate the table of contents.** This gathers together all table of contents entries (or headings) and displays them with page numbers in table of contents format.

This part of the chapter explains how to create a table of contents in a Word document.

✔ Tips

- If your document utilizes Word's built-in heading styles, you can view an onscreen table of contents by using Word's document map feature. Choose View > Document Map to display a table of contents with clickable links in a pane on the left side of the window (**Figure 66**). I discuss Word's document map feature in **Chapter 1**.

- A table of contents is created with Word fields. If pagination or document content changes after a table of contents has been generated, you'll need to update the table of contents before finalizing the document. I explain how to update tables at the end of this chapter.

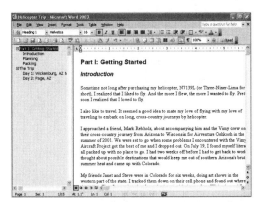

Figure 66 The document map feature displays a table of contents using Word headings in a pane on the left side of the document window.

Part I: Getting Started
Introduction

Sometime not long after purchasing my helicopter, N7139L (or Three-Niner-Lima for short), I realized that I liked to fly. And the more I flew, the more I wanted to fly. Pretty soon I realized that I loved to fly.

Figure 67 Position the insertion point anywhere in the heading's paragraph.

Figure 68 Choose a heading style from the Formatting toolbar's Style drop-down list.

Part I: Getting Started
Introduction

Sometime not long after purchasing my helicopter, N7139L (or Three-Niner-Lima for short), I realized that I liked to fly. And the more I flew, the more I wanted to fly. Pretty soon I realized that I loved to fly.

Figure 69 The heading is formatted with the heading style you choose.

To format headings for a table of contents

1. Make sure the heading is in its own paragraph. To do this, position the insertion point at the end of the heading and press Return.

2. Position the insertion point anywhere in the heading's paragraph (**Figure 67**).

3. Choose a heading style from the Style drop-down list on the Formatting toolbar (**Figure 68**). The heading is formatted with the style you applied (**Figure 69**).

4. Repeat steps 1 through 3 for each heading in the document.

✔ Tips

- The easiest way to generate an index based on heading styles is to apply Word's built-in heading styles (Heading 1 through Heading 9). You can, however, apply any style, as long as the styles you use meet the following criteria:

  ▲ The styles are used only for headings.

  ▲ There is a different style for each heading level.

  ▲ The styles are applied consistently to each heading level.

- Another way to format headings for a table of contents is to switch to Outline view and use its tools to convert paragraphs into headings. I discuss outlines in **Chapter 12**.

- If you created your document using Word's outline feature, you can skip this step. Your headings are already formatted and ready to use for a table of contents.

FORMATTING TABLE OF CONTENTS HEADINGS

To generate a table of contents from built-in heading styles

1. Position the insertion point where you want the table of contents to appear. This is usually at the beginning of the document, but it can be anywhere you like.

2. Choose Insert > Reference > Index and Tables (**Figure 1**) to display the Index and Tables dialog.

3. If necessary, click the Table of Contents tab to display its options (**Figure 70**).

4. Set formatting options as desired:

   ▲ **Show page numbers** displays the corresponding page number for each heading listed in the table of contents.

   ▲ **Right align page numbers** shifts page numbers to the right side of the page. This option is only available if you turned on the Show page numbers check box.

   ▲ **Tab leader** enables you to choose the characters that appear between the heading text and page number reference. This option is only available if you turned on the Right align page numbers check box.

   ▲ **Formats** enables you to choose one of several predefined table of contents formats.

   ▲ **Show levels** determines how many heading levels will be included in the table of contents.

5. Click OK. Word generates the table of contents and displays it at the insertion point (**Figure 71**).

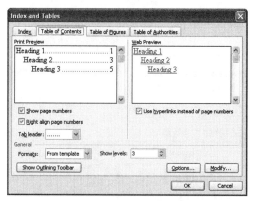

Figure 70 The Table of Contents tab of the Index and Tables dialog.

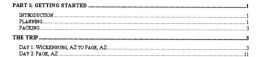

Figure 71 A table of contents using the Formal format.

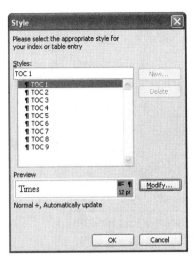

Figure 72 Use the Style dialog to modify the definition of TOC styles.

{TOC \O "1-3" \H \Z \U }

Figure 73 The TOC field codes for the table of contents in **Figure 71**.

✔ Tips

■ You can see the effect of changes you make in steps 4 through 6 in the Print Preview area of the Index and Tables dialog (**Figure 70**).

■ If the document will be saved as a Web page, you can toggle the Use hyperlinks instead of page numbers check box to specify whether table of contents entries appear as clickable links or include page numbers. I tell you about saving documents as Web pages in **Chapter 17**.

■ You can further define the appearance of a table of contents by clicking the Modify button in the Table of Contents tab of the Index and Tables dialog (**Figure 70**) when the From template format is chosen. This displays the Style dialog (**Figure 72**), which you can use to modify style definitions for TOC (table of contents) styles. I tell you more about modifying Styles in **Chapter 4**.

■ If you don't like the way a table of contents looks, you can delete it and start over. Just select the entire table of contents and press ⟨Backspace⟩, then follow the steps on the previous page to generate a new table of contents.

■ If your table of contents looks more like **Figure 73** than **Figure 71**, View preferences are set to display field codes. To display the table of contents instead, turn off the Field codes option in the Options dialog's View options (**Figure 55**).

GENERATING A TABLE OF CONTENTS

To generate a table of contents from custom heading styles

1. Follow steps 1 through 4 in the previous section to set basic options for the table of contents.

2. Click the Options button in the Table of Contents tab of the Index and Tables dialog (**Figure 70**) to display the Table of Contents Options dialog (**Figure 74**).

3. Make sure the Styles check box is turned on.

4. Scroll through the list of styles in your document and:

   ▲ Remove numbers in the boxes beside styles that should not be used for table of contents headings.

   ▲ Enter heading level numbers in the boxes beside styles that should be used for table of contents headings.

   For example, suppose the document headings used two styles called Main Heading and Subheading. You'd remove numbers beside every style except those, enter a 1 beside Main Heading, and enter a 2 beside Subheading (**Figure 75**).

5. Click OK to save your settings and dismiss the Table of Contents Options dialog.

6. Click OK in the Index and Tables dialog. Word generates the table of contents and displays it at the insertion point (**Figure 71**).

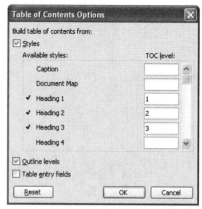

Figure 74 The default settings in the Table of Contents Options dialog.

Figure 75 You can set any style in the document to be used as a table of contents heading.

GENERATING A TABLE OF CONTENTS

Updating Reference Fields

When the content, pagination, or entry fields in a document change, any reference features created with Word fields that are already in the document must be updated to reflect the change.

For example, suppose you wrote a report, complete with bookmarks, cross-references, a table of contents, and an index. You submitted the report to management and although they liked it, they decided to expand the report scope. As a result, you had to write another 20 report pages and insert them in the middle of the report.

As part of the editing process, you created new cross-references, bookmarks, headings, and index entries. The existing references are no longer correct; they omit headings and index entries and have incorrect page references. These references must be manually updated for the revised document.

By "manually" I mean you must take some action to update the fields. Fortunately, updating them is as easy as selecting them and choosing a menu command or pressing a keyboard key. Or you can instruct Word to automatically update the fields that produce indexes and tables before a document prints.

In this part of the chapter, I explain how to update reference fields to ensure that they are accurate in your Word documents.

To manually update indexes & tables

1. Right-click anywhere in the reference field you want to update. A contextual menu like the one in **Figure 76** appears.

2. Choose Update Field from the contextual menu.

3. A dialog like the one in **Figure 77** may appear. Select an option to indicate what you want to update:

   ▲ **Update page numbers only** updates only the page numbers.

   ▲ **Update entire table** recreates the entire table from scratch.

   The reference is updated to reflect current document contents and information.

✔ Tips

- To update all reference fields in a document, choose Edit > Select All or press Ctrl A to select the entire document and press F9 . Follow step 3 if necessary to complete the update. This will update all Word fields in the selection.

- In step 2, choosing Toggle Field Codes displays captions and cross-references as Word field codes. Although you probably won't want to view them this way, you may find it interesting to see how Word tracks this information internally. You can choose the command again to view the references as they will print.

Figure 76 Right-clicking a reference field like this table of contents displays a contextual menu that enables you to update the field.

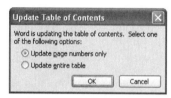

Figure 77 The Update Table of Contents dialog.

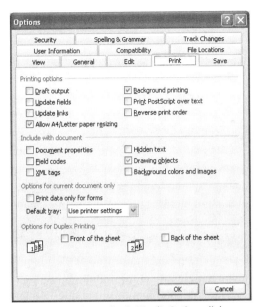

Figure 78 The Print option in Word's Options dialog.

To automatically update indexes & tables before printing

1. Choose Tools > Options to display the Options dialog.

2. Click the Print tab to display its options (**Figure 78**).

3. Turn on the Update fields check box.

4. Click OK.

   From that point forward, Word updates all Word fields—including reference fields— in the document before you print it.

✔ Tip

■ I recommend enabling this option for any document that contains reference fields. This can prevent you from printing the document with inaccurate information.

AUTOMATICALLY UPDATING REFERENCE FIELDS

Outlines

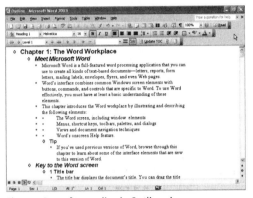

Figure 1 Part of an outline in Outline view.

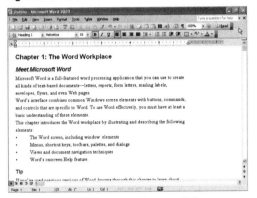

Figure 2 The outline in **Figure 1** in Normal view.

Outlines

An outline is a great tool for organizing ideas. By grouping topics and subtopics under main headings, you can set up the logical flow of a lengthy or complex document. A well-prepared outline is like a document "skeleton"—a solid framework on which the document can be built.

An outline has two components (**Figure 1**):

◆ *Headings* are topic names. Various levels of headings (1 through 9) are arranged in a hierarchy to organize and develop relationships among them.

◆ *Body text* provides information about each heading.

Microsoft Word's Outline view makes it easy to build and refine outlines. Start by adding headings that you can set to any level of importance. Then add body text. You can use drag-and-drop editing to rearrange headings and body text. You can also switch to Normal view (**Figure 2**) or another view to continue working with your document.

✔ Tips

■ Word's Outline feature automatically applies the Heading and Normal styles as you work. You can redefine these styles to meet your needs; **Chapter 4** explains how.

■ You can distinguish headings from body text in Outline view by the symbols that appear before them. Hollow dashes or plus signs appear to the left of headings while small hollow boxes appear to the left of body text (**Figure 1**).

Building an Outline

Building an outline is easy. Just create a new document, switch to Outline view, and start adding headings and body text.

✔ Tip

- You can turn an existing document into an outline by simply switching to Outline view and adding headings.

To create an outline

1. Create a new blank document.

2. Choose View > Outline (**Figure 3**).

   or

   Click the Outline View button at the bottom of the document window (**Figure 4**).

   The document switches to Outline view and the Outlining toolbar appears (**Figure 5**).

✔ Tip

- The Outlining toolbar (**Figure 6**) appears automatically any time you switch to Outline view. If it does not appear, you can display it by choosing View > Toolbars > Outlining. Displaying and hiding toolbars is covered in **Chapter 1**.

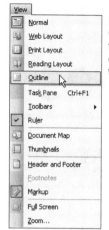

Figure 3
One way to switch to Outline view is to choose Outline from the View menu.

Outline View button

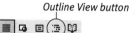

Figure 4 The View buttons at the bottom of the document window.

Figure 5 The document window in Outline view. The Outlining toolbar is right above the window.

Figure 6 The Outlining toolbar. Buttons on the far right end are for Word's master document feature, which I discuss near the end of this chapter.

CREATING OUTLINES

▫ Introduction to Word|

Figure 7 Enter the text that you want to use as a heading.

▫ **Introduction to Word**
▫ |

Figure 8 When you press (Enter), Word creates a new paragraph with the same heading level.

▫ **Introduction to Word**
▫ **The Word Workplace**
▫ |

Figure 9 To create a new heading at the same level, simply type it in.

▫ **Introduction to Word**
⊕ **The Word Workplace**
 ▫ *Introduction*
 ▫ *|*

Figure 10 To create a heading at a lower level, click the Demote button before typing it in. When you press (Enter), Word creates a new paragraph at the same (lower) heading level.

▫ **Introduction to Word**
⊕ **The Word Workplace**
 ▫ *Introduction*
▫ **New & Improved Features in Word**
▫ |

Figure 11 To create a heading at a higher level, click the Promote button while the insertion point is in the heading. When you press (Enter), Word creates a new paragraph at the same (higher) heading level.

Figure 12
You can assign a specific level to a paragraph by choosing the level from the Outline Level drop-down list.

To add headings

1. Type the heading text (**Figure 7**).

2. Press (Enter). A new paragraph at the same heading level appears (**Figure 8**).

3. Continue using one of these techniques:

    ▲ To add a heading at the same level, repeat steps 1 and 2 (**Figure 9**).

    ▲ To add a heading at the next lower level, press (Tab) or click the Demote button ⊞ on the Outlining toolbar. Then repeat steps 1 and 2 (**Figure 10**).

    ▲ To add a heading at the next higher level, press (Shift)(Tab) or click the Promote ⊞ button on the Outlining toolbar. Then repeat steps 1 and 2 (**Figure 11**).

    ▲ To add a heading at the Level 1 level, click the Promote to Heading 1 button ⊞ on the Outlining toolbar. Then repeat steps 1 and 2.

    ▲ To add a heading at a specific level, choose the level from the Outline Level drop-down list on the Outlining toolbar (**Figure 12**). Then repeat steps 1 and 2.

✔ Tips

■ By default, the first heading you create is Level 1—the top level. You can see the outline level in the Outline Level box on the Outlining toolbar when the insertion point is in the heading paragraph.

■ When you create a lower level heading beneath a heading, the marker to the left of the heading changes to a hollow plus sign to indicate that the heading has subheadings (**Figure 10**).

■ Don't worry about entering a heading at the wrong level. You can promote or demote a heading at any time—I tell you how next.

To promote or demote a heading

1. Click anywhere in the heading to position the insertion point within it (**Figure 13**).

2. To promote the heading, press [Shift][Tab] or click the Promote button ⟐ on the Outlining toolbar. The heading shifts to the left and changes into the next higher level heading (**Figure 14**).

    or

    To demote the heading, press [Tab] or click the Demote button ⟐ on the Outlining toolbar. The heading shifts to the right and changes into the next lower level heading.

✔ Tips

- You cannot promote a Heading 1 level heading. Heading 1 is the highest level.

- You cannot demote a Heading 9 level heading. Heading 9 is the lowest level.

- To promote or demote multiple headings at the same time, select the headings, then follow step 2 above.

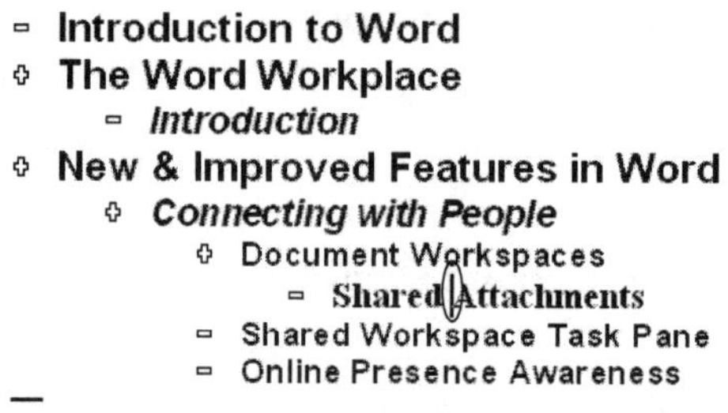

▫ **Introduction to Word**
⊕ **The Word Workplace**
    ▫ *Introduction*
⊕ **New & Improved Features in Word**
    ⊕ *Connecting with People*
        ⊕ Document Workspaces
            ▫ **Shared Attachments**
        ▫ Shared Workspace Task Pane
        ▫ Online Presence Awareness
___

Figure 13 Position the insertion point in the heading that you want to promote or demote.

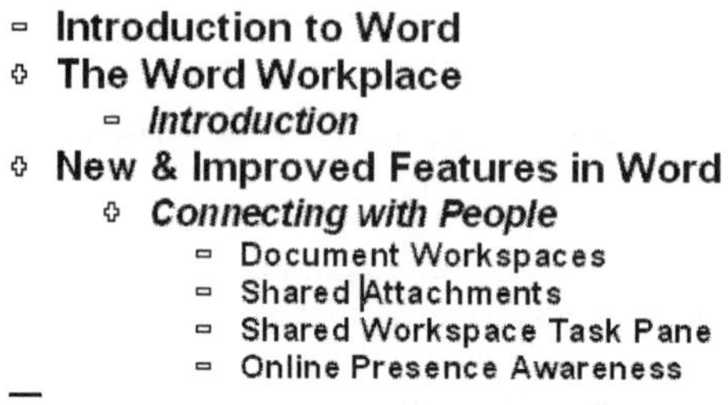

▫ **Introduction to Word**
⊕ **The Word Workplace**
    ▫ *Introduction*
⊕ **New & Improved Features in Word**
    ⊕ *Connecting with People*
        ▫ Document Workspaces
        ▫ Shared Attachments
        ▫ Shared Workspace Task Pane
        ▫ Online Presence Awareness
___

Figure 14 Clicking the Promote button shifts the heading to the left and changes it to the next higher heading level.

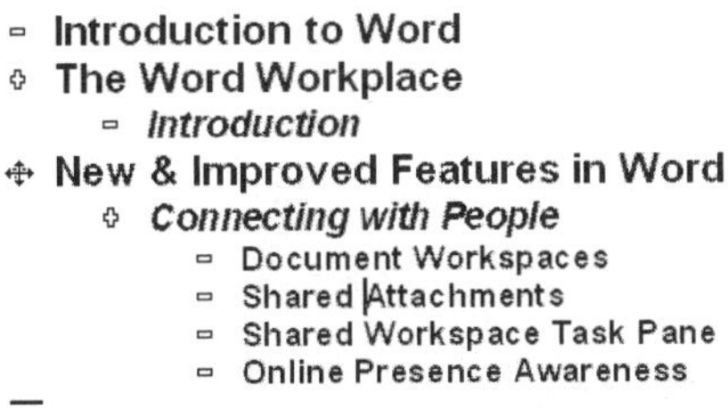

- Introduction to Word
- The Word Workplace
  - *Introduction*
- **New & Improved Features in Word**
  - *Connecting with People*
    - Document Workspaces
    - Shared Attachments
    - Shared Workspace Task Pane
    - Online Presence Awareness

Figure 15 Position the mouse pointer over a heading marker; it turns into a four-headed arrow.

- Introduction to Word
- The Word Workplace
  - *Introduction*
- **New & Improved Features in Word**
  - *Connecting with People*
    - Document Workspaces
    - Shared Attachments
    - Shared Workspace Task Pane
    - Online Presence Awareness

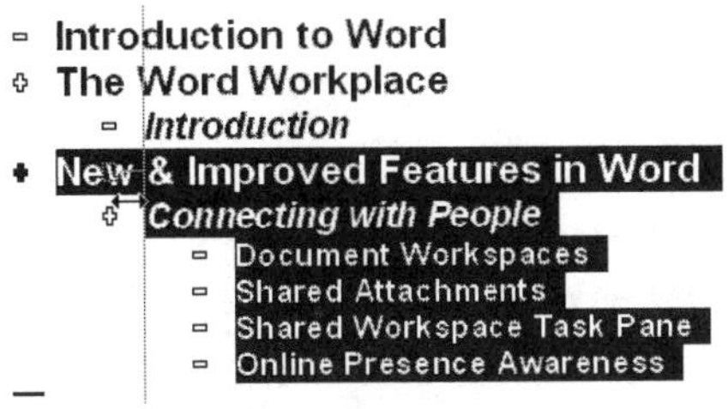

Figure 16 When you drag the heading marker, a line indicates the heading's level when you release the mouse button.

- Introduction to Word
- The Word Workplace
  - *Introduction*
  - *New & Improved Features in Word*
    - *Connecting with People*
      - Document Workspaces
      - Shared Attachments
      - Shared Workspace Task Pane
      - Online Presence Awareness

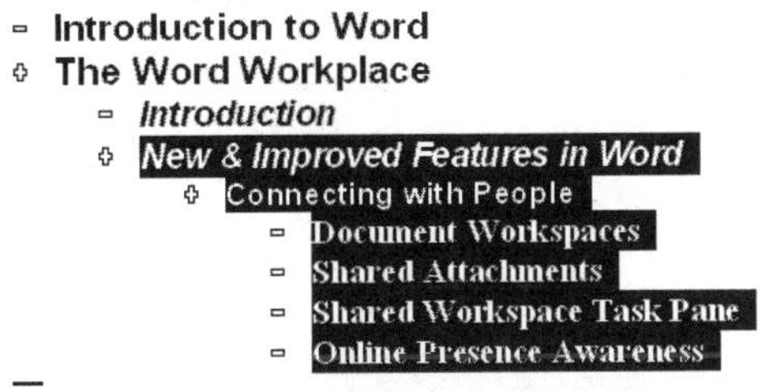

Figure 17 Release the mouse button to change the level of the heading and its subheadings.

To promote or demote a heading with its subheadings

1. Position the mouse pointer over the hollow plus sign to the left of the heading. The mouse pointer turns into a four-headed arrow (**Figure 15**).

2. To promote the headings, press the mouse button and drag to the left.

   or

   To demote the headings, press the mouse button and drag to the right (**Figure 16**).

   The heading and its subheadings are selected. As you drag, a line indicates the level to which the heading will be moved when you release the mouse button. You can see all this in **Figure 16**.

3. Release the mouse button to change the level of the heading and its subheadings (**Figure 17**).

✔ Tips

- You can also use this method to promote or demote a heading with no subheadings. Simply drag the hollow dash as instructed in step 2 to change its level.

- Another way to promote or demote a heading with its subheadings is with the Promote ⊞ or Demote ⊞ button on the Outlining toolbar. Just click the hollow plus sign marker (**Figure 15**) to select the heading and its subheadings. Then click the Promote or Demote button to change the selected headings' levels.

PROMOTING & DEMOTING HEADINGS

To add body text

1. Position the insertion point at the end of the heading after which you want to add body text (**Figure 18**).

2. Press (Enter) to create a new line with the same heading level (**Figure 19**).

3. Click the Demote to Body Text button ⇒ on the Outlining toolbar. The marker to the left of the insertion point changes into a small hollow square to indicate that the paragraph is body text (**Figure 20**).

4. Type the text that you want to use as body text (**Figure 21**).

✔ Tips

■ Word automatically applies the Normal style to body text. You can modify the style to meet your needs; I tell you how in **Chapter 4**.

■ Each time you press (Enter) while typing body text, Word creates a new paragraph of body text.

■ You can convert body text to a heading by clicking the Promote ⬆ or Demote ➡ button on the Outlining toolbar.

▫ **Introduction to Word**
◇ **The Word Workplace**
  ▫ *Introduction/*
  ◇ *New & Improved Features in Word*

Figure 18 Position the insertion point.

▫ **Introduction to Word**
◇ **The Word Workplace**
  ▫ *Introduction*
  ▫ */*
  ◇ *New & Improved Features in Word*

Figure 19 Press (Enter).

▫ **Introduction to Word**
◇ **The Word Workplace**
  ◇ *Introduction*
  ▪ |
  ◇ *New & Improved Features in Word*

Figure 20 When you click the Demote to Body Text button, the level changes to body text.

▫ **Introduction to Word**
◇ **The Word Workplace**
  ◇ *Introduction*
    ▪ Microsoft Word, a component of Microsoft Office, is a powerful word processing program for Windows users. Now more powerful and user-friendly than ever, Word enables users to create a wide variety of documents, ranging in complexity from simple one-page letters to complex, multi-file reports with figures, table of contents, and index|
  ◇ *New & Improved Features in Word*

Figure 21 Type the text that you want to appear as body text.

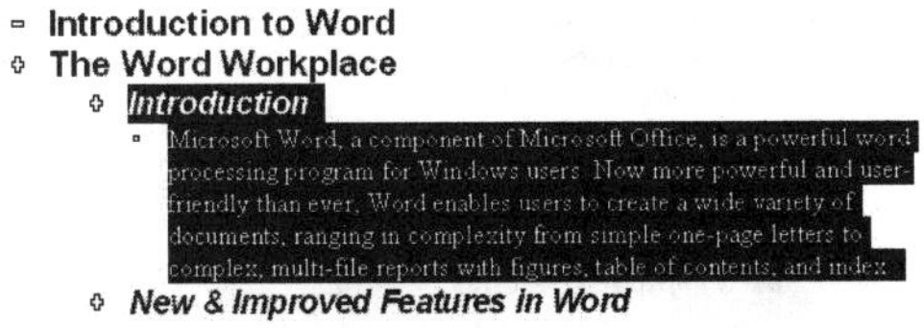

- Introduction to Word
- The Word Workplace
  - *Introduction*
    - Microsoft Word, a component of Microsoft Office, is a powerful word processing program for Windows users. Now more powerful and user-friendly than ever, Word enables users to create a wide variety of documents, ranging in complexity from simple one-page letters to complex, multi-file reports with figures, table of contents, and index.
  - *New & Improved Features in Word*

Figure 22 When you click the marker to the left of a heading, Word selects the heading and all of its sub-headings and body text.

To remove outline components

1. To remove a single heading or paragraph of body text, click the hollow dash or small square marker to the left of the heading or body text. This selects the entire paragraph of the heading or body text.

   or

   To remove a heading with its subheadings and body text, click the hollow plus sign marker to the left of the heading. This selects the heading and all of its subheadings and body text (**Figure 22**).

2. Press Backspace. The selection is removed.

✔ Tip

- You can edit an outline in any of Word's views. Just use commands under the View menu to switch to your favorite view and edit the outline as desired.

REMOVING OUTLINE COMPONENTS

Rearranging Outline Components

Word's Outline feature offers two methods to move selected outline components up or down:

◆ Click the Move Up ⊞ or Move Down ⊞ button on the Outlining toolbar.

◆ Drag heading or body text markers.

✔ Tips

■ Rearranging outline components using these methods changes the order in which they appear but not their level of importance.

■ Either of these methods can be used to move a single heading or paragraph of body text, multiple headings, or a heading with all of its subheadings and body text.

To move headings and/or body text with toolbar buttons

1. To move a single heading or paragraph of body text, click to position the insertion point within it (**Figure 23**).

    or

    To move a heading with its subheadings and body text, click the hollow plus sign marker to the left of the heading to select the heading, its subheadings, and its body text (**Figure 22**).

2. To move the heading up, click the Move Up ⊞ button on the Outlining toolbar. The heading moves one paragraph up.

    or

    To move the heading down, click the Move Down ⊞ button on the Outlining toolbar. The heading moves one paragraph down (**Figure 24**).

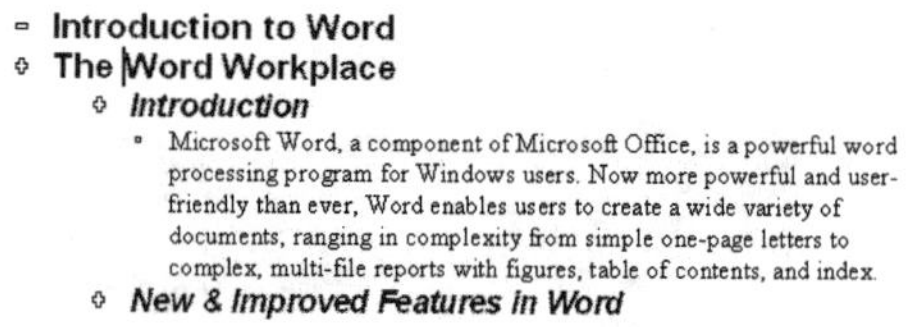

- Introduction to Word
- The Word Workplace
   - *Introduction*
      - Microsoft Word, a component of Microsoft Office, is a powerful word processing program for Windows users. Now more powerful and user-friendly than ever, Word enables users to create a wide variety of documents, ranging in complexity from simple one-page letters to complex, multi-file reports with figures, table of contents, and index.
   - *New & Improved Features in Word*

Figure 23 Click to position the insertion point.

- Introduction to Word
   - *Introduction*
- **The Word Workplace**
      - Microsoft Word, a component of Microsoft Office, is a powerful word processing program for Windows users. Now more powerful and user-friendly than ever, Word enables users to create a wide variety of documents, ranging in complexity from simple one-page letters to complex, multi-file reports with figures, table of contents, and index.
   - *New & Improved Features in Word*

Figure 24 When you click the Move Down button, the heading moves down.

REARRANGING OUTLINE COMPONENTS

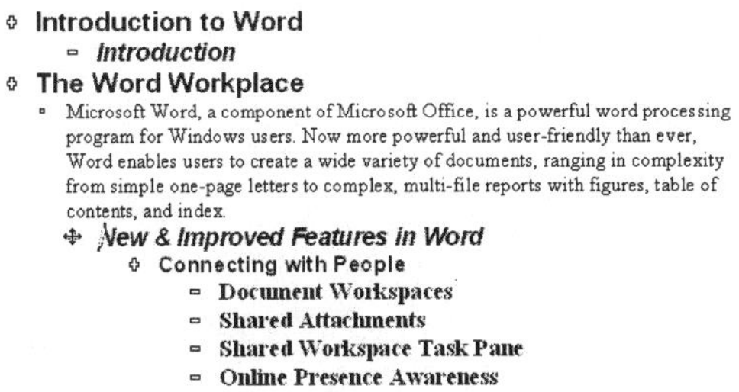

- ◊ **Introduction to Word**
  - ▫ *Introduction*
- ◊ **The Word Workplace**
  - ▫ Microsoft Word, a component of Microsoft Office, is a powerful word processing program for Windows users. Now more powerful and user-friendly than ever, Word enables users to create a wide variety of documents, ranging in complexity from simple one-page letters to complex, multi-file reports with figures, table of contents, and index.
    - ✦ *New & Improved Features in Word*
      - ◊ **Connecting with People**
        - ▫ **Document Workspaces**
        - ▫ **Shared Attachments**
        - ▫ **Shared Workspace Task Pane**
        - ▫ **Online Presence Awareness**

Figure 25 Position the mouse pointer over the heading marker.

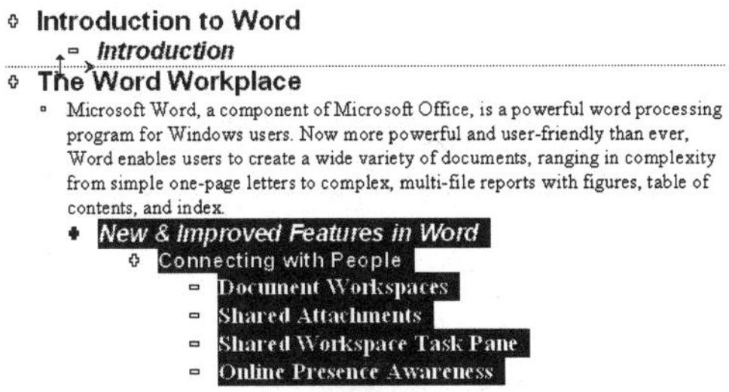

- ◊ **Introduction to Word**
  - ▫ *Introduction*
- ◊ **The Word Workplace**
  - ▫ Microsoft Word, a component of Microsoft Office, is a powerful word processing program for Windows users. Now more powerful and user-friendly than ever, Word enables users to create a wide variety of documents, ranging in complexity from simple one-page letters to complex, multi-file reports with figures, table of contents, and index.
    - ✦ *New & Improved Features in Word*
      - ◊ Connecting with People
        - ▫ Document Workspaces
        - ▫ Shared Attachments
        - ▫ Shared Workspace Task Pane
        - ▫ Online Presence Awareness

Figure 26 As you drag, a line indicates the new position when you release the mouse button.

- ◊ **Introduction to Word**
  - ▫ *Introduction*
  - ◊ *New & Improved Features in Word*
    - ◊ Connecting with People
      - ▫ Document Workspaces
      - ▫ Shared Attachments
      - ▫ Shared Workspace Task Pane
      - ▫ Online Presence Awareness
- ◊ **The Word Workplace**
  - ▫ Microsoft Word, a component of Microsoft Office, is a powerful word processing program for Windows users. Now more powerful and user-friendly than ever, Word enables users to create a wide variety of documents, ranging in complexity from simple one-page letters to complex, multi-file reports with figures, table of contents, and index.

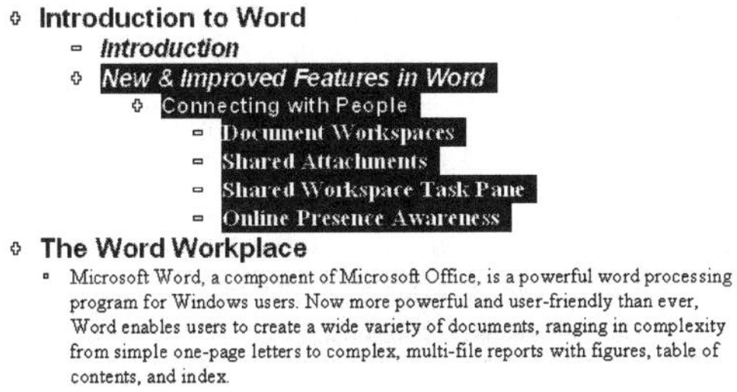

Figure 27 When you release the mouse button, the headings (and their body text, if any) move.

To move headings and/or body text by dragging

1. To move a single heading or paragraph of body text, position the mouse pointer over the hollow dash or small square marker to its left.

   or

   To move a heading with its subheadings and body text, position the mouse pointer on the plus sign marker to its left (**Figure 25**).

   The mouse pointer turns into a four-headed arrow (**Figure 25**).

2. To move the component(s) up, press the mouse button down and drag up (**Figure 26**).

   or

   To move the component(s) down, press the mouse button down and drag down.

   The components are selected. As you drag, a line indicates the location to which they will be moved when you release the mouse button. You can see this in **Figure 26**.

3. Release the mouse button to move the component(s) (**Figure 27**).

Viewing Outlines

Buttons on the Outlining toolbar (**Figure 6**) enable you to change your view of an outline:

◆ Collapse headings to hide subheadings and body text

◆ Expand headings to show subheadings and body text

◆ Show only specific heading levels

◆ Show all heading levels

◆ Show only the first line of text in each paragraph

◆ Show all lines of text in each paragraph

◆ Show or hide formatting

✔ Tip

■ These viewing options do not change the document's content—just your view of it.

To collapse a heading

1. Click the marker to the left of the heading that you want to collapse to select the heading, its subheadings, and its body text (**Figure 28**).

2. Click the Collapse button [▭] on the Outlining toolbar. The heading collapses to hide the lowest displayed level (**Figure 29**).

3. Repeat step 2 until only the levels you want to see are displayed (**Figure 30**).

or

Double-click the marker to the left of the heading that you want to collapse. The heading collapses to its level (**Figure 30**).

✔ Tip

■ When you collapse a heading with sub-headings or body text, a gray line appears beneath it to indicate hidden items (**Figures 29** and **30**).

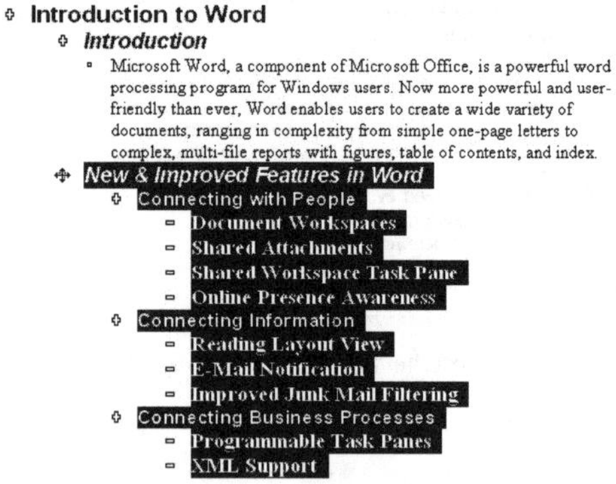

Figure 28 Click a heading's marker to select it, along with its subheadings and body text.

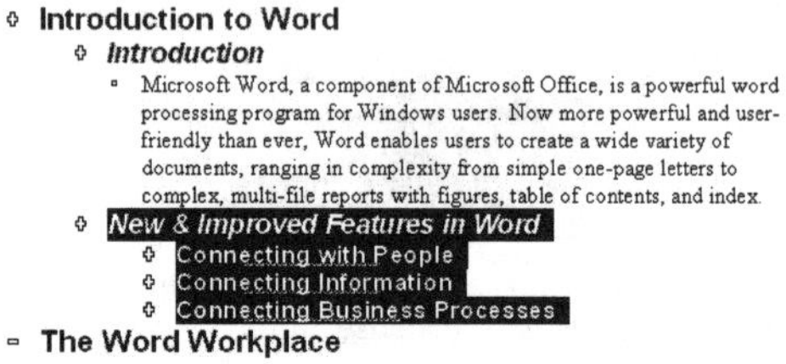

Figure 29 When you click the Collapse button, the lowest displayed level—in this example, Level 4—is hidden.

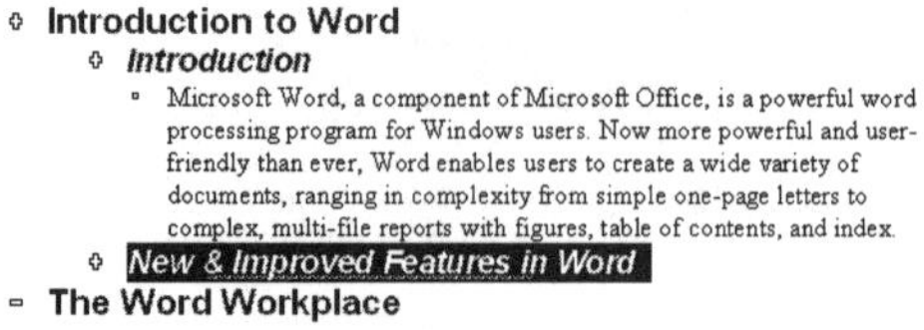

Figure 30 You can click the Collapse button repeatedly to hide multiple levels.

Figure 31
The Show Level drop-down list on the Outlining toolbar.

◊ Introduction to Word
   ◊ *Introduction*
   ◊ *New & Improved Features in Word*
      ◊ Connecting with People
      ◊ Connecting Information
      ◊ Connecting Business Processes
  ▫ **The Word Workplace**

Figure 32 In this example, the Show Level 3 option was chosen to display heading levels 1, 2, and 3.

◊ Introduction to Word
   ◊ *Introduction*
   ◊ *New & Improved Features in Word*
      ◊ Connecting with People
         ◊ Document Workspaces
         ▫ Shared Workspace Task Pane
         ▫ Online Presence Awareness
      ◊ Connecting Information
         ▫ Reading Layout View
         ▫ E-Mail Notification
         ▫ Improved Junk Mail Filtering
      ◊ Connecting Business Processes
         ▫ Programmable Task Panes
         ▫ XML Support
  ▫ **The Word Workplace**

Figure 33 In this example, the Show Level 4 option was chosen to display heading levels 1, 2, 3, and 4.

◊ Introduction to Word
   ◊ *Introduction*
      ▫ Microsoft Word, a component of Microsoft Office, is a powerful word processing program for Windows users. Now more powerful and user-friendly than ever, Word enables users to create a wide variety of documents, ranging in complexity from simple one-page letters to complex, multi-file reports with figures, table of contents, and index.
      ▫ This Visual QuickStart Guide will help you learn Word by providing step-by-step instructions, plenty of illustrations, and a generous helping of tips. On these pages, you'll find everything you need to know to get up and running quickly with Word—and more!
   ◊ *New & Improved Features in Word*
      ▫ Word includes many brand new features, as well as major improvements to existing features. Here's a list.
      ◊ Connecting with People
         ▫ One of Microsoft's objectives when developing this latest version of Word was to make Word and its documents more flexible when working in multiple-user environments. These new and improve features help meet that objective.
         ◊ Document Workspaces
            ▫ Document Workspaces utilize a Microsoft Windows

Figure 34 Choosing Show All Levels displays all levels of headings and the body text.

To expand a heading

1. Click the marker to the left of the heading that you want to expand to select the heading and all of its subheadings and body text.

2. Click the Expand button ⊞ on the Outlining toolbar. The heading expands to display the highest hidden level.

3. Repeat step 2 as desired to display all of the levels you want to see.

or

Double-click the marker to the left of the heading that you want to expand. The heading expands to show all levels.

To view only certain heading levels

On the Show Level drop-down list on the Outlining toolbar (**Figure 31**), choose the option that corresponds to the lowest level of heading that you want to display.

The outline collapses or expands to show just that level (**Figures 32** and **33**).

To view all heading levels

Choose Show All Levels from the Show Level drop-down list on the Outlining toolbar (**Figure 31**).

The outline expands to show all headings and body text (**Figure 34**).

VIEWING HEADING LEVELS

To display only the first line of every paragraph

Click the Show First Line Only button ▤ on the Outlining toolbar.

The Outline view changes to display only the first line of each heading and paragraph of body text (**Figure 35**).

✔ Tip

■ The Show First Line Only button ▤ works like a toggle switch. When turned on, only the first line of every paragraph is displayed. When turned off, all lines of every paragraph are displayed. This button is turned off by default.

To hide formatting

Click the Show Formatting button ✍ on the Outlining toolbar.

The Outline view changes to display all headings and body text in the default paragraph font for the Normal style (**Figure 36**).

✔ Tip

■ The Show Formatting button ✍ works like a toggle switch. When turned on, paragraph formatting is displayed. When turned off, all text appears in the default paragraph font for the Normal style. This button is turned on by default.

- ⬦ Introduction to Word
  - ⬦ *Introduction*
    - ▫ Microsoft Word, a component of Microsoft Office, is a powerful word ...
    - ▫ This Visual QuickStart Guide will help you learn Word by providing ...
  - ⬦ *New & Improved Features in Word*
    - ▫ Word includes many brand new features, as well as major ...
      - ⬦ Connecting with People
        - ▫ One of Microsoft's objectives when developing this latest ...
          - ⬦ **Document Workspaces**
            - ▫ Document Workspaces utilize a Microsoft Windows ...
          - ▭ **Shared Workspace Task Pane**
          - ▭ **Online Presence Awareness**
      - ⬦ Connecting Information
        - ▭ **Reading Layout View**
        - ▭ **E-Mail Notification**
        - ▭ **Improved Junk Mail Filtering**
      - ⬦ Connecting Business Processes
        - ▭ **Programmable Task Panes**
        - ▭ **XML Support**
  - ▭ **The Word Workplace**

Figure 35 Turning on the Show First Line Only button displays only the first line of each heading or paragraph of body text.

- ⬦ Introduction to Word
  - ⬦ Introduction
    - ▫ Microsoft Word, a component of Microsoft Office, is a powerful word processing program for Windows users. Now more powerful and user-friendly than ever, Word enables users to create a wide variety of documents, ranging in complexity from simple one-page letters to complex, multi-file reports with figures, table of contents, and index.
    - ▫ This Visual QuickStart Guide will help you learn Word by providing step-by-step instructions, plenty of illustrations, and a generous helping of tips. On these pages, you'll find everythign you need to know to get up and running quickly with Word—and more!
  - ⬦ New & Improved Features in Word
    - ▫ Word includes many brand new features, as well as major improvements to existing features. Here's a list.
      - ⬦ Connecting with People
        - ▫ One of Microsoft's objectives when developing this latest version of Word was to make Word and its documents more flexible when working in multiple-user environments. These new and improve features help meet that objective.
          - ⬦ Document Workspaces
            - ▫ Document Workspaces utilize a Microsoft Windows SharePoint Services site that is centered around one or

Figure 36 Turning off the Show Formatting button displays all text in the default paragraph font for the Normal style—in this case, 12-point New Times Roman.

VIEWING OUTLINE TEXT

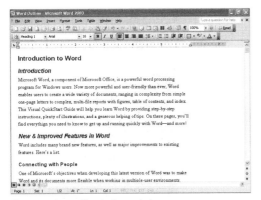

Figure 37 An outline in Normal view,...

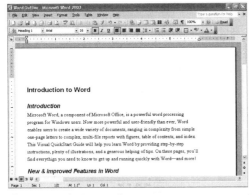

Figure 38 ...Print Layout view,...

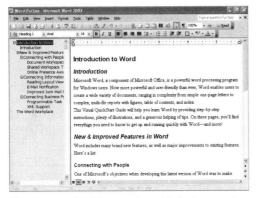

Figure 39 ...and Web Layout view with the Document Map showing.

Working with an Outline in Another View

You can switch to Normal (**Figure 37**), Print Layout (**Figure 38**), or Web Layout (**Figure 37**) view while working with an outline. There's nothing special about an outline except the additional outlining features available in Outline view. It's the same document when you switch to another view.

✔ Tips

- You can switch between any of Word's views at any time.

- I explain how to switch from one view to another in **Chapter 1**.

- Once the structure of a lengthy or complex document has been established in Outline view, you may find it easier to complete the document in Normal or Print Layout view.

- In Normal, Print Layout, and Web Layout views, you can apply the Heading and Normal styles using the Style menu on the Formatting toolbar. Styles are covered in **Chapter 4**.

- The Document Map lists all of the outline's headings (**Figure 39**). Double-click a heading to move quickly to that part of the document. You can show the Document Map in Normal or Web Layout view. The Document Map is discussed in **Chapter 1**.

Numbering Outline Headings

One of the more tedious aspects of working with a long, structured document is numbering (and renumbering) headings. This is especially cumbersome when dealing with legal documents that have multiple heading levels and strict heading or paragraph numbering requirements. But it can be almost as frustrating when dealing with a simple document that's frequently reorganized.

Fortunately, Word's paragraph numbering feature can automatically number—and renumber—paragraph headings. You can set up this feature as you build your document in Outline or Normal view so you don't have to worry about numbering. As long as you use Word's built-in heading styles, Word can handle all the numbering for you.

This part of the chapter explains how to set up outline numbering so Word can number your headings for you.

To automatically number headings in an outline

1. Select the outline for which you want to number headings (**Figure 40**).

2. Choose Format > Bullets and Numbering to display the Bullets and Numbering dialog.

3. If necessary, click the Outline Numbered tab to display its options (**Figure 41**).

4. Select the preview for the numbering format that most closely matches the format you want.

5. Click the Customize Button to display the Customize Outline Numbered List dialog (**Figure 42**).

6. Select a heading level from the Level list.

Figure 40 Select the outline you want to number.

Figure 41 The Outline Numbered tab of the Bullets and Numbering dialog.

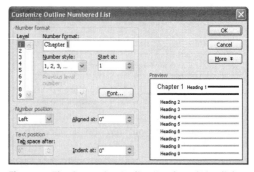

Figure 42 The Customize Outline Numbered List dialog.

Figure 43
The Number style drop-down list.

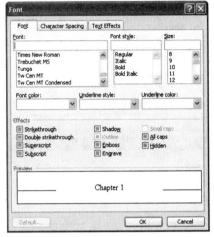

Figure 44 The Font dialog.

7. Edit the contents of the Number format box so it includes the text you want to appear with the number. Do not edit the gray highlighted number in the box.

8. Choose an option from the Number style drop-down list (**Figure 43**). The Number format box changes to reflect the option you chose.

9. If desired, enter a starting number in the Start at box.

10. If you chose a heading level other than 1 in step 6, indicate the previous heading level by choosing an option from the Previous level number drop-down list. Only those heading levels that are lower than the level you selected in step 6 appear; this option is not available if you chose heading level 1.

11. If desired, click the Font button and use the Font dialog that appears (**Figure 44**) to set the character formatting options for the contents of the Number format box. Click OK to save your settings.

12. To set the heading number position, choose an option from the Number position drop-down list (Left, Centered, Right) and enter an indentation setting in the Aligned at box.

13. To set the position of text that appears after the heading number, enter a value in the Indent at box.

14. Repeat steps 6 through 12 for each heading level used in your document.

15. Click OK to save your settings in the Customize outline numbered list dialog.

16. If necessary, click OK in the Bullets and Numbering dialog.

Continued on next page...

AUTOMATICALLY NUMBERING HEADINGS

Continued from previous page.

Figure 45 shows the outline in **Figure 40** with heading numbering set up for heading levels 1 and 2 and all number format options removed for heading 3.

✔ Tips

■ In step 4, if one of the previews indicates the exact formatting you want, you can skip steps 5 through 15.

■ In step 7, be sure to include (or remove) any punctuation you want to appear (or not appear).

■ If you skip step 11, the heading number will appear in the default paragraph font for the heading in which it appears.

■ After step 13, you can click the More button in the Customize Outline Numbered List dialog to expand the dialog and offer more options (**Figure 46**).

■ Once heading numbering has been set for an outline, rearranging outline levels automatically renumbers the outline. **Figure 47** shows an example.

◊ **Chapter 1: The Word Workplace**
 ▫ *Section I: Meet Microsoft Word*
 ◊ *Section II: The Word Screen*
  ▫ Title Bar
  ▫ Menu Bar
  ▫ Standard Toolbar
  ▫ Formatting Toolbar
  ▫ Task Pane
  ▫ Ruler
  ▫ Insertion Point
  ▫ End-of-Document Marker
  ▫ I-beam Pointer
  ▫ Document Window
  ▫ View Buttons
  ▫ Status Bar
  ▫ Browse Object Controls
 ◊ *Section III: The Mouse*
  ▫ Mouse Pointer Appearance
  ▫ To use the mouse
 ◊ *Section IV: Menus*
  ▫ To choose a menu command

Figure 45 The outline in **Figure 40** with automatic numbering applied to Level 1 and Level 2 headings.

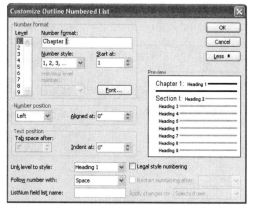

Figure 46 The Customize Outline Numbered List dialog, expanded to show additional options.

◊ **Chapter 1: The Word Workplace**
 ▫ *Section I: Meet Microsoft Word*
 ◊ *Section II: The Mouse*
  ▫ Mouse Pointer Appearance
  ▫ To use the mouse
 ◊ *Section III: The Word Screen*
  ▫ Title Bar
  ▫ Menu Bar
  ▫ Standard Toolbar
  ▫ Formatting Toolbar
  ▫ Task Pane
  ▫ Ruler
  ▫ Insertion Point
  ▫ End-of-Document Marker
  ▫ I-beam Pointer
  ▫ Document Window
  ▫ View Buttons
  ▫ Status Bar
  ▫ Browse Object Controls
 ◊ *Section IV: Menus*
  ▫ To choose a menu command

Figure 47 When you rearrange an outline, the headings are automatically renumbered.

- The Word Workplace
  - Meet Microsoft Word
  - The Word Screen
  - The Mouse
  - Menus
  - Shortcut Keys
  - Toolbars
  - The Task Pane
  - Dialogs
  - Views
  - Document Navigation
  - Windows
  - Word Help
- Word Basics
  - Word Processing Basics
  - Running Word
  - Exiting Word
  - Word Documents, Templates, & Wizards

Figure 48 Some of the Level 1 and Level 2 heads for the first few chapters of this book.

Master Documents

Very long documents, such as books, can be cumbersome to create. Creating the entire document in one document file can result in a monster file that slows performance when editing or scrolling text. But creating a separate file for each chapter makes it difficult to ensure consistent formatting and review the document as a whole. What's the solution?

Word's master document feature offers the best of both approaches. A *master document* is a Word document that includes a group of related documents called *subdocuments*. Master documents are commonly used to divide a long document into smaller, more manageable pieces.

Master documents normally start as outlines created in Word's Outline view. You can then use the master document feature to set up headings and their subheadings as subdocuments. For example, take the original outline for the first nine chapters of this book, part of which is shown in **Figure 48**. Chapter names are Heading 1 level headings that can be designated as subdocuments. The result is that each chapter becomes a separate document.

Although using outlines may be the best way to create a master document from scratch, you can also turn an existing document into a master document or add existing documents to a master document to make them subdocuments.

In this part of the chapter, I explain how to create and work with master documents.

✔ Tips

- A master document can also be used to manage a large document accessible by multiple users over a network. Users can work on different subdocuments at the same time.
- One of the benefits of using master documents to organize components of a lengthy document is that the template of the master document is automatically used by each subdocument. This ensures consistency in formatting and in other elements such as headers and footers.

To convert an outline into a master document

1. If necessary, click the Master Document View button [icon] on the Outlining toolbar to display the master document toolbar buttons on the far right end of the Outlining toolbar (**Figure 6**).

2. In the document window, click an outline symbol to select the heading and associated subheadings that you want to turn into a subdocument (**Figure 49**).

3. Click the Create Subdocument button [icon] on the Outlining toolbar.

   A subdocument icon appears near the heading and a gray box appears around the heading and its subheadings (**Figure 50**).

4. Repeat steps 2 and 3 for each heading you want to turn into a subdocument.

5. Save the document. Word automatically creates a separate document file for each subdocument (**Figure 51**).

✔ Tips

- Word inserts section breaks between each subdocument in a master document. I tell you more about section breaks in **Chapter 5**.

- To convert part of a document into a subdocument, the part of the document you want to convert must begin with a heading style.

Figure 49 Click an outline symbol to select a heading and all of its subheadings and body text.

Figure 50 A box appears around each subdocument.

Figure 51 When you save a master document, each of its subdocuments is saved as a separate document file. This example shows the master document's icon ("Word 2003 VQS Outline") and the icons for subdocuments created for the first three chapters in the outline.

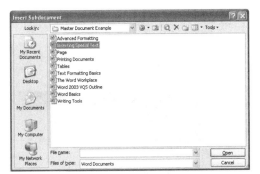

Figure 52 The Insert Subdocument dialog enables you to insert a Word document as a subdocument in a master document.

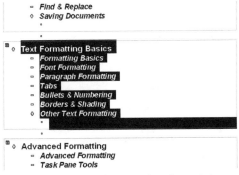

Figure 53 Click the subdocument icon for a subdocument to select it.

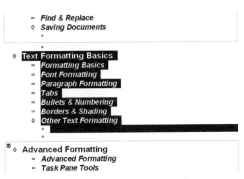

Figure 54 As shown here, removing a subdocument doesn't remove any text. Only the subdocument icon and the box around the text disappear.

To insert a subdocument into a master document

1. Position the insertion point where you want to insert the subdocument.

2. Click the Insert Subdocument button 🔲 on the Outlining toolbar.

3. In the Insert Subdocument dialog that appears (**Figure 52**), locate and select the document you want to insert as a subdocument and click Open.

   The document is inserted as a subdocument, with a subdocument icon near its heading and a gray box around its contents.

To remove a subdocument

1. In the document window, click the subdocument icon near the first heading for the subdocument to select the entire subdocument (**Figure 53**).

2. Click the Remove Subdocument button 🔲 on the Outlining toolbar.

   The subdocument icon and gray box around the subdocument disappear. The document becomes part of the master document (**Figure 54**).

✔ Tip

■ Clicking the Remove Subdocument button doesn't remove any text from your document. Instead, it converts the subdocument to part of the master document. If the master document had been saved before you removed the subdocument, the subdocument's contents still exist as a separate document file (**Figure 51**).

To merge two or more subdocuments

1. Click the subdocument icon for one of the subdocuments to select the entire subdocument.

2. Hold down (Shift) and click the subdocument icon for a subdocument you want to merge with the first subdocument. The subdocument is added to the selection (**Figure 55**).

3. Repeat step 2 for each subdocument you want to include in the merge.

4. Click the Merge Subdocument button ⊟ on the Outlining toolbar.

   The subdocuments are merged into one (**Figure 56**).

To split a subdocument into two subdocuments

1. Position the insertion point where you want the split to occur (**Figure 57**).

2. Click the Split Subdocument button ⊟ on the Outlining toolbar.

   A new subdocument is created at the insertion point (**Figure 58**).

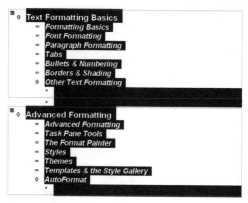

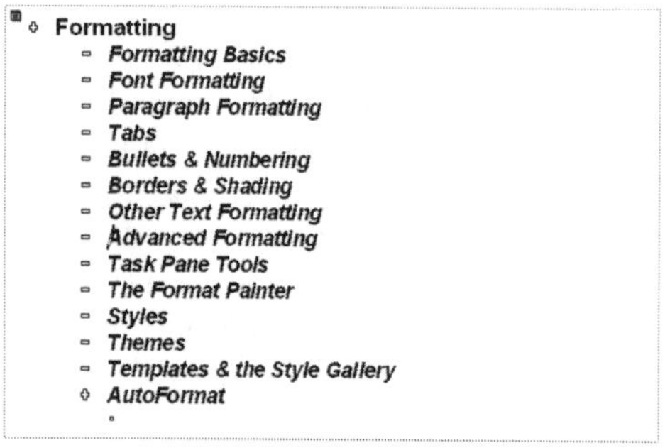

Figure 55 Select the subdocuments you want to merge by holding down (Shift) and clicking on their subdocument icons.

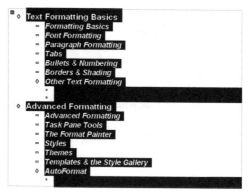

Figure 56 The two subdocuments selected in **Figure 55** after merging them into a single subdocument.

Figure 57 Position the insertion point where you want to split the document.

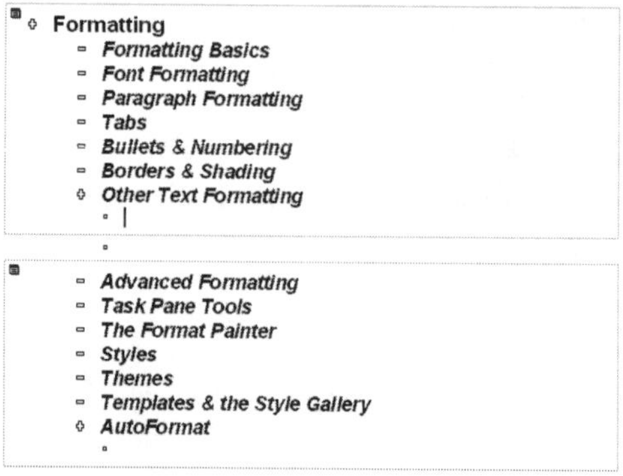

Figure 58 The subdocument is split into two subdocuments.

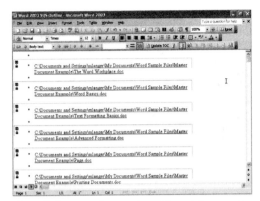

Figure 59 A master document with the subdocuments collapsed.

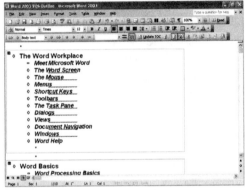

Figure 60 The master document from **Figure 59** with subdocuments expanded.

To collapse subdocuments

Click the Collapse Subdocuments button 🔲 on the Outlining toolbar.

The subdocuments are replaced with hyperlinks to their respective files (**Figure 59**).

✔ Tips

■ When you open a master document, it usually appears in a collapsed view (**Figure 59**).

■ Collapsing a master document makes it easy to see a list of all of its subdocuments.

To expand subdocuments

Click the Expand Subdocuments button 🔲 on the Outlining toolbar.

The subdocuments' hyperlinks are replaced with the contents of their files (**Figure 60**).

To edit a subdocument in its own document window

Double-click the subdocument icon for the subdocument you want to open. Its file opens in its own document window (**Figure 61**).

✔ Tips

■ It doesn't matter whether subdocuments are expanded (**Figure 60**) or collapsed (**Figure 59**) when you double-click a subdocument icon. Either way, the document opens.

■ Saving changes to a subdocument automatically saves changes to that document in the master document.

To prevent a subdocument from being edited

1. Position the insertion point anywhere in the subdocument you want to lock to prevent editing of its contents.

2. Click the Lock Document button on the Subdocument toolbar. A padlock icon appears beneath the subdocument icon (**Figure 62**). The document can no longer be edited.

✔ Tips

■ To allow editing of a locked subdocument, position the insertion point in the subdocument and click the Lock Document button on the Outlining toolbar. The document is unlocked.

■ To prevent an unauthorized user from editing a document, you can use Word's document protection features to password protect it. I tell you how in **Chapter 15**.

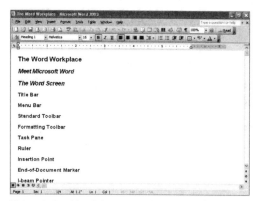

Figure 61 Double-clicking a subdocument icon opens the subdocument in its own document window.

Figure 62 A padlock icon beneath the subdocument icon indicates that the subdocument cannot be edited.

Envelopes & Labels

Envelopes & Labels

Microsoft Word's Envelopes and Labels feature can create and print addressed envelopes and mailing labels based on document contents or other information you provide. This feature makes it easy to print professional-looking envelopes and labels for all of your mailing needs.

✔ Tips

- Word supports a wide variety of standard envelope and label sizes and formats. Settings can also be changed for printing on nonstandard envelopes or labels.

- As discussed in **Chapter 14**, you can use the Mail Merge task pane to create envelopes and labels based on database information.

- Word is able to print postage on envelopes and labels—if you have installed and subscribed to the electronic postage feature. Although instructions for using electronic postage is beyond the scope of this book, you can learn more about it by visiting the Microsoft Office eServices page: office.microsoft.com/Services/.

- If you use Microsoft Outlook, you can use the Insert Address button that appears in the Envelopes and Labels dialog to automatically insert an Outlook address for an envelope or label. A detailed discussion of this feature is beyond the scope of this book; experiment with it on your own if you think it might be useful.

Creating an Envelope

In Word, you create an envelope with the Envelopes tab of the Envelopes and Labels dialog (**Figure 2**). This tab enables you to provide several pieces of information:

◆ **Delivery address** is the address the envelope will be mailed to.

◆ **Return address** is the address that appears in the upper-left corner of the envelope. You can use your own address, specify another address, or omit the address entirely.

From the Envelopes tab of the Envelopes and Labels dialog, you can also access the Envelope Options dialog (**Figure 3**), which enables you to set envelope and printing options.

Once you have set options for an envelope, you can either print it immediately or add it to the currently active document so it can be printed later.

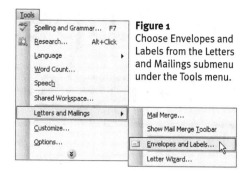

Figure 1
Choose Envelopes and Labels from the Letters and Mailings submenu under the Tools menu.

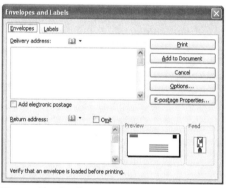

Figure 2 The Envelopes tab of the Envelopes and Labels dialog.

Figure 3
The Envelope Options tab of the Envelope Options dialog.

CREATING ENVELOPES

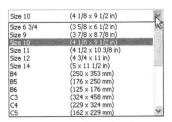

Figure 4 The Envelope size drop-down list includes many standard envelope sizes.

Figure 5 Use this dialog—which looks and works like the Font dialog discussed in **Chapter 3**—to set font options for the delivery and return addresses.

Figure 6
The Printing Options tab of the Envelope Options dialog.

To set up an envelope

1. Choose Tools > Letters and Mailings > Envelopes and Labels (**Figure 1**).

2. In the Envelopes and Labels dialog that appears, click the Envelopes tab to display its options (**Figure 2**).

3. Enter the name and address of the person to whom the envelope should be addressed in the Delivery address box.

4. If desired, enter a return address in the Return address box.

   or

   To create an envelope without a return address, turn on the Omit check box. This omits the return address from the envelope, even if one appears in the Return address box.

5. Click the Options button to display the Envelope Options dialog.

6. If necessary, click the Envelope Options tab to display its options (**Figure 3**).

7. Choose a size from the Envelope size drop-down list (**Figure 4**).

8. To set the font options for either address, click the Font button in its area. Then use the dialog that appears (**Figure 5**) to set formatting options and click OK.

9. In the Envelope Options dialog, click the Printing Options tab to display its options (**Figure 6**).

10. Check the Feed method options to make sure that they are properly set for your printer. If they are not, make changes as necessary.

Continued on next page...

SETTING UP ENVELOPES

Continued from previous page.

11. Select an option from the Feed from drop-down list. The options that appear vary depending on your printer.

12. Click OK to save your settings and dismiss the Envelope Options dialog.

✔ Tips

- In step 1, you cannot choose the Envelopes and Labels command unless a document window is open.

- If you are creating an envelope for a letter in the active document window, the Delivery address may already be filled in based on the inside address of the letter (**Figure 7**). You can "help" Word enter the correct address in this box by selecting the recipient's address *before* opening the Envelopes and Labels dialog.

- To override Word's automatic positioning of addresses, enter measurements in the From left and From top text boxes in the Envelope Options tab of the Envelope Options dialog (**Figure 3**) for the address you want to move.

- To include a postal barcode on the envelope, turn on the Delivery point barcode check box in the Envelope Options tab of the Envelope Options dialog (**Figure 3**). You can then also turn on the FIM-A check box if desired to add additional postal coding to the face of the envelope.

- In step 8, you can save font formatting changes as default settings by clicking the Default button in the dialog (**Figure 5**). Font formatting is covered in detail in **Chapter 3**.

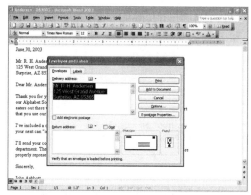

Figure 7 When you create an envelope for a letter, Word is usually "smart" enough to fill in the delivery address for you.

- In step 10, Word can usually set options correctly for printers capable of printing envelopes (**Figure 6**). Make changes to these options only if you know that the settings are incorrect.

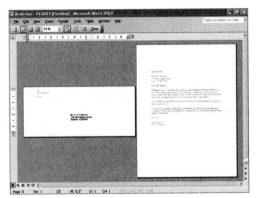

Figure 8 An envelope added as a separate document section when viewed in Print Preview.

To print an envelope

1. Set up the envelope as instructed on the previous two pages.

2. Click the Print button in the Envelopes tab of the Envelopes and Labels dialog (**Figure 2**).

   Word prints the envelope.

✔ Tip

- Printing is covered in greater detail in **Chapter 6**.

To save the envelope as part of the active document

1. Set up the envelope as instructed on the previous two pages.

2. Click the Add to Document button in the Envelopes tab of the Envelopes and Labels dialog (**Figure 2**).

   Word adds a new section to the document with the proper settings to print that section as an envelope (**Figure 8**).

✔ Tip

- I tell you about document sections in **Chapter 5**.

PRINTING & SAVING ENVELOPES

283

To create a default return address

1. Follow the instructions earlier in this chapter to set up an envelope with a new return address.

2. In the Envelopes tab of the Envelopes and Labels dialog (**Figure 2**), click either the Print button to print the envelope or the Add to Document button to add the envelope to the active document.

3. A dialog like the one in **Figure 9** appears. Click Yes.

✔ Tip

■ When you save a default return address, that address automatically appears in the Envelopes tab of the Envelopes and Labels dialog each time you create an envelope.

Figure 9 When you enter a new return address in the Envelopes and Labels dialog, Word offers to save it as the default.

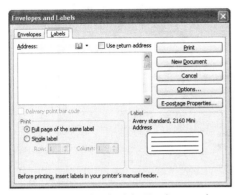

Figure 10 The Labels tab of the Envelopes and Labels dialog.

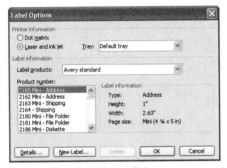

Figure 11 The Label Options dialog.

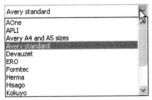

Figure 12 The Label products drop-down list includes all the major label manufacturers.

Creating Labels

In Word, you create labels with the Labels tab of the Envelopes and Labels dialog (**Figure 10**). This dialog enables you to set up labels by entering the address that should appear on the label and the number of labels that should be printed. You can also use the Label Options dialog to set additional options for the type of label on which you want to print.

Once you have set options for a label, you can either print it immediately or save it as a new document so it can be printed later.

To set label options

1. Choose Tools > Letters and Mailings > Envelopes and Labels (**Figure 1**) to display the Envelopes and Labels dialog.

2. Click the Labels tab to display its options (**Figure 10**).

3. Enter the name and address for the label in the Address box.

4. Select an option in the Print area:
   ▲ **Full page of the same label** prints the entire page of labels with the name and address that appears in the Address box.
   ▲ **Single label** prints only one label. If you select this option, be sure to enter the row and column number (if applicable) for the label to print.

5. To select the type of label you want to print on, click the Options button in the Label area to display the Label Options dialog (**Figure 11**). Select the appropriate Printer information option, then choose an option from the Label products drop-down list (**Figure 12**) and select the Product number for the label you want to use. Then click OK.

Continued on next page...

SETTING LABEL OPTIONS

Continued from previous page.

✔ Tips

- In step 1, you cannot choose the Envelopes and Labels command unless a document window is open.

- If you are creating a label for a letter in the active document window, the Address may already be filled in based on the inside address of the letter. You can "help" Word enter the correct address in this box by selecting the recipient's address before opening the Envelopes and Labels dialog.

- If you saved a default return address as instructed earlier in this chapter, you can automatically enter the return address by turning on the Use return address check box in the Labels tab of the Envelopes and Labels dialog (**Figure 10**). This is a handy way to create a sheet of return address labels.

- If you're not sure which Product number to select in step 5, consult the information on the box of labels.

- You can create your own custom label settings. In step 5, click the New Label button to display the New Custom dialog (**Figure 13**). Enter a name and measurements for the label, and click OK. The name of your new labels will appear in the Product number list in the Label Options dialog (**Figure 11**) when Other is selected from the Label products dropdown list (**Figure 12**).

- In step 5, you can customize the selected label by clicking the Details button. The dialog that appears looks and works very much like the one in **Figure 13**. Make changes as desired and click OK.

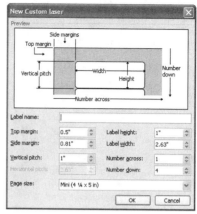

Figure 13 Use a dialog like this one to create your own custom label sizes.

SETTING LABEL OPTIONS

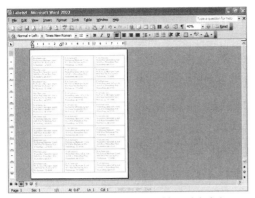

Figure 14 Here's a sheet of return address labels in Print Layout view. You can see the table gridlines (which don't print) separating each label.

To print labels

1. Set up the label as instructed on the previous two pages.

2. Click the Print button in the Labels tab of the Envelopes and Labels dialog (**Figure 10**).

   Word prints the labels.

✔ Tips

■ When printing single labels on a laser or inkjet printer, print on the labels at the bottom of the sheet first. This helps prevent printer jamming that could occur when labels at the top of the sheet have been removed.

■ Printing is covered in greater detail in **Chapter 6**.

To save the labels as a new document

1. Set up the label as instructed on the previous two pages.

2. In the Labels tab of the Envelopes and Labels dialog (**Figure 10**), click the Add to Document button.

   Word creates a new document containing the labels (**Figure 14**).

✔ Tips

■ This option is only available when creating a full page of the same label.

■ Word uses its table feature to create labels. Tables are covered in **Chapter 8**.

Mail Merge

14

Mail Merge

Microsoft Word's Mail Merge feature enables you to create mailing labels, form letters, and other documents based on database information. This feature merges fields or categories of information with static text to produce merged documents.

The mail merge process uses two special kinds of documents:

◆ A *main document* contains the information that remains the same for each version of the merged document. In a form letter, for example, the main document would consist of the letter text that appears in every letter.

◆ A *data source* contains the information that changes for each version of a merged document. In a form letter, the data source would consist of the names and addresses of the individuals who will receive the letter.

The results of a mail merge can be sent directly to the printer, sent as e-mail or saved as a file on disk.

✔ Tips

■ You can use a single main document with any number of data sources. Similarly, you can use a data source with any number of main documents.

■ You can create a data source with Word as discussed in this chapter or with another program such as Microsoft Excel or Microsoft Outlook.

■ Word's mail merge feature also includes powerful query and conditional functions. These are advanced features that are beyond the scope of this book.

The Mail Merge Task Pane

Word's Mail Merge task pane (**Figure 1**) leads you, step-by-step, through the process of performing a mail merge. Each step offers options based on selections you made in previous steps. At any point in the process, you can go back and change options.

To use the Mail Merge task pane: an overview

1. Open the Mail Merge task pane (**Figure 1**).

2. Select the type of document you want to create.

3. Open or create a main document.

4. Open or create a data source document and select the records to include in the merge.

5. If necessary, edit the main document to include static text and merge fields.

6. Preview the merge documents.

7. Perform the merge.

This chapter provides details for all of these steps.

To open the Mail Merge task pane

Choose Tools > Letters and Mailings > Mail Merge (**Figure 2**).

✔ Tips

■ You cannot open the Mail Merge task pane unless a document window is open.

■ The Mail Merge task pane, which was referred to as the *Mail Merge Wizard* in Word 2002, is a reworked version of the Mail Merge Helper from previous versions of Word.

Figure 1
The first step of the Mail Merge task pane.

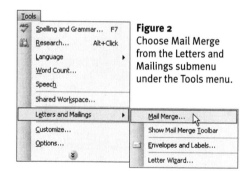

Figure 2
Choose Mail Merge from the Letters and Mailings submenu under the Tools menu.

THE MAIL MERGE TASK PANE

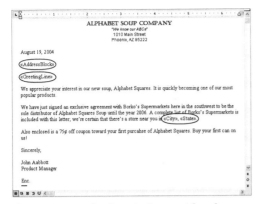

Figure 3 An example of a main document for a form letter. The merge fields are circled.

Creating or Opening a Main Document

A main document (**Figure 3**) has two parts:

◆ **Static text** that does not change. In a form letter, for example, static text would be the information that remains the same for each individual who will get the letter.

◆ **Merge fields** that indicate what data source information should be merged into the document and where it should go. In a form letter, the static text *Dear* might be followed by the field *«FirstName»*. When merged, the contents of the FirstName field are merged into the document after the word *Dear* to result in *Dear Joe, Dear Sally,* etc.

Normally, a main document can be created with one or two steps:

◆ Enter the static text first, then insert the fields when the data source is complete. This method is useful when you use an existing document as a main document.

◆ Enter the static text and insert the fields at the same time when the data source document is complete. This method may save time and prevent confusion when creating a main document from scratch.

✔ Tips

■ You cannot insert fields into a main document until after the data source has been created and associated with the main document.

■ You enter, edit, and format static text in a main document the same way you do in any other Word document.

■ As shown in **Figure 3**, Word includes predefined blocks of merge fields that make it easy to insert addresses and salutations into main documents.

To select a type of main document

1. Open a document on which you want to base the main document (**Figure 4**).

   or

   Create a new document.

2. Choose Tools > Letters and Mailings > Mail Merge (**Figure 2**) to open the Mail Merge task pane.

3. Select one of the options in the Select document type area of the Mail Merge task pane (**Figure 1**):

   ▲ **Letters** are form letters customized for multiple recipients.

   ▲ **E-mail messages** are like letters, but they are sent via e-mail.

   ▲ **Envelopes** are envelopes addressed to multiple recipients.

   ▲ **Labels** are labels addressed to multiple recipients.

   ▲ **Directory** is a collection of information about multiple items, such as a phone directory or a catalog.

4. Click the Next: Starting document link at the bottom of the Mail Merge task pane.

5. Continue following the appropriate instructions on one of the next two pages.

✔ Tips

■ You cannot open the Mail Merge task pane unless a document window is open.

■ You can find more information about working with envelopes and labels in **Chapter 13**.

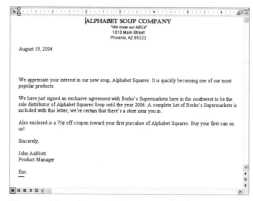

Figure 4 A form letter without merge fields.

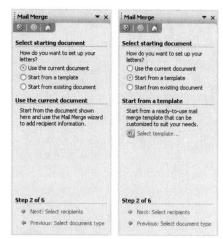

Figures 5, 6, & 7
The second step of the Mail Merge task pane prompts you for more information about your main document. You can use the current document (top left), start from a template (top right), or start from an existing document (bottom).

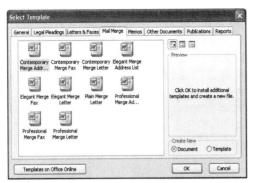

Figure 8 If you indicate that you want to start from a template, use the Select Template dialog to select the template you want to use.

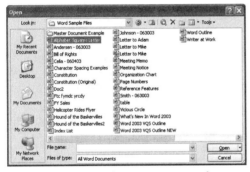

Figure 9 If you indicate that you want to start from an existing document, use the Open dialog to select and open the document you want to use.

✔ Tip

■ Templates are discussed in **Chapter 2**.

To start a main document for letters, e-mail messages, or a directory

1. Follow the instructions in the section titled "To select a type of main document." Be sure to select Letters, E-mail messages, or Directory in step 3.

2. In the Mail Merge task pane, select an option under Select starting document:

   ▲ **Use the current document (Figure 5)** sets the active document as the main document for the merge. If you select this option, skip ahead to step 4.

   ▲ **Start from a template (Figure 6)** enables you to base the main document for the merge on a template.

   ▲ **Start from existing document (Figure 7)** enables you to open an existing document to use as the main document for the merge.

3. Select the main document for the merge:

   ▲ If you selected Start from template in step 2, click the Select template link (**Figure 6**) to display the Mail Merge tab of the Select Template dialog (**Figure 8**). Select a template and click OK.

   ▲ If you selected Start from existing document in step 2, select a document listed in the Mail Merge task pane (**Figure 7**). If the file you want is not listed, select (More Files…), click Open, use the Open dialog that appears (**Figure 9**) to locate and select a document, and click Open. The document opens.

4. Click the Next: Select recipients link at the bottom of the Mail Merge task pane.

5. Continue following the appropriate instructions in the "Creating or Opening a Data Source" section.

To start a main document for envelopes or labels

1. Follow the instructions in the section titled "To select a type of main document." Select Envelopes or Labels in step 3.

2. In the Mail Merge task pane, select an option under Select starting document:

   ▲ **Change document layout (Figures 10 and 11)** lets you modify the active document for envelopes or labels. If you select this option, skip to step 4.

   ▲ **Start from existing document (Figure 12)** lets you open an existing document as a main document for your envelopes or labels.

3. Select one of the main documents listed in the Mail Merge task pane (**Figure 12**). If the file you want is not listed, select (More files…), click Open, and use the Open dialog that appears (**Figure 9**) to locate, select, and open a document.

4. Set options for your envelopes or labels:

   ▲ For envelopes, click the Envelope options link (**Figure 10**). Set options in the two tabs of the Envelope Options dialog that appears (**Figures 13 and 14**) and click OK.

   ▲ For labels, click the Label options link (**Figure 11**). Set options in the Label Options dialog that appears (**Figure 15**) and click OK.

5. Click the Next: Select recipients link at the bottom of the Mail Merge task pane.

6. Continue following the appropriate instructions in the "Creating or Opening a Data Source" section.

✔ Tip

■ Learn about envelope and label options in **Chapter 13**.

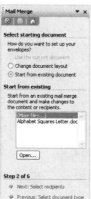

Figures 10, 11, & 12 The second step of the Mail Merge task pane prompts you for more information about your main document. You can change the current document layout for envelopes (top left) or labels (top right), or start from an existing document (bottom).

Figures 13, 14, & 15 Use the Envelope Options dialog tabs (top) or Label Options dialog (bottom) to set options for envelopes or labels.

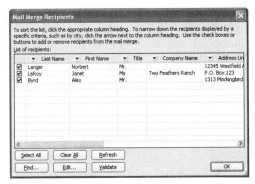

Figure 16 A data source with three records, created within Microsoft Word.

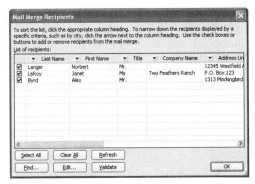

Figure 17 The data source in **Figure 16** merged into the main document in **Figure 3**.

Creating or Opening a Data Source

A data source (**Figure 16**) has two parts:

◆ **Fields** are categories of information. In a form letter, for example, *Last Name* and *City* might be two fields. Each field has a unique name that identifies it in both the main document and data source document.

◆ **Records** are collections of information for individual items. In a form letter, the John Smith record would include all fields for John Smith—his name, address, city, state, and postal code.

When you perform a mail merge, Word inserts the data from a data source record into a main document, replacing field names with field contents. It repeats the main document for each record in the data source (**Figure 17**).

✔ Tip

■ This chapter explains how to create or open a Word-based data source. You can also use Microsoft Outlook data or an Excel list as a data source; **Chapter 16** explains how.

To create a data source

1. Follow the instructions earlier in this chapter to select a main document type and start a main document.

2. In the Mail Merge task pane, select the Type a new list option (**Figure 18**).

3. Click the Create link to display the New Address List dialog (**Figure 19**). It lists commonly used field names for form letters, mailing labels, and envelopes.

4. Enter information for a specific record into each of the text boxes. You can press Tab to move to the next box or Shift Tab to move to the previous box.

5. To add another record, click the Add New button and repeat step 4.

6. When you are finished adding records, click Close.

7. A Save Address List dialog appears (**Figure 20**). Use it to name and save the data source file.

8. Word displays the Mail Merge Recipients dialog (**Figure 16**). Continue following instructions in the section titled "To select recipients."

Figure 18
When you indicate that you want to type a new list, the Mail Merge task pane includes a link for creating the data source.

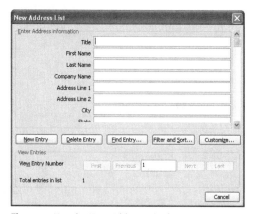

Figure 19 Use the New Address List form to enter information for each person you want to include in the data source.

Figure 20 Once you have created a data source, save it in the My Data Sources folder.

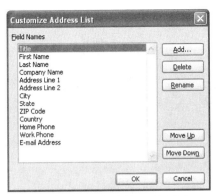

Figure 21 The Customize Address List dialog lists all of the fields in the data source and offers buttons for modifying them.

Figure 22
Use the Add Field dialog to enter the name for a new field.

Figure 23
Use the Rename Field dialog to enter a new name for a field.

✔ Tips

- You can use other buttons in the New Address List dialog (**Figure 19**) to scroll through, delete, search for, and sort records.

- You can customize the fields in the New Address List dialog (**Figure 19**) to include only the fields you need. Click the Customize button to display the Customize Address List dialog (**Figure 21**), then use its buttons to modify the Field Names list:

  ▲ To add a field name, click Add, enter the name in Add Field dialog that appears (**Figure 22**), and click OK.

  ▲ To remove a field name from the list, click to select it, then click Delete.

  ▲ To rename a field, click Rename, enter a new name in Rename Field dialog that appears (**Figure 23**), and click OK.

  ▲ To move a field name up in the list, click to select it, then click Move Up.

  ▲ To move a field name down in the list, click to select it, then click Move Down.

  When you are finished editing the list, click OK.

- In step 7, Word automatically displays the contents of the My Data Sources folder that it creates in the My Documents folder. Saving your data source documents in this folder makes it easy to find them for future merges.

- To edit a completed data source, click the Edit button in the Mail Merge Recipients dialog (**Figure 16**). This displays a dialog similar to the one in **Figure 19**, which you can use to add, modify, or delete records.

CREATING A DATA SOURCE

To open an existing data source

1. Follow the instructions earlier in this chapter to select a main document type and start a main document.

2. In the Mail Merge task pane, select the Use an existing list option (**Figure 24**).

3. Click the Browse link to display the Select Data Source dialog (**Figure 25**). Select a data source and click Open.

4. Word displays the Mail Merge Recipients dialog (**Figure 16**). Continue following instructions in the section titled "To select recipients."

✔ Tips

- Use this technique to associate an existing data source with a main document.

- To edit a data source, click the Edit button in the Mail Merge Recipients dialog (**Figure 16**). This displays a dialog similar to the one in **Figure 19**, which you can use to add, modify, or delete records.

To change the data source document associated with a main document

1. Follow the instructions earlier in this chapter to select a main document type and start a main document.

2. In the Mail Merge task pane, select the Use an existing list option (**Figure 26**).

3. Click the Select a different list link to display the Select Data Source dialog (**Figure 25**). Select a data source and click Open.

4. Word displays the Mail Merge Recipients dialog (**Figure 16**). Continue following instructions in the section titled "To select recipients."

Figure 24
When you indicate that you want to use an existing list, the Mail Merge task pane includes a link for selecting a data source.

Figure 25 Use the Select Data Source dialog to select the data source document to associate with the main document.

Figure 26
When a data source is already associated with a main document, the Mail Merge task pane offers a link to select a different list.

Figure 27 A check mark beside a recipient name indicates that the recipient will be included in the merge.

To select recipients

1. In the Mail Merge Recipients dialog (**Figure 16**), click to toggle the check boxes beside the records for recipients you want to include in the list (**Figure 27**). A check indicates that the record will be included; no check indicates that the record will be excluded.

2. Click OK to save your selections and dismiss the Mail Merge Recipients window.

3. Continue following the appropriate instructions in the "Completing a Main Document" section.

✔ Tip

- If the Mail Merge Recipients dialog (**Figure 16**) is not showing, click the Edit recipient list link in the Mail Merge task pane (**Figure 26**).

Completing a Main Document

Before you can perform a mail merge, you must complete the main document by entering static text (if necessary) and inserting merge fields. How you do this depends on the type of main document you have created.

To complete letters, e-mail messages, or a directory

1. Click the Next link near the bottom of the Mail Merge task pane:

   ▲ For letters, click Next: Write your letter (**Figures 18**, **24**, and **26**).

   ▲ For e-mail messages, click Next: Write your e-mail message.

   ▲ For a directory, click Next: Arrange your directory.

2. If you haven't already done so, enter static text into the document window by typing or pasting it in (**Figure 28**).

3. Position the insertion point where you want to insert a merge field (**Figure 28**). Then:

   ▲ To insert a predefined block of merge fields, click one of the first four options in the Mail Merge task pane (**Figure 29**). Then use the dialog box that appears to set options for the block. **Figures 30** and **31** show two examples.

   ▲ To insert an individual merge field, click the More items link in the Mail Merge task pane (**Figure 29**). In the Insert Merge Field dialog that appears (**Figure 32**), make sure Database Fields is selected, then select the field you want to insert and click the Insert button. Click Close to dismiss the dialog.

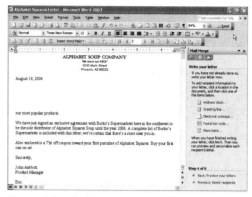

Figure 28 A main document window for letters, all ready for merge fields to be inserted.

Figure 29
The fourth step of the Mail Merge task pane enables you to insert merge fields into your main document.

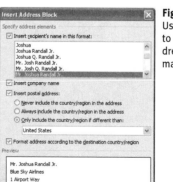

Figure 30
Use this dialog to set up an address block for a main document.

Figure 31 Use this dialog to set options for inserting a greeting line in a main document.

Figure 32
To insert an individual merge field, select the name of the field and click Insert.

4. Repeat step 3 for each merge field that you want to insert.

Figure 3 shows an example of a main document with merge fields inserted.

5. Click the Next link near the bottom of the Mail Merge task pane:

▲ For letters, click Next: Preview your letters (**Figure 29**).

▲ For e-mail messages, click Next: Preview your e-mail messages.

▲ For a directory, click Next: Preview your directory.

6. Continue following instructions in the section titled "Previewing the merge."

✔ Tips

■ When inserting predefined merge field blocks, consult the Preview area of the dialog box you use to set options (**Figures 30 and 31**) to see how your settings will appear in the merged document.

■ Be sure to include proper spacing and punctuation as necessary between merge fields. To do this, position the insertion point where you want the space or punctuation to appear and press the appropriate keyboard key to insert it.

■ If you insert a field in the wrong place, simply select it and drag it to the correct position within the document window.

■ To remove a field, select it and press Backspace.

To complete envelopes

1. Click the Next: Arrange your envelope link at the bottom of the Mail Merge task pane.

2. If you haven't already done so, enter static text into the document window by typing or pasting it in (**Figure 33**).

3. Position the insertion point in the address frame of the document window (**Figure 33**). Then:

   ▲ To insert a predefined block of merge fields, click one of the first four options in the Mail Merge task pane (**Figure 34**). Then use the dialog box that appears to set options for the block. **Figures 30** and **31** show two examples.

   ▲ To insert an individual merge field, click the More items link in the Mail Merge task pane (**Figure 34**). In the Insert Merge Field dialog that appears (**Figure 32**), make sure Database Fields is selected, then select the field you want to insert and click the Insert button. Click Close to dismiss the dialog.

4. Repeat step 3 for each merge field that you want to insert.

   Figure 35 shows an example of a main document for an envelope with the AddressBlock merge field inserted.

5. Click the Next: Preview your envelopes link at the bottom of the Mail Merge task pane (step 4, **Figure 34**).

6. Continue following instructions in the section titled "Previewing the merge."

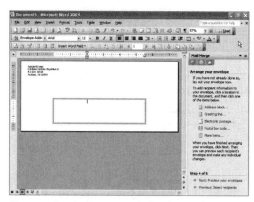

Figure 33 A main document window for envelopes, all ready for merge fields to be inserted.

Figure 34
The fourth step of the Mail Merge task pane enables you to insert merge fields into your main document.

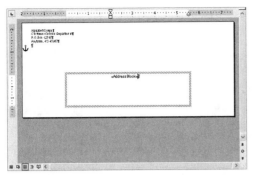

Figure 35 A main document for envelopes with the AddressBlock field inserted.

✔ Tips

- Word automatically inserts your default return address (if it has been saved) in the return address area of the envelope (**Figure 33**). You can edit or delete this text if desired. Saving a return address is discussed in **Chapter 13**.

- In step 3, if you cannot see the address frame, click the Show/Hide ¶ button ¶ on the Standard toolbar to display formatting marks. Then click beside the paragraph mark (¶) that appears in the middle of the document. The address frame appears around it. Formatting marks are covered in **Chapter 2**; frames are discussed briefly in **Chapter 10**.

- When inserting predefined merge field blocks, consult the Preview area of the dialog box you use to set options (**Figures 30** and **31**) to see how your settings will appear in the merged document.

- Be sure to include proper spacing and punctuation as necessary between merge fields. To do this, position the insertion point where you want the space or punctuation to appear and press the appropriate keyboard key to insert it.

- If you insert a field in the wrong place, simply select it and drag it to the correct position within the document window.

- To remove a field, select it and press Backspace.

To complete mailing labels

1. Click the Next: Arrange your labels link at the bottom of the Mail Merge task pane.

2. If necessary, enter static text into the first cell of the table by typing or pasting it in.

3. Position the insertion point in the first cell of the table (**Figure 36**). Then:

   ▲ To insert a predefined block of merge fields, click one of the first four options in the Mail Merge task pane (**Figure 37**). Then use the dialog box that appears to set options for the block. **Figures 30** and **31** show two examples.

   ▲ To insert an individual merge field, click the More items link in the Mail Merge task pane (**Figure 37**). In the Insert Merge Field dialog that appears (**Figure 32**), make sure Database Fields is selected, then select the field you want to insert and click the Insert button. Click Close to dismiss the dialog.

4. Repeat step 3 for each merge field that you want to insert.

5. When you are finished inserting fields in the first cell of the table, click the Update all labels button in the Mail Merge task pane (**Figure 37**) to copy the label layout to all of the labels in the table (**Figure 38**).

6. Click the Next: Preview your labels link at the bottom of the Mail Merge task pane (**Figure 37**).

7. Continue following instructions in the section titled "Previewing the Merge."

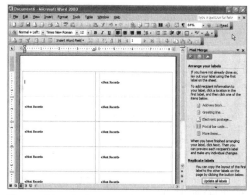

Figure 36 A main document for mailing labels, all ready for merge fields to be inserted.

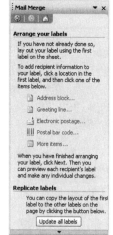

Figure 37
When creating labels, the fourth step of the Mail Merge task pane enables you to insert merge fields and copy the first label's layout to all labels in the document.

Word field

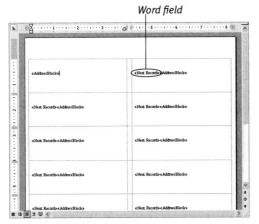

Figure 38 A completed main document for labels.

✔ Tips

- When inserting predefined merge field blocks, consult the Preview area of the dialog box you use to set options (**Figures 30** and **31**) to see how your settings will appear in the merged document.

- Be sure to include proper spacing and punctuation as necessary between merge fields. To do this, position the insertion point where you want the space or punctuation to appear and press the appropriate keyboard key to insert it.

- If you insert a field in the wrong place, simply select it and drag it to the correct position within the document window.

- To remove a field, select it and press Backspace.

- Do not change the Word fields included in the mailing labels main document (**Figure 38**). Altering or removing a field can prevent the mailing labels from merging or printing properly. I tell you more about Word fields in **Chapter 9**.

Previewing the Merge

Before you perform the merge, the Mail Merge task pane gives you an opportuntity to see what the merged documents will look like. If you like what you see, you can perform the merge. If you don't like what you see, you can go back and make changes to fine-tune the merge setup.

To preview the merge

Use the arrow buttons in the Mail Merge task pane to scroll through the recipients that appear in the document window (**Figures 39, 40,** and **41**).

✔ Tips

■ You can exclude a recipient from the merge by clicking the Exclude this Recipient button in the Mail Merge task pane while the recipient's record is displayed (**Figures 39** and **40**).

■ To edit the data source, click the Edit recipient list link in the Mail Merge task pane (**Figures 39, 40,** and **41**). This displays the Mail Merge Recipients dialog (**Figure 16**), which you can use to select recipients and modify the data source file.

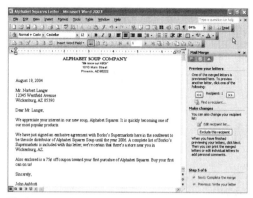

Figure 39 Previewing a mail merge for a letter, ...

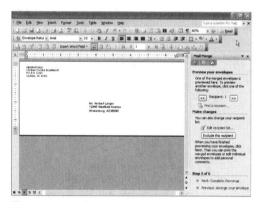

Figure 40 ... envelopes, ...

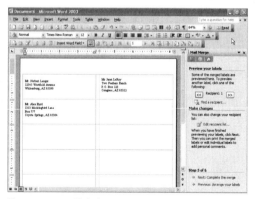

Figure 41 ... and labels.

Figures 42, 43, & 44
The last step of the Mail Merge task pane for letters (top left), envelopes (top right), and labels (bottom).

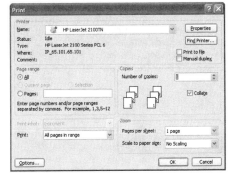

Figure 45
The Merge to Printer dialog.

Completing the Merge

The last step in performing a mail merge is to merge the main document and data source. Word offers three options for merging:

- ◆ **Print** merges the documents directly to a printer. This option is available for letters, envelopes, and labels.

- ◆ **Electronic mail** merges the documents directly to e-mail. This option is available for e-mail messages only.

- ◆ **Edit individual** *document type* or **To New Document** creates a file with all of the merged data. This option is available for letters, envelopes, labels, and directories.

To merge to a printer

1. Click the Complete the merge link near the bottom of the Mail Merge task pane (**Figures 39, 40,** and **41**).

2. In the Mail Merge task pane, click the Print link (**Figures 42, 43,** and **44**).

3. The Merge to Printer dialog appears (**Figure 45**). Select an option to indicate which records should print:

   - ▲ **All** prints all records in the data source that have been included in the merge.

   - ▲ **Current record** prints the record that is displayed in the document window.

   - ▲ **From / To** enables you to enter a range of records. Enter starting and ending record numbers in each text box.

4. Click OK.

5. Use the Print dialog that appears (**Figure 46**) to set options for printing the merged documents and click OK to print.

✔ Tip

- ■ Printing and the Print dialog (**Figure 46**) are covered in detail in **Chapter 6**.

Figure 46 The Print dialog.

MERGING TO A PRINTER

To merge to electronic mail

1. Click the Complete the merge link near the bottom of the Mail Merge task pane.

2. In the Mail Merge task pane, click the Electronic mail link (**Figure 47**) to display the Merge to E-mail dialog (**Figure 48**).

3. Choose the field containing the e-mail addresses for the recipients from the To drop-down list (**Figure 49**).

4. Enter a subject for the messages in the Subject line text box.

5. Choose a format from the Mail format drop-down list (**Figure 50**):

   ▲ **Attachment** sends the merged document as a Word document attached to an e-mail message. The recipient must have Word (or a program capable of opening Word documents) to view the merged document.

   ▲ **Plain text** sends the merged document as plain text inside an e-mail message. This format removes all document formatting.

   ▲ **HTML** sends the merged document with HTML encoding inside an e-mail message. This format preserves most document formatting, but the recipient must have an e-mail program capable of displaying HTML.

6. Select a Send records option to indicate which records should be sent via e-mail:

   ▲ **All** sends all records in the data source that have been included in the merge.

   ▲ **Current record** sends the record that is displayed in the document window.

   ▲ **From / To** enables you to enter a range of records. Enter starting and ending record numbers in each text box.

Figure 47
The sixth step of the Mail Merge task pane for e-mail messages.

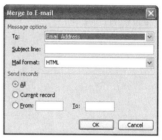

Figure 48 Use the Merge to E-mail dialog to set options for merging directly to e-mail messages.

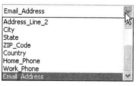

Figure 49 Use the To drop-down list to choose the field containing the e-mail addresses. (This is usually the Email_Address field.)

Figure 50 Choose an e-mail message format.

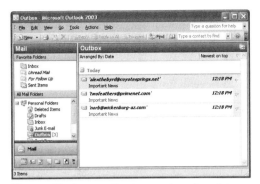

Figure 51 Word merges the documents and creates individual e-mail messages for each recipient.

Figures 52 & 53 These two dialogs may appear when you send e-mail messages as attachments or plain text. You must click Yes to send the messages.

7. Click OK. The document is merged and placed in your e-mail program's outbox (**Figure 51**) to be sent the next time you send e-mail messages.

✔ Tips

■ For an e-mail merge to work properly, you must have MAPI-compatible e-mail software installed (such as Microsoft Outlook) and set up as your default e-mail program. Consult the documentation that came with Windows or your e-mail program to learn how to configure your computer for e-mail.

■ After step 7, a series of dialogs like the ones in **Figures 52** and **53** may appear if you selected Attachment or Plain text in step 5. This is a security feature of Microsoft Word. You must click Yes in each dialog to send the messages.

■ After step 7, if your e-mail program is set up to automatically send outgoing e-mail messages, the messages will be sent rather than stored in the outbox.

To merge to a new document

1. Click the Complete the merge link near the bottom of the Mail Merge task pane (**Figures 39, 40,** and **41**).

2. In the Mail Merge task pane, click the link for Edit individual letters (**Figure 42**), Edit individual envelopes (**Figure 43**), Edit individual labels (**Figure 44**), or To New Document (**Figure 54**).

3. The Merge to New Document dialog appears (**Figure 55**). Select an option to indicate which records should be included in the document:

   ▲ **All** includes all records in the data source that have been included in the merge.

   ▲ **Current record** includes only the record that is displayed in the document window.

   ▲ **From / To** enables you to enter a range of records. Enter starting and ending record numbers in each text box.

4. Click OK. Word creates a new document with the records you specified.

✔ Tip

■ Once Word has created a new document containing all the merged information, you can edit, save, or print it as desired.

Figure 54
The sixth step of the Mail Merge task pane for a directory.

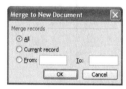

Figure 55
Use this dialog to indicate when records should be merged.

Working with Others

Collaboration Features

In office environments, a document is often the product of multiple people. In the old days, a draft document would be printed and circulated among reviewers. Along the way, it would be marked up with colored ink and covered with sticky notes full of comments. Some poor soul would have to make sense of all the markups and notes to create a clean document. The process was time consuming and was sometimes repeated through several drafts to fine-tune the document for publication.

Microsoft Word, which is widely used in office environments, includes features that make the collaboration process quicker and easier and help protect documents from unauthorized access and changes:

◆ **Properties** stores information about the document's creator and contents.

◆ **Comments** enables reviewers to enter notes about the document.

◆ **Versions** enables reviewers to save multiple versions of the same document. At any time, you can revert to a previous version.

◆ **Change Tracking** enables reviewers to edit the document while keeping the original document intact. Changes can be accepted or rejected to finalize the document.

◆ **Document Protection** limits how a document can be changed.

Document Properties

The Properties dialog enables you to view and store information about a document. This information can be viewed by anyone who opens the document.

The Properties dialog has five tabs of information; click a tab to view its contents:

◆ **General** (**Figure 3**) provides general information about a document.

◆ **Summary** (**Figure 4**) enables you to enter additional information about a document.

◆ **Statistics** (**Figure 7**) provides creation and editing information about the document, as well as statistics about its length.

◆ **Contents** (**Figure 8**) displays the document's title or the first line of the document.

◆ **Custom** (**Figure 9**) enables you to specify additional information about the document using a variety of predefined fields.

To open the Properties dialog

1. Open the document for which you want to view or edit properties.

2. Choose File > Properties (**Figure 1**).

or

1. Choose File > Open (**Figure 1**) to display the Open dialog.

2. Locate and select the document for which you want to view properties.

3. Choose Properties from the Tools menu on the Open dialog's toolbar (**Figure 2**)

✔ Tip

■ The instructions in this part of the chapter assume that you open the Properties dialog for an open document (see the first set of instructions above).

Figure 1
Word's File menu.

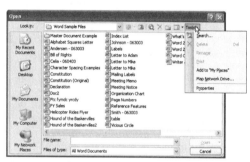

Figure 2 The Tools menu in the Open dialog.

Figure 3 The General tab of the Properties dialog.

To view general document information

1. Open the Properties dialog.

2. If necessary, click the General tab to display its icon, name, and other information (**Figure 3**):

   ▲ **Type** is the type of document.

   ▲ **Location** is the complete path to the document.

   ▲ **Size** is the size, in kilobytes and bytes, of the document.

   ▲ **MS-DOS name** is the name of the document as it appears in an MS-DOS file directory.

   ▲ **Created** is the creation date of the document.

   ▲ **Modified** is the most recent modification or save date of the document.

   ▲ **Accessed** is the most recent date that the document was opened.

   ▲ **Attributes** are Windows file attributes for the file.

3. When you are finished viewing statistics, click OK to dismiss the dialog.

✔ Tip

■ Information in the General tab (**Figure 3**) cannot be changed.

To enter summary information

1. Open the Properties dialog.

2. If necessary, click the Summary tab to display its options (**Figure 4**).

3. Enter or edit information in each field as desired:

   ▲ **Title** is the title of the document. This does not have to be the same as the file name. This field may already be filled in based on the first line of the document.

   ▲ **Subject** is the subject of the document.

   ▲ **Author** is the person who created the document. This field may already be filled in based on information stored in the User Information tab of the Options dialog.

   ▲ **Manager** is the person responsible for the document content.

   ▲ **Company** is the organization for which the author or manager works.

   ▲ **Category** is a category name assigned to the document. It can be anything you like.

   ▲ **Keywords** are important words related to the document.

   ▲ **Comments** are notes about the document.

   ▲ **Hyperlink base** is an Internet address or path to a folder on a hard disk or network volume. This option works in conjunction with hyperlinks inserted in the document.

4. To create a document preview image that will appear in the Preview area of the Open dialog when you select the document (**Figure 5**), turn on the Save preview picture check box.

5. Click OK to save your entries.

Figure 4 The Summary tab of the Properties dialog.

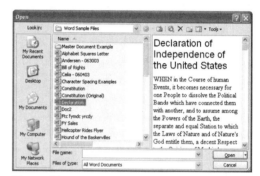

Figure 5 When you create a preview picture, it appears in the Open dialog.

ENTERING SUMMARY INFORMATION

Figure 6
Choose Preview from the View icon's menu to display a Word document's preview picture in the Open dialog.

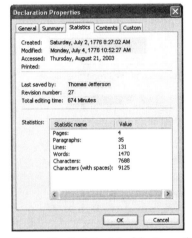

Figure 7 The Statistics tab of the Properties dialog.

✔ Tip

■ Information in the Statistics tab (**Figure 7**) cannot be changed.

✔ Tips

■ It is not necessary to enter information in any of the Summary tab boxes (**Figure 4**).

■ To view a document preview in the Open dialog (**Figure 5**), you may have to select Preview from the View icon menu in the Open dialog (**Figure 6**).

■ I tell you more about the User Information tab of the Options dialog in **Chapter 19**.

To view document statistics

1. Open the Properties dialog.

2. If necessary, click the Statistics tab to display its information (**Figure 7**):

   ▲ **Created** is the creation date of the document.

   ▲ **Modified** is the most recent modification or save date of the document.

   ▲ **Accessed** is the most recent date that the document was opened.

   ▲ **Printed** is the most recent print date for the document. This field will be blank if the document has never been printed.

   ▲ **Last saved by** is the name of last person who saved the document.

   ▲ **Revision number** is the number of times the document has been revised and saved.

   ▲ **Total editing time** is the total amount of time the document has been worked on.

   ▲ **Statistics** is the number of pages, paragraphs, lines, words, characters excluding spaces, and characters including spaces.

3. When you are finished viewing statistics, click OK to dismiss the dialog.

To view document contents

1. Open the Properties dialog.

2. If necessary, click the Contents tab to display its information (**Figure 8**). In most cases, this will be the document title or first line of the document.

3. When you are finished viewing contents, click OK to dismiss the dialog.

To enter custom information

1. Open the Properties dialog.

2. If necessary, click the Custom tab to display its options (**Figure 9**).

3. Select one of the field names in the Name scrolling list.

4. Choose one of the data types form the Type drop-down list (**Figure 10**).

5. Enter the value you want to record for that field in the Value box.

6. Click Add. The information you entered is added to the Properties list in the bottom of the dialog (**Figure 11**).

7. Repeat steps 3 through 6 for each piece of information you want to add.

8. When you are finished entering information, click OK to dismiss the dialog.

✔ Tip

- To delete custom properties information, select its name in the Properties list at the bottom of the Custom tab (**Figure 11**) and click Delete.

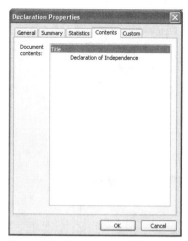

Figure 8 The Contents tab of the Properties dialog.

Figure 9 The Custom tab of the Properties dialog.

Figure 10
Choose a data type from the Type drop-down list.

Figure 11 Data you enter appears in the bottom of the Custom tab of the Properties dialog.

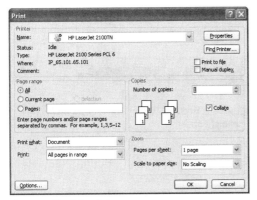

Figure 12 The Print dialog.

Figure 13
Use the Print what drop-down list to specify what part of the document you want to print.

To print document properties

1. Choose File > Print (**Figure 1**) or press ⌨Ctrl P to display the Print dialog (**Figure 12**).

2. Choose Document Properties from the Print what drop-down list (**Figure 13**).

3. Set other options as desired in the Print dialog.

4. Click OK.

   Word creates a document containing document properties and sends it to your printer.

✔ Tip

- Printing and the Print dialog are covered in detail in **Chapter 6**.

Comments

Comments are annotations that you and other document reviewers can add to a document. These notes can be viewed on screen but don't print unless you want them to.

To insert a comment

1. Select the text for which you want to insert a comment (**Figure 14**).

2. Choose Insert > Comment (**Figure 15**).

   A few things happen: The selected text becomes highlighted, a comment marker (colored parentheses) appears around the selected text, the Reviewing toolbar appears, the window splits, and the insertion point moves to the Reviewing pane at the bottom of the window under a color-coded heading with your name (**Figure 16**).

3. Type in your comment. It can be as long or as short as you like (**Figure 17**).

✔ Tips

- Word gets your name and initials from the User Information tab of the Options dialog. I tell you more about that in **Chapter 19**.

- The text highlighting and colored parentheses that appear in the document window (**Figure 16**) do not print.

To close the Reviewing pane

Click the Reviewing Pane button 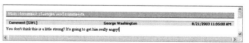 on the Reviewing toolbar.

✔ Tip

- If the Reviewing toolbar is not displayed, choose View > Toolbars > Reviewing to display it.

Figure 14 Start by selecting the text you want to enter a comment about.

Figure 15 Choose Comment from the Insert menu.

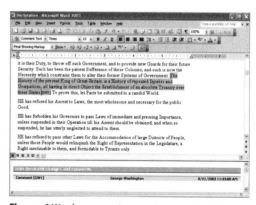

Figure 16 Word prepares to accept your comment.

Figure 17 Enter your comment in the Reviewing pane at the bottom of the window.

Figure 18 When you position the mouse pointer over commented text, the comment appears in a box.

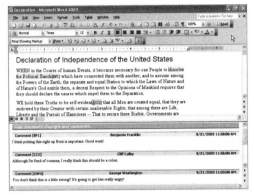

Figure 19 When the Reviewing pane appears, it shows all comments entered in a document.

Figure 20 Choose Final Showing Markup to show all comments and markups in a document.

To view comments

Position the mouse pointer over highlighted text enclosed in colored parentheses. A box appears. It contains the name of the person who wrote the comment, the date and time the comment was written, and the comment text (**Figure 18**).

or

Click the Reviewing Pane button 🔲 on the Reviewing toolbar to display the Reviewing pane and the comments it contains (**Figure 19**).

✔ Tips

- If the colored parentheses do not appear in the document, choose Final Showing Markup from the Display for Review drop-down list on the Reviewing toolbar (**Figure 20**).

- If the Reviewing toolbar is not displayed, choose View > Toolbars > Reviewing to display it.

- You can change the size of the Reviewing pane by dragging the border between it and the main document window.

To delete a comment

1. If necessary, choose View > Toolbars > Reviewing to display the Reviewing toolbar.

2. In the document window, position the insertion point anywhere within the parentheses surrounding commented text.

3. Click the Reject Change/Delete Comment button 🔲▾ on the Reviewing toolbar. All traces of the comment disappear.

To print comments

1. Choose File > Print (**Figure 1**) or press
   ⌃Ctrl ⌃P to display the Print dialog
   (**Figure 12**).

2. Choose one of the markup options from
   the Print what drop-down list (**Figure 13**):

   ▲ **Document showing markup** prints
   each page of the document, slightly
   reduced, with comments in the right
   margin. **Figure 21** shows what this
   looks like in Print Preview.

   ▲ **List of markup** prints the contents of
   the Reviewing pane.

3. Set other options as desired in the Print
   dialog.

4. Click OK to print the chosen markup
   option.

✔ Tip

■ Printing and the Print dialog are covered
  in detail in **Chapter 6**.

Figure 21 Here's the first page of a document printed with markup.

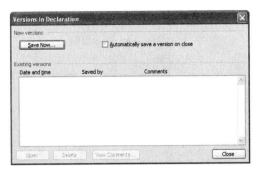

Figure 22 The Versions dialog before any versions have been saved.

Figure 23 Use this dialog to enter comments about the version you are saving.

Versions

Word's Versions feature enables you to save multiple versions of a document. You can then revert to any version to undo editing changes made over time.

To save a version

1. Choose File > Versions (**Figure 1**).

2. In the Versions dialog that appears (**Figure 22**), click Save Now.

3. The Save Version dialog appears (**Figure 23**). If desired, enter comments about the version, then click OK.

   The current state of the document is saved as a version within the document file.

To automatically save a version of the file when you close it

1. Choose File > Versions (**Figure 1**).

2. In the Versions dialog that appears (**Figure 22**), turn on the Automatically save a version on close check box.

3. Click Close.

   From that point forward, every time you close the document, it will be saved as a version.

To open a version

1. With a document that includes multiple versions open and active, choose File > Versions (**Figure 1**).

2. In the Versions dialog that appears (**Figure 24**), select the version you want to open.

3. Click Open.

   The version of the document that you selected opens. Word arranges both document windows—the one that was open in step 1 and the one that you opened in step 3—so you can see them at the same time (**Figure 25**).

✔ Tips

- You can click the View Comments button in the Versions dialog (**Figure 24**) to see the entire text of a comment. It appears in a dialog like the one in **Figure 23**.

- If you save an opened version of a document, it is saved as a separate document.

To delete a version

1. Choose File > Versions (**Figure 1**).

2. In the Versions dialog that appears (**Figure 24**), select the version you want to delete.

3. Click Delete.

4. A confirmation dialog like the one in **Figure 26** appears. Click Yes.

   The version you deleted is removed from the list in the Versions dialog.

✔ Tip

- Each time you save a file version, you increase the size of the file. If your file becomes too large, you can delete early versions to reduce its size.

Figure 24 The Versions that have been saved are listed in reverse chronological order.

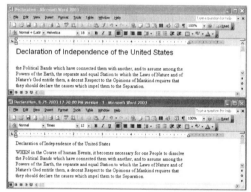

Figure 25 When you open another version of a document, it appears in its own window. Word automatically arranges the windows so you can see them both.

Figure 26 A dialog like this one appears when you delete a version.

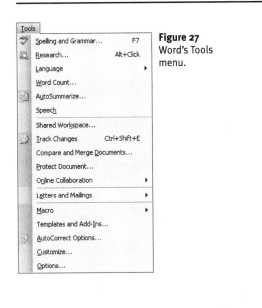

Figure 27
Word's Tools
menu.

Change Tracking

Word's Change Tracking feature makes it possible for multiple reviewers to edit a document without actually changing the document. Instead, each reviewer's markups are displayed in color in the document window.

At the conclusion of the reviewing process, someone with final say over document contents reviews all of the edits and either accepts or rejects each of them. The end result is a final document that incorporates only the accepted changes.

To turn change tracking on or off

Choose Tools > Track Changes (**Figure 27**) or press Ctrl Shift E.

◆ If change tracking was turned off, it is enabled and the Reviewing toolbar appears (**Figure 28**).

◆ If change tracking was turned on, it is disabled.

✔ Tip

■ You can tell whether change tracking is enabled by looking at the Track Changes button on the Reviewing toolbar (**Figure 28**). If the button is selected, change tracking is enabled.

Figure 28 The Reviewing toolbar with change tracking enabled.

CHANGE TRACKING

To track changes

1. Turn on change tracking as instructed on the previous page.

2. Make changes to the document.

   Your changes appear as colored markups and a vertical line appears in the left margin beside each edit (**Figure 29**).

✔ Tip

- If the document is edited by more than one person, each person's revision marks appear in a different color. This makes it easy to distinguish one editor's changes from another's.

To view revision information

Point to a revision mark. A colored box with information about the change appears (**Figure 30**).

✔ Tip

- This is a handy way to see who made a change and when it was made.

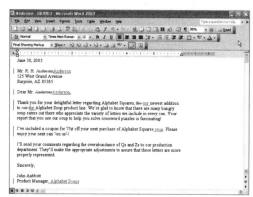

Figure 29 When you edit a document with change tracking enabled, your changes appear as revision marks.

Figure 30 When you point to a revision mark, a box appears with information about the change.

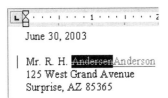

Figure 31 Word selects the change.

Figures 32a & 32b The change selected in **Figure 31** after it has been accepted (left) or rejected (right). As shown here, accepting the change (the deletion of the word *Andersen*) removes the selected text from the document and rejecting the change retains the selected text and removes revision marks from it.

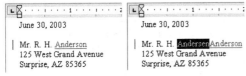

Figure 33 Use this menu to accept all changes in a document.

Figure 34 Use this menu to reject all changes in a document.

To accept or reject changes

1. If necessary, choose View > Toolbars > Reviewing to display the Reviewing toolbar (**Figure 28**).

Then:

2. Click the Next 📄 or Previous 📄 button on the Reviewing toolbar to select the next or previous change (**Figure 31**).

3. Accept or reject the selected change:

   ▲ To accept the change, click the Accept Change button 📄▾ on the Reviewing toolbar. The change is incorporated into the document and its revision mark disappears (**Figure 32a**).

   ▲ To reject the change, click the Reject Change/Delete Comment button 📄▾ on the Reviewing toolbar. The revision mark disappears (**Figure 32b**).

4. Repeat steps 2 and 3 until all changes have been reviewed and either accepted or rejected.

Or then:

2. Accept or reject all changes:

   ▲ To accept all changes, choose Accept All Changes in Document from the Accept Change button's menu on the Reviewing toolbar (**Figure 33**). All revisions are incorporated into the document and the revision marks disappear.

   ▲ To reject all changes, choose Reject All Changes in Document from the Reject Change/Delete Comment button's menu on the Reviewing toolbar (**Figure 34**). The revision marks disappear and the document is returned to the way it was before change tracking was enabled.

To compare & merge documents

1. Open one of the documents you want to compare.

2. Choose Tools > Compare and Merge Documents (**Figure 27**).

3. Use the Compare and Merge Documents dialog that appears (**Figure 35**) to locate and select the document you want to compare the open document to.

4. Use the merge button or its menu (**Figure 36**) to begin the merge:

   ▲ **Merge** merges the currently open document into the one you select in the dialog.

   ▲ **Merge into current document** merges the document you select in the dialog into the currently open document.

   ▲ **Merge into new document** creates a new document that compares the currently open document with the one you select in the dialog (**Figure 37**).

   Word displays the two documents together as one document. Differences between the two documents appear as revision marks (**Figure 37**).

5. Follow the instructions on the previous page to review, accept, or reject revisions, thus creating a final document based on two separate documents.

✔ Tip

■ This feature is especially useful when a document has been distributed to reviewers who neglect to use the change tracking feature to identify their revisions. Open the original document first, then merge the other document(s) into it and review the changes.

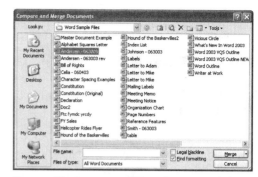

Figure 35 The Compare and Merge Documents dialog enables you to choose a document to compare the current document to.

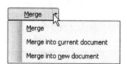

Figure 36 The Merge button is really a menu that offers three options.

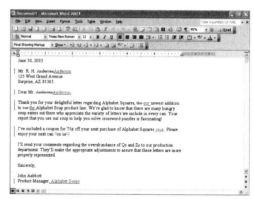

Figure 37 When you merge two documents, Word displays the differences as revision marks. In this example, I compared a revised version of a document with an original version of the same document.

Figure 38
The Protect Document task pane, which replaces the Protect Document dialog in previous versions of Word, offers additional protection options.

Document Protection

Word's Document Protection feature enables you to limit the types of changes others can make to a document. This feature has been greatly enhanced for Word 2003 to offer even more protection options.

Word's new Protect Document task pane (**Figure 38**) offers two types of restrictions to protect document contents:

◆ **Formatting restrictions** prevent users from applying certain styles that you specify.

◆ **Editing restrictions** enables you to limit changes based on the type of editing:

▲ **Tracked changes** enables users to change the document only with the change tracking feature turned on.

▲ **Comments** only enables users to add comments to the document.

▲ **Forms** enables users to enter information only into form fields. (This is an advanced feature of Word that is beyond the scope of this book.)

▲ **No changes** prevents users from making any changes to the document.

✔ Tip

■ Microsoft Office's Information Rights Management (IRM) feature adds additional protection options. Because these features are complex and require the installation of the Windows Rights Management client software, they are not covered in this book.

To display the Protect Document task pane

Choose Tools > Protect Document (**Figure 27**). The Protect Document task pane appears (**Figure 38**).

DOCUMENT PROTECTION

To set formatting restrictions

1. Display the Protect Document task pane (**Figure 38**).

2. Turn on the check box in the Formatting restrctions area.

3. Click the Settings link to display the Formatting Restrictions dialog (**Figure 39**).

4. Toggle check boxes beside style names to indicate which styles are allowed to be applied.

    or

    Click one of the buttons beneath the list of styles to select groups of styles:

    ▲ **All** turns on all style check boxes.

    ▲ **Recommended Minimum** turns on only the check boxes for the styles Word recommends.

    ▲ **None** turns off all style check boxes.

5. To allow formatting applied with Word's AutoFormatting feature to override the restrictions you set, turn on the check box at the bottom of the dialog.

6. Click OK.

7. A dialog like the one in **Figure 40** may appear. Click No.

✔ Tip

■ Formatting restrictions are not enabled until you start enforcing protection, as discussed in the section titled "To enforce protection" later in this chapter.

Figure 39 Use the Formatting Restrictions dialog to specify which styles may be applied in the document.

Figure 40 This dialog may appear if your document contains styles that are not allowed.

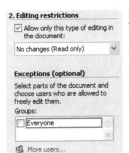

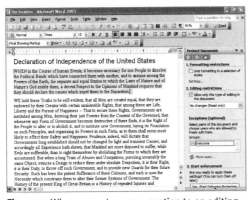

Figure 42 When you set up an exception to an editing restriction, the exception text is highlighted.

Figure 43 Use this dialog to add users for Editing restriction exceptions.

To set editing restrictions

1. Display the Protect Document task pane (**Figure 38**).

2. Turn on the check box in the Editing restrictions area. The area may expand to show additional options (**Figure 41**).

3. Choose a protection option from the drop-down list.

4. If you chose Comments or No changes in step 3, you can use the exceptions area to indicate parts of the document that can be changed by anyone or by specific users: Select a part of the document and turn on the check box beside Everyone or a specific user name in the Groups list. The selection is highlighted and placed within gray brackets, indicating that it can be edited (**Figure 42**).

✔ Tips

- You can add more user names to the Exceptions area (**Figure 41**). Click the More users link in the Exceptions area and use the Add Users dialog that appears (**Figure 43**) to enter Windows user names or e-mail addresses.

- Editing restrictions are not enabled until you start enforcing protection, as discussed in the section titled "To enforce protection" on the next page.

To start enforcing protection

1. Use the Protect Document task pane (**Figure 38**) to set up desired formatting and editing restrictions as instructed on the previous two pages.

2. Click the Yes, Start Enforcing Protection button at the bottom of the task pane to display the Start Enforcing Protection dialog (**Figure 44**).

3. Select the Password option.

4. If desired, enter the same password in each of the boxes in the dialog.

5. Click OK.

   The Protect Document task pane changes to provide information about protection and buttons to work with editable regions (**Figures 45a** and **45b**).

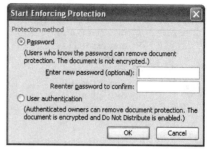

Figure 44 The Start Enforcing Protection dialog.

✔ Tips

■ The User authentication option in the Start Enforcing Protection dialog (**Figure 44**) requires IRM, which is discussed briefly earlier in this section.

■ Entering a password in the Start Enforcing Protection dialog (**Figure 44**) is optional. However, if you do not use a password with this feature, the document can be unprotected by anyone.

■ If you enter a password in the Protect Document dialog (**Figure 44**), don't forget it! If you can't remember the password, you can't unprotect the document!

■ As shown in **Figures 45a** and **45b**, the appearance of the Protect Document task pane varies depending on what restriction options are set and what text the user has selected.

Enabling Protection Options

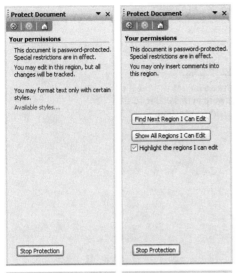

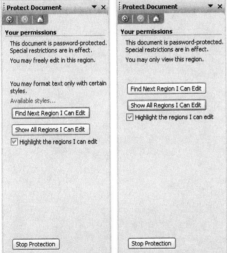

Figures 45a, 45b, 45c, & 45d The many faces of the Protect Document task pane when protection is enforced. The task pane explains what you can do depending on what restrictions are set up and whether the insertion point is in an exception region of the document. These examples all show formatting restrictions plus editing restrictions for Tracked changes (top left), Comments (top right), No changes with an exception region selected (bottom left), and No changes with an exception region not selected (bottom right).

To work with a protected document

What you can do with a protected document depends on how it was protected:

◆ If the document has formatting restrictions, you will only be able to apply certain styles. You can click the Available styles link in the Protect Document task pane (**Figures 45a**, **45b**, **45c**, and **45d**) to display the Styles and Formatting task pane, which lists available styles.

◆ If the document is protected for tracked changes (**Figure 45a**), you can edit the document, but all of your changes will be tracked and you will not be able to turn off the track changes feature. I tell you about tracking changes earlier in this chapter.

◆ If the document is protected for Comments (**Figure 45b**), you can only insert comments in the document—unless exceptions are set up. You can click the Find Next Region I Can Edit and the Show All Regions I Can Edit buttons in the Protect Document task pane to find the document sections you can edit. I tell you about comments earlier in this chapter.

◆ If the document is protected for forms, you can only fill in form fields.

◆ If the document is protected to prevent changes, you cannot edit the document at all (**Figure 45d**)—unless exceptions are set up (**Figure 45c**). You can click the Find Next Region I Can Edit and the Show All Regions I Can Edit buttons in the Protect Document task pane to find the document sections you can edit.

To stop enforcing document protection

1. In the Protect Document task pane, click the Stop Protection button (**Figures 45a, 45b, 45c,** and **45d**).

2. If protection is enforced with a password, a dialog like the one in **Figure 46** appears. Enter the password and click OK.

   Document protection is no longer enforced, although all protection settings remain unchanged.

Figure 46 Enter the protection password in this dialog to stop enforcing protection.

Using Other Programs

Using Word with Other Programs

Microsoft Word works well with a number of other programs. These programs can expand Word's capabilities:

♦ OLE objects created with other Microsoft Office and Windows programs can be inserted into Word documents.

♦ Word documents can be inserted into documents created with other Microsoft Office programs.

♦ Word documents can be e-mailed to others using Microsoft Outlook.

♦ Outlook address book information can be used as a data source for a Word mail merge.

This chapter explains how you can use Word with some of these other programs.

✔ Tip

■ This chapter provides information about programs other than Microsoft Word. To follow instructions for a specific program, that program must be installed on your computer.

OLE Objects

An *object* is all or part of a file created with an OLE-aware program. *OLE* or *Object Linking and Embedding* is a Microsoft technology that enables you to insert a file as an object within a document (**Figure 1**)—even if the file was created with a different program. Clicking or double-clicking the inserted object runs the program that created it so you can modify its contents.

Word's Object command enables you to insert OLE objects in two different ways:

◆ **Create and insert a new OLE object.** This method runs a specific OLE-aware program so you can create an object.

◆ **Insert an existing OLE object.** This method enables you to locate, select, and insert an existing file as an object.

✔ Tips

■ All Microsoft programs are OLE-aware. Many software programs created by other developers are also OLE-aware; check the documentation that came with a specific software package for details.

■ Microsoft Word comes with a number of OLE-aware programs that can be used to insert objects. The full Microsoft Office package includes even more of these programs.

■ You can learn more about inserting text and multimedia elements in **Chapters 9** and **10**.

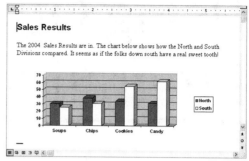

Figure 1 A Microsoft Graph Chart object inserted in a Microsoft Word document.

Figure 2
Choose Object from
the Insert menu.

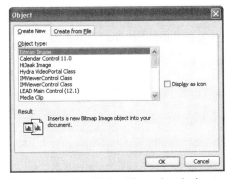

Figure 3 The Object dialog. The options in the
Object type list vary depending on the software
installed on your computer.

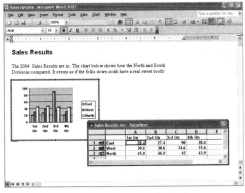

Figure 4 The default Microsoft Graph window.

To insert a new object

1. Position the insertion point where you
   want the object to appear.

2. Choose Insert > Object (**Figure 2**) to
   display the Object dialog.

3. If necessary, click the Create New tab to
   display its options (**Figure 3**).

4. In the Object type list, click to select the
   type of object that you want to insert.

5. Click OK. Word runs the program that
   you selected. It may take a moment for it
   to appear. **Figure 4** shows the default
   Microsoft Graph window and toolbar.

6. Use the program to create the object that
   you want.

7. When you are finished creating the
   object, click outside of the object. The
   program's toolbars and menus disappear
   and you can continue working with Word
   (**Figure 1**).

✔ Tips

- Some of the programs that come with
  Word and appear in the Object dialog
  may not be fully installed. If that is the
  case, Word will prompt you to insert the
  program CD to install the software.

- For more information about using one
  of the OLE-aware programs that comes
  with Word or Office, use the program's
  Help menu.

- Some OLE-aware programs may display
  a dialog or similar interface. Use the
  controls within the dialog to create and
  insert the object.

To insert an existing object

1. Position the insertion point where you want the object to appear.

2. Choose Insert > Object (**Figure 2**) to display the Object dialog.

3. Click the Create from File tab to display its options (**Figure 5**).

4. Click the Browse button.

5. Use the Browse dialog that appears (**Figure 6**) to locate and select the file that you want to insert. Then click Insert.

6. The pathname for the file appears in the Object dialog. Click OK. The file is inserted as an object in the document (**Figure 7**).

✔ Tip

- To insert a file as an object, the program that created the file must be properly installed on your computer or accessible through a network connection. Word informs you if the program is missing.

To customize an inserted object

Follow the instructions in the previous two sections to create and insert a new object or insert an existing object. In the Object dialog (**Figures 3** or **5**), toggle check boxes as desired:

- **Link to File** creates a link to the object's file so that when it changes, the object inserted within the Word document can change. This is similar to inserting linked text, which is explained in **Chapter 9**. This option is only available when inserting an existing file as an object.

- **Display as icon** displays an icon that represents the object rather than the object itself (**Figure 8**). Double-clicking the icon displays the document in the program in which it was created.

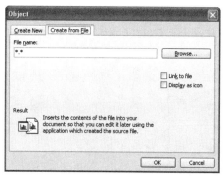

Figure 5 The Create from File tab of the Object dialog.

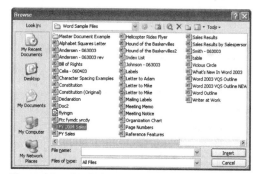

Figure 6 Use this dialog to select the file you want to insert.

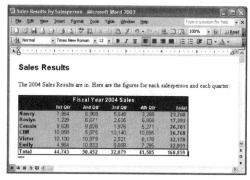

Figure 7 An Excel worksheet inserted into a Word document.

Figure 8 A Microsoft Excel 2003 worksheet displayed as an icon.

INSERTING & CUSTOMIZING OBJECTS

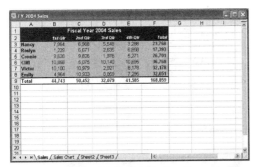

Figure 9 Spreadsheet software like Excel is most often used to create worksheets full of financial information.

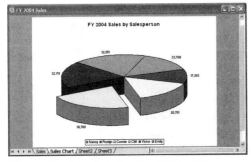

Figure 10 Excel has built-in features for managing lists of information.

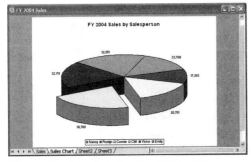

Figure 11 Excel also includes powerful charting capabilities.

Using Excel with Word

Microsoft Excel is the spreadsheet component of Microsoft Office. A *spreadsheet* is like a computerized accountant's worksheet—you enter information and formulas and the software automatically calculates results (**Figure 9**). Best of all, if you change one of the numbers in the worksheet, the results of calculations automatically change as necessary.

You can use Excel with Word to:

◆ Include information from an Excel document in a Word document (**Figure 7**).

◆ Perform a Word data merge with an Excel list as a data source.

✔ Tips

■ Spreadsheet software is especially handy for financial calculations, but it is often used to maintain databases, or simple lists of data (**Figure 10**).

■ Excel also includes powerful charting capabilities so you can create charts based on spreadsheet information (**Figure 11**).

■ To learn more about using Excel 2003, pick up a copy of *Excel 2003 for Windows: Visual QuickStart Guide*, a Peachpit Press book by Maria Langer. (Okay, so it's a shameless plug. But I have bills to pay, too!)

To include Excel document content in a Word document

To insert an Excel document as an object in a Word document, consult the section about OLE objects earlier in this chapter.

or

1. In the Excel document, select the cells (**Figure 12**) or chart (**Figure 13**) that you want to include in the Word document.

2. Choose Edit > Copy or press Ctrl C (**Figure 14**).

3. Switch to Word and position the insertion point in the Word document where you want the Excel content to appear.

4. Choose Edit > Paste or press Ctrl V (**Figure 15**). The selection appears in the Word document at the insertion point (**Figures 16** and **17**).

✔ Tips

- You can also use drag-and-drop editing techniques to drag an Excel document selection into a Word document. Drag-and-drop is discussed in **Chapter 2**.

- Worksheet cells are pasted into Word as a Word table (**Figure 16**). Tables are covered in **Chapter 8**.

- An Excel chart is pasted into Word as a picture (**Figure 17**). Working with pictures is discussed in **Chapter 10**.

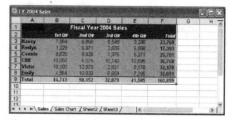

Figure 12 Select the cells...

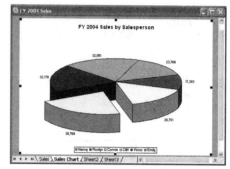

Figure 13 ...or the chart that you want to include.

Figure 14 Choose Copy from Excel's Edit menu.

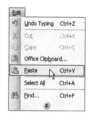

Figure 15 Choose Paste from Word's Edit menu.

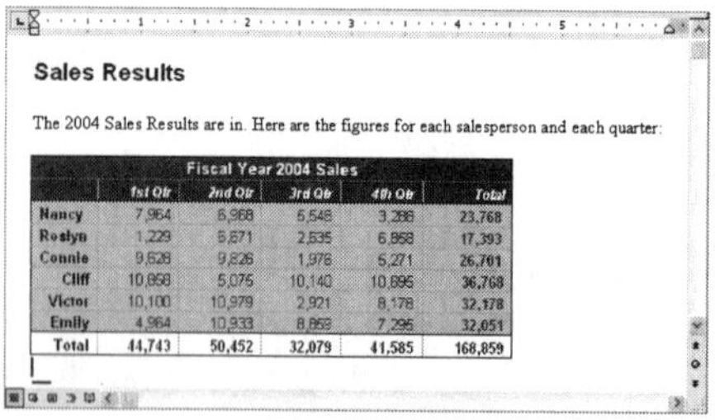

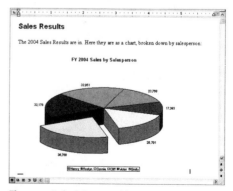

Figure 16 Worksheet cells are pasted into a Word document as a Word table.

Figure 17 A chart is pasted into a Word document as a picture.

Figure 18
Step 3 of the Mail Merge task pane enables you to specify a data source.

To use an Excel list as a data source for a mail merge

1. Follow the instructions in **Chapter 14** to display the Mail Merge task pane and create a main document.

2. In step 3 of the Mail Merge task pane (**Figure 18**), select the Use an existing list option.

3. Click the Browse link and then use the Select Data Source dialog that appears (**Figure 19**) to locate, select, and open the Excel file containing the list you want to use for the merge.

4. If the Select Table dialog appears (**Figure 20**), select the worksheet containing the data you want to use. If the first row of the Excel worksheet contains column headings, make sure the check box for First row of data contains column headers is turned on. Then click OK.

5. The Mail Merge Recipients dialog appears (**Figure 21**). It contains all of the data from the Excel list. Follow the steps in **Chapter 14** to complete the main document and merge the data.

✔ Tip

- Word's mail merge feature is covered in detail in **Chapter 14**.

Figure 19 Select the Excel file containing the data.

Figure 20 If the file contains more than one worksheet, select the worksheet containing the data.

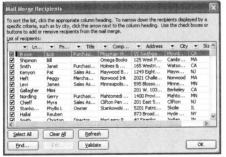

Figure 21 The Excel data appears in the Mail Merge Recipients dialog.

Using PowerPoint with Word

PowerPoint is the presentation software component of Microsoft Office. *Presentation software* enables you to create slides for use at meetings and seminars (**Figure 22**). The slides can be printed on paper, output as 35mm slides, saved as Web pages or graphic files, or shown directly from the computer.

You can use PowerPoint with Word to:

◆ Create a PowerPoint presentation from a Word outline.

◆ Include PowerPoint slides in a Word document.

✔ Tip

■ To learn more about using PowerPoint, consult the documentation that came with the program or its onscreen help feature.

To use a Word outline in a PowerPoint presentation

1. Display the Word outline document you want to use in PowerPoint (**Figure 23**).

2. Choose File > Send To > Microsoft PowerPoint (**Figure 24**).

   The outline is imported into PowerPoint. A new slide is created for each top-level heading. **Figure 22** shows what the outline in **Figure 23** looks like after being sent to PowerPoint and formatted using one of PowerPoint's built-in templates.

✔ Tip

■ Word's Outline feature is discussed in detail in **Chapter 12**.

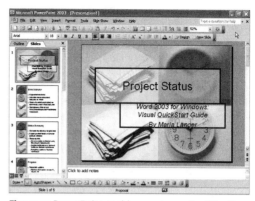

Figure 22 PowerPoint enables you to create slides for presenting information.

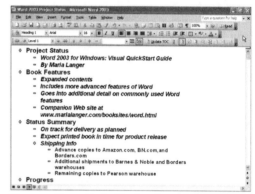

Figure 23 Start with the Word outline that you want to use in PowerPoint.

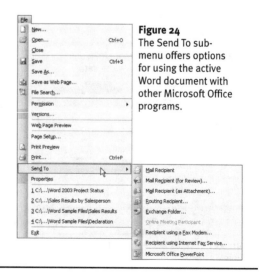

Figure 24 The Send To sub-menu offers options for using the active Word document with other Microsoft Office programs.

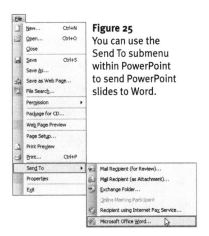

Figure 25
You can use the Send To submenu within PowerPoint to send PowerPoint slides to Word.

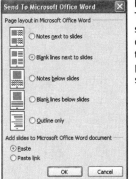

Figure 26
The Send To Microsoft Office Word dialog enables you to select layout and paste options for slides.

To insert PowerPoint slides into a Word document

1. Display the PowerPoint presentation that you want to use in a Word document.

2. Choose File > Send To > Microsoft Office Word (**Figure 25**). The Send To Microsoft Office Word dialog appears (**Figure 26**).

3. Select one of the page layout options in the top part of the dialog to determine how slides will be laid out on Word pages.

4. Select one of the options at the bottom of the dialog to specify whether the slides will be pasted in or pasted in as a link.

5. Click OK.

6. A new Word document is created. Slides are pasted into the document using the layout you specified in step 3. **Figure 27** shows an example of the slides from **Figure 22** pasted into Word with blank lines beside each slide.

✔ Tip

■ PowerPoint slides are pasted into Word as pictures (**Figure 27**). Working with pictures is discussed in **Chapter 10**.

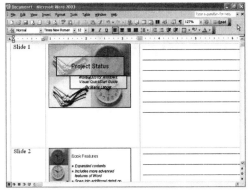

Figure 27 Slides are pasted into a new Word document using the layout you specified.

INSERTING POWERPOINT SLIDES INTO WORD

Using Outlook with Word

Outlook is the e-mail and personal information management software component of Microsoft Office. *E-mail software* enables you to send and receive electronic mail messages (**Figure 28**). *Personal information management software* enables you to store and organize calendar (**Figure 29**) and address book (**Figure 30**) data.

You can use Outlook with Word to:

◆ E-mail a Word document to a friend, family member, or co-worker.

◆ Perform a Word data merge with an Outlook contacts list as the data source.

✔ Tips

■ To learn more about using Outlook, consult the documentation that came with the program or its onscreen help feature.

■ As discussed in **Chapter 14**, performing a mail merge to e-mail messages uses Outlook (or another e-mail program) to send merged data as e-mail messages.

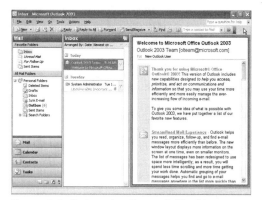

Figure 28 Outlook can handle e-mail (like this message that all new Outlook 2003 users get), ...

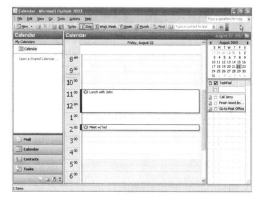

Figure 29 ... calendar events and to-do list items, ...

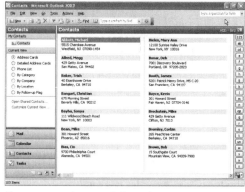

Figure 30 ... and contact information.

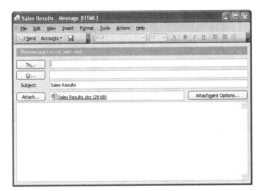

Figure 31 Outlook displays an e-mail form.

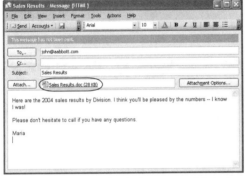

Figure 32 Here's what a finished message might look like. Note that the name of the Word document being sent appears in the Attachments area.

To send a Word document via e-mail

1. Display the Word document you want to send via e-mail.

2. Choose File > Send To > Mail Recipient (as Attachment) (**Figure 24**).

3. Word runs Outlook and displays an empty e-mail window with the To field selected (**Figure 31**). Enter the e-mail address for the person you want to send the document to.

4. If desired, edit the contents of the Subject field.

5. In the message body, enter a message to accompany the file. **Figure 32** shows an example.

6. To send the message, click the Send button. Outlook connects to the Internet and sends the message.

7. Switch back to Word to continue working with the document.

✔ Tips

■ These instructions assume that Outlook is the default e-mail program as set in the Internet control panel. If a different program has been set as the default e-mail program, ignore steps 3 through 6 and send the message as you normally would with your e-mail program.

■ Outlook (or your default e-mail program) must be properly configured to send and receive e-mail messages. Check the program's documentation or onscreen help if you need assistance with setup.

SENDING WORD DOCUMENTS VIA E-MAIL

To use an Outlook contacts list as a data source for a data merge

1. Follow the instructions in **Chapter 14** to display the Mail Merge task pane and create a main document.

2. In step 3 of the Mail Merge task pane (**Figure 33**), select the Select from Outlook contacts option.

3. Click the Choose Contacts folder link and then use the Select Contact List folder dialog that appears (**Figure 34**) to locate and select the folder containing the data you want to use for the merge. Click OK.

4. The Mail Merge Recipients dialog appears (**Figure 35**). It contains all of the data from the Outlook folder. Follow the steps in **Chapter 14** to complete the main document and merge the data.

✔ Tip

- Word's mail merge feature is covered in detail in **Chapter 14**.

Figure 33
Step 3 of the Mail Merge task pane enables you to specify a data source.

Figure 34 Use this dialog to select the Outlook contact folder containing the data.

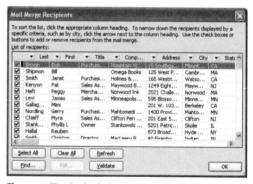

Figure 35 The Outlook data appears in the Mail Merge Recipients dialog.

Web Pages

Web Pages

The World Wide Web has had a bigger impact on publishing than any other communication medium introduced in the past fifty years. Web pages, which can include text, graphics, and hyperlinks, can be published on the Internet or an intranet, making them available to audiences 24 hours a day, 7 days a week. They can provide information quickly and inexpensively to anyone who needs it.

Microsoft Word 2003 has built-in Web page creation, modification, and interaction tools. With Word, you can build Web pages and open links to other Web pages and sites.

✔ Tips

- This chapter provides enough information to get you started using Word to create Web pages. Complete coverage of Web publishing, however, is beyond the scope of this book.

- Web pages are normally viewed with a special kind of software called a *Web browser*. Microsoft Internet Explorer and Netscape Navigator are two examples of Web browsers.

Continued on next page...

Continued from previous page.

- To access the Internet, you need an Internet connection, either through a network or dial-up connection. Setting up a connection is beyond the scope of this book; consult the documentation that came with Windows or your Internet access software for more information.

- To publish a Web page, you need access to a Web server. Contact your organization's Network Administrator or *Internet Service Provider* (*ISP*) for more information.

- A *hyperlink* (or *link*) is text or a graphic that, when clicked, displays other information from the Web.

- An intranet is like the Internet, but it exists only on the internal network of an organization and is usually closed to outsiders.

- Although Microsoft Word can create Web pages and simple Web sites, it is not the best tool for creating complex Web sites. If you're interested in creating a full-blown Web site, consider Web publishing software such as Microsoft FrontPage (part of Microsoft Office Professional Edition), Macromedia Dreamweaver, or Adobe GoLive.

WEB PAGES

Figure 1
Word's File menu.

Figure 2
The New Document task pane enables you to create all kinds of Word documents, including Web pages.

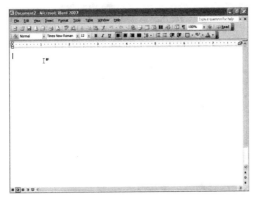

Figure 3 A blank document window for a Web page. Note that Word automatically switches to Web Layout view.

Creating a Web Page

Word offers three ways to create a Web page:

◆ The **Web Page** template lets you create a Web page from scratch, using appropriate formatting options.

◆ The **Save as Web Page** command lets you save a regular Word document as a Web page. This encodes the document and saves it as HTML.

◆ The **Batch Conversion Wizard** can convert a folder full of Word documents to HTML document format.

✔ Tips

■ *HTML* (or *HyperText Markup Language*) is a system of codes for defining Web pages.

■ I explain how to save a regular Word document as an HTML file near the end of this chapter.

To use the Web Page template

1. If necessary, choose File > New (**Figure 1**) to display the New Document task pane (**Figure 2**).

2. Click the Web Page link in the New area. Word creates a blank new Web page and displays it in Web Layout view (**Figure 3**).

3. Enter and format text in the document window as desired to meet your needs.

✔ Tip

■ I explain how to enter and format text for a Web page a little later in this chapter.

To convert Word documents to Web pages

1. Place all the documents you want to convert to Web pages in a single folder.

2. If desired, create a new empty folder for the converted documents.

3. Choose File > New (**Figure 1**) to display the New Document task pane (**Figure 2**).

4. Click the On my computer link under Templates to open the Templates dialog.

5. Click the Other Documents tab to display its contents (**Figure 4**).

6. Select the Batch Conversion Wizard icon.

7. Click OK.

8. The Start screen of the Conversion Wizard dialog appears (**Figure 5**). Click Next.

9. The From/To screen of the Conversion Wizard appears (**Figure 6**). Select the second option and choose HTML document from the drop-down list. Then click Next.

10. Use the Folder Selection screen that appears next (**Figure 7**) to select the Source and Destination folders. To do this, click a Browse button, use the Browse for Folder window that appears (**Figure 8**) to select the appropriate folder, and click OK. Do this for both the Source and Destination folders. Then click Next.

11. Use the File Selection screen that appears (**Figure 9**) to select the files you want to convert. Double-click a file name in the Available list to add it to the To Convert list. When you're finished, click Next.

Figure 4 The Other Documents tab of the Templates dialog.

Figure 5 The Start screen of the Conversion Wizard dialog.

Figure 6 Use the From/To screen to indicate the type of conversion you want to perform.

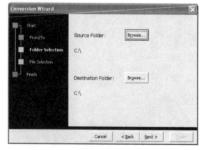

Figure 7 The Folder Selection screen enables you to specify Source and Destination folders.

Figure 8
Use the Browse for Folder dialog to select Source and Destination folders.

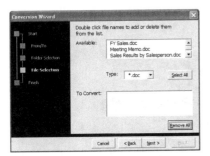

Figure 9 The File Selection screen lets you choose the files you want to convert.

Figure 10 The Finish screen of the Conversion Wizard.

Figure 11 A dialog like this one confirms that the conversion has been successfully completed.

12. In the Finish screen (**Figure 10**), click Finish.

13. Word displays a progress dialog while it converts the files. When it's finished, it displays a dialog like the one in **Figure 11**. You have two options:

▲ Click Yes to repeat steps 8 through 13 for another folder full of files.

▲ Click No to exit the Conversion Wizard.

✔ Tips

■ After step 7, Word may tell you that it needs to install software. Follow the instructions that appear on screen. You may have to insert your Word program disc.

■ As you can see in the drop-down lists in the From/To screen (**Figure 6**), the Batch Conversion Wizard handles more than just HTML conversions.

■ If you only want to convert one Word file, you don't need the Conversion Wizard. Instead, simply open it and use the Save as Web Page command to save it as an HTML document. I explain how near the end of this chapter.

Entering & Editing Web Page Text

You can add, edit, or delete text on a Web page the same way you add, edit, or delete text in a regular Word document. Consult **Chapter 2** for details.

Formatting Web Pages

You format text on a Web page the same way you format text in any other Word document: by using the Formatting toolbar, Format menu commands with their related dialogs, and shortcut keys. **Chapters 3** and **4** provide details about Word's formatting features.

Although the font and paragraph formatting techniques are the same for Web pages as they are for regular Word documents, there are three options that are especially useful for Web pages:

♦ **Background** enables you to set the background color, pattern, or image for the page.

♦ **Theme** enables you to set background patterns, graphic elements, and color schemes for an entire page all at once.

♦ **Horizontal Line** enables you to insert a graphic divider in the Web page.

✔ Tips

■ Formatting and multimedia element insertion techniques not specifically covered in this chapter either work exactly as they do for regular Word documents or they do not apply to Web pages.

■ Additional formatting options are available for Web pages saved to a Web server running FrontPage Server Extensions from Microsoft or SharePoint Team Services from Microsoft. If your Web server supports these options, you can access them from the Web Components command on the Insert menu. You can explore these options on your own if they are available to you.

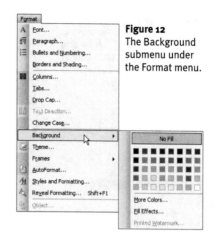

Figure 12
The Background submenu under the Format menu.

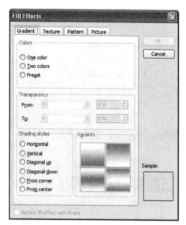

Figure 13 The Fill Effects dialog offers options for Gradient, …

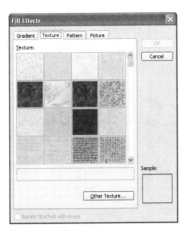

Figure 14 ... Texture, ...

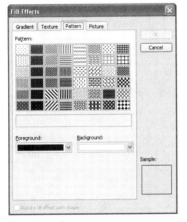

Figure 15 ... Pattern, ...

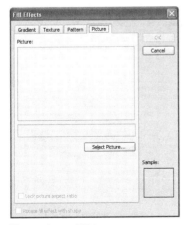

Figure 16 ... and Picture.

To set the page background color, pattern, or image

1. Choose Format > Background to display the Background submenu (**Figure 12**).

2. To set a background color, choose a color.

   or

   To set a background pattern or texture, choose Fill Effects. Then set options on one of the four tabs in the Fill Effects dialog that appears and click OK:

   ▲ **Gradient** (**Figure 13**) enables you to set a gradient fill pattern for the background. Select a color option and shading style to create the gradient you want. Other options appear in the dialog depending on the options you select.

   ▲ **Texture** (**Figure 14**) enables you to set a texture for the background. Click a texture button to select it.

   ▲ **Pattern** (**Figure 15**) enables you to set a standard fill pattern for the background. Select the pattern you want, then choose Foreground and Background colors from the drop-down lists.

   ▲ **Picture** (**Figure 16**) enables you to use an image as a background. The image is repeated to fill the page. Click the Select Picture button to locate and select a picture file on disk.

   or

   To remove a background color or pattern, choose No Fill.

To set the page theme

1. Choose Format > Theme (**Figure 17**) to display the Theme dialog (**Figure 18**).

2. In the Choose a Theme scrolling list, select the name of the theme you want to apply to the page. The Sample area changes to show what the theme looks like.

3. Set other options by toggling check boxes near the bottom of the Theme dialog:

   ▲ **Vivid Colors** makes styles and borders a brighter color and changes the document background color.

   ▲ **Active Graphics** displays animated graphics in the Web browser window when the theme includes them.

   ▲ **Background Image** displays the background image for the theme as the page background. Turning off this check box enables you to use a plain background color with a theme.

4. Click OK to save your settings. The page's colors and background change accordingly to match the theme (**Figure 19**).

✔ Tips

■ Themes are a great way to apply consistent formatting to multiple Web pages.

■ Not all of the themes may be installed in Word. If a theme is not installed, an Install button appears in the Sample area of the Theme dialog. Click that button to install the theme. You may have to insert your Office or Word program disc to complete the installation.

Figure 17
The Format menu.

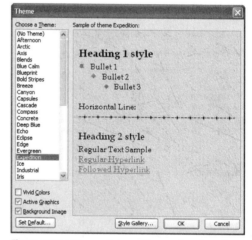

Figure 18 The Theme dialog with one of my favorite themes selected.

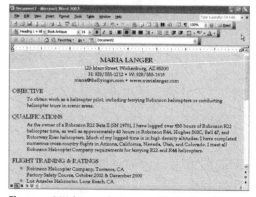

Figure 19 A Web page document with the Expedition theme applied.

SETTING PAGE THEMES

Figure 20 Position the insertion point where you want to insert the line.

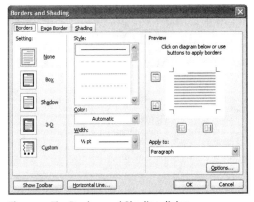

Figure 21 The Borders and Shading dialog.

Figure 22
The Horizontal Line dialog with a line selected.

Figure 23 The line you selected is inserted in the document.

To insert a horizontal line

1. Position the insertion point where you want the line to appear (**Figure 20**).

2. Choose Format > Borders and Shading (**Figure 17**) to display the Borders and Shading dialog (**Figure 21**).

3. Click the Horizontal Line button at the bottom of the dialog.

4. In the Horizontal Line dialog that appears (**Figure 22**), select the line you want to insert.

5. Click OK. The line is inserted in the document (**Figure 23**).

✔ Tips

- To find the horizontal line that corresponds to a specific theme, enter the name of the theme in the Search text box at the top of the Horizontal Line dialog (**Figure 22**) and click Go. The horizontal line for the theme you entered is selected. Click OK to insert it.

- Horizontal lines are graphic images and can be used with any Word document— not just Web pages. I explain how to work with graphics in **Chapter 10**.

- I explain how to use other options in the Borders and Shading dialog in **Chapter 3**.

Hyperlinks

A *hyperlink* is text or a graphic that, when clicked, displays other information. Word enables you to create two kinds of hyperlinks:

◆ A link to a *URL* (*Uniform Resource Locator*), which is the Internet address of a document or individual. Word makes it easy to create links to two types of URLs:

   ▲ **http://** links to a Web page on a Web server.

   ▲ **mailto:** links to an e-mail address.

◆ A link to a Word document on your hard disk or network.

By default, hyperlinks appear as colored, underlined text (**Figure 24**).

✔ Tip

■ Word can automatically format URLs as hyperlinks. Simply type the complete URL; when you press (Spacebar) or (Enter), Word turns the URL into a hyperlink. You can set this option in the AutoFormat tab of the AutoCorrect dialog, which I tell you about in **Chapter 4**.

To insert a hyperlink

1. Position the insertion point where you want the hyperlink to appear.

   or

   Select the text or picture that you want to convert to a hyperlink (**Figure 25**).

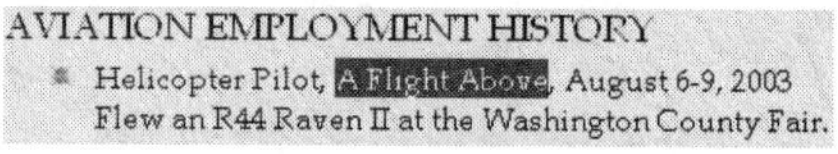

2. Choose Insert > Hyperlink (**Figure 26**), press (Ctrl)(K), or click the Insert Hyperlink button on the Standard toolbar.

   The Insert Hyperlink dialog appears (**Figure 27**).

Figure 24 This portion of a Web page includes three links. By default, they're underlined and appear in a different color text.

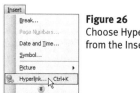

Figure 25 Select the text you want to turn into a link.

Figure 26 Choose Hyperlink from the Insert menu.

Figure 27 The Insert Hyperlink dialog for inserting a link to an existing file or Web page. In this example, the Browsed Pages button displays a list of recently viewed pages and I've clicked on the one I want to link to. Word automatically enters the page's URL in the Address box.

INSERTING HYPERLINKS

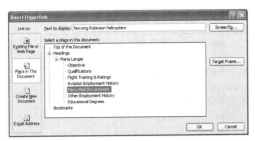

Figure 28 The Insert Hyperlink dialog for inserting a link to a place in the current document, ...

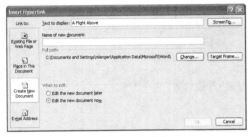

Figure 29 ... to a new document, and ...

Figure 30 ... to an e-mail address.

Figure 31 Use the Set Hyperlink ScreenTip dialog to create a custom ScreenTip for a hyperlink.

AVIATION EMPLOYMENT HISTORY

* Helicopter Pilot, *A Flight Above*, August 6-9, 2003
  Flew an R44 Raven II at the Washington County Fair.

Figure 32 The text you originally selected turns into a hyperlink.

3. Choose one of the Link to buttons on the left side of the dialog:

▲ **Existing File or Web Page** (**Figure 27**) enables you to link to a file on disk or a Web page. If you select this option, click one of the buttons along the left side of the scrolling list to change the display of files or Internet locations. You can either select one of the files or locations that appear in the list or type a path or URL in the Address box.

▲ **Place in This Document** (**Figure 28**) enables you to link to a specific location in the current document. If you select this option, choose a heading in the document hierarchy.

▲ **Create New Document** (**Figure 29**) enables you to create and link to a new document. If you select this option, you can either enter a path-name for the document or click the Change button and use the Create New Document dialog that appears to create a new document.

▲ **E-mail Address** (**Figure 30**) enables you to link to an e-mail address. If you select this option, you can either enter the e-mail address in the E-mail address box or select one of the recently used e-mail addresses in the list.

4. To create a custom ScreenTip for the hyperlink, click the ScreenTip button. Then enter the ScreenTip text in the Set Hyperlink ScreenTip dialog that appears (**Figure 31**) and click OK.

5. Click OK to save your settings and dismiss the Insert Hyperlink dialog.

The hyperlink is inserted.

or

The selected text turns into a hyperlink (**Figure 32**).

INSERTING HYPERLINKS

To follow a hyperlink

1. Position the mouse pointer on the hyperlink. A box containing the URL (**Figure 33**) or ScreenTip (**Figure 34**) for the link and some instructions appears.

2. Hold down Ctrl—the mouse pointer turns into a hand with a pointing finger (**Figure 35**)—and click the link.

   If the hyperlink points to an Internet URL, Word starts your default Web browser, connects to the Internet, and displays the URL.

   or

   If the hyperlink points to a file on your hard disk or another computer on the network, the file opens.

   or

   If the hyperlink points to an e-mail address, Word starts your default e-mail program and displays a new message form with the address included in the link.

kenburg, AZ http://www.marialanger.com/
W: 928/555- CTRL + click to follow link
www.marialanger.com

Figures 33 & 34 When you position the mouse pointer on a hyperlink, a box containing either the link's URL (above) or ScreenTip (below) appears.

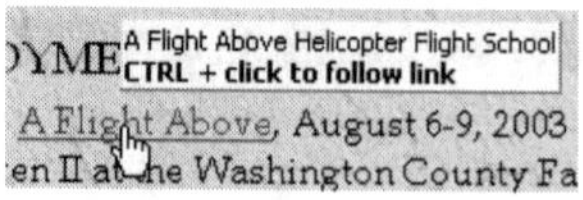

)YME A Flight Above Helicopter Flight School
CTRL + click to follow link
A Flight Above, August 6-9, 2003

)YME A Flight Above Helicopter Flight School
CTRL + click to follow link
A Flight Above, August 6-9, 2003
en II at the Washington County Fa

Figure 35 When you hold down Ctrl, the mouse pointer turns into a hand with a pointing finger.

Figure 36 The Edit Hyperlink dialog.

To remove a hyperlink

1. Position the insertion point anywhere within the hyperlink.

2. Choose Insert > Hyperlink (**Figure 26**) or press Ctrl K.

   or

   Click the Insert Hyperlink button 🔲 on the Standard toolbar.

3. In the Edit Hyperlink dialog that appears (**Figure 36**), click the Remove Link button.

4. Click OK.

   The link is removed from the text, but the text remains. All hyperlink formatting is removed.

or

1. Drag to select the hyperlink.

2. Press Backspace.

   Both the text and its hyperlink are removed from the document.

✔ Tip

■ You can also use the Edit Hyperlink dialog (**Figure 36**) to modify the link, as discussed earlier in this section.

Previewing Web Page Files

Not all Word formatting appears the same in a Web browser window as it does in Word. This means that a Web page you create in Word may look different when published on the Internet or a corporate intranet.

The Web Page Preview command on Word's File menu (**Figure 1**) enables you to see what a Web page you created in Word looks like when viewed with a Web browser. Previewing a Web page helps you ensure that its appearance is acceptable when viewed by others.

To preview a Web page

1. Choose File > Web Page Preview (**Figure 1**).

   Word runs your default Web browser. The Web page appears in the browser window (**Figure 37**).

2. When you are finished viewing the document in your Web browser, choose File > Exit or click the program window's close button to exit and return to Word.

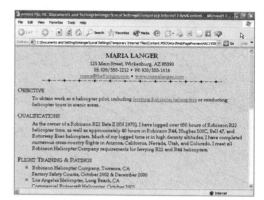

Figure 37 The Web page appears in your default Web browser's window.

Saving Web Page Files

Word enables you to save Web page files in three different formats:

◆ **Single File Web Page** saves all elements of a Web page or site, including text and graphics, into a single MHTML (MIME encapsulated aggregate HTML) document. This makes it possible to send the page or site as an e-mail file attachment. The drawback to single file Web page format is support—it is not supported by all Web browsers. As a result, it's possible to create a file that your intended audience can't open or view.

◆ **Web Page** saves the document text as an HTML document and saves the graphics that appear in the document as separate, linked files. This file format is more compatible with Web browsers. Word's Web Page format, however, includes Word-specific codes that make it possible to view the document as it was originally created if it is opened again in Word.

◆ **Filtered Web Page** removes all Word-specific coding from a Web page file and saves it using standard HTML codes. Like the Web page format, graphics that appear in the document are saved as separate files. This file format is supported by all Web browsers and servers, so it's the least likely to cause errors when viewed by others. It also creates smaller files than Web Page format. The drawback: if the file is opened again in Word, the instructions Word needs to display the document as it was originally created will be gone. Although the file will open, the formatting may be different.

✔ Tip

■ Using the Save As dialog is covered in **Chapter 2**.

To save a Word document as a Web page

1. Choose File > Save as Web Page (**Figure 1**) to display the Save As dialog (**Figure 38**).

2. Use the dialog to enter a name and select a disk location for the file.

3. Choose the desired Web page format from the Save as type drop-down list (**Figure 39**).

4. To specify a page title for the Web page, click the Change Title button. Then enter a new title in the Set Page Title dialog that appears (**Figure 40**) and click OK.

5. Click Save.

6. If you save the document as a single file Web page, a dialog like the one in **Figure 41** may appear. Click Continue.

   or

   If you save the document as a filtered Web page, a dialog like the one in **Figure 42** appears. Click Yes.

   Word saves the file as follows (**Figure 43**):

   ▲ If you saved the document as a single file Web page, Word saves the file and all the graphic elements within it into one MHTML document.

   ▲ If you saved the document as a Web page or filtered Web page, Word saves the file as an HTML document. It also saves each picture within the file as an individual JPEG or GIF format graphic file in a folder named for the Web page. If you saved the document as a Web page, Word also creates and saves a filelist file (**Figure 44**) that contains information Word needs to properly display the document within Word.

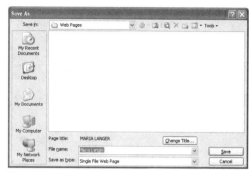

Figure 38 The Save As dialog, when saving a document as a Web page.

Figure 39 The Save as type drop-down list includes all three Web page formats.

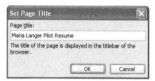

Figure 40 Use this dialog to set a page title.

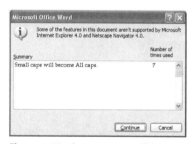

Figure 41 Word may warn you if the page you are saving includes formatting that is not supported by some Web browsers.

Figure 42 When you save a document as a filtered Web page, Word reminds you that Word-specific formatting may be lost.

SAVING WORD DOCUMENTS AS WEB PAGES

Figure 43
In this example, I saved the same document as a Web page in each of the three web page formats. The first icon illustrates the single file Web page. The next two illustrate Web page format. The last two illustrate filtered Web page format.

Figure 44
When you save a document in Web page format, Word saves each of the images individually, along with a filelist file.

✔ Tip

- A Web page *title* is the text that appears in the title bar of a Web browser.

- When copying Web pages to a directory on a Web server to make them available on the Internet or an intranet, be sure to include the Web page file and any associated image files.

To save a Web page as a Word document

1. With a Web page open, choose File > Save As (**Figure 1**) to display the Save As dialog (**Figure 38**).

2. Use the dialog to enter a name and select a disk location for the file.

3. Make sure Word Document is chosen from the Save as type drop-down list (**Figure 39**).

4. Click Save.

SAVING WEB PAGES AS WORD DOCUMENTS

Opening Web Pages with Word

Word can also open Web pages stored on your computer, on another computer on the network, or on the World Wide Web. This makes it possible to view and edit Web pages within Word, even if they were not created with Word.

To open a Web page

1. Choose File > Open (**Figure 1**).

2. Use the Open dialog that appears (**Figure 45**) to locate and select the file you want to open. Then click Open.

   Word opens the Web page you indicated, whether it is on your hard disk, another computer on the network, or the World Wide Web.

✔ Tips

- You can choose All Web Pages from the Files of type drop-down list (**Figure 46**) so only Web pages appear in the Open dialog.

- To open a Web page on the World Wide Web, your computer must be connected to the Internet. Word will initiate a connection if it needs to.

- Double-clicking the icon for a Web page created with Word will open it with your default Web browser—*not* Microsoft Word.

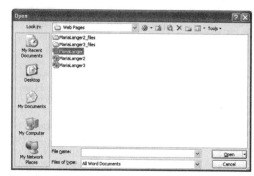

Figure 45 The Open dialog.

Figure 46 The Files of type drop-down list in the Open dialog.

Macros

Macros

Microsoft Word's macro feature enables you to automate repetitive tasks within Word. For example, suppose you often insert a table, with specific size and formatting settings, in your Word documents. You can turn on Word's macro recorder and perform the steps to insert the table. Word records each step as you work. You then save the resulting macro so you can run it at any time. This can be a real timesaver because not only will Word faithfully repeat all the steps you included in the macro, but it will do it much quicker than you could do it manually.

Word's macro feature uses Microsoft Visual Basic for Applications (VBA), a programming language that makes it possible to create complex macro routines for Word. Wizards, for example, which I discuss in **Chapter 2**, are created with VBA. VBA is extremely powerful. Unfortunately, however, it requires a solid understanding the VBA programming language. It has also become a popular tool for virus programmers who unleash their creations on unsuspecting Office users.

This chapter tells you how you can get started using Word's macro feature. It explains how you can record, run, and modify macros. It introduces the VBA programming environment and tells you how you can access VBA-specific help. It also covers Word's built-in macro virus protection feature and explains how you can use it to prevent Word viruses from infecting your computer.

✔ Tip

■ If you performed a custom installation of Office or Word and the macros feature doesn't work at all, it's probably because you did not install Visual Basic for Applications. Use the Office or Word Setup program to install this software if you want to work with Word's macro feature.

Using Word's Macro Recorder

The quickest and easiest way to get started using Word's macro feature is to use its macro recorder. The macro recorder records the steps you perform within Word, automatically writing the VBA code that makes up the macro. You can then run the macro to repeat the steps.

There are two potential "gotchas" that you may encounter when using the macro recorder:

◆ The macro recorder cannot record mouse movements within the document window. So if you want to select text or reposition the insertion point as part of a macro, you must use shortcut keys to do it.

◆ The macro recorder will record *every* keystroke and menu choice you make. So if you make a mistake, it's recorded as part of the macro, too.

To make the most of the macro recorder and record a macro correctly the first time, you should have a solid understanding of what you want the macro to do and what steps are required to complete the task. Don't be afraid to jot down a few notes before starting the recorder. A little advance preparation may save you time in the long run.

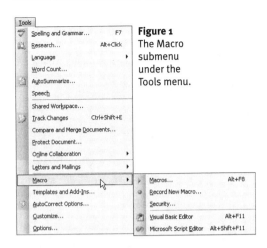

Figure 1
The Macro submenu under the Tools menu.

Figure 2 The Record Macro dialog.

Figure 3 The Store macro in drop-down list.

Figure 4 The tiny Stop Recording toolbar.

To record a macro

1. If necessary, open the document you want to have open when recording the macro steps and position the insertion point or select text as desired.

2. Choose Tools > Macro > Record New Macro (**Figure 1**) to display the Record Macro dialog (**Figure 2**).

3. Enter a name for the macro in the Macro name box. The name cannot contain any spaces or special characters.

4. Choose a location to store the macro from the Store macro in drop-down list (**Figure 3**).

5. If desired, enter a description for the macro by editing the contents of the Description box.

6. Click OK. The tiny Stop Recording toolbar appears (**Figure 4**).

7. Perform the steps you want to record. (Remember that the macro recorder won't record mouse movements or clicks within the document window.)

8. When you are finished performing all of the steps you want to include in the macro, click the Stop Recording button on the Stop Recording toolbar. The Stop Recording toolbar disappears and your macro steps are saved.

Continued on next page...

RECORDING MACROS

365

Continued from previous page.

✔ Tips

- In step 4, if you want to store the macro in a specific template or document, make sure that template or document is open before you open the Record Macro dialog.

- After step 5, you can click the Toolbars button or Keyboard button to display the Commands tab of the Customize dialog (**Figure 5**) or the Customize Keyboard dialog (**Figure 6**). I explain how to use these dialogs to assign toolbar buttons and shortcut keys to commands, including macros, in **Chapter 19**. Clicking OK in either of these dialogs starts the macro recorder.

- In step 3, if you enter the name of an existing macro, when you click OK to begin recording the macro a dialog like the one in **Figure 7** will appear. Click Yes to overwrite the macro; click No to return to the Record Macro dialog so you can rename the macro you want to record.

- In step 7, you can pause macro recording at any time by clicking the Pause Recording button on the Stop Recording toolbar. The button looks pushed in (**Figure 8**) or selected until you click it again to resume recording.

Figure 5 The Commands tab of the Customize dialog. Use this dialog to assign a macro to a toolbar button.

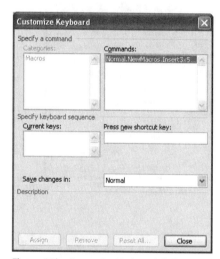

Figure 6 The Customize Keyboard dialog. Use this dialog to assign a shortcut key to a macro.

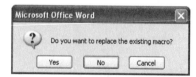

Figure 7 A dialog like this appears when you attempt to record a macro with the same name as an existing macro.

Figure 8 The Stop Recording toolbar with the Pause Recording button selected.

RECORDING MACROS

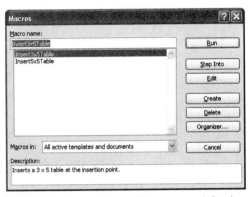

Figure 9 The Macros dialog with two macros defined.

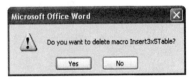

Figure 10 This dialog confirms that you really do want to delete a macro.

To run a macro

1. If necessary, open the document you want to have open when running the macro and position the insertion point or select text as desired.

2. Choose Tools > Macro > Macros to display the Macros dialog.

3. Select the name of the macro you want to run (**Figure 9**).

4. Click Run. The macro steps are performed, just the way they were recorded (but a heck of a lot quicker).

✔ Tip

- If this is the first time you're running a macro that modifies the contents of a document, you might want to save the document before running the macro. This way you can revert to the saved copy if something goes wrong during macro execution.

To delete a macro

1. Choose Tools > Macro > Macros to display the Macros dialog.

2. Select the name of the macro you want to delete (**Figure 9**).

3. Click Delete.

4. A confirmation dialog like the one in **Figure 10** appears. Click Yes.

RUNNING & DELETING MACROS

Working with the Visual Basic Editor

Microsoft Word comes with the Microsoft Visual Basic Editor (**Figure 11**). This program enables you to write macros from scratch and edit macros that were either manually written or written using the macro recorder. The Visual Basic Editor is a true programming environment that includes a variety of windows, commands, and buttons designed for programmers.

To take full advantage of the Visual Basic Editor, you need to know how to program in the VBA languge. But even without a full understanding of VBA, you may be able to edit macros you recorded to remove or modify macro steps. For example, suppose you made and fixed a mistake while recording a macro. You can edit the macro code to remove the step where you made the mistake and the step where you fixed it.

In this part of the chapter, I explain how you can use the Microsoft Visual Basic Editor to edit a macro. I also tell you how you can get started writing macros from scratch and where you can find more information about programming in VBA.

✔ Tip

■ One way to learn more about VBA is to use the Visual Basic Editor to examine macros written by others, including Microsoft Corporation. I explain how to install the Sample Macros file that comes with Word later in this chapter.

Menu bar *Standard toolbar*

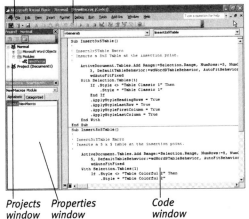

Projects   *Properties*   *Code*
window   *window*   *window*

Figure 11 The Microsoft Visual Basic Editor programming environment for Word 2003.

To edit a macro

1. Choose Tools > Macro > Macros to display the Macros dialog (**Figure 9**).

2. Select the macro you want to edit.

3. Click Edit. Microsoft Visual Basic Editor launches and displays its windows (**Figure 11**).

4. Edit the macro code in the Code window.

5. Choose File > Save *Template Name*, or press ⌗Ctrl⌗ ⌗S⌗.

6. Choose File > Close and Return to Microsoft Word, or press ⌗Alt⌗ ⌗Q⌗.

✔ Tip

- If you don't know a thing about VBA, in step 4, limit yourself to modifying commands that you can recognize. For example, in the macro shown in **Figure 11**, I could change the AutoFormatting options by changing some True settings to False or remove AutoFormatting completely by deleting the step that begins with With Selection.Tables(1). This is pretty easy to figure out, even without VBA programming experience.

EDITING MACROS

369

To write a macro from scratch

1. Choose Tools > Macro > Macros to display the Macros dialog (**Figure 9**).

2. Enter a name for the macro in the Macro name box.

3. Choose a location to store the macro from the Store macro in drop-down list (**Figure 3**).

4. If desired, enter a description for the macro by editing the contents of the Description box.

5. Click Create. Microsoft Visual Basic Editor launches and displays its windows. The Code window includes a new Sub procedure named for the macro (**Figure 12**).

6. Enter the macro code in the Code window for the new Sub procedure.

7. If desired, use commands under the Debug menu (**Figure 13**) to compile or step through your macro statements.

8. Choose File > Save *Template Name*, or press Ctrl S.

9. Choose File > Close and Return to Microsoft Word, or press Alt Q.

✔ Tips

- As you can see in **Figure 12**, the clean slate approach to writing macros requires an intimate knowledge of VBA.

- Using Debug menu commands (**Figure 13**) can help identify syntax errors (**Figure 14**) that will prevent the macro from running properly. These commands can't, however, fix errors. That's up to you. (And please don't ask me for help—I just told you everything I know about VBA!)

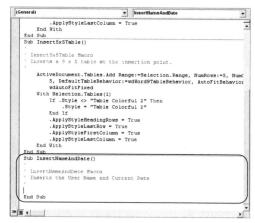

Figure 12 A new Sub procedure is created for the macro in the Code window.

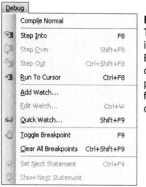

Figure 13 The Debug menu in the Visual Basic Editor. These commands help programmers find errors in VBA code.

Figure 14 If you use the Compile command on the Debug menu to check VBA code that contains an error, a dialog like this appears. When you click OK, the offending code is highlighted in the Code window.

Figure 15
The Microsoft Visual Basic Editor's Help menu.

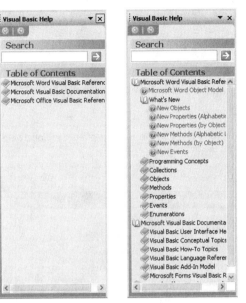

Figure 16 The Microsoft Visual Basic Help command displays three main Help topics in a task pane.

Figure 17 Clicking links in the task pane displays subtopic help document names.

Figure 18 Click the name of a Help document to display its contents in a window.

Getting VBA Help

The Microsoft Visual Basic Editor's Help menu offers commands for accessing an extensive onscreen help system. This help system provides a wealth of information about using the editor. It also provides valuable information about the VBA language to help you write, edit, or debug macros.

In this part of the chapter, I explain how to access Visual Basic Help and tell you what you can expect to find within it.

To access Visual Basic Help

While using the Visual Basic Editor (**Figure 11**), choose an option from the Help menu (**Figure 15**):

◆ **Microsoft Visual Basic Help** displays the Visual Basic Help task pane on the right side of the screen (**Figure 16**). The Table of Contents lists three resources:

▲ **Microsoft Word Visual Basic Reference** provides basic information about programming in Visual Basic for Word.

▲ **Microsoft Visual Basic Documentation** provides information about using the Visual Basic Editor, as well as conceptual and how-to topics.

▲ **Microsoft Office Visual Basic Reference** provides basic information about programming in Visual Basic for the Office suite of products.

Click links in the task pane to browse Help topics (**Figures 17** and **18**). You can also enter search words or a search phrase in the box at the top of the task pane box and click Search to view specific topics.

Continued on next page...

371

ACCESSING VBA HELP

Continued from previous page.

♦ **MSDN on the Web** runs your default
  Web browser, connects to the Internet
  (if necessary), and displays the MSDN
  (Microsoft Developer's Network) home
  page (**Figure 19**). Use this resource to
  search for documents, sample files, and
  products to help you with VBA.

♦ **About Microsoft Visual Basic** displays
  a dialog with information about the
  installed version of Microsoft Visual
  Basic (**Figure 20**).

✔ Tip

■ If a dialog like the one in **Figure 21**
  appears when you attempt to view a VBA
  help topic, the VBA help feature is not
  installed. Click the Yes button and follow
  the instructions that appear on screen to
  install Help. You may have to insert your
  Office or Word program disc.

Figure 19 The MSDN Home page offers additional help
for VBA programming.

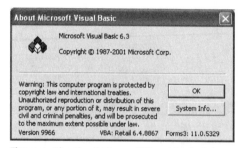

Figure 20 The About Microsoft Visual Basic dialog.

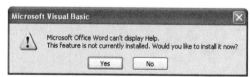

Figure 21 A dialog like this appears when you attempt
to view a Visual Basic Help topic and Help has not been
installed.

Macro Virus Protection

VBA is a powerful programming language that can be used to create applications that work within Microsoft Office. Unfortunately, virus programmers have embraced it as a perfect programming and distribution environment for creating and spreading their dirty deeds.

One of the benefits of Word's macro feature—from the programmer and user points of view—is that macros are stored in template files. This makes them easy to distribute. Send someone a Word file that contains a macro and that person can use the macro on his computer. He can even copy the macro to other templates and share them with others.

It's this feature that also makes macros dangerous to users. Opening a Word file that contains a malicious macro—one designed to do something annoying or damaging—can trigger its functions. Macros like this are known as *macro viruses*.

One particularly widespread example of a Word Macro virus appeared in March 2002. Dubbed "Melissa," it spread in a Word file that, once opened, sent e-mail messages to the first 50 people in the user's Outlook address book. The e-mail message included the infected file as an attachment, thus spreading the virus to other users.

Fortunately, the folks at Microsoft have developed a strategy for protecting Word users from unsuspectingly opening a Word file that includes a macro virus. In this part of the chapter, I explain how you enable macro virus protection and how you can use it to protect your computer from macro viruses.

✔ Tips

- You can protect your computer from all kinds of viruses by installing virus protection software, keeping it up to date, and using it regularly.

- You can learn more about macro viruses on the Microsoft Web site, www.microsoft.com; search for the phrase "macro virus".

To enable macro virus protection

1. Choose Macro > Security (**Figure 1**) to display the Security dialog.

2. If necessary, click the Security Level tab to display its options (**Figure 22**).

3. Select one of the security levels:

   ▲ **High** only allows you to run macros that have been digitally signed and are from a trusted source. When you open a file containing signed macros from an organization that is not on your list of trusted publishers, Word asks whether it should trust all signed macros from that publisher. If you open a file containing unsigned macros, the macros are disabled. No warning is displayed.

   ▲ **Medium** displays a warning like the one in **Figure 23** every time you open a macro from a source that is not one of your trusted sources. Click Disable macros to open the file with macros disabled, Enable Macros to open the file with macros enabled, or More Info to learn more about macro security and warnings.

   ▲ **Low** does not provide any macro virus protection at all. Use this option only if you trust all Word file sources.

4. To further enhance security, click the Trusted Publishers tab to display its options (**Figure 24**) and turn off the check box labeled Trust all installed add-ins and templates.

5. Click OK.

✔ Tips

■ Macro virus protection is set to High by default. You may want to follow these steps, however, to ensure that it hasn't been disabled since Word was installed.

Figure 22 The Security Level tab of the Security dialog.

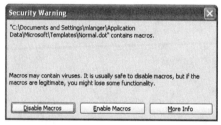

Figure 23 Word can display a dialog like this when you open a file containing macros.

Figure 24 The Trusted Publishers tab of the Security dialog.

■ A *digital signature* is an electronic authentication stamp that confirms that a macro or document from a specific source has not been altered since signed.

Customizing Word

Setting Word Options

Microsoft Word's Options dialog offers eleven categories of options that you can set to customize the way Word works for you:

- ◆ **View** options control Word's onscreen appearance.

- ◆ **General** options control general Word operations.

- ◆ **Edit** options control editing.

- ◆ **Print** options control document printing.

- ◆ **Save** options control file saving.

- ◆ **User Information** options contain information about the primary user.

- ◆ **Compatibility** options control a document's compatibility with other applications or versions of Word.

- ◆ **File Locations** options specify where certain Word files are stored on disk.

- ◆ **Security** options enable you to set file encryption, file sharing, and privacy options for a file.

- ◆ **Spelling & Grammar** options control spelling and grammar checker operations.

- ◆ **Track Changes** options control the track changes feature.

✔ Tip

- ■ Word's default preference settings are discussed and illustrated throughout this book.

To set options

1. Choose Tools > Options (**Figure 1**) to display the Options dialog (**Figure 2**).

2. Click the tab to display the category of options that you want to set.

3. Set options as desired.

4. Repeat steps 2 and 3 for other categories of options that you want to set.

5. Click OK to save your settings.

✔ Tips

- I illustrate and discuss all Options dialog options throughout this chapter.

- If Microsoft Word is installed on your computer as part Office 2003, you can use the Save My Settings Wizard to save your options settings on your computer, another network computer, or the Microsoft Web site. This makes it possible to restore your settings if they should become corrupted or changed by someone else. Choose Start > All Programs > Microsoft Office > Microsoft Office Tools > Microsoft Office 2003 Save My Settings Wizard to get started.

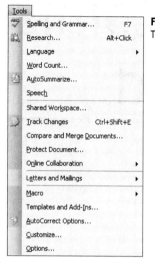

Figure 1
The Tools menu.

View Options

The View tab of the Options dialog (**Figure 2**) offers options in four categories: Show, Formatting marks, Print and Web Layout options, and Outline and Normal options.

Show

Show options determine what Word interface elements appear on screen:

◆ **Startup Task Pane** is the New document task pane that appears when you run Word from the Start menu.

◆ **Highlight** displays text highlighting.

◆ **Bookmarks** displays document bookmarks by enclosing their names in square brackets. If displayed, the bookmarks do not print.

◆ **Status bar** displays the status bar at the bottom of the window.

◆ **ScreenTips** displays information or comments in boxes when you point to buttons or annotated text.

◆ **Smart tags** displays purple dotted underlines beneath text for which there is a smart tag. Pointing to the text displays a pop-up menu you can use to perform tasks with the text. **Figure 3** shows an example of a smart tag that appears when you type in a date.

◆ **Animated text** displays animation applied to text. Turning off this option displays animated text the way it will print.

◆ **Horizontal scroll bar** displays a scroll bar along the bottom of the window.

◆ **Vertical scroll bar** displays a scroll bar along the right side of the window.

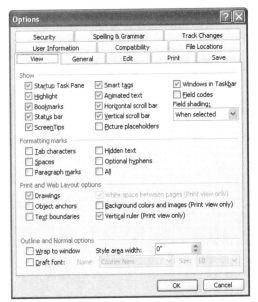

Figure 2 The default settings in the View tab of the Options dialog.

Figure 3
Smart tags enable you to perform tasks with certain text.

Continued on next page...

VIEW OPTIONS

Continued from previous page.

- ◆ **Picture placeholders** displays graphics as empty boxes. Turning on this option can speed up the display of documents with a lot of graphics.

- ◆ **Windows in Taskbar** displays a Taskbar icon for each open Word document window.

- ◆ **Field codes** displays field codes instead of results.

- ◆ **Field shading** enables you to specify how you want fields shaded. The options are:

  - ▲ **Never** never shades fields.
  - ▲ **Always** always shades fields.
  - ▲ **When selected** only shades a field when it is selected.

Formatting marks

Formatting marks options determine which (if any) formatting mark characters appear on screen (**Figure 4**).

- ◆ **Tab characters** displays gray right-pointing arrows for tab characters.

- ◆ **Spaces** displays tiny gray dots for space characters.

- ◆ **Paragraph marks** displays gray backwards Ps for return characters.

- ◆ **Hidden text** displays text formatted as hidden with a dotted underline.

- ◆ **Optional hyphens** displays L-shaped hyphens for optional hyphen characters.

- ◆ **All** displays all formatting marks. Turning on this option is the same as turning on the Show/Hide ¶ button ⸰¶⸰ on the Standard toolbar.

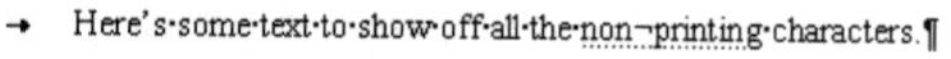

→   Here's·some·text·to·show·off·all·the·non‑printing·characters.¶

Figure 4 Formatting marks revealed!

Print and Web Layout options

Window options determine which elements are displayed in Print and Web Layout views.

◆ **Drawings** displays objects created with Word's drawing tools. Turning off this option can speed up the display and scrolling of documents with many drawings.

◆ **Object anchors** displays an anchor marker indicating that an object is attached to text. An object's anchor can only appear when the object is selected, this check box is turned on, and non-printing characters are displayed. You must turn on this option to move an anchor.

◆ **Text boundaries** displays dotted lines around page margins, text columns, and objects.

◆ **White space between pages** displays the full top and bottom margins of pages in Print Layout view. This option can only be modified if the currently active document is displayed in Print Layout view.

◆ **Background colors and images** displays background colors or images set for the page when in Print Layout view.

◆ **Vertical ruler** displays a ruler down the left side of the window in Print Layout view.

VIEW OPTIONS

Outline and Normal options

Window options determine which elements are displayed in Outline and Normal views.

◆ **Wrap to window** wraps text to the width of the window rather than to the right indent or margin.

◆ **Draft font** displays most character formatting as bold or underlined and displays graphics as empty boxes. If you turn on this option, you can set the font and size to use for the draft font (**Figure 5**). Using this option can speed up the display of heavily formatted documents.

◆ **Style area width** enables you to specify a width for the style area. When set to a value greater than 0, the style area appears along the left side of the window and indicates the style applied to each paragraph in the document (**Figure 6**).

Figure 5 When you turn on the Draft font option, you can choose a font and size.

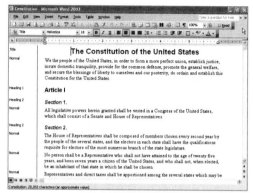

Figure 6 The Style area displayed in Normal view.

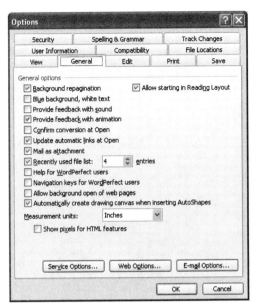

Figure 7 The default settings in the General tab of the Options dialog.

General Options

General options (**Figure 7**) control the general operation of Word:

- ◆ **Background repagination** paginates documents automatically as you work. (This option cannot be turned off in Page Layout view.)

- ◆ **Blue background, white text** displays the document as white text on a blue background—like the old WordPerfect software.

- ◆ **Provide feedback with sound** plays sound effects at the conclusion of certain actions or with the appearance of alerts.

- ◆ **Provide feedback with animation** displays special animated cursors while waiting for certain actions to complete.

- ◆ **Confirm conversion at Open** displays a dialog that you can use to select a converter when you open a file created with another application.

- ◆ **Update automatic links at Open** automatically updates linked information when you open a document containing links to other files.

- ◆ **Mail as attachment** sends the current document as an attachment to an e-mail message when you choose File > Send To: Mail Recipient (as Attachment). With this check box turned off, the contents of the current document are copied into an e-mail message rather than sent as an attachment.

- ◆ **Recently used file list** enables you to specify the number of recently opened files that should appear near the bottom of the File menu. This feature is handy for quickly reopening recently accessed files.

Continued on next page...

GENERAL OPTIONS

Continued from previous page.

◆ **Help for WordPerfect users** displays Word instructions when you press a Word-Perfect for DOS key combination.

◆ **Navigation keys for WordPerfect users** changes the functions of Page Up, Page Down, Home, End, and Esc to the way they work in WordPerfect.

◆ **Allow background open of web pages** enables you to open HTML documents in the background while you work with Word.

◆ **Automatically create a drawing canvas when inserting AutoShapes** creates a drawing canvas on the drawing layer of a document when you draw an AutoShape.

◆ **Allow starting in Reading Layout** opens documents in Reading Layout view.

◆ **Measurement units** enables you to select the measurement unit used throughout Word. Options are Inches, Centimeters, Millimeters, Points, and Picas.

◆ **Show pixels for HTML features** changes the default unit to pixels in dialogs while working with HTML features.

GENERAL OPTIONS

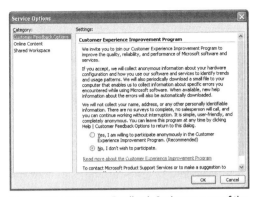

Figure 8 The Customer Feedback Options screen of the Service Options dialog.

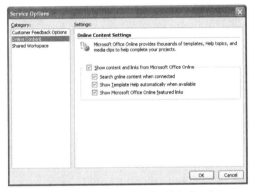

Figure 9 The Online Content screen of the Service Options dialog.

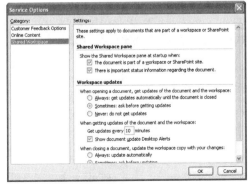

Figure 10 The Shared Workspace screen of the Service Options dialog.

Service Options

Clicking the Service Options button displays the Service Options dialog (**Figures 8** through **10**), which includes screens for Customer Feedback Options, Online Content, and Shared Workspace.

◆ **Customer Feedback Options** (**Figure 8**) enables you to indicate whether you want to participate in Microsoft's Customer Experience Improvement Program.

◆ **Online Content** (**Figure 9**) enables you to specify whether Word should include content from the Microsoft Office Online Web site in Word Help and elsewhere throughout Word software. To enable online content, turn on the top check box. Then toggle check boxes for the type of content you want to view.

◆ **Shared Workspaces** (**Figure 10**) enables you to set options for Word's Shared Workspace feature. This is an advanced feature of Word that requires special server software and is not covered in this book.

GENERAL OPTIONS

Web Options

Clicking the Web Options button displays the Web Options dialog (**Figures 11** through **15**), which has five different tabs of options for creating and working with Web pages. Although these options are advanced and far beyond the scope of this book, here's a quick overview of each.

◆ **Browsers** options (**Figure 11**) control various compatibility and formatting options for the Web pages you create.

◆ **Files** options (**Figure 12**) control file naming and locations and the default editor for Web pages.

◆ **Pictures** options (**Figure 13**) control the file formats of images and the resolution of the target monitor.

◆ **Encoding** options (**Figure 14**) control how a Web page is coded when saved.

◆ **Fonts** options (**Figure 15**) control the character set and default fonts.

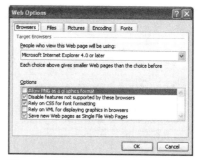

Figure 11 The Browsers tab of the Web Options dialog.

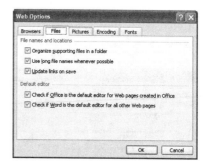

Figure 12 The Files tab of the Web Options dialog.

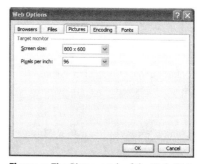

Figure 13 The Pictures tab of the Web Options dialog.

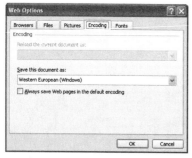

Figure 14 The Encoding tab of the Web Options dialog.

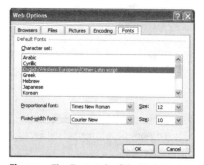

Figure 15 The Fonts tab of the Web Options dialog.

Figure 16 The E-mail Signature tab of the E-mail Options dialog.

Figure 17 The Personal Stationery tab of the E-mail Options dialog.

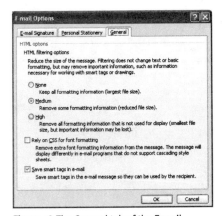

Figure 18 The General tab of the E-mail Options dialog.

E-mail Options

Clicking the E-mail Options button displays the E-mail Options dialog (**Figures 16** through **18**), which has three tabs of options related to e-mail. The options are advanced and beyond the scope of this book, but here's a quick look at each.

◆ **E-mail Signature** options (**Figure 16**) enables you to enter and save text that can appear at the bottom of every e-mail message you write.

◆ **Personal Stationery** options (**Figure 17**) enables you to specify the themes and font appearance used in e-mail messages you write.

◆ **General** options (**Figure 18**) enables you to set HTML options for e-mail messages you send.

GENERAL OPTIONS

385

Edit Options

Edit options (**Figure 19**) control the way certain editing tasks work. There are three categories: Editing options, Cut and paste options, and Click and type.

Editing options

Editing options set the way text is edited:

◆ **Typing replaces selection** deletes text when you start typing. If you turn this check box off, Word inserts typed text to the left of any text selected before you began typing.

◆ **Drag-and-drop text editing** allows you to move or copy selected text by dragging it.

◆ **Use the INS key for paste** enables you to press [Ins] to use the Paste command.

◆ **Overtype mode** replaces characters, one at a time, as you type. This is the opposite of Insert mode.

◆ **Use smart cursoring** moves the insertion point as you scroll up or down.

◆ **Picture editor** is the program you use to edit pictures within Microsoft Word.

◆ **Insert/paste picture as** enables you to determine how pictures are inserted or pasted into your document. The default is In line with text, but you can select a different option from the drop-down list (**Figure 20**).

◆ **Use smart paragraph selection** includes the paragraph mark when you select a paragraph.

Figure 19 The default settings in the Edit tab of the Options dialog.

Figure 20
Use this drop-down list to determine how pictures are inserted into your documents.

- **Use CTRL+Click to follow hyperlink** requires you to hold down Ctrl while clicking a hyperlink to follow it.

- **When selecting, automatically select entire word** selects entire words when your selection includes the spaces after words. This feature makes it impossible to use the mouse to select multiple word fragments.

- **Prompt to update style** tells Word to display a dialog when you format text containing a style and then choose the style again. The dialog enables you to update the style to match the new formatting or reapply the style.

- **Keep track of formatting** tells Word to record formatting commands as you type so you can apply the formatting again.

- **Mark formatting inconsistencies** applies a wavy blue underline to formatting that is similar but not exactly the same as other text in the document. To use this option, you must also enable the Keep track of formatting option.

EDIT OPTIONS

Cut and paste options

Cut and paste options set the way the cut, copy, and paste commands work.

Figure 21
Clicking the Paste Options button beneath pasted text displays options for the text.

◆ **Show Paste Options button** displays a button beneath pasted text that offers additional options for the text (**Figure 21**).

◆ **Use smart cut and paste** adds or removes spaces as necessary when you delete, drag, or paste text. This feature can save time when editing text.

◆ **Settings** displays the Settings dialog (**Figure 22**), which you can use to fine-tune the way the smart cut and paste feature works.

Figure 22 Use the Settings dialog to fine-tune the way the smart cut and paste feature works.

Click and type

Click and type options control the way the click and type feature works:

◆ **Enable click and type** turns on the click and type feature.

◆ **Default paragraph style** enables you to select the default style for click and type entries in a document.

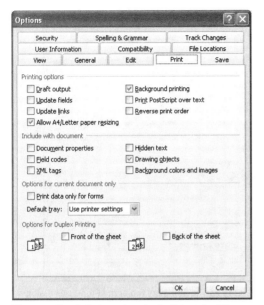

Figure 23 The default settings in the Print tab of the Options dialog.

Print Options

Print options (**Figure 23**) control the way documents print. There are four categories: Printing options, Include with document, Options for current document only, and Options for Duplex Printing.

Printing options

Printing options let you specify how the document content is updated and printed:

- ◆ **Draft output** prints the document with minimal formatting. This may make the document print faster, but not all printers support this option.

- ◆ **Update fields** automatically updates Word fields before you print. This feature prevents you from printing a document with outdated field contents.

- ◆ **Update links** automatically updates information in linked files before you print. This feature prevents you from printing a file with outdated linked file contents.

- ◆ **Allow A4/Letter paper sizing** automatically adjusts the paper size for documents created with another country's standard paper size (such as A4, which is used in Europe) to your standard paper size (which is Letter in the U.S.).

- ◆ **Background printing** allows your printer to print Word documents in the background while you continue to work with Word or other programs. With this option turned off, you would have to wait for a document to finish printing before you could continue working.

Continued on next page...

PRINT OPTIONS

Continued from previous page.

- **Print PostScript over text** prints any PostScript code in a converted Word for Macintosh document (such as a digital watermark) on top of document text instead of underneath it. This option only works with PostScript printers.

- **Reverse print order** prints documents in reverse order—last page first. This might be useful if your printer stacks output face up.

Include with document

Include with document options enable you to print or suppress specific information from the document:

- **Document properties** prints the document's summary information on a separate page after the document. This information is stored in the Summary tab of the Properties dialog (**Figure 24**).

- **Field codes** prints field codes instead of field contents.

- **XML tags** prints the XML tags applied to an XML document.

- **Hidden text** prints text formatted as hidden.

- **Drawing objects** prints objects drawn with Word's drawing tools.

- **Background colors and images** prints any background colors, patterns, or images applied to document pages.

Figure 24 The Summary tab of the Properties dialog.

Options for current document only

As the name implies, options for current document only affect the way the active document prints:

◆ **Print data only for forms** prints just the information entered in fill-in forms—not the form itself.

◆ **Default tray** is the default tray from which paper should be used when printing. (This option is printer-specific and may not appear for your printer.)

Options for Duplex Printing

These options control the order of pages printed on both sides.

◆ **Front of the sheet** prints the first page on the top sheet. With this check box turned off, the first page prints on the bottom sheet.

◆ **Back of the sheet** prints the second page on the top sheet. With this check box turned off, the second page prints on the bottom sheet.

PRINT OPTIONS

Save Options

Save options (**Figure 25**) control the way files are saved to disk. There are two categories of Save options: Save options and Default format.

Save options

Save options enable you to set file saving options for all files that you save.

◆ **Always create backup copy** saves the previous version of a file as a backup copy in the same folder as the original. Each time the file is saved, the new backup copy replaces the old one.

◆ **Allow fast saves** speeds up saving by saving only the changes to an existing file. If you turn off this check box, Word saves the entire file; this takes longer but results in slightly smaller files that are less likely to suffer from file corruption problems. This option is not available when the Always create backup copy option is enabled.

◆ **Allow background saves** allows Word to save a document in the background while you continue working with it. This option is especially useful for large or complex files.

◆ **Embed TrueType fonts** includes font information in the document so others can view your document with the fonts you applied, even if the fonts are not installed in their system. If you turn on this check box, you can turn on one or both of the options beneath it:

▲ **Embed characters in use only** embeds only the characters that are used in the document. This minimizes file size.

▲ **Do not embed common system fonts** does not embed the font if it is one of the commonly installed system fonts.

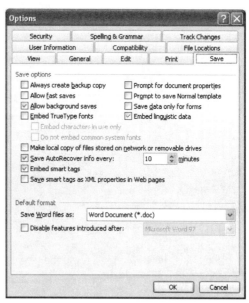

Figure 25 The default settings in the Save tab of the Options dialog.

◆ **Make local copy of files stored on network or removable drives** makes a copy on your hard disk of any file you store on a network or removable drive.

◆ **Save AutoRecover info every** enables you to set a frequency for automatically saving a special document recovery file. Word can use the AutoRecover file to recreate the document if your computer crashes or loses power before you get a chance to save changes.

◆ **Embed smart tags** saves smart tag information with the document.

◆ **Save smart tags as XML properties in Web pages** saves smart tags in files you save as HTML documents.

◆ **Prompt for document properties** displays the Summary tab of the Properties dialog (**Figure 24**) when you save a file for the first time. You can use this dialog to enter and store information about the file.

◆ **Prompt to save Normal template** displays a dialog that enables you to save or discard changes you made to the default settings in the Normal template. With this check box turned off, Word automatically saves changes to the Normal template.

◆ **Save data only for forms** saves the data entered into a form as a single, tab-delimited record that you can import into a database.

◆ **Embed linguistic data** saves speech and handwritten input data with the file.

Default format

The Default format options enables you to set the default format for files you save.

◆ **Save Word files as** enables you to choose a default format for saving Word files. The drop-down list (**Figure 26**) offers the same options found in the Save As dialog.

◆ **Disable features introduced after** enables you to select the features you want included with the file. Choose a version of Word from the drop-down list (**Figure 27**) to disable features introduced after that Word version.

User Information Options

The User Information options (**Figure 28**) store information about the primary user of that copy of Word. This information is used by a variety of features throughout Word. The fields of information here are self-explanatory, so I won't go into them in detail.

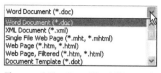

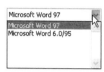

Figure 26 The Save Word files as drop-down list in the Save tab of the Options dialog.

Figure 27
Use this drop-down list to choose the features you want saved with files.

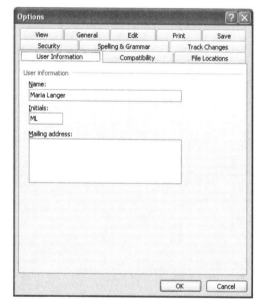

Figure 28 The User Information tab of the Options dialog.

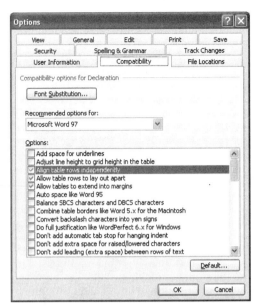

Figure 29 The default settings in the Compatibility tab of the Options dialog.

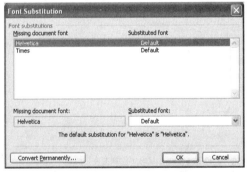

Figure 30 The Font Substitution dialog.

Figure 31
The Recommended options for drop-down list.

Compatibility Options

Compatibility options (**Figure 29**) control the internal formatting of the current Word document for compatibility with other applications or versions of Word.

◆ **Font Substitution** enables you to specify a font to be used in place of a font applied in the document but not installed on your computer. (This happens most often when you open a file that was created on someone else's computer.) Click this button to display the Font Substitution dialog (**Figure 30**). You can then select the missing font name and choose a substitution font from the Substituted font drop-down list. The menu includes all fonts installed on your computer. To reformat text by applying the substituted font, click the Convert Permanently button. If the document does not contain any missing fonts, Word does not display the Font Substitution dialog.

◆ **Recommended options for** enables you to select a collection of compatibility rules for a specific application. Choose an option from the drop-down list (**Figure 31**).

◆ **Options** enables you to toggle check boxes for a variety of internal formatting options. These options are automatically set when you choose one of the rule sets from the Recommended options for drop-down list, but you can override them as desired.

◆ **Default** applies the current dialog settings to all documents created with the current template from that point forward.

File Locations Options

File Locations options (**Figure 32**) enable you to set the default disk location for certain types of files. This makes it easier for Word (and you) to find these files.

To set or change a default file location

1. Click to select the name of the file type for which you want to set or change the file location (**Figure 32**).

2. Click the Modify button.

3. Use the Modify Location dialog that appears (**Figure 33**) to locate and select the folder in which the files are or will be stored.

4. Click OK.

   The pathname for the location appears to the right of the name of the file type (**Figure 34**).

Figure 32 The File Locations tab of the Options dialog.

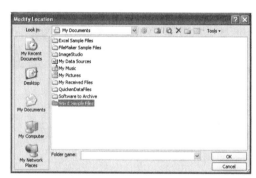

Figure 33 Use this dialog to set the location of a specific type of file.

Figure 34 The pathname for the folder you selected appears in the dialog.

FILE LOCATIONS OPTIONS

Security Options

Security options (**Figure 35**) help keep your documents and system secure. There are four categories of options: File encryption options for this document, File sharing options for this document, Privacy options, and Macro security.

File encryption options for this document

File encryption encodes a file so it is impossible to read without entering a correct password.

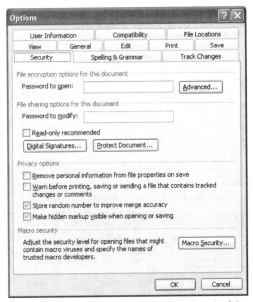

Figure 35 The default settings in the Security tab of the Options dialog.

Figure 36 Use this dialog to confirm that you know the password to open the file.

Figure 37 Use this dialog to enter a file's password when opening it.

◆ **Password to open** enables you to specify a password that must be entered to open the file. Entering a password in this box enables the encryption feature. When you click OK to save your settings and close the Options dialog, Word displays a dialog that prompts you to enter this password again (**Figure 36**). Later, when you reopen the document, Word displays a dialog that prompts you to enter the password (**Figure 37**). If you fail to enter the correct password, the file will not open.

◆ Advanced displays the Encryption Type dialog (**Figure 38**), which you can use to set advanced file protection options.

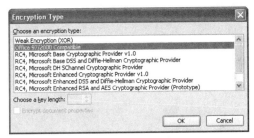

Figure 38 The Encryption Type dialog.

File sharing options for this document

File sharing options protect a document from unauthorized modification.

◆ **Password to modify** enables you to specify a password that must be entered to save modifications to the file. When you click OK to save your settings and close the Options dialog, Word displays a dialog similar to the one in **Figure 36** that prompts you to enter this password again. Later, when you reopen the document, Word displays a dialog that prompts you to enter the password (**Figure 39**). If you cannot enter the correct password, you can open the file as a read-only file.

◆ **Read-only recommended** displays a dialog that recommends that the file be opened as a read-only file (**Figure 40**) each time the file is opened. If the file is opened as read-only, changes to the file must be saved in a file with a different name or in a different disk location.

◆ **Digital Signatures** displays the Digital Signature dialog (**Figure 41**), which provides information about signatures attached to the document.

◆ **Protect Document** displays the Protect Document task pane (**Figure 42**), which you can use to limit the types of changes that can be made to the document. (This feature is covered in **Chapter 15**.)

Figure 39
This dialog appears when you open a document that has a password to modify it.

Figure 40 This dialog appears when you open a document that is set as Read-only recommended.

Figure 41 The Digital Signature dialog displays information about digital signatures in a document.

Figure 42
Use the Protect Document task pane to limit the types of modifications a user can make to a document.

SECURITY OPTIONS

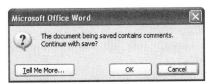

Figure 43 Word can warn you when you save, print, or e-mail a file that contains tracked changes or comments.

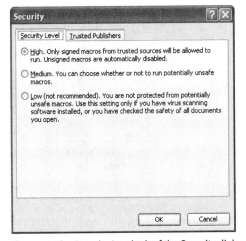

Figure 44 The Security Level tab of the Security dialog.

Figure 45 The Trusted Publishers tab of the Security dialog.

Privacy options

Privacy options help protect your privacy.

◆ **Remove personal information from this file on save** removes user information from the file when you save it.

◆ **Warn before printing, saving or sending a file that contains tracked changes or comments** displays a warning dialog (**Figure 43**) when you print, save, or e-mail a file that contains tracked changes or comments. This helps prevent you from sending draft files that may include confidential information.

◆ **Store random number to improve merge accuracy** tells Word to store a random number in the file for use with its compare and merge feature. This increases the accuracy of the merge.

◆ **Make hidden markup visible when opening or saving** displays all comments and revisions when you open or save the file. This ensures that markup is seen.

Macro security

The Macro security options enable you to protect your computer from viruses attached to macros that work with Word or other Microsoft Office products. Clicking the Macro Security button displays a dialog with two tabs of settings. (Macro security is discussed in **Chapter 18**.)

◆ **Security Level** (**Figure 44**) enables you to set a general security level for protecting your computer from macro viruses.

◆ **Trusted Publishers** (**Figure 45**) displays a list of the sources from which you have accepted files containing macros.

Spelling & Grammar Options

Spelling & Grammar options (**Figure 46**) control the way the spelling and grammar checkers work. There are three categories of options: Spelling, Grammar, and Proofing Tools.

Spelling

Spelling options control the way the spelling checker works:

◆ **Check spelling as you type** turns on the automatic spelling check feature.

◆ **Hide spelling errors in this document** hides the red wavy lines that Word uses to identify possible spelling errors when the automatic spelling check feature is turned on. This option is only available when the Check spelling as you type option is enabled.

◆ **Always suggest corrections** tells Word to automatically display a list of suggested replacements for a misspelled word during a manual spelling check.

◆ **Suggest from main dictionary only** tells Word to suggest replacement words from the main dictionary—not from your custom dictionaries.

◆ **Ignore words in UPPERCASE** tells Word not to check words in all uppercase characters, such as acronyms.

◆ **Ignore words with numbers** tells Word not to check words that include numbers, such as *MariaL1*.

◆ **Ignore Internet and file addresses** tells Word not to check any words that appear to be URLs, e-mail addresses, file names, or file pathnames.

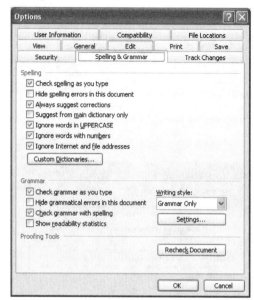

Figure 46 The default settings in the Spelling & Grammar tab of the Options dialog.

Figure 47 The Custom Dictionaries dialog.

Figure 48
Use this dialog to make changes to a custom dictionary.

◆ **Custom Dictionaries** enables you to create, edit, add, and remove custom dictionaries. Click this button to display the Custom Dictionaries dialog (**Figure 47**), which lists all the dictionary files open in Word. Then:

▲ To activate a dictionary file so it can be used by the spelling checker, turn on the check box to the left of its name in the Custom dictionaries list.

▲ To edit the selected dictionary, click the Edit button to display a dialog like the one in **Figure 48**. You can add a word to the dictionary by typing it into the Word box and clicking Add. You can delete a word from the dictionary by selecting the word in the list and clicking Delete. When you are finished making changes, click OK.

▲ To change the default dictionary (the one that words are automatically added to), select the dictionary you want to be the default and click Change Default.

▲ To create a new custom dictionary, click the New button and use the dialog that appears to name and save the new dictionary file.

▲ To add a dictionary to the Custom dictionaries list, click the Add button and use the dialog that appears to locate and open the dictionary file. This feature makes it possible to share dictionary files that contain company- or industry-specific terms with other Word users in your workplace.

▲ To remove a dictionary from Word, select the dictionary and click the Remove button. This does not delete the dictionary file from disk.

When you are finished making changes in the Custom Dictionaries dialog, click OK.

SPELLING & GRAMMAR OPTIONS

Grammar

Grammar options control the way the grammar checker works:

- ◆ **Check grammar as you type** turns on the automatic grammar check feature.

- ◆ **Hide grammatical errors in this document** hides the green wavy lines that Word uses to identify possible grammar errors when the automatic grammar check feature is turned on. This option is only available when the Check grammar as you type option is enabled.

- ◆ **Check grammar with spelling** performs a grammar check as part of a manual spelling check.

- ◆ **Show readability statistics** displays readability statistics (**Figure 49**) for a document at the conclusion of a manual spelling and grammar check. This option is only available when the Check grammar with spelling option is enabled.

- ◆ **Writing style** enables you to select a set of rules for the grammar checker. Use the drop-down list to select an option (**Figure 50**).

- ◆ **Settings** enables you to customize the rules for the grammar checker. Click this button to display the Grammar Settings dialog (**Figure 51**). Choose the set of rules that you want to modify from the Writing style drop-down list (**Figure 50**), then use the options in the dialog to set the style's rules. You can use the Reset All button to reset all writing style rule sets to the default settings.

Proofing Tools

The Proofing Tools area includes one button: Recheck Document. Clicking this button clears the list of ignored problems so you can recheck a document for errors.

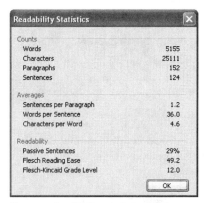

Figure 49 Readability statistics for the Constitution and Bill of Rights of the United States. (It seems that our founding fathers knew how to write in legalese, too.)

Figure 50 The Writing style drop-down list offers two predefined sets of rules.

Figure 51 The Grammar Settings dialog lets you fine-tune the settings for writing style rule sets.

Figure 52 The default settings in the Track Changes tab of the Options dialog.

Figure 53
Use a drop-down list like this to specify how you want insertions, deletions, and formatting to appear.

Figure 54
The Changed lines drop-down list enables you to set the position of the changed lines marker.

Figure 55
Use this drop-down list to specify how you want changes to be colored.

Track Changes Options

The Track Changes options (**Figure 52**) control the way the Track Changes feature works. There are three categories of options: Track Changes options, Balloons, and Printing (with Balloons).

Track Changes options

The Track Changes options enables you to control the appearance of the Track Changes feature.

◆ **Insertions** controls the appearance of text that is inserted into the document. Choose an option from the drop-down list (**Figure 53**).

◆ **Deletions** controls the appearance of text that is deleted from the document. Choose an option from the drop-down list (**Figure 53**).

◆ **Formatting** controls the appearance of text that has been reformatted. Choose an option from the drop-down list (**Figure 53**).

◆ **Changed lines** offers a drop-down list (**Figure 54**) for selecting the location of the changed lines marker.

◆ **Color** controls the color of revision marks. Choose an option from the drop-down list (**Figure 55**) beside a specific type of mark to change the color of that type of mark. The By author option color codes the changes by reviewer.

Balloons

The Balloons options enable you to display changes in a document's margin.

Figure 56 Use this drop-down list to specify when you want balloons to appear in Print and Web Layout views.

◆ **Use balloons in Print and Web Layout** (**Figure 56**) enables you to specify how you want balloons to appear in Print and Web Layout views:

▲ **Always** always displays balloons.

▲ **Never** never displays balloons.

▲ **Only for comments/formatting** only displays balloons for comments and formatting changes.

Figure 57 Choose an option from this drop-down list to set the paper orientation for a document with tracked changes.

◆ **Preferred width** enables you to set the width for the area in which changes appear.

◆ **Measure in** enables you to specify whether the Preferred width measurement is in inches or a percentage of the page or window width.

◆ **Margin** enables you to specify which margin the balloons should appear in: left or right.

◆ **Show lines connecting to text** displays lines connecting the change notations to the text that was changed.

Printing (with Balloons)

The sole option in this area is a drop-down list (**Figure 57**) for setting the paper orientation when printing pages with tracked changes. Choose one of the options:

◆ **Auto** lets Word decide what the best orientation for printing the document is.

◆ **Preserve** keeps the orientation setting in the Page Setup dialog.

◆ **Force Landscape** prints the page in landscape mode.

Customizing Word's Toolbars & Menus

Word's toolbars and menus enable you to access commands by clicking a toolbar button or choosing a menu command. This is pretty standard stuff that's available in many applications. But what isn't standard is your ability to customize Word's menus and toolbars as follows:

- Create new toolbars with any combination of buttons.

- Display any combination of toolbars.

- Show or hide ScreenTips with or without shortcut keys on toolbars.

- Display font names in plain text or font typefaces on font menus.

- Add and remove toolbar buttons, menu commands, and menus.

You customize Word's toolbars and menus with its Customize dialog. This part of the chapter explains how—and how to restore toolbars and menus to default settings when you need to.

To open the Customize dialog

Choose Tools > Customize (**Figure 1**).

To modify the appearance of menus & toolbars

1. In the Customize dialog, click the Options tab to display its options (**Figure 58**).

2. Toggle check boxes as desired in the Personalized Menus and Toolbars section:

   ▲ **Show Standard and Formatting toolbars on two rows** displays the Standard and Formatting toolbars on separate rows beneath the menu bar.

   ▲ **Always show full menus** disables the personalized menu feature.

   ▲ **Show full menus after a short delay** displays a personalized menu at first, then displays a full menu after a few seconds.

   ▲ **Reset menu and toolbar usage data** forgets your recent or frequent menu choices and restores the default personalized menus.

3. Toggle check boxes to set other appearance options:

   ▲ **Large icons** increases the size of toolbar and Formatting Palette buttons.

   ▲ **List font names in their font** displays font names in their typeface in font menus (**Figures 59a** and **59b**).

   ▲ **Show ScreenTips on toolbars** displays the name of a button in a small box when you point to it.

   ▲ **Show shortcut keys in ScreenTips** displays a command's shortcut key in the ScreenTip box when you point to its button (**Figure 60**).

   ▲ **Menu animations** (**Figure 61**)enables you to choose a special effect for displaying menus and commands.

4. Click OK to save your settings.

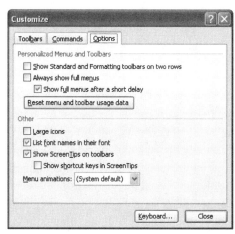

Figure 58 The Options tab of the Customize dialog.

Figures 59a & 59b The Font drop-down list on the Formatting toolbar with font names displayed in their font (left) and font names displayed as plain text (right).

Figure 60 A shortcut key displayed in a ScreenTip.

Figure 61 The Menu animations drop-down list.

MODIFYING MENU & TOOLBAR APPEARANCE

Figure 62 The Toolbars tab of the Customize dialog.

Figure 63
Use this dialog to set options and create a new toolbar.

Figure 64
An empty toolbar. As you can see, it isn't much to look at.

Figure 65 A new toolbar's name appears at the bottom of the Toolbar's list.

Figure 66
Use this dialog to rename a toolbar you created.

To create a new toolbar

1. In the Customize dialog, click the Toolbars tab to display its options (**Figure 62**).

2. Click the New button to display the New Toolbar dialog (**Figure 63**).

3. Enter a name for the toolbar in the Toolbar name box.

4. Choose a template or document name from the Make toolbar available to drop-down list to specify where the toolbar should be stored.

5. Click OK. A tiny empty toolbar appears onscreen (**Figure 64**) and the name of the toolbar you created appears at the bottom of the list in the Toolbars tab of the dialog (**Figure 65**).

✔ Tip

- I explain how to add buttons to a custom toolbar later in this chapter.

To rename a toolbar

1. In the Customize dialog, click the Toolbars tab to display its options (**Figure 62**).

2. Select the name of the toolbar you want to rename (**Figure 65**).

3. Click the Rename button to display the Rename Toolbar dialog (**Figure 66**).

4. Enter a new name for the toolbar in the Toolbar name box.

5. Click OK. The name of the toolbar changes in the list in the Toolbars tab of the dialog.

✔ Tip

- You can only rename a toolbar you created. You cannot rename Word's built-in toolbars.

CREATING & RENAMING TOOLBARS

To delete a toolbar

1. In the Customize dialog, click the Toolbars tab to display its options (**Figure 62**).

2. Select the name of the toolbar you want to delete (**Figure 65**).

3. Click the Delete button.

4. Click OK in the confirmation dialog that appears (**Figure 67**). The name of the toolbar is removed from the list in the Toolbars tab of the dialog.

✔ Tip

■ You can only delete a toolbar you created. You cannot delete Word's built-in toolbars.

To show or hide toolbars

1. In the Customize dialog, click the Toolbars tab to display its options (**Figure 62**).

2. To display a toolbar, turn on the check box beside the toolbar name.

   or

   To hide a toolbar, turn off the check box beside the toolbar name.

✔ Tips

■ You can also display or hide most toolbars by choosing the toolbar's name from the Toolbars submenu under the View menu (**Figure 68**). This submenu also includes the Customize command, which opens the Toolbars tab of the Customize dialog (**Figure 62**).

■ You must display a toolbar to make changes to its buttons as discussed on the following pages.

Figure 67 A dialog box like this appears to confirm that you really do want to delete the toolbar.

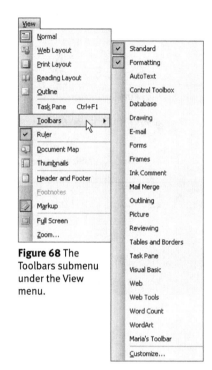

Figure 68 The Toolbars submenu under the View menu.

Figure 69 The Commands tab of the Customize dialog.

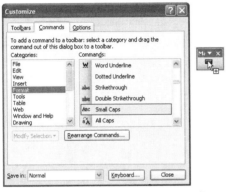

Figure 70a You can add a button to a new toolbar, ...

Figure 70b ... or an existing one.

To add buttons to a toolbar

1. In the Customize dialog, click the Toolbars tab to display its options (**Figure 62**).

2. Make sure the check box for the toolbar you want to change is turned on so the toolbar appears onscreen.

3. Click the Commands tab to display its options (**Figure 69**).

4. Select a command category in the Categories list. The commands that appear in the Commands list change.

5. Scroll through the Commands list to find the command you want to add to the toolbar.

6. Drag the command from the Commands list to the toolbar you want to add it to. A vertical bar appears where the button will be inserted (**Figures 70a** and **70b**). When the bar is in the desired location, release the mouse button. The toolbar button appears (**Figures 71a** and **71b**).

7. Repeat steps 4 through 6 for each button you want to add to a toolbar.

8. When you are finished adding buttons, click OK.

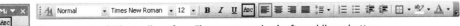

Figures 71a & 71b The toolbars from **Figures 70a** and **70b** after adding a button.

ADDING TOOLBAR BUTTONS

To remove buttons from a toolbar

1. In the Customize dialog, click the Toolbars tab to display its options (**Figure 62**).

2. Make sure the check box for the toolbar you want to change is turned on so the toolbar appears onscreen.

3. Drag a button off the toolbar (**Figure 72**). When you release the mouse button, the button disappears (**Figure 73**).

4. Repeat step 3 for each button you want to remove from the toolbar.

5. When you are finished removing buttons, click OK.

To restore a toolbar to default settings

1. In the Customize dialog, click the Toolbars tab to display its options (**Figure 62**).

2. Select the name of the toolbar you want to restore to its default settings.

3. Click the Reset button. The Reset Toolbar dialog appears (**Figure 74**).

4. If desired, choose a different template or document from the drop-down list. The reset toolbar will be saved in the document or template you choose.

5. Click OK. The toolbar is restored to its default settings.

✔ Tip

- You can only restore one of Word's built-in toolbars. You cannot restore a toolbar that you created.

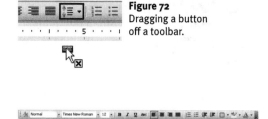

Figure 72
Dragging a button off a toolbar.

Figure 73 The button is removed from the toolbar.

Figure 74 The Reset Toolbar dialog.

REMOVING BUTTONS, RESETTING TOOLBARS

Figure 75 Drag a command from the Customize dialog to a menu.

Figure 76
The command is
added to the menu.

To add commands to a menu

1. In the Customize dialog, click the Toolbars tab to display its options (**Figure 62**).

2. Make sure the check box beside Menu Bar is turned on so the menu bar appears onscreen.

3. Click the Commands tab to display its options (**Figure 69**).

4. Select a command category in the Categories list. The commands that appear in the Commands list change.

5. Scroll through the Commands list to find the command you want to add to the menu.

6. Drag the command from the Commands list to the menu you want to add it to. The menu opens and a horizontal bar appears where the command will be inserted (**Figure 75**). When the bar is in the desired location, release the mouse button. If you click the menu to display it again, you'll see that the command has been added (**Figure 76**).

7. Repeat steps 4 through 6 for each command you want to add to a menu.

8. When you are finished adding commands, click OK.

✔ Tip

■ In step 6, if you drag the command over a submenu name, the submenu opens so you can insert the command on it.

ADDING MENU COMMANDS

To remove a command from a menu

1. In the Customize dialog, click the Toolbars tab to display its options (**Figure 62**).

2. Make sure the check box beside Menu Bar is turned on so the menu bar appears onscreen.

3. Click the name of the menu containing the command you want to remove to display the menu.

4. Drag the command off the menu (**Figure 77**). When you release the mouse button, the command is removed (**Figure 78**).

5. Repeat steps 3 and 4 for each command you want to remove from a menu.

6. When you are finished removing commands, click OK.

To remove a menu

1. In the Customize dialog, click the Toolbars tab to display its options (**Figure 62**).

2. Make sure the check box beside Menu Bar is turned on so the menu bar appears onscreen.

3. Drag the name of the menu you want to remove off the Menu toolbar. When you release the mouse button, the menu is removed.

4. Repeat step 3 for each menu you want to remove.

5. When you are finished removing menus, click OK.

✖ Warning!

- Removing menu commands and menus can make Word commands inaccessible!

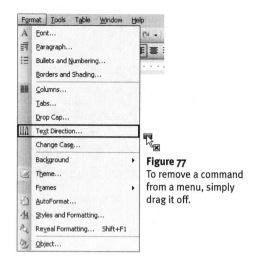

Figure 77
To remove a command from a menu, simply drag it off.

Figure 78
The command is removed from the menu.

To restore menus to default settings

1. In the Customize dialog, click the Toolbars tab to display its options (**Figure 62**).

2. Select Menu Bar in the scrolling list.

3. Click the Reset button. The Reset Toolbar dialog appears (**Figure 74**).

4. If desired, choose a different template or document from the drop-down list. The reset toolbar will be saved in the document or template you choose.

5. Click OK. The menu bar is restored to its default settings.

✔ Tip

- Use this technique to get back menus you removed from the menu bar in error.

RESTORING MENUS

Customizing Word's Shortcut Keys

Word comes preconfigured with a surprising number of shortcut keys assigned to menu commands and other options. This enables you to perform many commands without menus or dialogs.

Word's Customize Keyboard dialog enables you to modify existing shortcut keys or add new ones.

This part of the chapter tells you how you can create a list of assigned shortcut keys, and then explains how you can modify them.

To create a list of existing shortcut keys

1. Choose Tools > Macro > Macros to display the Macros dialog.

2. Choose Word Commands from the Macros in drop-down list (**Figure 79**).

3. Select ListCommands from the list of macros (**Figure 80**).

4. Click Run.

5. In the List Commands dialog that appears (**Figure 81**), select the Current menu and keyboard settings option.

6. Click OK. Word creates a document that lists all commands that appear on menus or have shortcut keys assigned to them (**Figure 82**).

✔ Tips

- You can print or save the command list document Word creates (**Figure 82**).

- If you make changes to keyboard or menu settings, recreate this document to get an updated list.

LISTING SHORTCUT KEYS

Figure 79 The Macros in drop-down list in the Macros dialog.

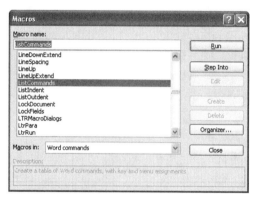

Figure 80 Select the ListCommands macro.

Figure 81 The List Commands dialog.

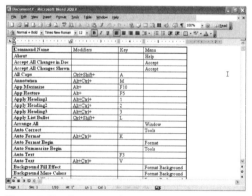

Figure 82 Word creates a document that lists all commands that appear on menus or have shortcut keys.

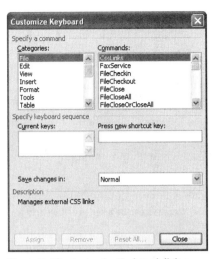

Figure 83 The Customize Keyboard dialog.

Figure 84 The keystroke you type appears in the box and the status of that keystroke appears beneath it.

To customize shortcut keys

1. Choose Tools > Customize (**Figure 1**) to display the Customize dialog.

2. Click the Keyboard button to display the Customize Keyboard dialog (**Figure 83**).

3. Select a command category from the Categories list.

4. Select the command you want to modify from the Commands list.

5. Customize the shortcut key as follows:
   - ▲ To remove an existing shortcut key, select the keystroke in the Current keys box and click Remove.
   - ▲ To add a shortcut key, position the insertion point in the Press new shortcut key box and press the keystroke you want to assign. The keystroke status appears (**Figure 84**). If the keystroke is unassigned, click Assign to assign it to the current command.

6. Repeat steps 3 through 5 to add or remove as many shortcut keys as you like.

7. If desired, choose a different template or document from the drop-down list. The customized shortcut keys will be saved in the document or template you choose.

8. Click OK to save your changes in the Customize Keyboard dialog.

9. Click OK to dismiss the Customize dialog.

Continued on next page...

CUSTOMIZING SHORTCUT KEYS

✔ Tips

- In step 5, if the keystroke is already assigned to another command (**Figure 85**), remove it from that other command before assigning it to the current command.

- In step 5, you can enter a series of keystrokes to invoke a command. For example, pressing Alt Ctrl Shift W and then 1 (**Figure 86**) creates a shortcut key that requires you to press that series of keystrokes.

- A command can have more than one shortcut key.

To restore all shortcut keys

1. Choose Tools > Customize (**Figure 1**) to display the Customize dialog.

2. Click the Keyboard button to display the Customize Keyboard dialog (**Figure 83**).

3. Click the Reset All button.

4. Click Yes in the confirmation dialog that appears (**Figure 87**).

5. Click OK to dismiss the Customize Keyboard dialog.

6. Click OK to dismiss the Customize dialog.

✔ Tip

- The Reset All button can only be clicked if there have been changes to shortcut keys.

Figure 85 In this example, the keystroke I typed is already assigned to another command.

Figure 86 Shortcut keys can be a series of keystrokes.

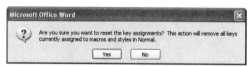

Figure 87 Use this dialog to confirm that you really do want to reset shortcut keys.

Menus & Shortcut Keys

Menus & Shortcut Keys

This appendix illustrates all of Microsoft Word's standard menus and provides a list of shortcut keys—including many that don't appear on menus.

To use a shortcut key, hold down the modifier key (usually Ctrl) and press the keyboard key corresponding to the command. For example, to use the Save command's shortcut key, hold down Ctrl and press S.

✔ Tips

- I explain how to use menus and shortcut keys in **Chapter 1**.

- I tell you how you can customize menus and shortcut keys in **Chapter 19**.

File Menu

Ctrl N	New Default
Ctrl O	Open
Ctrl W	Close Document
Ctrl S	Save
F12	Save As
Ctrl F2	Print Preview
Ctrl P	Print
Alt F4	Close or Exit

Permission submenu

Send To submenu

Edit Menu

Ctrl Z	Undo
Ctrl Y	Redo or Repeat
Ctrl X	Cut
Ctrl C	Copy
Shift F2	Copy Text
Ctrl V	Paste
Ctrl A	Select All
Ctrl F	Find
Shift F4	Repeat Find
Ctrl H	Replace
Ctrl G	Go To
Shift F5	Go Back

Clear submenu

Formats	
Contents	Del

Del	Contents

View Menu

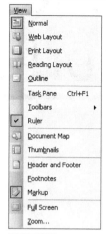

Alt Ctrl N	Normal
Alt Ctrl P	Print Layout
Alt Ctrl O	Outline
Ctrl F1	Task Pane

Toolbars submenu

FILE, EDIT, & VIEW MENUS

Insert Menu

Ctrl Enter	Page Break
Ctrl Shift Enter	Column Break
Alt Shift D	Date Field
Alt Shift T	Time Field
Alt Ctrl M	Comment
Ctrl Shift F5	Bookmark
Ctrl K	Hyperlink

AutoText submenu

F3	AutoText
Alt F3	New

Reference submenu

Alt Ctrl F	Footnote Now
Alt Ctrl D	Endnote Now
Alt Shift x	Mark Index Entry
Alt Shift O	Mark Table of Contents Entry
Alt Shift I	Mark Citation

Picture submenu

Format Menu

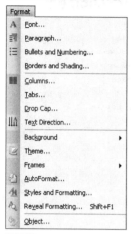

<table>
<tr><td>Ctrl D</td><td>Font</td></tr>
<tr><td>Ctrl Shift Q</td><td>Symbol Font</td></tr>
<tr><td>Ctrl B</td><td>Bold</td></tr>
<tr><td>Ctrl I</td><td>Italic</td></tr>
<tr><td>Ctrl U</td><td>Underline</td></tr>
<tr><td>Ctrl Shift W</td><td>Word Underline</td></tr>
<tr><td>Ctrl Shift D</td><td>Double Underline</td></tr>
<tr><td>Ctrl Shift H</td><td>Hidden</td></tr>
<tr><td>Ctrl Shift A</td><td>All Caps</td></tr>
<tr><td>Ctrl Shift K</td><td>Small Caps</td></tr>
<tr><td>Ctrl =</td><td>Subscript</td></tr>
<tr><td>Ctrl Shift =</td><td>Superscript</td></tr>
<tr><td>Ctrl Shift .</td><td>Grow Font</td></tr>
<tr><td>Ctrl]</td><td>Grow Font One Point</td></tr>
<tr><td>Ctrl Shift ,</td><td>Shrink Font</td></tr>
<tr><td>Ctrl [</td><td>Shrink Font One Point</td></tr>
<tr><td>Ctrl M</td><td>Indent</td></tr>
<tr><td>Ctrl Shift M</td><td>Unindent</td></tr>
<tr><td>Ctrl T</td><td>Hanging Indent</td></tr>
<tr><td>Ctrl Shift T</td><td>Unhang Indent</td></tr>
<tr><td>Ctrl L</td><td>Left Align Paragraph</td></tr>
</table>

<table>
<tr><td>Ctrl E</td><td>Center Paragraph</td></tr>
<tr><td>Ctrl R</td><td>Right Align Paragraph</td></tr>
<tr><td>Ctrl J</td><td>Justify Paragraph</td></tr>
<tr><td>Ctrl 1</td><td>Single Space Paragraph</td></tr>
<tr><td>Ctrl 5</td><td>1.5 Space Paragraph</td></tr>
<tr><td>Ctrl 2</td><td>Double Space Paragraph</td></tr>
<tr><td>Ctrl 0</td><td>Open or Close Up Paragraph</td></tr>
<tr><td>Ctrl Shift L</td><td>Bulleted List</td></tr>
<tr><td>Shift F3</td><td>Change Case</td></tr>
<tr><td>Ctrl Shift C</td><td>Copy Format</td></tr>
<tr><td>Ctrl Shift V</td><td>Paste Format</td></tr>
<tr><td>Alt Ctrl K</td><td>AutoFormat</td></tr>
<tr><td>Ctrl Shift S</td><td>Style</td></tr>
<tr><td>Ctrl Shift N</td><td>Normal Style</td></tr>
<tr><td>Alt Ctrl 1</td><td>Apply Heading 1</td></tr>
<tr><td>Alt Ctrl 2</td><td>Apply Heading 2</td></tr>
<tr><td>Alt Ctrl 3</td><td>Apply Heading 3</td></tr>
<tr><td>Shift F1</td><td>Reveal Formatting</td></tr>
</table>

Background submenu

Frames submenu

Tools Menu

F7	Spelling and Grammar
Alt F7	Next Misspelling
Ctrl Shift O	Research
Ctrl Shift G	Word Count
Ctrl Shift E	Track Changes

Language submenu

| Alt Shift F7 | Translate |
| Shift F7 | Thesaurus |

Online Collaboration submenu

Letters and Mailings submenu

Alt Shift F	Merge Field
Alt Shift K	Mail Merge Check
Alt Shift E	Mail Merge Edit Data Source
Alt Shift N	Mail Merge to Document
Alt Shift M	Mail Merge to Printer

Macro submenu

Alt F8	Macros
Alt F11	Visual Basic Editor
Alt Shift F11	Microsoft Script Editor

TOOLS MENU

Table Menu

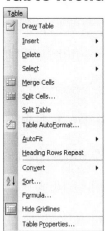

Window Menu

[Alt][Ctrl][S] Split/Remove Split

[F6] Other Pane

Help Menu

[F1] Microsoft Office Word Help

Insert submenu

Delete submenu

Select submenu

AutoFit submenu

Convert submenu

Index

INDEX

INDEX